JOSEPH BRODSKY AND THE CREATION OF EXILE

JOSEPH BRODSKY AND THE CREATION OF EXILE

David M. Bethea

PRINCETON UNIVERSITY PRESS   PRINCETON, NEW JERSEY

Library of Congress Cataloging-in-Publication Data

Bethea, David M., 1948–
Joseph Brodsky and the creation of exile / David M. Bethea.
p.   cm.
Includes bibliographical references (p.) and index.
ISBN 0-691-06773-2
1. Brodsky, Joseph, 1940–   —Criticism and interpretation.
I. Title.
PG3479.4.R64Z57   1994
811'.54—dc20   93-31178

This book has been composed in Adobe Sabon

10   9   8   7   6   5   4   3   2   1

For Emily

Our eyes and ears refused obedience
the princes of our senses proudly chose exile

Zbigniew Herbert,
"The Power of Taste"

Contents

Preface

THE PRESENT STUDY is what the Russians call a *postanovka voprosa*—nothing more or less than a propaedeutical "posing of the question." Since the time is not yet right for a serious (not to speak of "definitive") critical biography of Joseph Brodsky, what follows is an attempt to frame the issue of who he is as international man of letters and how he arrived at his present role as Russian-born American poet laureate. I decided early on in the project that to understand Brodsky required a formidable implied reader, for here was a poet who both was steeped in the Russian tradition from Skovoroda to Mandelstam and Tsvetaeva and who, in his anglophone (or rather anglicized russophone) incarnation, could speak in the cadences of Donne, Auden, and Lowell. To read Brodsky properly one would have to see and hear Auden not with native anglophone eyes and ears but with the eyes and ears of a young Russian poet whose generation had recently discovered, say, the sublime deep breathing of Mandelstam's hexameters or the stroboscopic speed of Tsvetaeva's dashes and enjambements. The puzzle of who precisely Brodsky was writing for and how to get "inside" (when so much was "outside") that relationship became intriguing. It became clear that the key to Brodsky, perhaps the last of the great Russian poets in the "bardic" mode, was in his relation to others, or the other (or the Other). His essence was in a poetic *askesis*, a shedding of self that, miraculously, *became* (in both senses) him. His voice rose as he muffled his own bel canto urgings against the background of a prior master's poetic speech. Consequently, the best way to define him, to pose the question of who he is, is to demonstrate, with the help of another, who he is not. Soon there arose the notion of comparing Brodsky and different aspects of his exile status to his favorite models: Donne, Auden, Mandelstam, and Tsvetaeva. In each instance it could be shown how Brodsky used the model and then, with no apparent Bloomian overtones (quite the opposite in fact), veered from it.

Over time, and with additional research and thought, the book grew into its present shape. The introduction (chapter 1) has a threefold thrust: to pose, somewhat polemically, the problem of Brodsky's bardic voice (or, as he would call it, "vector") within the present context of American letters; to explain Brodsky's complex attitude toward the issue of a poet's biography even as we are largely forced to avoid it; and to examine the concept of exile as it relates to Brodsky's life and art. Here and elsewhere certain critical paradigms, including Said's "Orientalism," Kristeva's "foreigner" and "semiotic"/"symbolic" orders, Bloom's "anxiety of influence," Gilman's "Jewish self-hatred," Tomashevsky's "biographical legend," and Lipking's "the life of the poet," are used as foils to Brodsky's thinking. Chapter 2 sets up a master trope for the remainder of the study: what I call Brodsky's "triangular vision," his tendency to mediate a prior model (Dante) with a closer model (Mandelstam) in the creation of a palimpsestlike text in which he, as speaker, is implicated as a triangulated hybrid of these earlier incarnations. Needless to say, such triangulated texts are often alive with an "East-West" force field, especially with regard to the interpenetration of the Russian and Anglo-American traditions, that has become in many ways Brodsky's special signature as poet.

In the following chapters I investigate these findings as they apply to Brodsky's appropriation of favorite models and to his continuously expanding notion of exile. In Donne, for example, Brodsky found a method (English metaphysical verse) that allowed him to conceptualize the problem of psychic exile (chapter 3); in Auden and Eliot, he did something analogous—he wrote himself out of internal exile by expanding further the notion of native tradition and by "ventriloquizing" the voice of one foreign precursor (Auden) to speak of the death of another (Eliot) (chapter 4); from Mandelstam and Pasternak, he took his cue as marginalized ("Jewish") outsider who, paradoxically, is better able to speak for the majority ("Christian") culture and to embody its principle of "creative destiny" (chapter 5); by fixing on Tsvetaeva, perhaps his favorite poet after Auden, he discovered someone whose physical exile and loss of love and youth in foreign places paralleled his own, but through the optic of a different gender (chapter 6); and finally in Nabokov, the only Russian writer of Brodsky's stature to rival him as a bilingual phenomenon, he confronted the issue of exile in its relation to, and translation of, genre—Nabokov the prose writer versus Brodsky the poet (chapter 7). All these comparisons and contrasts follow logically from focal points and emphases in Brodsky's essays and interviews (the poet, for example, has written separate prose eulogies of Mandelstam, Tsvetaeva, and Auden, and he has given a radio interview on the 350th anniversary of John Donne's death). The exception of course is Nabokov, a figure to whom Brodsky presumably would *not* compare himself and about whom, despite his admiration for Nabokov's Russian novels, he has not written. But Nabokov as foil suggests a useful stepping-off point for the study because his interest in translation and his transition to the anglophone environment parallel—again, with crucial differences—Brodsky's own. Each of the later chapters (3–7), therefore, frames the question of Brodsky's creative identity from a slightly different angle: national tradition (the poetic word as "ours" or "theirs"), ethnic origins (culture or originary myth as "ours" or "theirs"), personal relations (love as absence or "exilic desire"), and genre (poetry as language "exiled" from prose).

It is a virtual topos in such preliminaries to claim that one's subject has been "neglected" or unfairly passed over by literary history. Not so in Brodsky's case. Books and dissertations, some excellent, have been written about him and collections of articles by experts have been published, especially recently, in the wake of the awarding of the Nobel Prize in 1987. Moreover, literary history is still very much being made as far as Brodsky is concerned; many would argue that we need more distance on him, we need the ulterior vantage offered by a *completed* career and a generation of patient sleuthing and stock-taking, before we can say anything genuinely useful about this complex poet and person. But the real dangers involved in writing about a living figure are more than compensated for by the sense that one is participating in, if only obliquely and at a secondary (or even tertiary) remove, an evolving process. As a critic like Frank Kermode might say, quoting Valéry, not only have we lost our appetite for poetry, we have lost our appetite for the risk and sacrifice inherent in the creative process itself, of which poetry is simply the most distilled example. If the author is dead, either actually or metaphorically, then there is nothing in principle to keep us from making his or her words say what we want. But if the author is alive, then this option is riskier, more patently irresponsible. It is this sensation of risk that must surely have played some role in the writing of "classical" works about (then) living poets: Boris Eikhenbaum's and Viktor Vinogradov's studies of Akhmatova in the twenties or F. O. Matthiessen's "Tradition and the Individual Talent" (1935), a piece that eventually formed part of *The Achievement of T. S. Eliot* (1958). Could it be said that these works have not lost their currency precisely because their authors had their fingers on the pulse of the literary process at the time and because, with the ante thus raised, they could not indulge, as we might say today, the free play of their signifiers? In any event, I have enjoyed the presence of this risk. And I do not, by the way, expect the subject of this study to agree with my readings. That I have tried to take his words seriously and to meet him if only part way on that risky road spanning two languages and cultures is enough.

Acknowledgments

I WOULD LIKE to take this opportunity to acknowledge the many friends and colleagues who either generously offered relevant materials or who read parts (or all) of the present study and gave much-needed words of advice, including adjustments of emphasis and corrections of outright factual error: Vladimir Alexandrov, Stanislaw Baranczak, Clare Cavanagh, Alexander Dolinin, Galya Diment, Svetlana Elnitsky, Caryl Emerson, Mikhail Epstein, Viktor Erofeev, Efim Etkind, Gregory Freidin, the late Lydia Ginzburg, Judith Kornblatt, Michael Kreps, Lev Loseff, George Kline, Mikhail Meilakh, Catharine Nepomnyashchy, Eric Pervukhin, Valentina Polukhina, Evgeny Rein, Gary Rosenshield, Peter Scotto, Yury Shcheglov, G. S. Smith, Carol Ueland, Tomas Venclova, Irina Voskresenskaya, and Laura Weeks. I would particularly like to thank those colleagues who took part in a faculty seminar on Brodsky at the Middlebury College Russian School in the summer of 1990—Sophia Bogatyreva, Sergei Davydov, Svetlana Elnitsky, Mikhail Epstein, Efim Etkind, Michael Kreps, Vadim Liapunov, Lev Loseff, and Yuna Morits— and those students who participated in my graduate seminar on Brodsky in Madison in the fall of 1991—Anne Berggren, Rachel Kilbourn, Paul Klanderud, Galina Patterson, Roman Shcheglov, Alyssa Turner, Dan Ungurianu, and Adam Weiner. From both these latter groups I learned a great deal. Considerable help along the way was rendered by several able research assistants: Dianne Goldstaub, Maya Hoptman, Donald Loewen, Jennifer Ryan, and Dan Ungurianu. Rita Bernhard did a superb job of copyediting and the eventual book has been much enhanced by her efforts. I am particularly grateful to Joseph Brodsky himself, who patiently suffered my questions on several occasions. The entire project was made possible by an extended leave (1989–91) provided by the National Endowment for the Humanities, the Guggenheim Foundation, and the Graduate School at the University of Wisconsin-Madison. Parts of this study, modified for publication, have appeared or are scheduled to appear elsewhere and are here so noted: "Exile, Elegy, and Auden in Brodsky's 'Verses on the Death of T. S. Eliot'" (*PMLA* 107 [March 1992]: 232–45); "Exile as Pupation: The Image of the Butterfly in Nabokov and Brodsky" [Izgnanie kak ukhod v kokon: Obraz babochki u Nabokova i Brodskogo] (*Russkaia literatura* [St. Petersburg] [1991, #3]; 167–75); "Mandelstam, Pasternak, Brodsky: Judaism and Christianity in the Making of a Modernist Poetics" (in *American Scholars on Twentieth-Century Russian Literature*, ed. Boris Averin and Elizabeth Neatour

[St. Petersburg: Rif, forthcoming]); "The Exilic Imagination, Russian Style" (in *CULTURE/KULTURA: Soviet-American Dialogues on Literature*, ed. Emory Elliot, Ellen Chances, and Robert Maguire [Durham: Duke University Press, forthcoming]); "Mother(hood) and Poetry: Tsvetaeva and the Feminists" (in *Festschrift* for Simon Karlinsky, ed. Michael S. Flier and Robert P. Hughes [forthcoming]); "Joseph Brodsky as Russian Metaphysical: A Reading of 'Bol'shaia elegiia Dzhonu Donnu' " *Canadian-American Slavic Studies* 27 [1–4, 1993]: 69–89).

The quotations from *W. H. Auden: Collected Poems* by W. H. Auden, edited by Edward Mendelson, copyright 1940 and renewed 1968 by W. H. Auden, are reprinted by permission of Random House, Inc., and by permission of Faber and Faber Limited. The quotations from *Chast' rechi. Stikhotvoreniia 1972–1976*, copyright 1977 by Joseph Brodsky, are reprinted by permission of Farrar, Straus & Giroux, Inc. The quotation from "History of the Twentieth Century: A Roadshow," copyright 1986 by Joseph Brodsky and first appearing in *Partisan Review*, vol. 53, no. 3 (1986), is reprinted by permission of Joseph Brodsky. The quotations from *Konets prekrasnoi epokhi. Stikhotvoreniia 1964–1971*, copyright 1977 by Joseph Brodsky, are reprinted by permission of Farrar, Straus & Giroux, Inc. The quotations from *Less Than One: Selected Essays*, copyright 1986 by Joseph Brodsky, are reprinted by permission of Farrar, Straus & Giroux, Inc. The quotations from *Ostanovka v pustyne*, copyright 1970 by Joseph Brodsky, are reprinted by permission of Farrar, Straus & Giroux, Inc. The quotations from *A Part of Speech*, copyright 1980 by Joseph Brodsky, are reprinted by permission of Farrar, Straus & Giroux, Inc. The quotations from *Primechaniia paporotnika*, copyright 1990 by Joseph Brodsky, are reprinted by permission of Farrar, Straus & Giroux, Inc. The quotation from *Uraniia*, copyright 1987 by Joseph Brodsky, is reprinted by permission of Farrar, Straus & Giroux, Inc. The quotations from *Selected Poems*, copyright 1973 by Joseph Brodsky, are reprinted by permission of Farrar, Straus & Giroux, Inc. The quotation from *To Urania*, copyright 1988 by Joseph Brodsky, is reprinted by permission of Farrar, Straus & Giroux, Inc. The quotation from "Little Gidding" in *Four Quartets*, copyright 1943 by T. S. Eliot and renewed 1971 by Esme Valerie Eliot, is reprinted by permission of Harcourt Brace & Company and by permission of Faber and Faber Limited, Publishers. The quotation from "In verse," copyright 1993 by Alexander Kushner, is reprinted by permission of Indiana University Press from *Contemporary Russian Poetry: A Bilingual Anthology*, edited by G. S. Smith. The quotations from *Pale Fire: A Novel* by Vladimir Nabokov, copyright 1962 by Vera Nabokov and Dmitri Nabokov, is reprinted by permission of Vintage Books, a Division of Random House, Inc. The quotation from "The Monastery," copyright 1993 by Evgeny Rein, is reprinted by permission of Indiana University Press from *Contemporary Russian Poetry: A Bilingual Anthology*, edited by G. S. Smith. The quotation from "Any beginning," copyright 1993 by Boris Slutsky, is reprinted by permission of Indiana University Press from *Contemporary Russian Poetry: A Bilingual Anthology*, edited by G. S. Smith.

I dedicate this labor of love to my favorite aspiring pianist and purple-belt in karate.

A Note on the Transliteration _____

THE SYSTEM OF transliteration I have used is that recommended by Professor J. Thomas Shaw in his *The Transliteration of Modern Russian for English-Language Publications* (Madison, 1967). In the text itself, as well as in the substantive notes section, I have used Shaw's "System I," which is a modified version of the Library of Congress system for the purpose of normalizing personal and place names for the generalist Western reader. References to secondary literature in the text and notes are to *abbreviated* titles (the complete bibliographical information being found in the "Works Cited" section). In the "Works Cited" section and in transliteration of words as words, I have used "System II," which is the unmodified Library of Congress system, with the diacritical marks omitted. It is hoped that any confusion that might arise from the combination of these two systems (e.g., "Solovyov" in the text but "Solov'ev" in the "Works Cited" section) will be compensated for by the increased readability afforded the nonspecialist and the greater precision afforded the specialist.

Principal Abbreviations _____

ChR   Joseph Brodsky, *Chast' rechi. Stikhotvoreniia 1972–1976* (Ann Arbor: Ardis, 1977).
KPR   Joseph Brodsky, *Konets prekrasnoi epokhi. Stikhotvoreniia 1964–1971* (Ann Arbor: Ardis, 1977).
Less Joseph Brodsky, *Less Than One: Selected Essays* (New York: Farrar, Straus, and Giroux, 1986).
OVP   Joseph Brodsky, *Ostanovka v pustyne* (New York: Chekhov, 1970; rpt. Ann Arbor: Ardis, 1989).
Part Joseph Brodsky, *A Part of Speech* (New York: Farrar, Straus, and Giroux, 1980).
PP   Joseph Brodsky, *Primechaniia paporotnika* (Bromma, Sweden: Hylaea, 1990).
SP   Joseph Brodsky, *Selected Poems*, trans. George Kline (New York: Harper, 1973).
SiP   Joseph Brodsky, *Stikhotvoreniia i poemy* (Washington: Interlanguage Literary Associates, 1965).
U   Joseph Brodsky, *Uraniia* (Ann Arbor: Ardis, 1987).

Note: Other abbreviated titles are keyed to the "Works Cited" section.

JOSEPH BRODSKY AND THE CREATION OF EXILE

1

Joseph Brodsky and the Creation of Exile: A Polemical Introduction

When amorists grow bald, then amours shrink
Into the compass and curriculum
Of introspective exiles, lecturing.
  (Wallace Stevens, *Le Monocle de Mon Oncle*)

The Problem

The twentieth century, now nearing its end, seems to have had its way with all the arts except poetry. Viewed less chronologically and more exaltedly, history has imposed its reality on the arts. What we imply when we speak of modern aesthetics is nothing but the noise of history jamming or subjugating the song of art. Every ism is both evidence, direct or indirect, of art's defeat and a scar covering up the shame of this defeat. Though it may be crass to say so, existence has proved capable of defining the artist's consciousness, and proof of this can be found in the means the artist uses. For that matter, any mention of means is, in itself, a sign of adaptation. (Brodsky, "Poetry as a Form of Resistance," 220)

Thus begins one of the many forewords and afterwords that Joseph Brodsky has written for fellow poets since arriving on the shores of his adoptive country twenty years ago. Almost all these celebratory framings, these sturdy and sometimes antique-sounding bookends placed on the shelf of time to shore up a worthy volume against the "moral deafness" of contemporary reader expectation, reveal the same sensibility and tone of voice ("Beyond Consolation," 14). But this instance is particularly fascinating, and perhaps for that reason is as good a place as any to make our entry. This foreword was penned for a Polish edition of the selected verse of Tomas Venclova, the émigré Lithuanian poet and professor of Slavic at Yale. The edition itself was prepared by Stanislaw Baranczak, another poet (this time Polish) and professor at Harvard. Brodsky's original comments were made in Russian, which means in effect that three languages, three cultures, and three poets came together for the sole purpose of presenting Venclova to Polish readers. Perhaps little should be made of this demonstration of cultural solidarity, other than that Brodsky's reputation and Baranczak's considerable translating skills were necessary to give Venclova's verse the best chance of finding a larger audience. And yet there is more here than meets the untrained eye, especially when Brodsky's words are translated *into English*, as they were in a recent issue of *PMLA*. Now the audience is dramatically different, with the result that the speaker could be seen as a postmodern Pnin who has picked up the wrong lecture for the Cremona Women's Club. Presumably Brodsky himself experiences none of this, but the English translation of his Russian *sententiae* creates the impression in a reader aware of both contexts that the utterer of these words has, as though in a dream sequence, come to his own lecture, begun to speak, literally, *ex cathedra*, and then discovered to his chagrin that he has forgotten to get dressed. Why is this so? Let us investigate further, since it is this crease across the well-pressed seam of cultural habit, this *sdvig* (shift), as the Russian formalists might call it in another context, that goes to the heart of Brodsky's calling as poet and man of letters.

First of all, it takes a certain kind of consciousness to produce the sentences of this opening quotation, just as it takes a certain kind of audience to understand them fully. To claim that a century can "have its way" with anything human, including the creation of art, is to make a conventional temporal marker into a manipulative Greek god. (This is all the more startling when one realizes that on many occasions Brodsky has included among his most basic beliefs the Marxist-mocking idea that, for the genuine artist, "consciousness determines being.") Why the *volte-face*? One can imagine many contemporary readers recoiling almost instinctively from the statement's summary boldness. All the century's decades except the 1990s and all the arts except poetry collapse into a topic sentence. Mandelstam, we recall, could speak of his century within the Russian context as a beast with a broken back, but he was a high modernist and myth weaver of the most haunting power, and so we allow him his metaphorical stitching of time and animation. Brodsky, however, is writing in 1989. These words come across as a kind of verbal gauntlet hurled down in defiance (Of whom? Of what?). They are sure to the point of arrogance, combative, almost Olympian in their—Again, what is it? Scorn? Bitter resignation? Where could this man be standing, culturally speaking, in order to pronounce these thoughts? They could belong to a modern Underground Man, except that the speaker does not seem to care if they are heeded, at least in the *now* of their initial utterance. They do not invite qualification and they are indifferent to potential interlocutors. They are expressed by a man who appears to know his mind and who frames his insights within a system of values that is intensely, fiercely his own. They are, in short, the very opposite of "open." Where, we are justified in asking, does this tone come from?

"Every ism is . . . evidence . . . of art's defeat" is the verbal equivalent of a stone engraving: it gives the appearance of being there for all time, or, what is the same, of being outside time, unconditional. What we have here is discursive writing as a kind of epitaph, or possibly cenotaph, *avant la lettre*. The "punch" in Brodsky's lines comes more from *images* than from the incremental pace of a logically unfolding argument—the "jamming" noise of history or the "scar" covering the shame of defeat. And this force is constantly amplified by what Jakobson called the poetic function, by the fact, for example, that *shram* (scar) and *sram* (shame) rhyme in the original, being identical in sound except for the initial consonant (*Russkaia mysl'*, no. 3829 [25 May 1990]). The "cool, reflective, nonrepresentational" qualities associated with "aesthetic distance" in poetic language are thus elided with the "concrete, motor, representational" qualities of "iconicity" (Hartman, *Beyond Formalism*, 338). After all, how can one argue with metaphor, a trope that in this instance seems to do nothing so much as to take its own argument by the throat? Moreover, why would one choose to study this speaker, so peremptory in his judgments, at a time when those judgments are so clearly out of season with the current intellectual climate? Does not a phrase like the "song of art" sound musty and dated? Who among contemporary critics is comfortable speaking of "art" as a meaningful rubric (Is it not elitist?) or, worse, anthropomorphizing it with a singing voice? And finally, one wonders at the wisdom of Brodsky's anti-Marxist sentiment. By saying that "existence has proved capable of defining the artist's consciousness" he seems to be both admitting defeat and ridiculing, from his viewpoint, the diminution in human potential inherent in this economy. Whose existence and whose consciousness? How can a statement this large and porous be truth-bearing in any meaningful way? We might conclude, therefore, that this is writing which in all likelihood would find few champions among academy-trained humanists. It belongs, in short, to what can only be called a different type of discourse.

But that, it seems, is Brodsky's point. He is a poet who has agreed, provisionally, to descend into prose,[1] much the same as the Mandelstam who wrote "The Fourth Prose" or the Tsvetaeva who wrote "The Poet on the Critic [or Criticism[2]]." He is not writing to gain enfranchisement in the here and now, nor has he ever written for an academic—or narrowly "artistic," for that matter—audience, including an American one. Statements such as "Nothing is more appealing to the sensitive imagination than vicarious tragedy; it provides the artist with a sense of 'world crisis' without direct threat to his own anatomy" (Brodsky, "Poetry as a Form of Resistance," 221) immediately draw blood with their irony and their implication of hypocrisy. They are bound, therefore, to annoy certain readers and to push Brodsky still further to the margins of the regnant discourse. Should we question his motives? Certainly. Yet we should also recall that he has never sought solidarity with any group or "interpretive community" other than his own private "dead poets' society." Homer, Virgil, Ovid, Martial, Catullus, Horace, Dante, Donne, Mandelstam, Akhmatova, Tsvetaeva, Auden, Frost, Lowell—these are his jury of peers, his writing must meet their standards. "Joe Brodsky's List of Good Books," a two-page photocopy of more than a hundred texts central to Western civilization, enjoys legendary status among Brodsky's literature students at Mount Holyoke.[3] Not fortuitously, Greek and Roman authors are especially well represented. The fact is that Brodsky has always been out of step with intellectual priestly castes passing judgment on the topicality of his poetic word. In the Soviet Union he was tried for political crimes (although he had no explicit political agenda) and made into an icon by the dissident movement while still in his early twenties; in the United States precisely the opposite situation has obtained—he is considered a kind of gadfly New York intellectual, whose views might be swiftly dismissed as reactionary if it were not for his long-suffering past and status as illustrious outsider.[4]

Brodsky is an American poet laureate whose primary audience is in another language and culture and, in some cases, not even of this world. Perhaps more striking from our vantage, he would prefer to have the past interrogate the present rather than the present the past. His reactions to the maps and fault lines associated not only with geopolitical empire but with a Foucauldian power struggle for the dominant discourse range from the indifferent to the positively inimical and, in any case, tend to the "longer view" of spatial and temporal removes. There is no place in Brodsky's poetics or worldview for what the critic Gary Saul Morson calls "presentism"—that is, the tendency to see and judge all the past through the lens of a late-twentieth-century intellectual. Everything exists in a kind of reverse perspective where the past is rich and various (though inevitably tragic), the present impoverished and barely adequate, and the future a series of ciphers. As Brodsky continues in the same foreword to the Venclova poems,

> The suggestion that the modern artist's perception of the world is more com- plex and intricate than that of the audience (not to mention that of his creative forebears) is ultimately undemocratic and unconvincing . . . The proposition that the artist feels, comprehends and expresses something unattainable by the ordinary person is no more convincing than the suggestion that the artist's physical pain, hunger, and sexual satisfaction are more intense than those of a commoner. True art is always democratic precisely because there is no denom- inator more common, either in society or history, than the sense that reality is imperfect and that a better alternative should be sought. ("Poetry as a Form of Resistance," 221)

We might get closer to a preliminary understanding of what "author-izes" Brodsky by returning to the occasion for his remarks. Brodsky is a strikingly occasional writer, though each entry into the fray on behalf of a fellow poet is never fully, or even primarily, ad hoc, but rather a subtle variation on a central and unwavering theme. Poetry is the ultimate aske-sis. It is prior to all else, including life, politics, history, and love. What Brodsky, Venclova, and Baranczak have in common is a past, both per-sonal and historico-cultural, lived under the shadow of the late (in both senses) Soviet empire. They represent national cultures that have been dangerously corrupted by the "belle époque" (*prekrasnaia epokha*) of Soviet rule, as Brodsky ironically describes it in his poetry, and that, in some basic sense, have ceased to be their own. And yet, despite this wide-spread malaise and the curse of ideology, they have all found ways to write authentic verse. Indeed, some would say that this curse, which is only that in terms of daily life, has been a blessing, or at least a solid point d'appui, for poetry. Brodsky, this logic goes, would not be "Brodsky" without the defining crucible of the persecution, penury, trials, imprison-ment, and exile. These, however, are imponderables, and Brodsky himself is the first to dismiss the aureole of biographical legend that others have constructed around him.[5]

What can be said by way of comparison is done so with special elo-quence by Seamus Heaney, a poet with whom Brodsky has much to share:

> When poets of the Free World "envy" their Eastern European successors, they do so not in the simple-minded spirit sometimes attributed to them and which is a caricature of their subtler, more shadowy complexes. Western poets do not assume that a tyrannical situation is somehow mitigated by the fact that it produces heroic artists and last-ditch art. Their envy is not at all for the plight of the artists but for the act of faith in art which becomes manifest as the artist copes with the tyrannical conditions. They stand in awe as life rises to the chal-lenge of Yeats's imagined "Black out; Heaven blazing into the head:/ Tragedy wrought to its uttermost." In the professional literary milieu of the West, the poet is susceptible to self-deprecation and scepticism; the poet in the United States, for example, is aware that the machine of reputation-making and book distribution, whether it elevates or ignores him or her, is indifferent to the moral and ethical force of the poetry being distributed. . . . I am reminded of Stephen Dedalus's enigmatic declaration that the shortest way to Tara was via Holyhead, implying that departure from Ireland and an inspection of the coun-try from the outside was the surest way of getting to the core of the Irish expe-rience. I wonder if we might not nowadays affirm, analogously, that the short-est way to Whitby, the monastery where Caedmon sang the first Anglo-Saxon verses, is via Warsaw and Prague. (Heaney, "The Impact of Translation," 6–7)

The difference between, say, Brodsky, Venclova, Baranczak, Milosz, and Zbigniew Herbert, on the one hand, and, on the other, those equally talented Western poets "susceptible to self-deprecation and scepticism" and therefore caught in the cogs of a "machine of reputation-making and book distribution . . . indifferent to the moral and ethical force" of poetry is, as Heaney correctly points out, "the act of faith in art which becomes manifest as the artist copes with tyrannical conditions." "When an entire community is struck by misfortune, for instance, the Nazi occupation of Poland, the 'schism between the poet and the great human family' [a quotation from Oscar Milosz's *A Few Words about Poetry*] disappears and poetry becomes as essential as bread," writes Czeslaw Milosz (*Witness*, 31). Or to recast Heaney's argument in Milosz's terms, "Is noneschatological poetry possible?" (*Witness*, 37). Yeats imagines the Black Out through which these poets have lived and *out of which* they have written. This is where Brodsky's discourse has its provenance, and we cannot understand how he arrived at Whitby until we begin to reconstitute the precise meaning of "via Leningrad/Petersburg."[6]

The present book is about Joseph Brodsky, the metaphysical implications of exile,[7] and the poetry that is written when the first and second enter into dialogue. It cannot be about all three at the same time—unless it itself is a poem—which immediately raises the issue of origins. What comes first, Joseph Brodsky the man, the status of exile with which he and his work have traditionally been associated, or the poems themselves? It is a choice that lies at the center of his biographical legend and of his "creative path" (*tvorcheskii put'*), as the Russians are wont to say. Brodsky himself would take bitter issue with any outside attempt to place a causal conjunction ("because," "as a result of") between the facts of his life and, as he puts it in an English phrase that owes its birth to the Russian (*izgiby stilia*), his "twists of language" (*Less*, 3). We of course are perfectly entitled to differ with Brodsky, to claim that he qua poet is a product of this experience or that aspect of character or background, and we would be, logically, right. But Brodsky would counter, and here he would be "more right," by saying that his knowledge of Mandelstam, Tsvetaeva, Auden, and Donne or his persecution at the hands of Soviet authorities have not *made* his poetry, even as they have, through their collective residue, helped to make it possible. The most that can be said, according to the poet himself, is that such factors and considerations were present at his poetry's birth, but that its life, that initial benevolent fillip in the delivery room of consciousness when image, rhyme, meter, strophic pattern, and spiritual "vector" (one of the poet's favorite words) all commence to pulsate and breathe in homeostatic movement, is its own. In Brodsky's celebrated butterfly poem, the hand moves across the blank sheet of paper to create a line of verse, just as the insect's wing flutters in the air, separating its viewer from the nothingness (*nichto*) beyond, but neither the hand nor the wing knows *why* this movement is called forth.

It is a truism, but it bears repeating: assiduous study (the "life of the mind") or personal tragedy is not a precondition for the creation of serious art, particularly in an age when the very notion of "major poet" is under scrutiny. It is not perhaps fair, for example, to compare someone like Alexander Kushner, a fine academic poet and contemporary Leningradian, to Brodsky, since Kushner's very status as foil is bound to elicit certain literary couplings: Laertes to Hamlet, Salieri to Mozart (see Solov'ev, *Roman s epigrafami*, 81–96). And yet enough time has passed since the "Brodsky affair" to make the statement that Kushner's commitment to "career" is somehow of a piece with his art. The Christian sacrifice that stands at the center of Brodsky's poetic worldview and the tradition he inherited does not consist merely of toil—the "Forward, my loyal ox" of Valery Bryusov's famous credo—but *of risk*, of giving of oneself without the guarantee of recompense. Despite moments of splendid erudition and technical brilliance, Kushner's efforts have not eventuated in poetry of the magnitude, grandeur, and nearly Promethean vitality of that written by Brodsky over the past three decades (see below). In this regard, Brodsky is a unique phenomenon on the cultural landscape of contemporary Russia. "We have in Brodsky," says the poet Bella Akhmadulina, "one whose greatest feature is his innate ability to take on board the culture of the whole world. . . . There is no poet at the moment who i better than Brodsky" (Loseff and Polukhina, *Brodsky's Poetics*, 197 199). Even Brodsky's lapses, including his occasional long-windedness (*dlinnoty*),[8] are remarkable and immediately recognizable as "Brod skian." Countless analogies, therefore, can, and presumably should, b made between Brodsky and his cherished predecessors, but they, in th end, are only that—analogies that point to certain paradigmatic affinitie For example, both Mandelstam and Brodsky are Jews who, as outcas (*izgoi*), speak with special eloquence for the Christian values in Russi culture; both Tsvetaeva and Brodsky write repeatedly about betrayal love and the aging process against the background of exile; both Aud and Brodsky assume an essentially "anti-heroic posture" (*Less*, 367) ev when presenting a world at war or the passing of a fellow poet; bc Donne and Brodsky pinch, knead, and beat their most complica thoughts into the "ayery thinnesse" of a poetic *concetto*; and so on. this is helpful and apposite, and we will have more to say about su affinities in due course, but it does not isolate the secret essence of "Brodskian" within Brodsky.

In this epoch of the death of the author and the rubbing out of tr scendental signifiers, including that of the humanistic tradition it there is the assumption that we can, through a kind of critical knig move, step outside myth, analyze it and domesticate it, and ultima make sense of how it enabled the given poet. The assumption, perl typified most forcefully in a "metapsychological" critic like Leo Ber

is that we need to break through these false codes, beginning with that of the subject itself. There are, apparently, no subjects who are not, by definition, ideologically suspect, and thus, directly or indirectly, responsible for various social and political ills.[9] The exercise of power, it is argued, motivates any and every urge to write. What is required, therefore, is nothing less than a literature that continually mounts an assault on the "myth of personality" and ends, in Robert Alter's words, by "pulveriz[ing] . . . the unitary self" ("Revolt Against Tradition," 293). "Ruin the sacred truths," exclaims the archromantic oedipal warrior Harold Bloom in his recent book about the relentless interpenetration of the categories of sacred and secular in any authentic literary work. But this step to the outside of originary myth is fraught with its own peril. A major premise of this study and a reason for writing it is that we may be witnessing the death of poetic language in our own culture and that the least that can be said is that many of us have grown indifferent, at times profoundly so, to how poetic language works and lives *from the inside*. The language we use to talk about poetry is often positively inimical to the poetry itself. This, for example, is what Frank Kermode, one of our most eminent critic-scholars, means when he says, invoking Valéry, that we have lost our appetite for poetry. To make this claim from within the academy is, to be sure, itself hopelessly mired in ideology and, if the reader wishes, "reactionary" and nostalgic for the values of "high literature." Joseph Brodsky, however, did not become a leading poet by defining himself exclusively within the value system of his parent culture, but rather against it, and by trying to write the kind of Russian poetry that is both mindful of its native inheritance and committed to invigorating that inheritance through repeated inoculations of the foreign.[10] By following the twists of his language we can learn something about Brodsky as well as our own cultural insularity.

At this point it might be well to invoke a poet and exile who inspired Brodsky and, earlier, those Acmeists, namely Mandelstam and Akhmatova, from whom Brodsky took the central tenet of his *ars poetica*—the poetic word as Christian Logos. Dante would say of a postmodernist step beyond myth or belief system that it is like finding firm footing on one's sinister (i.e., to the left) descent into the Inferno, for *which* foot, that of will (*appetitus*) or that of intellect (*ratio*), remains fixed? Which pushes off into new territory? And as Mandelstam understood perhaps better than T. S. Eliot, Dante's quest was shod first and foremost in the footwear of his tercets, it was about the myth of language, the Word itself. Dante's "other-speaking" (*al + goria*) is to be separated out from the "inner-speaking" of the *Commedia*'s poetic form only by stilling the movement of his massive pilgrimage. In this regard, there is no critical unmasking of a poet or his poem that is not itself another masking, just as there is no

uncompromised "outside" position, save that of the same *selva oscura*, from which to step into the fray. Every age and polis have their Black Guelphs and White Guelphs, their Florentine careerists, their future "neutral angels," and of course their *veltro* who appears in the text of life only to die. Yet the combination of sound and sense (the prosodic *restructuring* of time, as Brodsky would say) that imbues Dante's stubbornly vertical and totalizing worldview, even now, with a haunting substantiality is the myth we keep returning to, in fact the same one Dante himself returned to, in the steps of Virgil. The mythical beasts change shape (though the poetic function, the *l* in the *lonza, leone,* and *lupa,* does not), as do the lineaments of the sun-domed hill, but what poet does not try to attain the summit by retreating into a forest of words and taking the way down?

The models of Roland Barthes ("death of the author"), Michel Foucault ("what is an author?"), and Paul de Man ("autobiography as defacement") may work for the "poet without a biography," such as Mallarmé. But they work less well for the Russian context, as Svetlana Boym has recently shown in her *Death in Quotation Marks: Cultural Myths of the Modern Poet.* For poets such as Mandelstam, Tsvetaeva, and Brodsky, who have, consciously or unconsciously, cultivated a *mystical* connection between the actual facts of their lives (*byt*) and their created legends (the poet-martyr), the terms of Boris Tomashevsky (*biographical legend*), Yury Tynyanov (*literary fact, literary evolution*), and Lydia Ginzburg (*lyrical hero*) work better. They do so because they are context-sensitive and because they presuppose a genuine symbiotic bond between the charismatic poet who suffers in life for the sake of Culture (the enabling myth) and the people (*narod*) who are continually "redeemed" by this spectacle of suffering in which they participate and for which they are to some extent responsible (see Freidin, *A Coat*, 1–33). The poet Vladislav Khodasevich called this relationship between kenotic poet and benighted, tormenting folk at the foot of the cross *krovavaia pishcha*—a bloody repast. Those of us who study Russian poetry are made frightfully uncomfortable by notions of the "death of the author" and the "pleasure of the text" when applied, say, to Mandelstam, perhaps the greatest of all twentieth-century poets, who died a terrible death in a Stalinist camp and was last seen alive foraging about in refuse in a state bordering on insanity, his fabled birdlike features realized in a gruesome metaphor come to death-in-life.[11] Given a political system that could do this to a poet, and given Mandelstam's own beautiful plea to "preserve my speech" even as he provides the axe handle for his own execution, how can we write him and his life off? This is what Brodsky means when he says in his Nobel speech, "It is precisely their [Mandelstam's, Tsvetaeva's, and Akhmatova's[12]] lives, no matter how tragic and bitter they were, that make me

often—evidently, more often than I ought—regret the passage of time"
(Loseff and Polukhina, *Brodsky's Poetics*, 1). In Brodsky's world, as in
Nabokov's and Mandelstam's, poetry teaches *ethics through aesthetics*:
prosodic structure, the right word in the right place at the right time, is
that maximal blend of *simultaneous* giving and receiving (not the exercise
of power!) which, if translated to the realm of ethics (not vice versa),
means that every individual is a unique and precious instance.

The best way to talk about Brodsky, then, is through his poetry. So
before turning to the important and complex issues of biography and
exile, let us look briefly at how his unique tone and "vector" surface in
the kinds of words—those prosodically embalmed against time—that
matter to him most.

> Я входил вместо дикого зверя в клетку,
> выжигал свой срок и кликуху гвоздем в бараке,
> жил у моря, играл в рулетку,
> обедал черт знает с кем во фраке.
> С высоты ледника я озирал полмира,
> трижды тонул, дважды бывал распорот.
> Бросил страну, что меня вскормила.
> Из забывших меня можно составить город.
> Я слонялся в степях, помнящих вопли гунна,
> надевал на себя что сызнова входит в моду,
> сеял рожь, покрывал черной толью гумна
> и не пил только сухую воду.
> Я впустил в свои сны вороненый зрачок конвоя,
> жрал хлеб изгнанья, не оставляя корок.
> Позволял своим связкам все звуки, помимо воя;
> перешел на шепот. Теперь мне сорок.
> Что сказать мне о жизни? Что оказалась длинной.
> Только с горем я чувствую солидарность.
> Но пока мне рот не забили глиной,
> из него раздаваться будет лишь благодарность.

(*U*, 177)

> I have braved, for want of wild beasts, steel cages,
> carved my term and nickname on bunks and rafters,
> lived by the sea, flashed aces in an oasis,
> dined with the devil-knows-whom, in tails, on truffles.
> From the height of a glacier I beheld half the world, the earthly
> width. Twice have drowned, thrice let knives rake my nitty-gritty.
> Quit the country that bore and nursed me.
> Those who forgot me would make a city.

I have waded the steppes that saw yelling Huns in saddles,
worn the clothes nowadays back in fashion in every quarter,
planted rye, tarred the roofs of pigsties and stables,
guzzled everything save dry water.
I've admitted the sentries' third eye into my wet and foul
dreams. Munched the bread of exile: it's stale and warty.
Granted my lungs all sounds except the howl;
switched to a whisper. Now I am forty.
What should I say about life? That it's long and abhors transparence.
Broken eggs make me grieve; the omelette, though, makes me vomit.
Yet until brown clay has been crammed down my larynx,
only gratitude will be gushing from it.

(*To Urania*, 3)

The poem was written on 24 May 1980, the day Brodsky turned forty, a
ripe old age for a major Russian poet of this century. It is an exceptionally
powerful poem in Russian, especially if one has heard Brodsky read it
aloud. Sadly, much of that power is lost in translation (the author's
own).[13] Anyone writing a serious critical biography of Brodsky could
point to certain details in the poem and trace them to real-life events: the
"steel cages" (*kletki*) referring to prison cells, the "height of a glacier"
that probably recalls an early geological expedition, the drunken binges
and knife fights with fellow "prols," the extensive travel (both voluntary
and involuntary), the "pigsties and stables" (*gumna*) of the northern
exile, the quitting of his homeland, and so forth.[14] But that is not the point
here, to tack from the poem back to the life and then, presumably, back
to the poem, in a trajectory that rewards the scholar-sleuth for uniting
and decoding the two "texts." Rather, our point is *the tone and the voice*
of this poet.

To repeat, how many contemporary poets—and anglophone poets a
fortiori—can write with such moral authority, such supreme control of
the medium, such, so to speak, (raspy) full-throatedness? The late Robert
Lowell had the feral intensity but not the distance on himself and his
story; what is more, the *blagodarnost'* (gratitude) at the end of Brodsky's
poem is not his. Perhaps a Seamus Heaney or Derek Walcott, poets who
write in English yet operate existentially at the edges of our culture and
who are constantly fed by different, non-native originary myths?[15] We
think of Heaney's poetic rendering of his father pulling potatoes out of
the Irish soil ("Digging") or of Walcott's Caribbean seascapes[16] and we
immediately recall Brodsky, the Russian transplant, who has been
haunted since childhood by the siren call of the Neva and who, in the
absence of native soil (the notorious "cosmopolitanism"), was reared in
the shadow of classical columns and porticoes. That Heaney, however,

will metapoeticize his forebears' physical gestures into digging for words (that is, direct his attention back to the myth of the soil), while Brodsky will metapoeticize his efforts into the movement of a butterfly's wing (that is, direct his attention back to the myth of the air, to the "nothingness" of time itself), is telling. And above all there is Milosz, the poet whose Wilno roots took him back to ancient Polish-Lithuanian rivalries and whose urges were toward witness and detachment. "One should appreciate, after all, the advantages of one's origin. Its worth lies in the power it gives one to detach oneself from the present moment" (*Native Realm*, 35). Because Milosz is "allergic to 'Polishness'" yet writes in Polish, and because his Lithuanian past has become a "metaphor for 'coming from the outside'" (*Prywatne obowiązki*, 81–82; cited in Fiut, *Moment*, 95–96), the links with Brodsky, the Jew in Russian culture, appear particularly strong. No two poets writing today are more "metaphysical" in their passion for ideas and in their gnomic presentation of them, more "stoic" in their worldview, more inspired and at the same time repulsed by the "martyrial-messianic reflex" of their respective cultures (*Prywatne obowiązki*, 86; cited in Fiut, *Moment*, 96).[17] Of the two, however, Brodsky is ultimately the more angular and centrifugal.

In "I have braved" Brodsky is composing his own legend, to be sure, but there is not an ounce of Mayakovskian swagger in his narrative. The irony, the sudden and brutal descents in word choice, such as the "with the devil-knows-whom" (*chert znaet s kem*), are aimed as much at himself as they are at "society." The poet has lived this long, and has survived these various brushes with death, in order to "preserve the same speech" that Mandelstam preserved. That is why, he believes, he has made it to forty. He thus *takes control* of the searing residue of these events by releasing it into the service of his prosodic structure, in this instance the rhymes, which become more foregrounded when we recognize the free *dol'nik* form of the lines. The rhymes, so difficult to manage in contemporary English unless they are half- or slant-, are remarkable for their precision and near-physical reality. A poet who can rhyme the genitive singular of "Hun" (*gunna*) with the accusative plural of "barns" (*gumna*) is, other issues aside, vivid and bold in his associative leaps. John Hollander's argument that a good rhyme is both the poet's formal manacle (constraint) and his bridge (freedom) to larger vistas comes to mind, as does Valéry's suggestive comparison of a rhyme to a clock ticking outside a poem's theme (Hollander, *Vision and Resonance*, 117–19). Brodsky deflates his own significance as a human being with a biography—I was a kind of caged circus animal, I wasted my youth in the same banal way that youth has always been wasted, many more have forgotten me than remember me, I drank everything one could drink except for dry water,

and so forth—in order to raise, on the wings of his rhymes, his significance as a poet, or rather, the significance of his calling. Joseph Brodsky
himself is not what is important, and that is strangely liberating. This, in
short, is a poet who knows his own worth and, through some compensatory alchemical formula, is incapable of uttering a single false note about
it. Is not a closing like "Yet until brown clay has been crammed down my
larynx, / only gratitude will be gushing from it"[18] close to unthinkable in
the context of contemporary American poetry?

A second example comes from Brodsky's 1989 poem on the centenary
of Akhmatova's birth. It is equally illustrative, but from a slightly different angle. And it also offers a useful point of transition, since it shows
rather compactly what happens to Brodsky's diction and tone when he
confronts the ghosts of his great forebears:

Страницу и огонь, зерно и жернова,
секиры острие и усеченный волос—
Бог сохраняет все; особенно—слова
прощенья и любви, как собственный свой голос.

В них бьется рваный пульс, в них слышен костный хруст,
и заступ в них стучит; ровны и глуховаты,
затем что жизнь—одна, они из смертных уст
звучат отчетливей, чем из надмирной ваты.

Великая душа, поклон через моря
за то, что их нашла, —тебе и части тленной,
что спит в родной земле, тебе благодаря
обретшей речи дар в глухонемой вселенной.

(*PP*, 30)

Fire and paper, millstone and seed,
the blade of the pole-ax, the hair freshly split—
God saves them all, but words He saves indeed,
of love and mercy, as from His own lips.

They pulsate in terror, they crack in one's bones,
they knock at the grave; in steady cadence they pound,
because life is just once, because their lips' mortal moan
rises still sharper athwart the heavens' dull sound.

Great soul, it is to you across the sea,
to you who found them, and to you who disappear
asleep in native soil, I now bend my knee,
for gift of speech in a universe's deaf ear.[19]

(my translation)

I have tried to give some approximation in English of Brodsky's Alexandrines, but the attempt is admittedly imperfect. It is very difficult to convey the combined tone of dignity and compassion in the poem—the sense that Brodsky is himself a major poet speaking to another major poet across the table of death. Yet every formal aspect of the manifold points in this direction: the choice of meter (the caesura in the middle of the line slows things down and, as it were, "prosodizes" the seriousness of the occasion); the choice of diction (the archaic and high-sounding *sekira* [pole-ax] and the Biblical *obretshaia*—the sense of "seek and ye shall find"); and the typically—for Brodsky—convoluted syntax (the phrasal and clausal "unpacking" necessary to understand what precisely is happening in the final stanza, again, impedes the flow of the sentiment and causes us to dwell at greater length on the significance of Akhmatova's passing). The "great soul" of the last stanza is a wonderful touch for the very reason that only Brodsky could manage it, only he, the greatest living Russian poet and the only genuine successor to Akhmatova and Mandelstam in the tradition, could call his "godmother" this and not be accused either of immodesty or, worse, ingratiation. We will have more to say about Brodsky's "authorizing" tone throughout the study, but for now the reader should note that there is no Bloomian anxiety in his tribute, and that Brodsky can be positively ferocious in the irony he directs against himself and the world order (a good example of which is the "I have braved" poem just cited), but he can be just as serene and tenderly dignified when that same poetic intelligence is directed toward a deceased (but not for him silent) great interlocutor.

The Context: In Place of Biography

The time is not yet right for a serious scholarly biography of Joseph Brodsky.[20] The very genre superimposes a distancing frame on its subject—a frame not compatible with the notion of a life still being lived. Brodsky is too much in the foreground of our thoughts about the contemporary state of Russian (and not only Russian) letters to allow us to assume a position of what Bakhtin would call *vnenakhodimost'* (lit., "outsideness"). Still, something does need to be said about the poet's biography for the simple reason that the Western reader at home with postmodern notions of the "death of the author" may not be equipped to understand the bioaesthetic nexus in this case. Mallarmé may have consciously cultivated the sense that he was, in Tomashevsky's terms, a "writer without a biography," but this model has limited application to the Russian context (see Boym, *Death in Quotation Marks*, 1–36). Poets writing in the tradition of Pushkin's "Prophet" (Prorok, 1826), where the seer in the desert has his "sinful, idle and cunning" tongue ripped out by a six-winged seraphim and his faint heart replaced by a flaming verbal coal capable of searing all it touches, are not apt to spin themselves into increasingly attenuated versions of nonbeing with each exquisite toss of the dice. It is this Pushkinian model, played out as it was in the tragic lives of such modern forebears as Mandelstam, Akhmatova, and Tsvetaeva, that exerted a profound influence on Brodsky during his formative years. Even today, when he speaks of these poets and the way their lives and works conjoined in a mystery play of Christian Logos, Brodsky is operating within this tradition (see, e.g., "Nobel Lecture," in Loseff and Polukhina, *Brodsky's Poetics*, 1–11).

Thus, we might say, Brodsky's life to date is complicated by several factors, not least of which are his legitimate need for privacy and the competing aureole of biographical legend that attends so relentlessly on the reader's understanding of any major Russian writer in the vatic mode. That the poet has said on more than one occasion that his essence as a person is to be found in the "twists of his language" does not mean that his reputation as the "second Osya" (the first being Mandelstam) is a mere conceit. It simply means that Brodsky will not be martyr (or "dissident") first, and poet second. Biography is real, yet not more real than prosody, the "restructured time" of poetic speech. In this respect, Brodsky's response to his most famous public statement is characteristic. When at his trial in February 1964 Judge Savelyeva asked him in a crudely provocative manner who had enlisted him in the ranks of the poets, that is, who had *authorized* him to write, Brodsky answered that he thought such a right came "from God" (*ot Boga*) ("Zasedanie," 280). The implication of the judge's query had been that if Brodsky did not hold an appropriate post in the literary establishment, then he had no right to call himself a poet.[21] But Brodsky, true to his tradition, shifted the discourse and the authorizing power from this world to the other world. Years later, when asked in an interview what he had been thinking about at the time, Brodsky said he did not know (Interview with author; 28–29 March 1991, South Hadley, Mass.). Whatever he was thinking about, it was not, presumably, Mandelstam, *imitatio Christi*, and "greatness." In other words, the precise moment in his biography (as opposed to his poetry) when he became, as it were, the "second Osya" and his two personas (private poet and public martyr) elided for the first time was not apparently etched in his own consciousness with images of a thorny crown. "Biography" does not operate on this grand romantic scale, at least as far as Brodsky himself is concerned (or is willing to admit). So the question becomes, at this preliminary stage, how can the poet (or reader) have it both ways, how can he be a rightful heir to the Pushkinian legacy of sacred sacrifice *and* claim that his life really does not matter, or that it matters only to the point that it has enabled him to write in the first place?

The purpose of this section is modest: to acquaint the reader with some skeletal information about Brodsky's background and his views on "reality." The focus will be on those personal areas—family, friends, hometown, shared values—that stand out in a certain relief in his autobiographical writings, especially in *Less Than One*. It is, not suprisingly, in response to such topics that Brodsky seems to address most directly the relation of *Wahrheit* to *Dichtung*. What follows, then, is a *vector* (Brodsky's own term) that may be of use to a future biographer.

Joseph Brodsky was born on 24 May 1940, in Leningrad, the only child of Alexander Brodsky and Maria Volpert. To his father, a native St. Petersburgian and photojournalist by training who became a well-traveled naval officer during the Second World War, the son owes his love of the sea and his affection for Russian naval history, lore, and "nobility of spirit" (*Less*, 466). Water, beginning with the Neva, would always be an essential element in Brodsky's native idiom, its Stevensian "ghostlier demarcations" setting off thoughts on time, origins, death, and eternity. The future poet's stated preference for the elegant rigors of naval "trigonometry" and the regular angles of Peter's "intentional" city over the "shoddy planimetry of ideologues" (*Less*, 466–67) dovetails poignantly with childhood memories of a duty-officer father in smart uniform who would allow the child to roam about the Navy Museum and then, on leisurely strolls homeward, explain the city's architectural monuments. One of the lessons the boy had to internalize early on was that the simple "either/or" morality of this decent man was hopelessly ill matched against the nuances and gradations of Soviet evil. Brodsky's mother came from Latvian merchant stock (her father had been a Singer sewing machine salesman in the Baltic provinces) and was adept at foreign languages. She served briefly during the war as an interpreter in a camp for German prisoners of war. However, because of the anti-Semitism that confronted many Jewish Russian families in the immediate postwar years prior to Stalin's death in 1953 (in fact, Alexander Brodsky himself lost his job in the navy and had a difficult time finding employment in civilian life), Maria Brodsky suppressed her own culture and intelligence and contented herself by working most of her adult life as a clerk in a borough "development council."

In general, the question of Brodsky's Jewishness and the notorious "fifth paragraph" (i.e., the blank in one's passport where one had to make a choice between "Russian" and "Jewish" as nationality) was less traumatic to him than it was to Mandelstam and Pasternak, his poetic uncles. He was, in any event, never "ethnic" or religious in an organized way, and he came to see this widespread prejudice as simply another convenient reason to "switch off" (*Less*, 6) and further estrange himself from the societal norm. Is his professed lack of interest in ethnic roots per se and his studied calm (save for moments of cathartic sarcasm) in the face of painful memories a compensatory facade, a kind of false bravado? One suspects not. This, for example, is how Brodsky remembers his first public clash with the nationality issue and his first lie, that is, his first recollection of stepping outside the bounds of the socium:

> The real history of consciousness starts with one's first lie. I happen to remember mine. It was in a school library when I had to fill out an application for membership. The fifth blank was of course "nationality." I was seven years old and knew very well that I was a Jew, but I told the attendant that I didn't know. With dubious glee she suggested that I go home and ask my parents. I never returned to that library, although I did become a member of many others which had the same application forms. I wasn't ashamed of being a Jew, nor was I scared of admitting it. . . . I was ashamed of the word "Jew" itself—in Russian, "*yevrei*"—regardless of its connotations.
>
> A word's fate depends on the variety of its contexts, on the frequency of its usage. In printed Russian "*yevrei*" appears nearly as seldom as, say, "mediastinum" or "gennel" in American English. In fact, it also has something like the status of a four-letter word or like a name for VD. . . . [S]omehow it goes against one's sense of prosody. I remember that I always felt a lot easier with a Russian equivalent of "kike"—"*zhyd*" (pronounced like André Gide): it was clearly offensive and thereby meaningless, not loaded with allusions. . . . All this is not to say that I suffered as a Jew at that tender age; it's simply to say that my first lie had to do with my identity. (*Less*, 7–8)

Note that while the ostensible topic is his Jewishness (as opposed to his Russianness—a Kafkaesque distinction, especially if applied linguistically), the more important topic is language itself. That is, even from this early age Brodsky derived his identity more from the internal workings of words than from general categories applied from without. What was most offended, if we are to believe his version (and we must in the absence of others), was his "sense of prosody." That the child did not suffer and that this sort of crude ostracism left no permanent traces is, of course, a moot point. But what can be argued is that Brodsky has a unique angle of vision on his first lie and his first embrace of "ambivalence" (*Less*, 10). Nowhere in *Less Than One*, throughout the handful of instances where the topic of anti-Semitism is broached, does the temperature, so to speak, of the author's prose rise, and this is true a fortiori of any self-reference. It was simply a fact of life in a world not distinguished for its fairness to begin with.

Brodsky's independence as poet and thinker originates, as he is the first to admit, with his family and upbringing. His rather low expectations for fellow human beings outside his immediate circle, his stoicism and lack of complaint in the face of adversity, his passion for privacy, his links to

Petersburg/Leningrad as hearth and home, and his deeply held belief in the values of memory, culture, and sacrifice also begin here. For those who suspect Brodsky of a kind of misanthropy, the following passage describing his family's life in a *kommunalka* (communal apartment) needs to be cited:

> For all the despicable aspects of this mode of existence, a communal apartment has perhaps its redeeming side as well. It bares life to its basics: it strips off any illusions about human nature. By the volume of the fart, you can tell who occupies the toilet, you know what he/she had for supper as well as for breakfast. You know the sounds they make in bed and when the women have their periods. It's often you in whom your neighbor confides his or her grief, and it is he or she who calls for an ambulance should you have an angina attack or something worse. (*Less*, 454–55)

This description, so raw and brutally "real," forces us to confront, if only verbally, the fishbowl that is Soviet communal life. There is absolutely no veneer here, with four families and eleven people sharing one kitchen, one bathroom, one toilet (actually the figures were not inhuman by Soviet standards). Everyone was basically a "good neighbor," despite the—by Western standards—unbearable closeness, and there was, happily, only one police informer. And so it was in the "tribal" atmosphere of this "dimly lit cave" that Alexander and Maria Brodsky made a "nest" for themselves and their son (*Less*, 455). Little wonder that Brodsky places such a premium on his own privacy and freedom of movement.

As every Soviet *intelligent* knows, the "life of the mind" becomes more of a sine qua non when basic physical privacy is hard to come by. It is the last place the state can look when one is forced on a daily basis to share toilets and kitchens with neighbors. The "room and a half" described in such loving detail in the last essay of *Less Than One* refers to the space (forty square meters) alloted to the Brodsky family. Since this was thirteen square meters more than the norm (nine square meters × 3 family members), it meant that the Brodskys had an extra half room to their name which in any event could not be made separate or self-enclosed without violating the rules. It is this partial space that Brodsky *fils* made, with a regiment of curtains, armoires, and bookcases, into his little medieval principality. One mentions the truncated aspect of what Brodsky calls his *Lebensraum* because it is precisely this sort of existential "whittling" (*vychitanie*) that would eventually become second nature to the poet.[22] He needed less than an entire room, in fact what for many would be nothing more than a good-sized closet, to read his forbidden texts, to initiate his relations with the opposite sex, and to begin typing his first literary efforts on his father's cast-off "Royal Underwood." "[T]hese ten square meters were mine, and they were the best ten square meters I've ever known" (*Less*, 477).

In general, Brodsky's philosophy of life, evident from the titles framing his book of essays ("Less Than One" and "In a Room and a Half"), is one of metaphysical expansion in the face of physical subtraction. Life picks over its human prey, leaving only, as the poet says in one of his better-known lyrics, a verbal carcass—"a part of speech." If his parents' apartment (postal address: Liteiny Blvd. #24, Apt. 28), the actual private space they did not have to share with others, could be reduced to a synecdoche, then it would be the large bed on which the family made all its important decisions and to which, in the poet's own words, "I owe my life" (*Less*, 473). Because this bed was certainly *more* than it needed to be, particularly in a space so physically cramped and to three people so materially constrained, one thinks of Brodsky's own verse, itself an infinitely expanding series of metaphysical arabesques and curlicues set against a background of stark human pain and relentless diminution. "It was a . . . king-sized affair whose carvings, again, matched to a certain degree the rest, yet they were done in a more modern fashion. The same vegetation motif, of course, but the execution oscillated somewhere between Art Nouveau and the commercial version of Constructivism" (*Less*, 473). Needless to say, the bed was the source not of one crucial and buried primal scene but of many secondary and tertiary ones (family fights, reconciliations, plans, musings), which were important and real because they were *theirs*. Brodsky will, for example, use a bed as a central motif in one of his finest love lyrics in the Donnean mode, where the metaphysical notion of "This bed thy center is, these walls, thy spheare" will preside over a triangle of betrayal and a couple's parting.

Perhaps the epithet most widely used when referring to the mature Brodsky is "stoic." "Tears," he writes, "were infrequent in our family; the same goes to a certain extent for the whole of Russia" (*Less*, 480). His own carapacelike exterior is given similar treatment in an already quoted poem: "[I have] granted my lungs [lit., vocal cords] all sounds except the howl." But stoicism itself, at least as a modern application of Zeno's doctrine of "detachment from, and independence of, the outer world" (Harvey, *Oxford Companion*, 407), is not entirely apposite. Brodsky's position is always both "in exile from" *and* "in liberation to." In this respect the poet is decidedly not postmodern. Only someone who believed in something more than flinty self-containment could say, as Brodsky does in a recent interview:

> One starts to write poems in order not to write poems but to get better, and not to get better as a poet but to get better as a—well, all right, I am going to use the word—soul. I am not concerned with the failure of my soul vis-à-vis the

Supreme Being. I am convinced, in parentheses, that what I've been doing [i.e., writing poetry] is to His (if He does exist) liking, because otherwise there would be no reason for Him to keep me around [a reference to Brodsky's long-standing heart condition]. (Interview with author; 28–29 March 1991, South Hadley, Mass.)

Thus, Brodsky's is not so much a realist's response to the injustice in this world as a glimmer of insight from the next. One need not underestimate the frequent moments when the poet's doubt and corrosive irony seem to make any affirmation, even the most tentative, impossible. Brodsky very much belongs to his time. Nevertheless, his stoicism is, as Nabokov imagined Gumilyov in the final seconds before a bolshevik firing squad, the wry smile of one who knows something that his killers do not (Alexandrov, *Nabokov's Otherworld*, 223–24).[23] It has its roots perhaps in his father's military bearing, in the older Brodsky's conviction that one rises, with whatever one has, to a challenge:

> He [Alexander Brodsky] was a proud man. When something reprehensible or horrendous was drawing near him, his face assumed a sour yet at the same time a challenging expression. It was as if he were saying "Try me" to something that he knew from the threshold was mightier than he. "What else could you expect from this scum?" would be his remark on those occasions, a remark with which he would go into submission. (*Less*, 480)

The difference, of course, between a Gumilyov and the elder Brodskys (and presumably countless more like them) is that the former had the blessing of a quick death, while the latter had to live out what was left of their lives as best they could. Can Varlam Shalamov be called a stoic? Is there not a point, and not only for those in the Gulag, when inner virtue becomes a luxury? Brodsky's reasoning is that his parents never lost sight of the fact that they had become "slaves" and that, if their modified stoicism had a function, it was to prevent the outward acts of submission from becoming inner ones.

Brodsky's idiosyncratic playing at causes and effects, his insistence on keeping the narrative authority for his life story to himself, is also, and perhaps most movingly, an homage to his parents. One reason origins may be interrogated so thoroughly at the end of *Less Than One* is to thwart the notion of a linear argument and a standard biography. Effects are not necessarily ethically superior to causes; they simply come after. "I am them [i.e., his dead parents], of course; I am now our family" (*Less*, 500) is again, according to Brodsky, not an expansion but a shrinkage. The distilled message of the eulogy in "A Room and a Half" is that Alexander and Maria Brodskys' "nest" made possible their son's *Lebensraum*, that their commitment to the "filiation" of family enabled his commitment to the "affiliation" of culture and poetry,[24] that their cognizance of "slavery" allowed and encouraged his cognizance of "freedom." "The main issues were bread on the table, clean clothes, and staying healthy. Those were their synonyms for love, and they were better than mine" (*Less*, 497). Brodsky, though he and they tried to arrange it many times, did not see his parents during the last twelve years of their life: the state did not consider such a visit "purposeful" (*Less*, 460). The combined residue of their unattended deaths and his survival is, not unexpectedly, guilt and gratitude:

> After all, every child feels guilty toward his parents, for somehow he knows that they will die before him. So all he needs to alleviate his guilt is to have them die of natural causes [as Brodsky's parents did]: of an illness, or old age, or both. Still, can one extend this sort of cop-out to the death of a slave? . . . [W]hat about someone born free but dying a slave? . . . A deflected river running to its alien, artificial estuary. Can anyone ascribe its disappearance at this estuary to natural causes? And if one can, what about its course? What about human potential, reduced and misdirected from the outside? . . . I am asking these questions precisely because I am a tributary of a turned, deflected river. (*Less*, 478–79, 482–83)

So it is here, in the conclusion to "A Room and a Half," that Brodsky comes as close as he is capable of to positing a causal connection between biography and a poet's work. The answer to the deflected river with its alien, artificial estuary is neither conscious nor premeditated. Such accounts can never be balanced on the paper of this world. And that is the son's point, the reason for his questions. Poetry is a permanent state of imbalance, an always returning need whose momentary fulfillment is made possible by those who came before (in various senses). Brodsky's trials as poet and man are not those of his parents, but on a good day, and if the illumination is coming from the right direction, his poetry may reveal a foolscap that is the imprint of their sacrifice and love. "I am grateful to my mother and my father not only for giving me life but also for failing to bring up their child as a slave." "The quality of their genes" was such, concludes Brodsky in a rare moment of immodesty, that their "fusion produced a body the system found alien enough to eject" (*Less*, 499). If it can be said that Alexander and Maria Brodsky "conceived their way out" of the chimneys of the state crematorium, then it was in the English prose, with its own "verbs of motion," of their Russian poet son (*Less*, 460, 500).

An only slightly less potent presence hovering around the edges of Brodsky's origins is that of his hometown. The last major study of St. Petersburg as mytho-cultural filter was published by N. P. Antsyferov in 1922 (*Dusha Peterburga*). Understandably, Antsyferov could not include the city's subsequent history as Soviet orphan. Petersburg/Leningrad, with its classical architecture and stern symmetries, its Lethean waterways and familiarity with suffering and death, was the site for what can only be termed a profound and ongoing Orphic rite. Russian poetry of the so-called Silver Age thrived, as it were, on its own *amor fati*. Petropolis gradually became a ghost town—a Necropolis. The desolation of the first great war and revolution had given the city's countenance a kind of somber grandeur, as more than one memoirist noted. There were poems, such as Khodasevich's mesmerizing "Ballad" (Ballada, 1921), written as the ties with the old culture were dying out, that joined poet and city in a *danse macabre*. Mandelstam spoke in one of his most oft-quoted lyrics of "burying the sun" of Russian culture, that is, Pushkin, in a funeral rite-cum-incantatory prayer whose very utterance ("a blessed, meaningless word") held the promise of sacred reunion for those left behind ("In Peterburg we shall meet again" [V Peterburge my soidemsia snova, 1920]). Thus, Russia's culture was driven underground during the "Soviet night" that eventuated in Stalinism. We see it in Akhmatova's great "Northern Elegies" (1943–53), in her *Requiem* cycle (1935–40), and in *Poem Without a Hero* (Poema bez geroia, 1940–62), and we see it in Mandelstam's piercing "Leningrad" (1930)—

Я вернулся в мой город, знакомый до слёз,
До прожилок, до детских припухлых желёз.

I've returned to my city, familiar to the point of tears,
to veins, to a child's swollen glands.

—where the poet is caught in the overlay of his epoch's palimpsest, in the hideous limbo between the two names for the city. He is not ready to die but feels himself and his Petersburg culture being buried alive in the altered surroundings. He wanders about like a tormented shade in Dante's *Inferno*.

Brodsky shares this underworld culture; it is the legacy of every Petersburg *intelligent*. To some it is a reserve and to others an arrogance. "The most characteristic features of Leningraders," summarizes the ex-Soviet *eiron*, "are . . . bad teeth (because of lack of vitamins during the siege), clarity in pronunciation of sibilants, self-mockery, and a degree of haughtiness toward the rest of the country" (*Less*, 93). It is the difference, one might say, between the restrained classicism of a Pushkin, Mandelstam, or Akhmatova and the unbuttoned exuberance of a Muscovite such as Pasternak or Tsvetaeva. The city is virtually awash in its own cultural history, as though what was unleashed in the flood described in the city's most famous poem, Pushkin's *Bronze Horseman* (Mednyi vsadnik, 1833), was nothing less than a massive anamnesis. Writers' homes become landmarks by which average citizens take their bearings. "Toward the middle of the nineteenth century, these two things merged: Russian literature caught up with reality to the extent that today when you think of St. Petersburg you can't distinguish the fictional from the real" (*Less*, 80). Moreover, the city's foreign architecture, faded pastel colorings, and unforgiving, at times "unreal" climate (e.g., White Nights), coupled with its tragic history, make it an ideal place for one inclined toward self-estrangement.

Brodsky quickly recognized this withdrawal as native to him. In these surroundings it was "somehow easier to endure loneliness" because "the city itself [was] lonely" (*Less*, 89–90). Leningrad entered his bloodstream, like the cod-liver oil in Mandelstam's poem, along with stoicism and stubbornness.

> I must say that from these facades and porticoes—classical, modern, eclectic, with their columns, pilasters, and plastered heads of mythic animals or people—from their ornaments and caryatids holding up the balconies, from the torsos in the niches of their entrances, I have learned more about the history of our world than I subsequently have from any book. . . . And from the gray, reflecting river flowing down to the Baltic, with an occasional tugboat in the midst of it struggling against the current, I have learned more about infinity and stoicism than from mathematics and Zeno. (*Less*, 5)

What the young man saw as he glanced out at the Neva or looked down the embankment had an almost abstract, clinical quality that we immediately recognize as "Brodskian" as well. The "absolute zero" of consciousness with which some of the poet's more far-flung metaphysical speculations can be characterized seems strangely at home in this context:

> The lower the thermometer falls, the more abstract the city looks. Minus 25 Centigrade is cold enough, but the temperature keeps falling as though, having done away with people, river, and buildings, it aims for ideas, for abstract concepts. With the white smoke floating above the roofs, the buildings along the embankments more and more resemble a stalled train bound for eternity. (*Less*, 90)

In "A Guide to a Renamed City" (1979), Brodsky explains as eyewitness how his hometown finally earned its name the hard way, through the horrendous suffering of the blockade. Up to that point its rechristening in the Soviet era had seemed so vulgar and ludicrous ("A survivor cannot be named after Lenin" [*Less*, 4]). But the nine hundred-day long siege anchored that absurdly floating signifier in a sea of blood, killing nearly a million people on the alternating racks of bombardment and starvation. The city grew so accustomed to the death of its own that death itself, to quote a survivor (Olga Berggolts), finally took fright. And when Brodsky refers to Leningrad as "unconquered," one feels both his bond to that ordeal and his pride. In any event, the grandeur of the dying city, already described movingly by postrevolutionary memoirists, is reincarnated with particular force in Brodsky's words. Orphism for this tradition is anything but a figure of speech:

> The siege is the most tragic page in the city's history, and I think it was then that the name "Leningrad" was finally adopted by the inhabitants who survived, almost a tribute to the dead; it's hard to argue with tombstone carvings. The city suddenly looked much older; it was as though History had finally acknowledged its existence and decided to catch up with this place in her usual morbid way: by piling up bodies. Today, thirty-three years later, however repainted and stuccoed, the ceilings and facades of this unconquered city still seem to preserve the stain-like imprints of its inhabitants' last gasps and last gazes. (*Less*, 91)

Brodsky is a private person. It will be up to a future biographer to track his friendships and fallings-out over the years. Presumably the interested reader will want to know more about how he quit school at the age of fifteen; his thirteen different jobs and peregrinations across the Soviet Union in the years 1956–62; his immediate circle of friends in Leningrad (Evgeny Rein, Anatoly Naiman, Lev Loseff, Vladimir Uflyand, Yakov Gordin, and others); his early work as translator; his long and painful affair with Marina Basmanova, and his conflicted feelings toward their son Andrei; his relationships with Akhmatova and Nadezhda Mandelstam; the circumstances surrounding his various arrests (1959–64) and betrayal(s); his stay in the Kashchenko Psychiatric Hospital (Moscow, December 1963–January 1964); the campaign of vilification mounted against him, and the impact his trial for "parasitism" had on the Leningrad intellectual community (February–March 1964); the honorable role in these proceedings of such senior cultural figures as Efim Etkind and Frida Vigdorova; his sentence (five years of hard labor) and exile to a small village (Norinskaya) in the far north (Arkhangelsk Province), and the course of study he plotted out for himself in those surroundings (March 1964–November 1965); his premature return and eventual banishment from the Soviet Union in June 1972; his gradual adaptation to life in the West under the benevolent guidance of those such as Auden and Carl Proffer; his work as teacher and cultural "post horse" at various institutions, including the University of Michigan, Columbia University, New York University, and Mount Holyoke College; his ties to prominent Russian and Eastern European cultural figures in exile, such as Mikhail Baryshnikov, Czeslaw Milosz, and Tomas Venclova; his attempts to maintain independence in the often volatile atmosphere of "third-wave"

Russian émigré literary politics; his acquaintances and friendships with Robert Lowell, Derek Walcott, Richard Wilbur, Susan Sontag, and other Western poets and intellectuals; his relationships to various women in the years of exile as he still "carried the torch" for Basmanova; his serious health problems and open-heart surgeries; his institutionalization as American man of letters (Guggenheim, MacArthur, Doctor of Letters from Yale, American Academy and Institute of Arts and Letters, National Book Critics Circle Award, and so forth); the politics surrounding the awarding of the Nobel Prize in 1987; his many travels and his continuing ties to New York; his unexpected marriage in 1990 to Maria Sozzani; and his work as poet laureate of the United States and consultant in poetry to the Library of Congress. All this will have to be carefully researched and studied against the record of available correspondence, published and unpublished writings, and personal interviews.

Yet even in the absence of this patient sifting, certain patterns can be observed. First of all, real friendship and love are never trivial, and where they do exist, which is rare, they are usually cemented by a shared belief in the transcendent value of culture. The future record will probably show how Brodsky was at his most loyal and solicitous when a friend was in genuine need, such as the gifted balletomane and critic Gennady Shmakov, who died of AIDS in New York in 1989 (see "Pamiati Gennadiia Shmakova," in *PP*, 45–48). No modern Russian poet has written more elegies on the deaths of friends than Brodsky. Brodsky's sacred trivium of culture, memory, and love, often set against the ultimate border-crossing to the other world, is the only basis for a lasting relationship ("Beyond Consolation"). Again, *Less Than One* gives us a firsthand impression of what it meant to be a friend among the "generation of 1956":

> We [Brodsky and his circle] were avid readers and we fell into a dependence on what we read. . . . Dickens was more real than Stalin or Beria. More than anything else, novels would affect our modes of behavior and conversations, and 90 percent of our conversations were about novels. . . . Books became the first and only reality. . . . Nobody knew literature and history better than these people, nobody could write in Russian better than they, nobody despised our times more profoundly. For these characters civilization meant more than daily bread and a nightly hug. This wasn't, as it might seem, another lost generation. This was the only generation of Russians that had found itself, for whom Giotto and Mandelstam were more imperative than their personal destinies. (*Less*, 28–29)

One's identity as a social being is indistinguishable from the volumes on one's bookshelf, a lesson learned first from another "upstart intellectual" (*raznochinets*), the same Mandelstam of *The Noise of Time*.[25] Edward Said, on the other hand, might describe these reactions as a beleaguered intelligentsia's inevitable postmodern passage from biological "filiation" to cultural "affiliation" (see above). Still others might speak of this generation's "marginalization" and disenfranchisement. Is it not a pity, the logic would go, that these young people have been forced to seek value outside the prevailing discourse and power structures of the state? In the last analysis, however, who should be learning from whom?

A final issue regarding context has to do with Brodsky's poetic origins. It is something of an enigma, certainly to Western readers but even to Russians, where this new voice came from. It will be a central argument of this study that Brodsky became "Brodsky" only with the thorough study and incorporation into his native tradition of certain Western, especially Anglo-American, sources, sources which up to that point had been little known and virtually untapped. Yet it would be a misrepresentation to claim that Brodsky emerged as it were ex nihilo, full-blown from the forehead of Donne or Auden. What space, for example, did he fill in the literary scene of the late fifties and early sixties? This is a complex question, and as in the case of his biography, one that cannot be answered fully at present. To posit the question correctly, however, one would need to examine carefully the full range of poetry being produced in Brodsky's milieu at the time he appeared on the scene. Moreover, one would need to compare Brodsky's earliest efforts, say those in his *Lyric and Narrative Verse* (Stikhotvoreniia i poemy, 1965), a volume whose publication the poet did not oversee and substantial portions of which he did not include in later collections, with other examples of contemporary poetry then in fashion. These juvenilia were Brodsky's "creative laboratory," his first attempts at trying on other styles and voices; in them lies the secret of when he first "became himself." And in this respect, of the various names that have since earned a niche in the literary history of post-Stalinist Soviet poetry (Arseny Tarkovsky, Naum Korzhavin, Bulat Okudzhava, Evgeny Evtushenko, Andrei Voznesensky, Novella Matveeva, Bella Akhmadulina, Dmitry Bobyshev, Natalya Gorbanevskaya, Aleksei Tsvetkov, Yury Kublanovsky, and so forth), three seem most promising—Boris Slutsky, Evgeny Rein, and Alexander Kushner.

Many of the pieces found in *Lyric and Narrative Verse* share qualities that the scholar Galina Gordeeva identifies as being characteristic of the works of Leningrad writers of the late fifties and sixties: a playful (perhaps at times even "metaliterary") attitude toward reality, an intentional mixing of levels of diction, an ironic intonation, a fascination with the myth of Orpheus, and an interest in antiquity ("Svobodnaia taina," 230–39).[26] But such a thematic approach, while not unhelpful, is insufficiently fine-grained. It is my hypothesis that there are elements of the mature Brodsky that are, *mutatis mutandis*, "Slutskian," "Reinian," and "Kushnerian," but there was no poet then on the scene who combined these elements in one "poetic world." What is more, when these elements came

together with the English metaphysical strain, first with Donne in 1963
("Large Elegy to John Donne") and then with Auden in 1965 ("Verses on
the Death of T. S. Eliot"), a kind of spontaneous combustion occurred.
Much more, of course, was going on in Brodsky's life and studies than
this version allows: readings of Dostoevsky, the Bible, the Polish metaphysicals (especially Zbigniew Herbert and Milosz),[27] the great Russian
moderns (especially Mandelstam and Tsvetaeva); arrest and exile; a pivotal love relationship. But the anglophonic element was crucial and trans-
figurative.

First, Boris Slutsky (1919–1986). In almost every way, Slutsky did not
seem a likely candidate to influence a young *izgoi* (outcast) like Brodsky.
Considerably older, a member of the party, and a Moscow-based war
veteran whose first book of verse appeared only in 1957, Slutsky had
establishment ties that in some ways could be seen as compromising him.
This impression was only heightened when he voted with other members
of the Writers' Union to expel Pasternak in 1958.[28] Yet Brodsky is slow
to judge, and there is evidence that this incident ("The Pasternak Affair")
left Slutsky consumed with guilt.[29] Furthermore, much of his poetry remained unpublished in his lifetime, written "for the desk drawer" (*v
iashchik*), which means that Slutsky himself had an ambiguous attitude
toward both literary politics and his own place (Slutsky was a Jew) in the
tradition. In any event, at his best Slutsky is a punning, epigrammatic,
antiheroic poet whose condensed forms and domestic settings were
bound to appeal to the future author of *A Part of Speech*. Brodsky once
wrote, for example, that "It is Slutsky who almost single-handedly
changed the diction of post-war Russian poetry. His verse is a conglomer-
ation of bureaucratese, military lingo, colloquialisms and sloganeering,
and it employs with equal ease assonance, dactylic and visual rhymes,
sprung rhythm and vernacular cadences" (*Times Literary Supplement*,
17 May 1985).

The following short poem by Slutsky demonstrates what Brodsky had
in mind:

Любое начало—начало конца.
Поэтому мы начинаем с яйца,
кончаем же битою скорлупою
этим венчаем начало любое.

Но нас обучили, но нас накачали
не думать о горьком исходе вначале,
не думать, не знать, не стараться узнать,
а—раз мы решили начать—начинать.

Начнем. Поиграем жестокой судьбой,
затем сражение, ввяжемся в бой.

Any beginning is the beginning of the end.
That's why we begin with an egg,
but end up with a smashed shell
and this is the way we crown any beginning.

But we've been taught, but we've been drilled
not to think about the bitter outcome in the beginning,
not to think, not to know, not to try to find out,
but—once we've decided to begin—to make a beginning.

Let's begin. Let's play with cruel fate,
let's start the conflict, let's plunge into the fray.

                                        (Smith, *Anthology*, 2–3)

Even from this miniature piece, it is clear that Slutsky plays a kind of Louis MacNeice role to the high modern tradition (Yeats followed by Auden) coming before him. He domesticates, simplifies, humanizes. He avoids cant and hyperbole and prefers instead precision and subtle emotional calibration. In this respect, he was for Soviet poetry of the fifties what Georgy Ivanov was for the Parisian emigration. Both poets were masters of the small form and a wry, self-deflecting manner. Here Slutsky builds an entire poem around a banality (to make an egg one must break its shell), and yet how much human pain and compromise lurk beneath the surface (we see here the poet who could come to regret his vote against Pasternak). Brodsky would like the vicious circularity of the poem (also quite Ivanovian), particularly the way the amphibrachs in the first stanza turn around to bite their own tail: "Liuboe nachalo . . . nachalo liuboe."[30] Despite the poem's surface simplicity, syntax and meter seem to be tugging at each other. The strikingly conversational cadence and the irony are clearly "proto-Brodskian": both poets employ a deflation of the traditional poetic idiom to register their sense of betrayal by an entire system of values (cf. "Pamiatnik," in *SiP*, 45–46). There is, moreover, a potential absurdist streak here that the mature Brodsky will put to good use. The wordplay in the poem, beginning with the distinction between a figurative *ab ovo* and a literal broken egg (the "cracking" of human lives), is not yet "metaphysical," but it certainly holds promise for Brodsky.[31] One of the poems in *Lyric and Narrative Verse* ends with a powerful—though ultimately too obvious—pun on the difference between poets and soldiers: the latter "fertilize" ("*udóbrit'*") the earth, presumably with blood, while the former celebrate or "approve" ("*odóbrit'*") it ("Piligrimy," in *SiP*, 67). Slutsky is a strong finisher; so too is Brodsky. Indeed, the sharp sarcasm of Slutsky's concluding couplet, with its stirring calls to battle and sacrifice indicating precisely the opposite (soulless careerism, lack of nobility), appears familiar. Here, then, is one arrow in the mature Brodsky's quiver—his special mix of existentialist concerns with absurdist intonations.

Brodsky is personally very attached to Evgeny Rein (b. 1935), who was probably chief among his early mentor figures. *A Halt in the Desert* (Ostanovka v pustyne, 1970), for example, opens with "Christmas Romance" (Rozhdestvenskii romans, 1962), which is dedicated "with love, to Evgeny Rein." Rein's poetry, though, is the opposite in nearly every way from that of Slutsky. Rein is expansive and freewheeling, where Slutsky is pinioned and tight. He is something of a Jewish gypsy or minstrel, even a *balagur* (clown), and he seems to draw energy from his outcast status. His poems can give the impression of feasting on their own outlandishness and buffoonery. In this respect, Rein's persona occasionally comes close to resembling a character out of Dostoevsky, a kind of bardish Lebedev (*The Idiot*). Here, for instance, is how he opens "The Monastery" (Monastyr', 1973?):

За станцией «Сокольники», где магазин мясной
И кладбище раскольников, был монастырь мужской.
Руина и твердыня, развалина, гнилье—
В двадцатые пустили строенье под жилье.
Такую коммуналку теперь уж не сыскать.
Зачем я переехал, не стану объяснять.
Я, загнанный, опальный, у жизни на краю
Сменял там отпевальню на комнату свою . . .
Шел коридор верстою, и сорок человек,
Как улицей Тверскою, ходили целый день.
Там газовые плиты стояли у дверей,
Я был во всей квартире единственный еврей.

Behind Sokolniki metro station, where there's a meat shop
And Old Believer cemetery, there was a monastery for men.
A ruin and a fortress, a wreck, decayed,
In the 1920s it was made into accommodation.
You couldn't find a communal dwelling like that these days.
Why I moved in there I won't start to explain.
Oppressed, in disfavor, on the edge of life
I made the funeral chapel my room . . .
The corridor was one verst long, and forty people
Walked along it every day, like along Tverskaya Street.
Gas stoves stood by the doors,
I was the only Jew in the whole building.

(Smith, *Anthology*, 70–71)

This is clearly the underside of Soviet life, descriptions of which were not admitted into the canon at the time of writing. A former place of worship has been turned into a flophouse à la Gorky's *Lower Depths*. Further on in the poem Rein alludes to knife fights, heavy drinking, sly cripples, and

mothers of easy virtue—every sort of flotsam and jetsam tossed on the
monastery's banks from the steamship of state. This is the "Dead House"
that a modern Dostoevsky might be sentenced to in order to find himself.
Such people are "obscene," "beyond the pale," and Rein's speaker fits
right in. Moreover, the work's modified ballad form and playful use of
caesura and internal rhyme are ideally suited to the poet's vivid story-
telling skills. For Rein's moral is as Dostoevskian as his speaker:

И все-таки при этом, когда она могла,
С участием и приветом там наша жизнь текла.
Там зазывали в гости, делилися рублем,
Там были сплетни, козни, как в обществе любом.
Но было состраданье, не холили обид . . .

And all the same, whenever it could
Our life flowed along with people to listen to and make you welcome.
There, guests were invited in, a ruble shared,
There, there was gossip, practical jokes, like in any group of people.
There was compassion, no one took offense . . .

(Smith, *Anthology*, 70–71)

The point for us is that Rein taught Brodsky, among other things, to
celebrate his own marginalization. And once beyond the pale, an entire
range of thematics suddenly opened up—pre-Soviet culture (Rein devotes
one fascinating piece to an updating of the lost "Psyche" celebrated in
Khodasevich's famous "Automobile" poem), suppressed history (in another work Rein superimposes thoughts upon viewing Rembrandt's
"Night Watch" in Amsterdam on paranoid anxieties about the Stalinist
purges), and so forth. This ballad, however, ends on a wonderful crescendo of thanks "to whom it may concern," as Nabokov might say. The
God who places a Jew in a Russian Orthodox monastery-cum-flophouse
has a better sense of humor and poetic justice than any state. The high
and the low, the singing of drunks and Mandelstam's "singing of Muses"
(pen'e aonid), are joined in a seriocomic *buffonada* that would certainly
appeal to the irreverent younger poet. Brodsky's virtuoso-style "Speech
about Spilt Milk" (Rech' o prolitom moloke, 1967), for instance, though
more bilious and angular than anything Rein might write, fairly bursts
with the energy that comes when its Underground Man speaker turns the
blade of indignation in his own entrails. This energy is especially apparent in Brodsky's self-ironizing rhymes and in his careful juxtaposing of
parts of speech to produce the effect of a chain reaction of minor explo-
sions. It is a lesson he may also have learned from Rein: "Iosif," as Brodsky recalls the older poet's words of admonishment in a later interview,
"a poem should have more nouns than adjectives, more nouns even than

verbs. A poem should be written in such a way that if you cover the paper with a magic cloth which would absorb all the adjectives and verbs, and then removed the cloth, the paper still should be dark because the nouns would remain" (Interview with N. Gorbanevskaia; *Russkaia mysl'*, 3 February 1983).

From the appearance of his first collection in 1962, Alexander Kushner (b. 1936) has been remarkably productive. As of this writing, he has published some ten books of verse together with three volumes of selected poetry. A portion of this verse has now been collected and translated into English under the title *Apollo in the Snow* (1991), a volume Brodsky presumably helped to place and for which he wrote an introduction.[32] Moreover, and more important for our purposes, Kushner is perhaps the most "academic" and deeply read poet writing in the former Soviet Union today and the one whose culture comes closest to rivaling Brodsky's—a fact both poets seem to realize.[33] His poetry is full of the classical reminiscences we associate most readily with Brodsky: Lethe, Apollo, ancient Rome, Pluto, Elysian Fields, bronze statues, Oedipus, Catullus, and so forth.[34] Also intriguing is the fact that after passing through earlier stages of intertextual dialogue (and apprenticeship) with poets such as Zabolotsky, Fet, Pasternak, Tyutchev, and Annensky, Kushner has, since his 1984 collection *Garden of Taurida* (Tavricheskii sad), fixed on Mandelstam as chief precursor.[35] In Kushner's best verse we experience that Acmeist "warmth of the hearth" and "longing for world culture" that Mandelstam himself immortalized. A superb technician, Kushner has also mastered Mandelstam's themes (swallows, eyelashes) and even his capacious heroic breath—the iambic hexameter of "Solominka" (The Straw) and "Est' ivolgi v lesakh i glasnykh dolgota" (Orioles are in the forests and vowels are drawn out) (Ueland, "Echoes," 5, 9). In sum, Kushner is the only poet from among Brodsky's contemporaries who can compete with Brodsky for the "mantle of Mandelstam."

Brodsky's relations with Kushner are, understandably, more complicated than those with either Slutsky or Rein. On the one hand, Brodsky can praise Kushner as "one of the best lyric poets of the twentieth century," a "name . . . destined to rank with those close to the heart of everyone whose mother tongue is Russian" (in Kushner, *Apollo*, ix [Introduction]). On the other hand, this praise has a de rigueur, almost "clenched teeth" quality to it: it strikes perhaps too close to home. When Brodsky writes about Kushner, he is apt to use terms that others have often used in characterizing him, a fact that is bound to cause a certain unease: "Kushner's poetics . . . is the poetics of stoicism"; or "Kushner's poems are remarkable for their tonal reserve, their absence of hysteria, their sharp horizons, and their nervous gestures; he is rather dry where somebody else would boil, ironic where another would despair" (Kushner,

Apollo, xi [Introduction]). The difference, poetically speaking, between
the manner of Kushner and the manner of Brodsky is that the former is "a
combination of the Harmonious School [whose roots go back to Batyush-
kov, Zhukovsky, and the early Pushkin] and Acmeism" (Kushner,
Apollo, xi [Introduction]), while the latter, though clearly tied to Acmeist
principles, cannot be fully contained by them, nor has it much to do with
the Harmonious School.

At risk of invoking a crude biographism that Brodsky himself rejects,
I would suggest that Kushner's verse dovetails neatly with the notion of
a "writer without a biography" and that his subtle chamber music, his
utter self-containment, his harmonious precision and "Flemish" caressing of detail, and, especially, his remarkable skill at ventriloquizing voices
from the past are not unmotivated. At some level Brodsky himself no
doubt understands this. Such "harmony" in poetry and in life are not and
cannot be for him. In typical fashion, he defends Kushner for his lack of
poetic biography, and his words are aimed at those who would automatically eulogize him (Brodsky) over his contemporary: "In the course of
these thirty years, Kushner covered an extraordinary distance, although
his life is not rich in spectacular events and doesn't conform to our image
of the poetic biography. (We are, I must say, almost corrupted by poetic
biographies, with their predominantly tragic denomination—in this century especially.)" (Kushner, *Apollo*, x [Introduction]). But here I would
argue that Brodsky himself is wrong, no matter how loudly he protests
that discussion must be limited to the poetry itself. The distinction has to
do with an approach to the world that is made manifest in words. That
Kushner has quietly yet persistently made a career for himself at home
while Brodsky has made his reputation in more *à rebours* fashion is not
only a biographical fact, it is a fact in and of their poetry. And for all
Brodsky's praise of Kushner's manifold accomplishments, one senses here
a kind of sibling rivalry, not altogether un-Bloomian, in the way each
poet views the other (see, e.g., Solov'ev, *Roman s epigrafami*, 81–100,
esp. 84–87).[36]

Perhaps a recent poem by Kushner, in fact one of his finest recontextu-
alizations of Mandelstam, will demonstrate our point:

В стихах сверкает смысл, как будто перестрелка
В горах,—и нелегко нам уследить за ним.
Вот так еще, обняв ствол, радуется белка:
Она уже не там, куда еще глядим.

Неуловимый взгляд и яркий мех опрятный.
А сидя, чем она так странно занята?
Как будто инструмент какой-то непонятный
Все время удержать старается у рта.

Ты к ней не подходи в своей широкой шубке.
Я вспомнить шкурки две в чужих стихах могу:
Две радости, два сна, две маленьких зарубки.
Мы третью проведем, чтоб нам не быть в долгу.

Я знаю, что сказать под занавес, шуршащий,
Сползающий в конце столетья, шелестя:
Нам все-таки связать с вчерашним настоящий
День рифмой удалось, по ельнику бродя.

Суровый выпал век, но белочка как дома
В нем чувствует себя: наверное, чутье
Подсказывает ей, что место перелома
Залечено, в когтях не флейта ль у нее?

In verse, meaning sparkles like an exchange of gunfire
In the mountains, and it's hard for us to follow it.
In just the same way too a squirrel has fun as it hugs the trunk:
It's already gone from the place we're looking at.

Glance you can't catch and bright, cared-for fur.
When it sits down, what is it busy doing in that odd way?
It's as if it were trying to keep some unknown instrument
To its mouth all the time.

Don't you go near it in your wide fur coat.
There are two other pelts I remember in other people's poems:
Two joys, two dreams, two small notches.
We'll make another, so we won't be indebted.

I know what to say at this curtain, rustling,
Coming down at the end of the century, swishing.
In spite of everything, we have been able to connect this day
With yesterday through rhyme, as we wander through the firs.

A stern century it's turned out to be, but the squirrel
Feels at home in it: probably, instinct
Is suggesting to it that the place where the break was
Is healed, and isn't that a flute in its claws?

                                        (Smith, *Anthology*, 116–19)

This marvelous poem makes every effort to inhale the air of Mandelstam—not, after all, a simple exercise, since so much of Mandelstam's
poetry has to do with breathing and the presence or absence of cultural
oxygen. Kushner takes exquisite pains to reconstruct Mandelstam's intonation (iambic hexameter) and even his image clusters. The allusions to
squirrels and pelts hark back to a poetic potlatch between the Akhmatova

of *Evening* (Vecher, 1912) and the Mandelstam of *Tristia* (1922) over such time-honored customs as fortune-telling. In the verbal fur both older poets shared to keep out the piercing cold of their century we also sense the rekindling of simple human values—the attempt to relume the fire in Mandelstam's beloved acropolis ("Tristia," 1918). The final reference to the "stern century" with its broken spine (the break that is here healed) evokes yet another famous Mandelstam poem—"The Age" (Vek, 1922). Yet be all this poignant archaeology as it may, the poem does not finally breathe the *spirit* of Mandelstam, nor is its evocation anything like that of Brodsky in similar circumstances. It is metapoetry of a high order (e.g., the movement of the squirrel = the movement of the poetic line), but without the pain and the tragedy.[37] It is difficult for Kushner to bond with Mandelstam in a capacity other than that of "culture uncle." Even in Kushner's splendid poem on Mandelstam's death ("Mozart's Skull"), beautiful in its evocation of the tragedy, there are a distancing and wan sadness that are not finally "Brodskian." Mandelstam's (and Brodsky's for that matter) *izgoistvo* (outcast status) are alien to Kushner. This particular squirrel was skinned alive in the Stalinist Gulag. It never felt at home in its century and its broken back was in actual fact never mended. Kushner's version, so carefully crafted and touched up, does not ring true; it possesses the too sweet aftertaste of what Russians call *poshlost'*. One wonders, similarly, what sort of flute is in the paws of the author of the *Voronezh Notebooks*, the half-crazed little tramp of the poems of the thirties?[38] Brodsky would say that rhyme is worth living for, but what he would not say is that it is capable of patching up anything worldly. To quote his hero Auden, "Poetry makes nothing happen."

Exile

Joseph Brodsky is an exile.[39] As of this writing, he has not returned to his homeland since 1972. It is a rather facile calculation to claim that his marginalization at home and his ultimate loss of Russia as geographical umbilicus *enabled* his poetry, that he drew verbal power from what, existentially, was wrested from him. At some level this may even be true, but it is not a satisfactory explanation. Brodsky refuses to have himself singled out for more attention than any other *Gastarbeiter* or refugee, just as he will not endow the word *exile* with any more freight than that of point of exit/entry: "'Exile' covers, at best, the very moment of departure, of expulsion; what follows is both too comfortable and too autonomous to be called by this name, which so strongly suggests a comprehensible grief" ("The Condition," 16, 18). *Épatage* and latter-day Nabokovian mystification? No, not if one looks carefully at the record, which is consistent in Brodsky's case. Perhaps Milosz, who shares Brodsky's emphasis on the *metaphysical* nature of exile, captures best the Russian's almost congenital recalcitrance in the face of self-definition when he writes in his autobiography *Native Realm* that,

> I feel both a native and a foreigner. Undoubtedly I could call Europe my home, but it was a home that refused to acknowledge itself as a whole; instead, as if on the strength of some self-imposed taboo, it classified its population into two categories: members of the family (quarrelsome but respectable) and poor rela-tions. . . . My roots are in the East; that is certain. Even if it is difficult or painful to explain who I am, nevertheless I must try. (*Native Realm*, 2)

Brodsky, too, has always been *both* a native *and* a foreigner, no matter where his physical self happens to be located. Moreover, he has always felt himself to be *both* European *and* something else, say, for lack of a better word, *Eastern*. Finally, Brodsky is no less aware than Milosz of how literal and linguistic borders can become, willy-nilly, coterminous with a poet's life. It is the mapping of himself by others that he resists.

Exile derives from *ex* ("out of") and the Latin root *salire* ("to leap") (see Seidel, *Exile*, 1). It is at base a political category, which is why Brod-sky will not have the word, unless metaphysically attenuated, applied to his poetry.[40] For those concerned with the word's literal, as opposed to figurative, meaning, it is hard not to see that a person in this condition is less apt to leap and more apt to be pushed. In *The Captive Mind* the same Milosz opts for defenestration into "the abyss of exile" only as a last resort, when socialist realism has been forcibly introduced into postwar Poland and there is no other alternative (*Captive Mind*, xi–xii). A writer is not usually expelled from society because the artistry of his work does not meet, as it were, industry standards. Instead, whether implicitly or explicitly, that artistry, and the individual projecting that artistry, some-how violate the social contract, the norms of the majority that grant the minority a place within its midst. This inability or, what is more likely, willful refusal to think, act, or write like others can be interpreted, regard-less of whether the individual is calling for emulation, as political treason. When Brodsky was tried for "social parasitism" (*tuneiadstvo*) in Febru-ary–March 1964 it was because, as the so-called crime suggested, he lived outside, or "on," the host. He had held many odd jobs and, though they rewarded him poorly, he gave the impression of hopping from one host's back to the other, of doing as he pleased; he was not, in a word, a solid citizen of Soviet letters. Regardless of how bizarre and Kafkaesque it may seem to pose the relationship in these terms, there is a kernel of truth even here, since the state recognized rightly that it had an alien element in its midst. It was not that there was anything openly seditious or even politi-cal in Brodsky's early verse (although feelings of alienation and corrosive questioning were definitely present from the start) but rather that what was there could not be defined as belonging to the regnant idiom. Aesthetic discourse becomes unsettling to a tyrant when its statements move off in too many directions at once and its memory is older than the current social contract.

Brodsky's exilic plight is in many ways emblematic of virtually every major Russian writer in the vatic mode and, analogously, of the fictions each creates to encode his struggles with an authority other than that of his language and its tradition. Consider, for example, Cincinnatus's crime in Nabokov's *Invitation to a Beheading*, the perfect grounds for incarceration, that is, physical exile from the group: "the most terrible of crimes, gnostical turpitude, so rare and so unutterable that it was necessary to use circumlocutions like 'impenetrability,' 'opacity,' 'occlusion'" (*Invitation*, 72). Cincinnatus is segregated from others because he is not transparent (that is, his creative essence is hidden, private, uniquely his own) and because he cannot be other than he is. Likewise, any state which insists that its citizens give up their "opacity" as the price of membership is, however well meaning, totalitarian. The Kafkaesque world that Cincinnatus walks away from at the end of the novel may be composed of cardboard characters (including the executioner) and stage props, but considering the work's context (Germany in the mid-thirties as experienced by a Russian émigré with a Jewish wife), the real-life consequences of exile and totalitarianism were certainly near at hand. Characteristically, Cincinnatus the emerging writer leaves his tormentors behind (he *banishes* them) at precisely the moment when his execution, his exile from this world, is said to be taking place. In other words, to the artist and conjurer who successfully transfers his patrimony from concrete space and time (lost homeland) to what Nabokov calls elsewhere the "un-real estate" of imaginative literature, the question eventually becomes *who exiles whom*. Agency is all.

Those of us with what has come to be called a Eurocentric view are apt to look at the issue of exile in terms of certain favored names—Ovid, Dante, Swift, Rousseau, Madame de Staël, Hugo, Lawrence, Mann, Joyce, Brecht, and others—and certain Ur-situations—the expulsion of Lucifer from heaven, the banishment of Adam and Eve from Eden, the voyage of the Argonauts, the exodus of the Jews, the wanderings of Odysseus, the journey of Dante the pilgrim (Seidel, *Exile*, x, 8). These examples and this typology have so entered into our cultural bloodstream that they have become second nature. Indeed, some critics, Marxist ones in particular, have seized on exile as a master category for describing modern forms of social and political alienation, while others have investigated the homologies between the experiential state (living "outside," "beyond," alongside borders separating the familiar and the alien) and the master trope of allegory (from *al* = "other" and *goria* = "voicing") (Seidel, *Exile*, xii, 14). And yet, as intriguing and apposite as these definitions and extensions may be, it is important not to lose sight of the term's literal root meaning: "an exile is someone who inhabits one place and remembers or projects the reality of another" (Seidel, *Exile*, ix).[41] Moreover, this ambiguous or liminal situation has clear linguistic consequences, beginning with the fact that for writers such as Bunin, Tsvetaeva, Nabokov, Milosz, Kundera, and Brodsky two very different languages and cultures are involved (see Beaujour, *Alien Tongues*, esp. 1–57). To romanticize the notion of exile is to mute its tragic tongue-tie and to turn it, inevitably, into something compensatory—an "enabling fiction" that permits the artist "to transform the figure of rupture back into a 'figure of connection'" (Seidel, *Exile*, x, xii). Lest we forget, more often than not exile has had a disabling and crippling function precisely because the dual vision which is its essence has been not liberating but oppressive, a kind of linguistic death sentence.[42] It is for this reason that "artists in exile are decidedly unpleasant, and their stubborness insinuates itself into even their exalted works" (Said, "Mind of Winter," 53). And it is for this same reason that Brodsky will not allow himself and fellow writers in exile to fetishize their plight, since their anguish, just because it is the anguish of a writer, is not more acute than the anguish of the next *Gastarbeiter*. To be sure, not all are capable of walking away from their gaol like Nabokov.

A number of contemporary critics have written on the conceptual origins of *exsilium*. Among them are Elizabeth Beaujour, Julia Kristeva, Harry Levin, Michael Seidel, Edward Said, George Steiner, and Paul Tabori. Inevitably they come to focus on exile's dual or stereoscopic vision, a concept that, though helpful, is in need of refinement. Perhaps Said puts the issue most pointedly:

> For an exile, habits of life, expression, or activity in the new environment inevitably occur against the memory of these things in another environment. Thus both the new and the old environments are vivid, actual, occurring together contrapuntally. There is a unique pleasure in this sort of apprehension, especially if the exile is conscious of other contrapuntal juxtapositions that diminish orthodox judgment and elevate appreciative sympathy. There is also a particular sense of achievement in acting as if one were at home wherever one happens to be. (Said, "Mind of Winter," 55)

Needless to say, the Russian context offers countless examples of this very contrapuntal thinking; it is particularly foregrounded among the so-called first wave of émigré writers who wrote for dwindling audiences in Berlin and Paris during the interwar period. Vladislav Khodasevich, for example, says virtually the same thing as Said but does so poetically, in his marvelous *poema* (narrative poem) *Sorrento Photographs* (Sorrentinskie fotografii), where the photographic negative of life in revolutionary Russia shows through, as in a double exposure, on the snapshots of life in and around Gorky's villa near Sorrento. So, too, does the poet Georgy Ivanov, who recalls from the sunny south of Nice his friend Mandelstam's prediction that "we will meet again" amid the snowstorms of Petersburg ("A quarter century has passed by abroad" [Chetvert' veka proshlo za granitsei]). And, above all, so does Nabokov, whose autobiographical hero Ganin returns to Russia and his first love as he sprawls on his bed in a Berlin boardinghouse and is shaken into bittersweet reverie by the trains (time machines?) rumbling nearby (*Mashen'ka*). For each of these writers the contrapuntal sensation of which Said speaks creates the *frisson* of discovery, the *entre deux* of epiphany and time travel recognizable to readers of Proust. What is more, the past that coexists in the present has either an unmistakable pastoral quality (particularly evident in Nabokov and his childhood memories of Vyra, his family estate) or the implication of a poetic Golden or "Silver" Age—here the poetic word in revolutionary Petersburg, epitomized by Blok and his generation and experienced by Khodasevich and Ivanov as a last flash of brilliance before the onset of the "Soviet night."

Yet this notion of counterpoint, so useful when comparing an Eliadean Great Time to a drab and homeless present, does not apply, at least in any simple or predictable way, to Brodsky. The poet will not allow us to write him into this scenario either. What was left behind was not a Silver but rather an Iron, or better, Stone Age, and what was acquired was not only loss but also the freedom to be alone with time, eternity, and his ever attenuating notions of poetic discourse. Brodsky, it should be noted, was *always* exiled within his homeland, between the "Soviet" state and "Russian" culture; his "generation of 1956" had no living memory, except through aging cultural relics like Anna Akhmatova and Nadezhda Mandelstam and through books themselves, of anything *prior*. There is, then, little consolation for the traditional exile, the inheritor of Ovid and Dante, in Brodsky's thinking:

> Whether we like it or not, *Gastarbeiters* and refugees of any stripe effectively pluck the carnation out of an exiled writer's lapel. Displacement and misplacement are this century's commonplace. And what our exiled writer has in common with a *Gastarbeiter* or a political refugee is that in either case a man is running away from the worse toward the better. The truth of the matter is that from tyranny one can be exiled only to a democracy. For the old gray mare of exile ain't what it used to be. It isn't leaving civilized Rome for savage Sarmatia anymore, nor is it sending a man from, say, Bulgaria to China. No, as a rule what takes place is a transition from a political and economic backwater to an industrially advanced society with the last word on individual liberty on its lips. ("The Condition," 16)

Ironically, these statements were prepared for a conference on exiled writers that Brodsky himself did not attend.[43] One imagines, again, how the words of the absent poet could offend those present, how his refusal to grant himself, and those who share his station, even a modicum of self-pity could appear harsh. The sarcastic, epigrammatic quality of Brodsky's assertions—"*Gastarbeiters* and refugees of any stripe pluck the carnation out of an exiled writer's lapel"; "The truth of the matter is that from a tyranny one can be exiled only to a democracy";—is certain, in this context as well, to draw blood. From the plight of the exile, from the political forces that have, ostensibly, eventuated in the "displacement and misplacement" of these writers, Brodsky has shifted the focus elsewhere. Why is this? Why will he not allow the traditional counterpoint of which Said speaks?

The reason, it seems, has to do with the entire question of agency and poetic language. This is also apparently why no explanatory theory of exilic consciousness can fully account for the bio-aesthetic phenomenon of "Joseph Brodsky." Let us test out for a moment this assertion against the works of Kristeva and Said, the two individuals who have been most influential in recent debate on the topic. Both in her essay "A New Type of Intellectual: The Dissident" (1977)[44] and more recently in her book *Strangers to Ourselves* (1991),[45] Kristeva has used psychoanalytic theory to explain the ubiquitous tendency to isolate the foreign(er) in our midst and in ourselves. To the critic who wishes to analyze the poet in terms of psychic patterns and proclivities, there is much in Kristeva that could be seen to fit Brodsky's portrait. For example,

> A secret wound, often unknown to himself, drives the foreigner to wandering. Poorly loved, however, he does not acknowledge it: with him, the challenge silences the complaint. . . . He is dauntless: "You have caused me no harm," he disclaims, fiercely, "it is I who chose to leave"; always further along, always inaccessible to all. As far back as his memory can reach, it is delightfully bruised: misunderstood by a loved and yet absent-minded, discreet, or worried mother, the exile is a stranger to his mother. He does not call her, he asks nothing of her. Arrogant, he proudly holds on to what he lacks, to absence, to some symbol or other. . . . Riveted to an elsewhere as certain as it is inaccessible, the foreigner is ready to flee. No obstacle stops him, and all suffering, all insults, all rejections are indifferent to him as he seeks that invisible and promised territory, that country that does not exist but that he bears in his dreams, and that must indeed be called a beyond.
>
> The foreigner, thus, has lost his mother. (*Strangers*, 5)

Brodsky, indeed, has had anything but a happy personal life, a fact about which we will have more to say in subsequent chapters. The first great love of his life (with Marina Basmanova) ended in duplicity and a hopelessly "triangulated" relationship, just as his great love for Russia ("Russia is my home; I lived there all my life [until June 1972], and for everything I have in my soul I am obliged to Russia and its people" ["A Writer," 78]) ended in banishment. So, if one likes, it can be argued that Brodsky's passion for responsibility and agency, for the "challenge" over the "complaint," is directly attributable to his "secret wound" and to the fact that he has "lost his mother," meaning in this case that he has lost not only his biological mother, the mother of his son (Basmanova), and his motherland, but most important, he has for twenty years been in danger of losing his *Muttersprache*. This Brodsky is "arrogant"; he does not call out to his mother, nor does he ask anything of her. Riveted to his stoic mask, he steals agency from the jaws of the patient ("You have caused me no harm; It is I who chose to leave"), and in the end he appears to be indifferent to "all suffering, all insults, all rejections."

And yet, even as Kristeva's psychoanalytic emplotment appears to empower the reader to see through certain of Brodsky's coping mechanisms, it is powerless to account for an actual concrete occurrence of his poetic language. That is, it can predict a type of *behavior* (coping mechanisms) but it cannot predict poetic speech. There is always some remainder, a factor *in excess* of the explanation.[46] The most that Kristeva's model can do is appropriate the poet, and by association his language, to a type—the "foreigner," the "exile." This is why both Brodsky and Nabokov, the two Russian exile writers who have spoken most eloquently for the sovereign agency of art, have been especially harsh on the subject of Freud and his legacy. Kristeva's thinking *subsumes*; like a massive theorizing exhaust fan, it draws its subject *up* into generalizations across several linguistic and psychological fronts simultaneously (biological mother, lover, homeland, native language), so that ultimately Brodsky's transgression is against what the critic would call the *semiotic* (i.e., preconscious, undifferentiated, "maternal") core of language in the name of the *symbolic* (i.e., conscious, differentiated, verbal, postoedipal) order of the Father.[47] Her powerful model can explain a "revolution in poetic language" after the fact, but it cannot show what Brodsky terms *poetic thinking*: "Poetic thinking, which is called metaphorical, is in fact synthetic thinking. As such, it contains analysis, but cannot be reduced to analysis. Analysis is neither the only nor the final form of cognition. . . . In the case of the poet it is through intuitive synthesis, i.e., when the poet—according to the poet—steals left and right and *does not even experience a sense of guilt* as he does so" (*Modern Russian Poets*, 7; my emphasis).

For Brodsky and his tradition, therefore, great poetry always telescopes the simultaneity of semiotic and symbolic. Let us return to Brodsky's tribute to Akhmatova. When the middle-aged exile says to his long-deceased godmother, "Великая душа, поклон через моря" (Lit., Great soul, [to you I extend] a bow across the seas), we are witness to a *specific* and unrepeatable instance where mother and son, tradition and absence, heroic meter (Alexandrine, with hemistichs divided by caesura) and unheroic age come together to create a moment of healing harmony. Brodsky divests himself (this is decidedly *not* how he would speak if the subject were his own person) in order to take on the voice and cadence, the "classical symmetry" and reserve, of his beloved interlocutor. It is a sacrifice he feels lies at the core of any poem. The "greatness" of Akhmatova demands an appropriate response, so the *lik* (the countenance of holiness) "entombed" in the initial ictus of the first hemistich ("Ve*lik*aia") is echoed by its partner in the second hemistich ("po*klon*"). The bow is literalized as the one poet pays tribute, so to speak, prosodically to the other. Similarly, the sonorous internal rhyme joining the third foot of each hemistich—"dush*a*" (soul)/"mor*ia*" (seas)—superimposes the metaphysical semantics characteristic of both poets on the notion of physical displacement. The open space, the "across the seas," collapses into a homecoming, a maternal embrace. Hence what is celebrated is not only Akhmatova on her birthday but her language, the "gift of speech" for which she in turn sacrificed herself. There is not the slightest trace of oedipal upstaging or "guilt" in this utterance. Indeed, semiosis and symbolism, what Kristeva calls the maternal *chora* and the signifying "thetic" phase, coexist in a poetic construct and, as it were, *interrogate each other*. To isolate them in time and to claim that "the exile is a stranger to his mother" does not do justice to the "moving stasis" of Brodsky's language.

If Kristeva's master grid is psychoanalytic, then Edward Said's is political and heavily indebted to, among others, Michel Foucault. In *Orientalism* (1978), *The World, the Text, and the Critic* (1983), and in various essays, including "The Mind of Winter: Reflections on Life in Exile" (1984), Said has made the argument repeatedly that "texts have ways of existing that even in their most rarefied form are always enmeshed in circumstance, time, place, and society—in short, they are in the world, and hence worldly" (*The World*, 35). In principle, this is a not unhelpful corrective, particularly when directed at the "mystical and disinfected subject matter of literary theory" known as "textuality" (*The World*, 3).[48] However, Said has given this subtle return to context potent ideological mandibles.[49]

It is a short step from Said's case for recognizing the Orient for what it is—not "an inert fact of nature" (*Orientalism*, 4) but a fact of political life and institutions—to giving voice to the quintessential other—the refugee and exile.[50] *The World, the Text, and the Critic* begins with a moving tribute to Erich Auerbach, the Jewish refugee from Nazi Europe who wrote one of the masterful critical texts of Western civilization, *Mimesis*, while living out the Second World War in Istanbul. "Auerbach explicitly makes the point," writes Said, "that it was precisely his distance from home—in all senses of that word—that made possible the superb undertaking of *Mimesis*. How did exile become converted from a challenge or risk, or even from an active impingement on his European selfhood, into a positive mission, whose success would be a cultural act of great importance?" (*The World*, 7). It is, parenthetically, a question that would certainly interest Brodsky as well. Said goes on to answer the query by citing a passage from Hugo of St. Victor's *Didascalicon* which the great philologist happened to single out in another of his essays ("Philologie der Weltliteratur"): "The man who finds his homeland sweet is still a tender beginner; he to whom every soil is as his native one is already strong; but he is perfect to whom the entire world is as a foreign land" [the Latin text is more explicit here—*perfectus vero cui mundus totus exilium est*]" (cited in *The World*, 7). This progression is a precise encapsulation of Brodsky's own relentlessly centrifugal, "self-estranging" exilic consciousness. Only through a kind of "willed homelessness," only by shedding one's cultural bias and creating a work, such as *Mimesis*, which "owe[s] its existence to the very fact of Oriental, non-Occidental exile," can one become a self for whom every soil is native and, ultimately, *mundus totus exilium est* (*The World*, 7–8). And yet, if this is Brodsky's stance *in nuce*, then how would he regard Said's underlying political message?

Said's notion of culture and exile as different sides of "discourse formation" encounters problems when applied to the Russian context. Here the Foucauldian lens, so strikingly francophonic even as it attempts to shatter itself, seems strangely out of focus:

> Culture is used to designate not merely something to which one belongs but something one possesses and, along with that proprietary process, culture also designates a boundary by which the concepts of what is extrinsic and intrinsic to the culture come into forceful play. . . . This means that culture is a system of discriminations and evaluations . . . for a particular class in the State able to identify with it; and it also means that culture is a system of exclusions legislated from above but enacted throughout its polity, by which such things as anarchy, disorder, irrationality, inferiority, bad taste, and immorality are identified, then deposited outside the culture and kept there by the power of the State and its institutions. (*The World*, 8–11)

Brodsky would be the first to say that culture is indeed a possession, in fact the only possession worth having. But whereas Said sees the Orientalist *episteme* as an Occidental "system of discriminations and evaluations" that excludes those it seeks, consciously or unconsciously, to subjugate, what happens to that same system when it is moved eastward to Russia? Here the model is turned squarely on its head, a fact that can only mean that the issue is not the texts per se but the manner in which they (or rather the "archive" that selects them) can be manipulated. Brodsky is living proof from someone clearly outside the dominant discourse(s) of Anglo-American culture that there is nothing *inherently* exclusionary or oppressive in the writing of, say, a poet and preacher like John Donne—except, perhaps, the intelligence and imaginative empathy necessary to reenter his time and place. The texts that Brodsky and his generation read in their formative years (Mandelstam, Tsvetaeva, Dostoevsky, the Bible) were precisely the ones that the state was furiously attempting to identify as "anarchic," "irrational," "inferior," and "immoral" and to deposit outside the culture. Moreover, these texts were the ones that reestablished continuity with a worthy past (Russian literature prior to 1917) and with Western culture. The genuinely anonymous and monolithic discourse of the Soviet state wielded massive power, but its efforts to deposit those such as Brodsky outside its midst only *empowered* the latter's language—unique, eccentric, commanding attention because of its difference. In the upside-down world of Soviet-Russian culture, the forbidden texts, which we from our perspective as late-twentieth-century "Euro-" and "logocentric" intellectuals are apt to see as enforcers in a "hegemonic" canon, emerged as the ones that helped Brodsky and his colleagues become free individuals. The irony here is that one has to be an exile in a sense from one's own culture to see this.

To say the least, Brodsky has an ambivalent attitude toward Russia's Eastern roots, a point about which we will have more to say in a later chapter. And his notion of Byzantium is certainly a far cry from, say, Yeats's. Just as Said is trying to give voice to the Eastern exile too often neglected in our Western tradition, Brodsky will not let us forget the Western heritage that had been selectively distorted and exiled from the "Eastern" discourse, authoritarian to the core, of his Soviet schooling.[51] This is how Brodsky speaks of Mandelstam—for whom he coins the term *homo culturus*—a man whose culture could not be "higher" and yet whose exclusion and punishment by the "discourse" of the state could not be more tragic:

> This is a book [i.e., Nadezhda Mandelstam's memoir *Hope Abandoned*] about how to live without consolation. Without consolation one can only live on love, memory, and culture. In the author's consciousness these three categories are inseparable and are present as a single entity. . . . Culture is a part of their [i.e., Russians', especially Mandelstam's] "ego," a physiological category, a characteristic as functional as their sex. Culture is their sex; it is the primary characteristic of their biological species, and hence their incompatibility with specimens of lower, or more often higher, species. . . . There is no love without memory, no memory without culture, no culture without love. Therefore every poem is a fact of culture as well as an act of love and a flash of memory—and, I would add, of faith. ("Beyond Consolation," 14)

As any reader of *Conversation about Dante* knows, Mandelstam's version of high culture and one of its chief representatives is anything but static, anonymous, monologic. Quite the contrary, Mandelstam's Dante is cranky, idiosyncratic, ever willing to set himself off against a Florentine center that will not have him—in a word, he is Mandelstam himself, the Soviet *izgoi* (outcast). Mandelstam's motile culture arms him against the fixed and bloated middle of what was soon to become socialist realism. So, too, do the love, memory, and culture entering into Brodsky's appropriation of Donne, Auden, Lowell, and Frost help him to redraw the boundaries of Russian poetic speech in his day. Ultimately, for Brodsky at least, it is poetic speech (the relationship to language in its most condensed form) that *empowers*, not the names and biographies of poets who, regardless of the system, become pawns (objects of power) in an exclusionary struggle for the chessboard (canon).

So Brodsky's response to the academy's politicization of exile is characteristically prickly, inasmuch as it resists this intrusion on the notion of agency like any other. He was force-fed on the curdled milk of "regularizing collectivities" in his youth, and even now he is hypersensitive to any rhetorical sleight of hand or "inflation of speech" ("says poet Brodsky," 11) that absolves one of individual responsibility. Whether a totalitarian regime or a Western-style democracy, whether it be, in Khodasevich's bitter pun, the *sotsial'nyi zakaz* (societal demand) or the *sotsial'nyi otkaz* (societal rejection), the "state" will find a way to segregate the writer ("Pered kontsom"). Do not ask for recognition and justice, the poet says, since it is not social integration and happiness you should seek, but linguistic discovery: "To be an exiled writer is like being a dog or a man hurtled into space in a capsule (more like a dog, of course, than a man, because they will never bother to retrieve you). And your capsule is your language. To finish the metaphor off, it must be added that before long the passenger discovers that the capsule gravitates not earthward but outward in space" ("The Condition," 18). The utopian writes in hopes that the capsule will gravitate earthward; the poet follows his own lonely, centrifugal trajectory. In the final analysis, Brodsky is, like Tsvetaeva, an exile among exiles. He stands alone, neither a character in the primal scene of someone else's family romance nor a rebel in the square of someone else's political unconscious. He chooses his own roles and takes responsibility for the success or failure of the performance:

> All I am trying to say is that, given an opportunity, in the great causal chain of things, we may as well stop being just its rattling effects and try to play at causes. The condition we call exile gives exactly that kind of opportunity. . . . [I]f we want to play a bigger role, the role of a free man, then we should be capable of accepting—or at least imitating—the manner in which a free man fails. A free man, when he fails, blames nobody. ("The Condition," 19)

It is, then, this *creation of exile*, this sense that Brodsky is, despite all the vagaries of history and a genuinely tragic fate, the source and shaper of his own alienation from life as well as of his bonding to language, to which the present study is devoted. The ambiguity of the preposition—Is the "exile" that follows the "of" the cause or the effect of the "creation"?—is precisely what Brodsky has wrestled with more than any other Russian writer has in the second half of the century. And with the coming of the post-*glasnost'* era and the inevitable demise of the "bardic mode" in Russian literature, Joseph Brodsky may be the last great poet in the tradition about whom it can be said that he created himself and in turn *was created* by what he wrote.[52]

2

Brodsky's Triangular Vision: Exile as Palimpsest

И щегол разливается в центре проволочной Равенны.

And the goldfinch bursts into song in the center of its wire Ravenna.
  (Brodsky, "December in Florence")

FOR ANYONE who has halted among the ruins of Western civilization that is Joseph Brodsky's poetry, a question often poses itself: what is the function of these shards from the past, these Martials, Ovids, Virgils, Horaces, and Dantes? Are they primarily decorative, verbal Elgin Marbles lifted out of their settings in order to grace the British Museum of a late-twentieth-century text? Is Brodsky simply interested, à la Khodasevich, in grafting the "classical rose to the Soviet wilding" (see *Less*, 395–96) or in modernizing Mandelstam's famous "nostalgia for world culture" formula? What poetic economy is at work here?

The answer is found throughout Brodsky's essays, but we might begin by citing "The Child of Civilization," his piece on Mandelstam:

> It is not that Mandelstam was a "civilized" poet; he was rather a poet for and of civilization. Once, on being asked to define Acmeism . . . he answered: "nostalgia for a world culture." This notion of a world culture is distinctly Russian. Because of its location (neither East or West) and its imperfect history, Russia has always suffered from a sense of cultural inferiority, at least toward the West. Out of this inferiority grew the ideal of a certain cultural unity "out there" and a subsequent intellectual voracity toward anything coming from that direction. This is, in a way, a Russian version of Hellenicism, and Mandelstam's remark about Pushkin's "Hellenistic paleness" was not an idle one. (*Less*, 130)

Like so much else in *Less Than One*, these statements are perceptive both in what they tell us about Mandelstam and in what they tell us about their author. With the possible exception of Tsvetaeva, no Russian poet has influenced Brodsky more powerfully than Osip Mandelstam. Mandelstam's "intellectual voracity" for a "cultural unity" that is "out there" and that continues to emanate "from that direction," that is, from the West, is, *mutatis mutandis*, Brodsky's.

It would be well to remind our reader in this connection how *personally* Brodsky, again like Mandelstam, takes his culture. In an essay devoted to Mandelstam's widow, Brodsky writes, "Culture is a part of their [i.e., Russians', especially the Mandelstams'] 'ego,' a physiological category, a characteristic as functional as their sex. Culture is their sex; it is the primary characteristic of their biological species, and hence their incompatibility with specimens of lower, or more often higher, species" ("Beyond Consolation," 14). He is, of course, speaking also of himself. Hence Brodsky's deployment of classical motifs is "Mandelstamian" in the sense that what is at issue is not their "archaeological" correctness or validity (e.g., the Caesar-bating "Martial" invoked in "Letters to a Roman Friend" was not nearly so cynical or blatantly critical of his government as the first century A.D. epigrammatist) but the way they speak to the poet and serve as distancing filter for his own concerns.[1] At the moment he is writing a poem, Brodsky *becomes* the Odysseus who is saying farewell to Telemachus or the Theseus who has won a pyrrhic victory over the Minotaur because Ariadna is left in the embraces of Bacchus (see Brodsky, *ChR*, 23 and *OVP*, 92–93). That a real son is being left behind or a real woman is exposed in the act of betrayal makes the process of Yeatsian masking both more necessary and more poignant. Perhaps harking back to Mandelstam's great Pindaric fragment "The Horseshoe Finder" (Nashedshii podkovu, 1923) but just as likely owing to the poet's own experience as a marginalized ex-*homo sovieticus*,[2] Brodsky's work over the years has become increasingly fixated on the notion of antiquity as busts, torsos, Ovidian candlesticks metamorphosed by time—in short, disfigured ruins. The Greek theme (Hector, Orpheus, Artemis, etc.) is gradually replaced by the Roman theme (Martial, Tiberius, etc.), particularly in the latter's incarnation as "empire."[3] This trajectory is deeply "Mandelstamian" as well.[4]

To understand how Brodsky encodes Mandelstam's "nostalgia for world culture" formula in his own work I propose a different term—*triangular vision*.[5] What is meant by this is that Brodsky, one of the most cosmopolitan poets in the history of Russian poetry and certainly the one most at home in the Anglo-American tradition, constantly looks *both ways*, both to the West and to Russia, as he continues Mandelstam's dialogue with Hellenicism. His vision can be called triangular in that a Russian source, say Mandelstam, is subtly implanted within a Western source, say Dante, so that each source comments on the other, but as they do so they also implicate a third source—Brodsky himself. Shortly I will demonstrate how this takes place in Brodsky's fine Dante poem "December in Florence," but for now I would simply like to suggest to the reader that this ingenious triangularity happens often enough to be, for the mature Brodsky, a kind of signature. It is, moreover, crucial for our entire study, since it serves as an overarching frame for other notions of exile, including ethnic origins, geographical homeland, national tradition, and personal relationships. In essence, Brodsky constantly "outflanks" his own marginal status through cultural triangulation.

Several examples should suffice for these preliminaries. Brodsky's elegy "Verses on the Death of T. S. Eliot" (1965), to be discussed in chapter 4, invokes as primary model Auden's "In Memory of W. B. Yeats," which in turn has Yeats's own "exegi monumentum,"[6] "Under Ben Bulben," in mind. But that is not where the dialogue ends, since underlying the conceptual framework of the Russian-language elegy, with its body-soul debate, is Tsvetaeva's "New Year's Greeting" (Novogodnee), her famous elegy to Rilke. The same might be said for "Nunc Dimittis" (Sreten'e), Brodsky's poem about Simeon, the *pravednik* (devout man), who was present at the temple for the presentation of the Christ child. This work is both an elaborate and moving homage to Anna Akhmatova, the ever-constant "prophetess Anna" (prorochitsa Anna), and a riddle of absence involving three Josephs: the biblical husband of Mary, present in the Luke text but not in "Sreten'e"; Mandelstam, the "first Osya" implicated in certain of the poem's images and phrases; and Brodsky, the "second Osya" figured in the future torments of the child (see chapter 5). The poem was written late enough that it is possible Brodsky was aware of the well-known "Simeons" of Eliot and (especially) Auden.

Or we have "Lullaby of Cape Cod" (Kolybel'naia Treskovogo Mysa, 1975), which situates Mandelstam's moving imperative "preserve my speech"[7] (*ChR*, 106, 108) within the tradition of the great American seashore poem about origins, such as Eliot's "Dry Salvages" or Stevens's "The Idea of Order at Key West." Indeed, the persevering reader might turn up a striking palimpsest in this instance.[8] The "Shoals of cod and eel / that discovered this land before Vikings or Spaniards still / beset the shore," a stanza from Brodsky's English-language "Elegy: for Robert Lowell" (1977; *Part*, 136), turns out to be a translation from the earlier Russian "Lullaby" (*ChR*, 103). The cod did not originate there, however; instead it goes back still further to Lowell's own morbid fascination with the intrusion of lower forms of life into American culture and with the deeply ironic "weathervane cod" in "For the Union Dead." (The weathervane then resurfaces at the end of Brodsky's elegy in the "false song of the weathercock" [*Part*, 137].) "Lullaby of Cape Cod" emerges, therefore, as a verbal petri dish of images and phrases out of Lowell and Mandelstam, from which the recently arrived poet will construct his hybrid self. On the one hand, there are Lowell-engendered thoughts on the sea as watery grave (e.g., "In Memory of Arthur Winslow") or threatening primordial hatchery (e.g., "Near the Ocean" and "Waking Early Sunday Morning"). And on the other, there are Mandelstamian thoughts on the sea as point of origin in a massive evolutionary chain (e.g., "Lamarck"), where intuitive poetic language is the only key, inversely and retrospectively applied, to the "ontogeny recapitulates phylogeny" formula. Energized by the oxygen of these native and foreign precursors, Brodsky's speaker, like the seriocomic cod that is the poem's central image, appears to rise linguistically out of the sea and pass into the broad continent of American letters.

One of Brodsky's boldest triangular statements to date comes from his essay and travelogue "Flight from Byzantium" (1985). As Tomas Venclova has pointed out, the essay "enters into two textual spaces" ("A Journey," 135, in Loseff and Polukhina, *Brodsky's Poetics*). That is, the English-language version, with its emphatic *from* in the title, is meant to enter into polemical dialogue with the golden bough, the singing bird, and the "artifice of eternity" of Yeats's ideal poetic culture in "Sailing *to* Byzantium" and "Byzantium." Conversely, the Russian-language version, which is translated as "Journey to Istanbul" (Puteshestvie v Stambul), invokes an entirely different tradition: the philosophical travel sketches of Radishchev (*Journey from Petersburg to Moscow*), Pushkin ("Journey to Arzrum"), and, of course, Mandelstam ("Journey to Armenia") (Venclova, "A Journey," 136, in Loseff and Polukhina, *Brodsky's Poetics*). Last but not least, however, the essay enters into a third textual space—that of Brodsky's own work on the interrelations of time, space, poetry, and empire. It turns out to be a way of reading Brodsky himself.

Brodsky's haunting odyssey is based on a controversial assumption. What happens if the Yeatsian destination is achieved and we are delivered into the hands of "Orientalist" myth—in this instance the original seat of Eastern Christianity and the source of both Russian Orthodoxy and the Russian historical imagination? Well, it depends on which side of the myth one is situated. Raised in the *kosnost'* (sluggishness) and *zastoi* (stagnation) of the aging Soviet empire, Brodsky has no illusions about his country's roots. Indeed, the essayist is terrified and repulsed by what he sees as the—pace Yeats—"formlessness" (*bezobrazie*) of the East. In this idiosyncratic reading, the formlessness expressed itself first and foremost as a disregard for the individual: "Socrates would simply have been impaled on the spot, or flayed, and there the matter would have ended. There would have been no Platonic dialogues, no Neoplatonism, nothing" (*Less*, 413). It penetrated into the West via Rome and the "linear" principle of empire (*lineinost'*) celebrated first by Virgil (this as opposed to the symmetry and circular movement of the Greek cosmos; see "Puteshestvie," 75). Brodsky's preference for the many voices of paganism over the one voice of monotheism, and for the individualism of the Greeks over the anti-individualism of the Romans, is, again, unmistakably akin to the Mandelstam who was influenced by the famous classicist

Tadeusz Zielinski and who authored "Pushkin and Scriabin" ("Puteshe-stvie," 82-83). Significantly, the transformation of the Hagia Sophia (also the title of one of Mandelstam's famous cathedral poems) into a mosque by the mere erection of four minarets on each side of the cathedral is, for Brodsky, an ominous metaphor for the triumph of the crescent over the cross and "for profound Eastern indifference to problems of a metaphys-ical nature" (*Less*, 432).

If the travelogue is read against Yeats, Mandelstam, and especially Brodsky, the following formula emerges: poetry is the temporalization (or dematerialization) of space, while empire, including social utopias and applied Christianity (e.g., Marxism), is the spatialization of time. Hence Mandelstam, the sacrificial victim of empire (the triumph of space), wrote verse whose "heavily caesuraed" lines give the "viscous sensation of time's passage" and whose words and even letters "are al-most palpable vessels of time" (*Less*, 125–26). In the end Brodsky comes to Istanbul not as a Western tourist or journalist but as a belated repre-sentative of Mandelstam's Hellas. He is confronting the specter of those same despotic "Eastern" roots that banished him from his homeland and swallowed Mandelstam whole. His occidentalism, nearly as hard-earned as his great forebear's, is a counterweight to the romantic (and false) Ori-entalism of Yeats. The golden bough and the bird singing out of time of the latter become the tragically caged goldfinch of Mandelstamian song, about which we will have more to say in the final pages of this chapter.

Eliot, Mandelstam, and Dante

I would like now to turn to Brodsky's triangulation of Dante, the *echt* Western poet, and Mandelstam, his greatest Russian follower. As our examples have made clear, Brodsky will both mediate between these two precursors and implicate himself as the "hybrid" result of that dialogue. But before addressing this instance, it might be well to make a slight detour.

In 1929 T. S. Eliot wrote an essay entitled "Dante," a piece that, ac-cording to Frank Kermode, is "arguably the centre of Eliot's critical work" (*Selected Prose*, 19).[9] We recall, for the sake of precision, that this was seven years after the publication of the epoch-making *The Waste Land* (a work that drew on, among other things, the experience of Eliot's disastrous first marriage to Vivienne Haigh-Wood) and two years after the poet's conversion and the (not unrelated) renewal of his contact with Emily Hale, the New England drama teacher-cum-Beatrice who would serve as the muse of *Ash Wednesday* (1927–30) and would call the poet to a *Vita Nuova* that was nothing less than a crossing *back* to his Massachusetts roots. Hence "Dante" is autobiographical in the way that the prose of poets is often autobiographical; it tells about poetic language in a narrative that is instructive for the historical moment (high modernism) even as it constantly reinscribes itself back into the poet's life. A given tradition, here English, and one's individual talent and place within it dictate which approach to the poetic word is appropriate for the moment:

> Dante is, in a sense to be defined (for the word means little by itself), the most *universal* of poets in the modern languages. . . . To enjoy any French or German poetry, I think one needs to have some sympathy with the French or German mind; Dante, none the less an Italian and a patriot, is first a European. . . . The style of Dante has a peculiar lucidity—a *poetic* as distinguished from an intellectual lucidity. The thought may be obscure, but the word is lucid, or rather translucent. In English poetry words have a kind of opacity which is part of their beauty. I do not mean that the beauty of English poetry is what is called 'verbal beauty.' It is rather that words have associations, and the groups of words *in* association have associations, which is a kind of local self-consciousness, because they are a growth of a *particular* civilization; and the same thing is true of other modern languages. The Italian of Dante, though essentially the Italian of today, is not in this way a modern language. The culture of Dante was not of one European country but of Europe. (Kermode, *Selected Prose*, 206–207)

This passage (as well as several others in the vicinity) is fascinating, particularly if we juxtapose it with Brodsky's earlier comments on Mandelstam's "nostalgia for world culture." Both poets experience similar nostalgias, but for different reasons and from different directions. It may have angered William Carlos Williams, for example, that Eliot absconded to Europe with "[the] heat [that was] in us, [the] core and . . . drive that was gathering headway upon the theme of a rediscovery of a primary impetus, the elementary principle of all art, in local conditions" and "gave the poem back to the academics" (cited in Kermode, *Appetite*, 97). But this would not have surprised the student of Mandelstam, another poet who felt constrained by the provincialism of his country's new art and who, forced to the margins by the literary establishment, took up the banner of Dante the outcast and exile—which of course was none other than his own banner—in "Conversation about Dante" (Razgovor o Dante, 1933). He, too, felt the need for a language that was defiantly other,[10] authentic because it was free of the contamination of current norms and therefore in its way "unauthorized."

Like Prufrock, Eliot wanted desperately to spit out the butt-ends of his days and ways; like Gerontion, to purge the "decayed house" of contemporary values, including his own; to get beyond the lukewarm spirituality of a Madame Sosostris to some fiery core where he could "be redeemed from fire by fire" (*Little Gidding*). But this process led back inevitably to his own roots in the New World. What was lacking in his original crossing from America to Europe, New to Old World, was precisely the pioneer spirit and Puritan resolve that had fired Andrew Eliot's departure, in 1669, from a village in Somerset (East Coker) for a "city on a hill." Young Eliot's was an escape, from family, origins, and the expected Harvard professorship, rather than a confrontation with destiny. "[Eliot's] own unwillingness to acknowledge his native tradition until late in his career was not snobbery," writes Lyndall Gordon, "but a fear, repeated in the essays, of 'provincialism' " (*New Life*, 94). Hence "Eliot's dreamvoyage [i.e. *East Coker*] points toward a new life" and, one might add, toward an ultimate confrontation with the demons (and angels) of that provincialism. "East Coker is a point of departure, and it is there that the poet re-enacts the about-face which gained its energy from rejection, the annihilating force of a condemnation of the comfortable Old World. His journey towards perfection takes its initiating impulse from a rejection of the earthly life and its obvious pleasures" (Gordon, *New Life*, 103). As in so much else, Dante the pilgrim is the model here as well: it matters not that this crossing is horizontal, for embedded in its trajectory is the "way down" (*via negativa*) that eventually becomes the "way up," pivoting at the *volte-face* (the ninth circle?) which leads forward, and back, to the mystical frontier/center where the poet, "alone with the Alone" (*Selected Prose*, 187), says (or hears),

> Quick now, here, now, always—
> A condition of complete simplicity
> (Costing not less than everything)
> And all shall be well and
> All manner of thing shall be well
> When the tongues of flame are in-folded
> Into the crowned knot of fire
> And the fire and the rose are one.

> (*Complete Poems*, 145)

This Eliot, the Eliot of the *Quartets*, is no longer, or at least not primarily, the social satirist and repressed misogynist, with his "personal and wholly insignificant grouse against life" and his "rhythmical grumbling" (in some ways the more interesting Eliot). Gone are Lil and Albert, Tiresias with his wrinkled dugs, the typist and the young man carbuncular. Instead we have the poet qua prophet, martyr, New England man of God, who has passed through the "flickering tongue" of dive bombers during the blitz of London to pause, like his model, at the threshold of "dovetailing" resolution, where the infernal fire and the paradisiacal rose are one.

But to return to the Dante essay. Dante's universality, his "peculiar lucidity," which shines through because European culture is as yet "undissociated," is precisely what is lacking in a civilization that has become demoralized and deracinated. Both Eliot and Mandelstam apply Dante's exile status to their own situations as repositories of a national tradition under siege, but they focus on different, even opposing aspects of Dante's poetic manifold. Eliot looks exclusively to Dante's imagery, the freshness and vividness of which are meant to rescue allegory from its ill repute (again, there is no perceived disjunction between the "real" and the "figurative"). "Dante's attempt is to make us see what he saw. He therefore employs very simple language, and very few metaphors, for allegory and metaphor do not get on well together" (*Selected Prose*, 210). In fact Eliot goes so far as to make the remarkable claim that "more can be learned about how to write poetry from Dante *than from any English poet*" (*Selected Prose*, 217; my emphasis). That is, any English poet writing in 1929 can, according to Eliot, learn more about writing English verse by studying Dante's fourteenth-century Italian than by studying the language of his own precursors or contemporaries. This exile from America suggests that English poetry has lost its way in a dark wood and that it must emerge from its immediate tradition into a prior and *foreign* one in order to reacquire its authenticity. He is, in this connection, obsessed with the *visual* or *metaphysical* (the joining of thought and feeling) aspects of the *Commedia*. Curiously, he has little to say about the sound of Dante's Italian. His willingness to impute associations to English words[11] but only a seamless lucidity to Dante's Italian appears counterintuitive to anyone who has immersed himself in a foreign language and culture, even one at a considerable temporal remove.

Why, the noninitiate might ask, is this so? How can Eliot arm himself against his and his generation's homelessness with a foreign language that is, in his rendering, peculiarly silent? Because in his view English poetry has been deafened by the roar of Milton's magniloquence, so much so that it has lost the capacity to envision what Dante once did. "At no point," says Eliot, "is the visual imagination conspicuous in Milton's poetry"; and "Milton may be said never to have seen anything" (*Selected Prose*, 259, 263).[12] Milton and his followers write in a "dead language"; their "syntax is determined by the musical significance, by the auditory imagination, rather than by the attempt to follow actual speech or thought" (*Selected Prose*, 261–62). A poet such as Tennyson can allude to Dante but he cannot, because of the split between thought and feeling that produces "rhetoric," write like Dante, even a nineteenth-century Dante. Dante's language was both universal enough (it was close to medieval Latin) and specific (or "vulgar") enough to enable the "vision" to happen. Hence the visionary Dante is one, salutary extreme (*opsis*) and the auditory Milton is another, pernicious extreme (*melos*). Again, what may get forgotten in Eliot's archmodernist appraisal of English poetry is the latter's need for a foreign transfusion in order to overcome the "blindness" of provincialism.[13] Even the interest in Laforgue and in the metaphysicals, whose predecessors were, predictably, "Dante, Guido Cavalcanti, Guinicelli, or Cino" (*Selected Prose*, 64), suggests that in Eliot's search for a unified sensibility there was no one "at home" to whom he could comfortably turn. Eliot the nostalgic monist has made a myth of Dante's Italian to gird himself against the Heraclitan movement of modern values.[14]

What is striking if we turn now to the Russian context is that Osip Mandelstam's Dante mediates in a similar way (one must go outside the native tradition to make it new) but for entirely different reasons and, linguistically, with entirely different results.[15] In 1933, just a few years after the writing of Eliot's Dante essay, Mandelstam was summering in Koktebel in the Crimea and composing his own, high modernist Russian version of the Dante legend. Recall that by this late date the new order promised by 1917 and appropriately "Christianized" by Mandelstam in the "Pushkin and Scriabin" essay (begun in 1915, completed in the early 1920s) had solidified into its own version of an inquisitorial historical church, armed with its own patriarchal dogma. And Mandelstam had, after years of trying in vain to find a place for himself within this order, come to accept and indeed defiantly affirm his heterodox role beyond the pale of official culture.[16] "Conversation about Dante" is, along with the earlier "Fourth Prose" (1929–30), precisely his own Aesopian (or "allegorical") statement about that role. Within months of this provocative statement the poet would write his self-destructive epigram on Stalin (November 1933), the Grand Inquisitor himself, see himself arrested (May 1934), and begin his internal exile to Cherdyn. Hence Dante's epic was not only the constant companion of his last years, but the poet's life and biographical legend were as well, this being one of those prototypical cases, so prevalent among Russian poets, where literary material seems to prefigure and shape the real-life outcome. Mandelstam wrote, and therefore in the Russian context *lived*, in such a way that he was as it were "fated" to go into exile and take Dante's way down.

Here we need to make an additional distinction, one that has interesting reverberations for Eliot, the displaced Puritan become British royalist. Mandelstam, like Pasternak and Brodsky, is a Jew writing for the larger Russian and "Christian" culture, and his eventual martyrdom and canonization depend on the perception of a kind of cultural "royalism." Yet the royalism is more than a little suspect, particularly if we, as in Eliot's case, dig deeper. There is never one simple process of rejection and acceptance, after which the searching and border-crossing and taboo-breaking come to rest. This is, to be sure, a complex issue, which I discuss elsewhere,[17] but suffice it to say for now that this primal "border"—in order to speak for the host culture the poet is required to traduce his own roots and "tribal" affiliations—adds yet another, perhaps ultimate and irresolvable dimension to Mandelstam's exile status. The past, what Mandelstam described in *Noise of Time* (wr. 1923–25) as "Judaic chaos," is overcome, in cultural terms, by becoming more Catholic than the Pope, or by wearing, as did Eliot, a white rose on the anniversary of the battle of Bosworth. But even this, as we know from studies of Jewish self-hatred (Gilman, Cuddihy), is never enough for total incorporation. Nor indeed should it be, since Mandelstam's goal was always more than "assimilation." To some, Mandelstam's eloquence would remain suspect, not "ours." Whatever he wrote and however much he suffered in the name of what he wrote, he could only be "Zinaida's [Zinaida Gippius's] little Jew" (*zinaidin zhidenok*).[18] Eliot (the anti-Semite!) was never at home, either in Boston or in London; he was, in Kermode's words, a "perpetual exile . . . banished and banishing, honored and deplored" (*Appetite*, 113–14). Yet while similar statements could be made about Mandelstam the person, the likeness ends there, and this is where the two Dantes, and the two different national traditions, enter the picture.

Mandelstam's Dante is diametrically opposed in every way to Eliot's Dante: he is all movement (as opposed to stability), metaphor (as opposed to allegory), opacity (as opposed to lucidity), verbal incantation (as opposed to vision), Wandering Jew (as opposed to quintessential Christian), unauthorized native language (as opposed to preferred lingua franca).[19] Mandelstam begins his "conversation" by stressing its oral and aural qualities: poetic speech is a "hybrid process" (skreshchennyi protsess) growing out of the self-perpetuating interplay of its own devices (orudiia) and their "intonational" and "phonetic" embodiment in the actual speech act (*SS*, 2:363). If there is any Christian message in this quirky presentation of the greatest of all Christian poets, it is located in the Acmeist notion of logos, of the miracle of poetic speech, which holds that the essential nature of that speech can never be "told," except through itself—through metaphor. Hence Mandelstam's essay is itself a kind of prose poem, an extended string of metaphoric arabesques that "accrete" a very different Dante. "Dante is the master of the instruments of poetry [orudiinyi master poezii], and not a manufacturer of images. He is a strategist of transformations and crossbreedings, and least of all a poet in the 'general European' and superficially cultural meaning of the word" (*SS*, 2:364). Nowhere can we say precisely what Mandelstam means, for that is his point. Crossbreeding means messiness, murkiness, illicit family planning, and shady genealogy. It is decidedly not "lucidity" he is after.

Note, for example, how Mandelstam uses Dante's Italian to authorize a radically unorthodox (for the Soviet Union in 1933) version of poetic speech:

> The art of speech precisely distorts our face, explodes its tranquility, disturbs its mask . . .
>
> When I began to study the Italian language and barely got acquainted with its phonetics and prosody, I suddenly realized that the center of gravity in speech production [lit., "speech work"—rechevaia rabota] had shifted: [it was now] nearer to the lips, to the outer [portions of the] mouth. The tip of the tongue suddenly held pride of place. Sound rushed toward the clamping shut of the teeth. Something else struck me more—that is the infantility of Italian phonetics, its wonderful childishness, proximity to baby's babble, to a kind of eternal Dadaism. (SS, 2:365–66)

If in life the poet sees himself as the wolf being run to earth by the wolf-hound (SS, 1:162),[20] he can still take perverse pleasure in feeling the out-law sounds of Italian on his lips. And even though this is prose it is often the *poetic* principle (assonance, internal rhyme, onomatopoeia, alliteration, paronomasia, etc.) that brings words together in meaning units. These sounds are "revolutionary" for their time—playful instead of stern, childish instead of patriarchal, foreign instead of domestic, "Dadaist" instead of politically correct, explosive for the facial "mask" instead of stolid and fixed. Dante's terza rima,[21] which Eliot has little to say about, is for Mandelstam a source of constant motion and fascination, as if mastery of the language and the goal of comprehension (lucidity) exist *in an inverse relationship*: "The reading of Dante is an endless labor, which distances us from our goal to the extent that we succeed." And the procession of metrical and physical feet (the pun exists in Russian as well) describes profoundly similar activities. In this respect Mandelstam anticipates intuitively a scholar such as John Freccero, who has demonstrated with exhaustive ingenuity the regenerative resources of terza rima ("The Significance," 258–71). "The *Inferno* and especially the *Purgatorio* glorify the human gait, the meter and rhythm of steps, the foot and its form. The step, accompanied by breathing and filled with thought, is understood by Dante as the origin of prosody" (SS, 2:367). What is undissociated for Eliot is the Dantesque vision; what is impenetrable and irreducible and "sacred" for Mandelstam is the logos where physical and metrical feet, joints that do not make sounds until they are *in motion*, coexist in the same metaphoric space.

As was suggested earlier, Mandelstam takes matters much more personally than Eliot. Dante is not an allusive scaffold, as in *The Waste Land*, or an anterior source of visionary truth, as in the essay. He is rather an actual human being, wounded, tetchy, bitter. For Mandelstam, exile, in all its nuances, is not a choice to start over elsewhere but an affront and a spiritual slap in the face, what readers of Dostoevsky know by the name of *obida*:

> Dante is a poor man. Dante is an internal *raznochinets* [the "upstart intellectual" whom Mandelstam had cited as model for himself and his generation in *Noise of Time*] of ancient Roman blood. What is characteristic of him is not at all civility [liubeznost'], but something quite the opposite. One has to be a blind mole not to notice that during the entire *Divina Commedia* Dante is unable to behave himself, does not know how to proceed, what to say, how to bow. (*SS*, 2:372)

Mandelstam goes on to say that the entire charm of the *Commedia* derives precisely from the pathos of this awkwardness and "internal anxiety," this inability of the "tormented and driven man" to fit in and find a place for himself in the "social hierarchy" (*SS*, 2:372–73). We should focus, in other words, not on the poem's lapidary message and allegorical structure (the mistake of prior Dante scholarship), but on the bile, the vengeful thoughts (hence the exquisite *contrapassi*), and the emotional "instability" seething underneath.

While all this may be found in Dante, it is decidedly *Mandelstam's* version we are confronting; indeed, as Clare Cavanagh has demonstrated, it is Mandelstam himself we are confronting. Dante's fear of answering anything directly is Mandelstam's fear, for his poetry and for his life, of answering anything directly (*SS*, 2:385). The reason why the shades of the three prominent Florentines (Canto XVI, *Inferno*) quake in the presence of their interlocutor is that his damning assessment of their native city (read Petersburg/Leningrad) allows no other interpretation (*SS*, 1:180). The words are delivered with the poet's head thrown back: "Cosi gridai colla faccia levata"—an immediately recognizable Mandelstamian gesture.[22] And they are filled with the dark passions of the interrogation ("tiuremnaia strastnost'"; *SS*, 2:385). It is not enough to say, as Eliot might, that here Mandelstam is writing within a certain tradition, a "sense of the timeless as well as of the temporal and of the timeless and the temporal together" (*Selected Prose*, 38). No High Culture this, no moment of sublime synchronicity in the bosom of illustrious precursors. Because Dante is "antimodernist" and because his contemporaneity is "inexhaustible" (*SS*, 2:389), he exists, according to Mandelstam's contrary logic, as the poet's companion and coeval. There is no Virgil (and no Beatrice for that matter), no room (or time) for reverence and pantheons. All that exists is the love for the Florence/Petersburg that should have been and the hatred for the Florence/Leningrad that is and the "babbling" language that hovers between the two: "Love of the city, passion for the city, hatred of the city—this is the material of the *Inferno*. The rings of Hell are nothing other than the Saturnian circles of emigration.[23] For the exile his one and only, forbidden and irrevocably lost city is dispersed everywhere; he is surrounded by it" (*SS*, 2:402).

Brodsky

In this final section of the chapter we will shift the time frame by roughly a half century and center discussion around Joseph Brodsky's most Dantesque creation, the poem "December in Florence" (Dekabr' vo Florentsii, 1976). Brodsky is the ideal summary interlocutor for several reasons, but principally because his own work, coming as it does at "the end of a *belle époque*" (the phrase is of course heavily ironic), is mediated brilliantly by all three of our authors—Eliot, Mandelstam, and Dante. Not without significance, Brodsky is also the quintessential Wandering Jew, having traveled more often and to more places than any other Russian poet in history.[24] "Perhaps exile is the poet's natural condition," writes Brodsky, echoing his favorite Tsvetaeva, "I felt a certain privilege in the coincidence of my existential condition with my profession" (Interview with Giovanni Buttafava, *L'Espresso*, 6 December 1987; cited in Kline, "Variations," 56).

Brodsky initially became aware of Eliot as poet and exile in the early 1960s, when the latter "reigned supreme in Eastern Europe" (*Less*, 361). First reading him in translation and then, as his (Brodsky's) English improved, in the original, the process of assimilation reached a new plateau in January 1965 when, sentenced to internal exile in the far northern village of Norinskaya, Brodsky wrote "Verses on the Death of T. S. Eliot." And while the poet has never said as much in print, aligning himself temperamentally with the more "anti-heroic" Auden (*Less*, 367), one divines a deep and abiding affinity with Eliot, especially the émigré haunted by the specter of his country's backwardness and provincial culture. It seems in a way fated that Brodsky, like Eliot, has seen fit to contemplate the historical mission or manifest destiny of one (massive yet in its own way "orphaned") empire from the boundaries of another. The rivers (Mississippi, Thames), oceans (Atlantic), and cities (St. Louis, Boston, London) that entered into Eliot's personal mythology find direct analogues in Brodsky's (and Mandelstam's as well) Neva and Petersburg-Leningrad.[25]

The links with Mandelstam run deeper still. To begin with, both Brodsky and Mandelstam, like Pushkin before them, have experienced the humiliation and deprivation of internal exile to a remote area (Norinskaya,

Voronezh). Moreover, like Dante their model, they know what it means to lose "the most beautiful city [Leningrad] on the face of the earth" (*Less*, 32). Mandelstam was present at the birth of the Soviet order when Petersburg/Petrograd became Leningrad: not only do cities banish poets but history banishes cities. In Khodasevich's classic formula, 1917 was the border dividing the era of "Petropolis" as capital of the empire and the Russian lyric tradition from the era of "Necropolis," an underworld city of shades and prior glories (see chapter 1). Now Petersburg, whose outward skeleton still exists in the city's stately architecture, must be sought *within* the poet, in the underworld of his psyche. "I'd rather call it [the city] 'Peter,'" muses Brodsky, "for I remember a time when it didn't look like 'Leningrad'—right after the [Second World] war" (*Less*, 4). And just as Mandelstam presided, uneasily, at the inception of Soviet time, Brodsky has written more powerfully than anyone of his generation about the shabby end of that saeculum. "In the national experience, the city is definitely Leningrad; in the growing vulgarity of its content, it becomes Leningrad more and more" (*Less*, 4). Yet even this, the loss of his Florence, is insufficient to capture the full poignancy of Brodsky's exile status. His enforced isolation has, in some ways, gone even further than the internal banishment that unhinged Mandelstam. When Brodsky was expelled from the Soviet Union in June 1972, he also lost his homeland and his primary audience (crucial factors, for example, lending support to Mandelstam and Akhmatova in their martyrdoms) as well as his linguistic tether—a not insignificant detail to be taken up in the "December" poem. That Brodsky, again like Mandelstam (and to a lesser degree the Muscovite Pasternak), has spoken eloquently for the Christian values central to Russian culture from the vantage of a Jewish outsider has only strengthened the remaining links.[26] In fact, Nadezhda Mandelstam confirmed this genealogy by dubbing Brodsky "the second Osya" (Joseph).[27]

But perhaps the most potent link with Mandelstam lies in Brodsky's special and, I would submit, characteristically Russian views on the ontology of language. These views owe their existence to an essentially Acmeist understanding of the concept of Christian logos. Over and over again in his essays and poetry Mandelstam makes the point that the word become flesh, the miracle of metaphorical eucharist, is the basis of all poetic speech. A word has its own soul or "psyche" (*dusha, psikheia*) and is completely free—this is the Christian miracle of new or redeemed time—to choose its own body—its form in a poetic utterance.[28] *Nothing is higher or prior to this word.* "The Christian, and now every cultured person is a Christian," writes Mandelstam in "The Word and Culture" (Slovo i kul'tura, 1921), "does not know mere physical hunger, mere spiritual sustenance. For him the word is both flesh and simple bread— gaiety and mystery" (*SS*, 2:223). That is, the mystery of the word is not to be found in the other worlds and higher reality of Vyacheslav Ivanov and the Symbolists (*a realibus ad realiora*), but in itself, as it takes on the flesh of its choosing *in this world.*

This means, further, that the state (gosudarstvo) and everything related to it are posterior to, and hence dependent on, this linguistic moment of sacrificial embodiment:

> The externality [vnepolozhnost'] of the state in relation to cultural values places that state in a position of complete dependence on culture. Cultural values color statehood [gosudarstvennost'], impart to it color, form, and, if you like, even gender. . . .
>
> There has arrived in the life of the word an heroic era. The word is flesh and bread. It shares the fate of bread and flesh: suffering. People are hungry. But hungrier still is the state. But there is something even more hungry: time. Time wants to swallow the state. . . . He who shall raise the word and display it to time, as the priest displays the eucharist, will be a second Joshua of Nun. ("Slovo i kul'tura," *SS*, 2:225–26)

Not only would Brodsky agree with these ideas and values, he could have authored them (see chapter 1). Mandelstam speaks in metaphors (here the eucharist) because language is above all else the *freedom* to say, and of course believe, *this is that.* To say the word is fleshlike is a figure of speech; to say the word is flesh and bread is an article of faith, an assertion of what today might be termed *a transcendental signified.* Yet Mandelstam, implicitly aware of this dilemma (the intentional fallacy of the Symbolists), resolves the issue by returning to its, the word's, immanent reality. The word can mean anything it wants (a potentially deconstructive notion), and yet, thanks to its Psychelike nature, its choice is intentional and "motivated." People are hungry and they turn to governments, which consume them; governments are more hungry still and they turn to time/history, which consumes them. Only the word, whose form (flesh) and essence/function (bread) are inseparable and complementary, can, according to Mandelstam, satisfy the craving for meaning and, by sacrificing itself to the jaws of time, perform a spiritual feat of heroism (podvig). The poet who utters the word is merely an occasion in space and time, a voicebox around which the butterfly *dusha* (soul) flutters before it passes through the organs of articulation and lights on a form in the material world. This implied hierarchy—state → time → language—is, as we have seen, quite typical of the mature Brodsky but typical in a distinctly late-twentieth-century way.[29]

Brodsky writes in an expository prose style more earthy and idiomatic than that of the intentionally opaque and incantatory Mandelstam. Be this as it may, the Acmeist *logology* (the term is Kenneth Burke's) informs many of his statements that otherwise might appear to be sheer rhetorical fireworks and mystification to the uninitiated Western reader. Note, for example, how he concludes "The Keening Muse" (1982), his prose homage to Anna Akhmatova:

> At certain periods of history it is only poetry that is capable of dealing with reality by condensing it into something graspable, something that otherwise couldn't be retained by the mind. . . .
>
> These two perspectives [that of "the individual heart" and that of "history"] were brought into sharp focus through prosody, which is simply a repository of time within language. . . . This is also why her verses are to survive whether published or not: because of the prosody, because they are charged with time in both these senses. They will survive because *language is older than state and because prosody always survives history.* (*Less*, 52; my emphasis)

Note also how he introduces "the modern Orpheus," Mandelstam himself, in "The Child of Civilization" (1977):

> [Art] is *a spirit seeking flesh but finding words.* In the case of Mandelstam, the words happened to be those of the Russian language. . . . Writing is literally an existential process; it uses thinking for its own ends, it consumes notions, themes, and the like, not vice vera. *What dictates a poem is the language,* and this is the voice of the language, which we know under the nicknames of Muse and Inspiration. It is better, then, to speak not about the theme of time in Mandelstam's poetry, but about the presence of time itself. (*Less*, 123–25; my emphasis)

By insisting that language (prosody, poetic structure) is older than the state (a profoundly anti-Marxist notion) and that it has a mind and heart of its own, Brodsky has in effect "leap-frogged" back to an earlier poetic culture in order to gird himself against his own imminent exile and orphanhood. The belief that language possesses its own internal logic (a logos that is anything but the idle play of the signifier) and that it exists independent of all parties, including the poet himself, is what continues, even now, to give Russian poetry its "moral purity and firmness" (*Less*, 142).[30]

Let us now look more closely at "December in Florence," keeping in mind the poem's ultimate placement in Brodsky's first collection written in exile. The poem opens with a distinctly "estranged" view of the city:

> Двери вдыхают воздух и выдыхают пар; но
> ты не вернешься сюда, где, разбившись попарно,
> населенье гуляет над обмелевшим Арно,
> напоминая новых четвероногих. Двери
> хлопают, на мостовую выходят звери.
> Что-то вправду от леса имеется в атмосфере

этого города. Это—красивый город,
где в известном возрасте просто отводишь взор от
человека и поднимаешь ворот.

(ChR, 111)

The doors take in air, exhale steam; you, however, won't
be back to the shallowed Arno where, like a new kind
of quadruped, idle couples follow the river bend.
Doors bang, beasts hit the slabs. Indeed,
the atmosphere of this city retains a bit
of the dark forest. It
is a beautiful city where at a certain age
one simply raises the collar to disengage
from passing humans and dulls the gaze.

(Part, 119)

The doors of Florence open and close with the rhythms of a sinister living body. They breathe in the air of the streets and breathe out its false double or "shade": *par* is a play on sound suggesting both close or "hellish" air (steam) and a truncated (genitive plural) version of "couple," another important theme in the poem.[31] These hinged orifices conjure up the gates of Hell, described so powerfully at the beginning of the third canto of the *Inferno*: "DINANZI A ME NON FUOR COSE CREATE / SE NON ETTERNE, E IO ETTERNA DURO. / LASCIATE OGNI SPERANZA, VOI CH' ENTRATE" (BEFORE ME NOTHING WAS CREATED BUT ETERNAL / THINGS AND I ENDURE ETERNALLY./ ABANDON EVERY HOPE, YE THAT ENTER) (Dante, *Inferno*, 46–47). The "you" of the second line (in the original) is a typically rich Brodskian evasion. Dante remains unnamed in the poem, although many details point to his identity as the primary addressee. This is the city, for one, that exiled him and permanently forbade his return: "*you* will not return here." Athwart his path are the beasts—the leopard, lion, and she-wolf?—which make that return anything but straightforward. Presumably this is why there is something of the *selva oscura* ("chto-to . . . ot lesa") about this city and why, *at a certain age*, one tends to turn away from one's fellow man and proceed inward. Dante was, we recall, precisely in the middle of life's journey (his age thirty-five, the year 1300) when he lost his path and took the way down. Although the city itself is "beautiful," it is also monstrous and potentially "underworldly." The reflection on the Arno changes people into four-legged predators. Here it is the law of the jungle that obtains (*homo homini lupus est*) and every man is an exile because no one has a home.[32]

The Dante connection clearly applies to the formal features of the poem as well. "December in Florence" is composed of nine stanzas, each of which is composed in turn of three "terzinas." We know that the numbers 3 and 9 were deeply symbolic to the author of *Vita Nuova* and the *Commedia*, and Brodsky has pointedly chosen to play on this tradition.[33] Not only, for example, does each of Dante's *terzine* consist of thirty-three syllables (three hendecasyllabic lines) but each of the three *cantiche* of the *Commedia* consists of thirty-three *canti* (the first canto of the *Inferno* being a "prologue"). Perhaps, for example, given the allusions to the beasts and the forest in the opening lines of "December," Brodsky has arranged the poem in nine equally symmetrical stanzas to suggest the nine circles of Hell in the *Inferno*? Significantly, however, Brodsky's terzinas are *not* Dantesque in one interesting particular: the middle member of the three-line unit does not have an opposing end-rhyme (*ABA, BCB*, etc., in the *Commedia* versus *AAA, BBB*, etc., in Brodsky's scheme). Brodsky is invoking, and at the same time subverting, the earlier tradition, with its implication of simultaneous progression and return. In this respect, his triple rhymes do not reflect the "reconciliation of motion that *terza rima* implies: a forward motion, closed off with a recapitulation that gives to the motion its beginning and end" (Freccero, "The Significance," 262). Likewise, on a thematic level, this sameness cannot anticipate the thud and counterthud of the Dante character's footfall, his "forward motion . . . toward a goal," which becomes "the transformation of the pilgrim into the author" at the story's end (Freccero, "The Significance," 262–63).[34] In short, there is no geometry of salvation, no "anagogic" plan or progression leading first down, then up and "out of itself" in Brodsky's rhyme scheme. Counterposed against the dyadic beginning and ending— the so-called *rime rilevate*—of each of Dante's cantos, a pattern that enforces the sense of proper entry and exit, is the absolute, and therefore in a way deadly, symmetry of Brodsky's poem. What *is* different about Brodsky's rhymes is their free deployment within grammatical and lexical categories: a noun/conjunction combination (*pár; no*—"steam; but") rhymes with an adverb (*popárno*—"in pairs") which in turns rhymes with a proper noun (Arno). Thus, coexisting with the fixed elitism and stayed elegance of the modified terzinas is a wild and fractious egalitarianism—perhaps Brodsky's way of saying that within the "a priority" and "restructured time" of prosodic forms all things, as in the flux of history, are possible.

But Brodsky is not only speaking about Dante. He is, of course, speaking also about himself. His "poetics of subtraction"[35] are so effective because the removal of the subject as physical body results in the proliferation of "other-voicing" and choral accompaniment.[36] Nowhere in the poem does Brodsky allude directly to the place or circumstances of his own banishment, a ruse that only causes the reader to look more vigilantly for the connection and project it into nearly every line. In the complete absence of a lyrical "I" the speaker becomes, a little later, a "body

in a raincoat" (telo v plashche),[37] described with a third-person verb.
Indeed, the only intrusion of the first person in the entire poem comes as
a wry aside ("O, the inevitability of [the Cyrillic letter] 'ы' in the spelling
of 'жизни' ['of life']") at the end of the eighth stanza, but even here the
"I" is only implied. We may assume, therefore, that the "you" of the
second line can and does refer to the poet who in December 1975 (the
poem was written in 1976) was himself thirty-five years old and had been
in exile in the West for more than four years.[38] He has come to Florence
as an outsider to consider his own beautiful city, Leningrad, populated as
it is by its own beasts and only too willing to rid itself of another unadap-
tive "parasite." Perhaps in this regard the Arno is not itself but the Neva?
In any event, to insist that the mirror of contemporary reality (the river's
surface) gives off a monstrous image would, in the minds of city fathers,[39]
be expected of a perversely narcissistic and untrustworthy "cosmopolite"
like Brodsky. Thus "you, however, won't be back" can be a line Brodsky
is speaking to his (pre-exile?) self: the "you" is not "out there" (the shade
of Dante) but within. Brodsky is indeed masterful in his use of tense and
aspect to telescope viewpoints. The first "you," presented together with a
perfective future construction, appears categorical and calculated to summon up the shade of the great precursor. In effect, the reader thinks of
Brodsky only *after* thinking of Dante. But the second "you," attached to
a verb form in the imperfective present ("you/one simply raises the collar
to disengage"), is more matter-of-fact and nonspecific, its referent a kind
of existential tourist. And here we think first of the poet Brodsky general-
izing from the particulars of his own exile experience.

There is, however, yet one more "you" hidden in this Dantesque colloquy. It is embedded in Brodsky's epigraph ("This one, as he left, did not
look back"),[40] which he borrowed from Akhmatova's Dante poem
("Dante," 1936). Since this work is short, I will cite it in full:

> Он и после смерти не вернулся
> В старую Флоренцию свою.
> Этот, уходя, не оглянулся,
> Этому я эту песнь пою.
> Факел, ночь, последнее объятье,
> За порогом дикий вопль судьбы.
> Он из ада ей послал проклятье
> И в раю не мог ее забыть, —
> Но босой, в рубахе покаянной,
> Со свечей зажженной не прошел
> По своей Флоренции желанной,
> Вероломной, низкой, долгожданной . . .

(S, 1:236)

Even after death he did not return
to his old Florence.
This one, as he left, did not look back,
and it is to this one that I sing this song.
A torch, night, a final embrace,
beyond the threshold fate's wild howl.
He sent her his curse from hell
and in paradise he still could not forget her;
but barefoot, in his penitential rags,
with lighted candle he did not pass
through his precious Florence,
treacherous, base, so long-awaited.

(my translation)

On the surface, Akhmatova's poem is about one poet, faced with her own manifest hardships, looking to another for support and inspiration. And yet we need to keep in mind the dating of the poem and the prior history of Akhmatova's interest in Dante to recover its second, and perhaps more important, addressee. Our point is that Akhmatova's poem is mediated by an unmentioned but no less present interlocutor in precisely the way that Brodsky's is. In the fall of 1933, directly after the writing of "Conversation about Dante," Akhmatova and Mandelstam spent considerable time together reading and discussing the great Italian. It was in November of that fall that Mandelstam wrote his fatal Stalin epigram and the following May that he was arrested for the first time and exiled to Cherdyn, where he feared for his sanity and attempted suicide. Eventually, through the intervention of influential friends of the poet (Bukharin, Pasternak), Stalin decided to "isolate but preserve" Mandelstam, commuting what would certainly have been a death sentence to three years of exile in the southern city of Voronezh. It was during these years (1935–37) that Mandelstam wrote his magnificent late poetry (the so-called Voronezh Notebooks) and that Akhmatova wrote, in 1936, her little Dante poem.

It is, then, not only to Dante but to the dear friend who wrote "For the exile his one and only, forbidden and irrevocably lost city is dispersed everywhere; he is surrounded by it" that Akhmatova silently dedicates her poem. Again, without naming the addressee, the "this one" (etot) is both vague and specific enough (at least to Akhmatova) to refer to both Dante and Mandelstam. Nearly every detail in the poem is simultaneously Dantesque and Mandelstamian: the emphasis on parting (cf. *Tristia*), the wild howl of fate (the beasts of the forest and the beasts of the security police waiting "beyond the threshold" to arrest the poet), the rags of the exile, the mixed feelings of love and hatred toward the city (*gorodoliubie* versus *gorodonenavistnichestvo*; cf "Razgovor," in *SS*,

2:402), and so on. The poem appears as well to resonate with one of Mandelstam's most famous poems, written in December 1930: entitled "Leningrad," this short and haunting piece refers repeatedly to the city as "Petersburg" and begins "I've returned to my city, familiar to [the point of] tears" (Ia vernulsia v moi gorod, znakomyi do slez) (*SS*, 1:158–59).[41] Its principal message is that the poet has come to a city of shades (his old Petersburg, with its addresses and telephone numbers of those since departed) where he no longer has a place among the living (the city of Lenin). The line "Petersburg! I still don't want to die" anticipates with grim irony Akhmatova's opening, which in 1936 could only refer to Dante, "Even after death he did not return / to his old Florence." Even living in Leningrad, Mandelstam could not live in Petersburg. His "one and only, forbidden and irrevocably lost city" was "dispersed" around him.

Mandelstam died in *December* 1938, probably in a transit camp near Vladivostok following his second arrest (in May 1938, in Samatikha) and sentencing. Brodsky was born a year and a half later in May 1940. His only physical link to Mandelstam was Akhmatova, who was among the first to recognize his gift and to make the connection between the two Josephs. My point is that Brodsky's "you" is the first as well as the second "Joseph." We know this for two reasons: because, first, the details of the earlier Mandelstam "December" poem ("Leningrad") are scattered throughout "December in Florence"—the notion of forbidden return, the tears of recognition, the swallowing of damp air, the streetlamps, the Lethean river, the time of year, the poet's position on life's "backstairs" (chernaia lestnitsa), the frightening doorbell/death knell, the themes of death and memory; and because, second, the central image in another related "December" poem ("My goldfinch, I will raise my head" [Moi shchegol, ia golovu zakinu]), this one written in 1936 in Voronezh, is implicated directly in perhaps the most Dante-inspired stanza of Brodsky's text. Let us quote first the Mandelstam text and then follow it by the stanza from Brodsky:

> Мой щегол, я голову закину—
> Поглядим на мир вдвоем:
> Зимний день, колючий, как мякина,
> Так ли жестк в зрачке твоем?
>
> Хвостик лодкой, перья—черно-желты,
> Ниже клюва в краску влит—
> Сознаешь ли, до чего, щегол, ты,
> До чего ты щегловит?
>
> Что за воздух у него в надлобье:
> Черн и красен, желт и бел!—

В обе стороны он в оба смотрит—в обе!
Не посмотрит, улетел.

(SS, 1:224–25)

My goldfinch, I will raise my head,
let us look at the world as two:
a winter's day, prickly like chaff,
does it seem so harsh in your eye?

Tail shaped like a boat, feathers dark-yellow,
Below the beak all poured into color:
Do you realize, goldfinch, do you,
how much you are goldfinch-like?

What is this air in his crest:
Black and red, yellow and white!
He looks attentively to both sides—to both!
He will not look, he's flown away.

(my translation)

В пыльной кофейне глаз в полумраке кепки
привыкает к нимфам плафона, к амурам, к лепке;
ощущая нехватку в терцинах, в клетке
дряхлый щегол выводит свои коленца.
Солнечный луч, разбившийся о дворец, о
купол собора, в котором лежит Лоренцо,
проникает сквозь штору и согревает вены
грязного мрамора, кадку с цветком вербены;
и щегол разливается в центре проволочной Равенны.

(ChR, 112)

In a dusty café, in the shade of your cap,
eyes pick out frescoes, nymphs, cupids on their way up.
In a cage, making up for the sour terza-rima crop,
a seedy goldfinch juggles his sharp cadenza.
A chance ray of sunlight splattering the palazzo
and the sacristy where lies Lorenzo
pierces thick blinds and titillates the veinous
filthy marble, tubs of snow-white verbena;
and the bird's ablaze within his wire Ravenna.

(Part, 120)

This is truly a remarkable instance of intertextual "triangulation." And yet, as suggested at our outset, it is not untypical of Brodsky. The entire poem, indirectly though insistently, refers us to Dante as primary addressee. At the same time, an educated Russian reader would recognize the goldfinch as a Mandelstamian spirit.[42] Indeed, that Brodsky had Mandelstam squarely in mind is confirmed in the Mandelstam essay: "[Mandelstam's later poetry] became more a song than ever before, not a bardlike but a birdlike song, with its sharp, unpredictable turns and pitches, something like a goldfinch tremolo" (*Less*, 134). Dante's exile is mediated by Mandelstam's, which in turn is mediated by Brodsky's. All are different—the Italian not at home in Italy, the Russian not at home in Russia, the Russian not at home in Italy—yet all are also the same, each in its way reflecting the central paradox of banishment: "an exile is someone who inhabits one place and remembers or projects the reality of another" (Seidel, *Exile*, ix). What is unique about Brodsky's rendering is that it requires not a double but a triple vision: the reader must know both Dante and Mandelstam and the Akhmatova link as it applies to the two Josephs.[43] The scruffy goldfinch is Dante because it senses a need for terzinas and breaks into song within its cage, described as a wire Ravenna (the place of Dante's exile and death).[44] On the other hand, a wire place of entrapment could easily, in the Russian context, be "barbed" (*koliuchaia* provoloka); as a reference, it points to both the "prickly" winter day in Mandelstam's poem and to the actual border of Mandelstam's final resting place.[45] So when Mandelstam sees himself matched (vdvoem) with a bird preparing to sing (right down to the characteristic "signature" of the raised head), we automatically recall the earlier line from Dante cited in "Conversation": "Cosi gridai colla faccia levata." All these Decembers (1930, 1936, 1938, 1975) come together and compete with one another for attention in Brodsky's poem. The main impression with which we are left, however, is that the goldfinch breaks out in song *despite everything*, including the death of its human alter ego. Not exactly a golden bird to keep a drowsy emperor awake, it sings of what is past, or passing, or to come through the cage erected around it by history. The words escape, the man does not.

The poem has numerous other examples of intertextual mediation, most of them pointing to Dante in a mordant inversion of the primary sources: the "your doorway" (tvoi pod"ezd) near the Piazza della Signoria that suggests Dante's home but that also, because it uses a Sovietism (pod"ezd), may apply to Brodsky (that is, again the "you" is ambivalent) (stanza II); the sighting of an angelic golden-haired woman rummaging through the wares of dark tradeswomen, an episode of potential "beatific" intrusion upstaged by its vulgar commercial context (stanza III);[46] houses sunk "waist deep" into their crumbling foundations like sinners awash in torment (stanza V); the assertion, contradicting the famous dance of the stars around Beatrice and the pilgrim in the *Paradiso* (stanza X), that "it is untrue / that love moves the stars" (stanza VII); and so on. But Brodsky's point is not, or at least not only, to weave a subtle tissue of ironic allusion. Rather, it is to turn this elaborate scaffolding of cultural syncretism on its head in order to examine the central myth of poetry itself—that of the Christian logos.

We should not lose sight of the fact that, for Dante and Mandelstam, poetry and life are mystically intertwined and the peregrinations of the pilgrim become emplotted in the progress of the poet, who must write for himself and his time a fitting end. Their poetry is testimony to the belief that not only could the word become flesh but that, in their cases, it had. The hidden meaning of Brodsky's poem is precisely the opposite, that *the flesh has become word*:

Человек превращается в шорох пера по бумаге, в кольца,
петли, клинышки букв и, потому что скользко,
в запятые и точки. Только подумать, сколько
раз, обнаружив «м» в заурядном слове,
перо спотыкалось и выводило брови
то есть, чернила честнее крови.
И лицо в потемках, словами наружу—благо
так куда быстрей просыхает влага—
смеется, как скомканная бумага.

(ChR, 112)

A man gets reduced to pen's rustle on paper, to
wedges, ringlets of letters, and also, due
to the slippery surface, to commas and full stops. True,
often, in some common word, the unwitting pen
strays into drawing—while tackling an
"M"—some eyebrows: ink is more honest than
blood. And a face, with moist words inside
out to dry what has just been said,
smirks like the crumpled paper absorbed by shade.

(Part, 120)

The stanza invokes the medieval tradition, alluded to directly in the twenty-third canto of *Purgatorio*, where the word for man (the *h* being dropped from *omo*) is written on a person's face in the form of two *o*'s (the eye-sockets) straddling an *m* (cheekbones, eyebrows, and nose).[47] (Dante has been witnessing the Gluttonous on the Sixth Terrace of Purgatory; the *contrapasso* of their emaciating hunger would make the *omo* stand out in still more haunting relief.) But the poet's own *contrapasso* involves a different sort of excess—that of love. Exile has taken everything from him, including his Beatrice (the *m* could be Marina Basmanova, his great passion and the mother of his only son), and has left him with his writing, his letters, his punctuation marks, his "parts of speech." He has *turned into* these things; instead of God's word made flesh in the coming of the first and second Adam (the primary Acmeist models), his flesh is dying away into these scattered hieroglyphics. It is a kind of inner hell ("man gets reduced to . . . ringlets"), and yet it is all he has. Ink is more honest than blood because she, with her eyebrows, is "there" and he, with his letters, is "here." Such a Beatrice will never descend to his limbo. By turning her into a crumpled piece of paper and a pun (*vlaga* [moisture] refers both to his tears and his ink), he can deflect his pain, regain his composure, and carry on. This explains why, for this postmodernist, love does not move the stars but only splits everything in two ("ibo ona delit vse veshchi na dva" [stanza VII]). People are no longer people but letters: a policeman directing traffic becomes the Russian ж (zh), arms pointing "neither up nor down"; and the letter ы appears "inevitable" in the spelling (actually the pronunciation) of жизни (life) because it is written separately while и is written together, as one unit (stanza VIII). Hence Brodsky cannot return to his native city for the additional reason that his love no longer resides there. The image of that love has not risen to the stars whence it beckons the poet "from the future." It has died and entered the underworld of the past even if its object has not.

Still, and this is our final message, the goldfinch bursts out in song amid its (barbed-)wire Ravenna even now. Brodsky's notes are these letters and sounds that stubbornly assert their existence despite all evidence to the contrary. His last stanza, with its theme of nonreturn, in fact returns to the first on the wings of language. Here again is the city by the river criss-crossed by six bridges (Florence/Leningrad); here the lost stellar or lunar regions impregnable to sunlight; here the sacred scenes of love (lips meeting lips) and creativity (pen meeting paper) where an implied "he" or "I" (Dante/Brodsky) first came of age; and last but not least, here the linguistic remains of the pilgrim/goldfinch who has, and has not, left:

Есть города, в которые нет возврата.
Солнце бьется в их окна, как в гладкие зеркала. То
есть, в них не проникнешь ни за какое злато.
Там всегда протекает река под шестью мостами.
Там есть места, где припадал устами
тоже к устам и пером к листам. И
там рябит от аркад, колоннад, от чугунных пугал;
там толпа говорит, осаждая трамвайный угол,
на языке человека, который убыл.[48]

(*ChR*, 113)

There are cities one won't see again. The sun
throws its gold at their frozen windows. But all the same
there is no entry, no proper sum.
There are always six bridges spanning the sluggish river.
There are places where lips touched lips for the first time ever,
or pen pressed paper with real fervor.
There are arcades, colonnades, iron idols that blur your lens.
There the streetcar's multitudes, jostling, dense,
speak in the tongue of a man who's departed thence.

(*Part*, 121)

3 _____

The Flea and the Butterfly:
John Donne and the Case for Brodsky as
Russian Metaphysical

> Verse embalmes vertue; and Tombs, or Thrones of rimes,
>   Preserve fraile transitory fame, as much
>   As spice doth bodies from corrupt aires touch.
>   (John Donne, "To the Countesse of Bedford")

> And in this flea, our two bloods mingled be.
>   (John Donne, "The Flea")

> Такая красота
>   И срок столь краткий,
>   соединясь, догадкой
>   кривят уста . . .

> Such beauty
>   and such a short span of time,
>   uniting, twist the lips
>   in a riddle . . .
> (Joseph Brodsky, "The Butterfly")

JOSEPH BRODSKY has never been one to come by poetic or ontological truths straightforwardly. He is less afraid of heights and depths than he is of level ground, especially the flatland of cliché. His prosodic footfall is reminiscent of the movement of Mandelstam's little peasant horse in "Clacking on purple granite" (O porfirnye tsokaia granity, 1930), whose hoofs scrape defiantly against verbal (and existential) matter in their ascent up the mountainside of the Russian lyric tradition. Brodsky, too, tends to halt before the beaten path and prefers the steep incline of new and ever more difficult challenges. A single frontal assault is alien to his poetics. Indeed, to anyone who has ever heard Brodsky read aloud one of his longer poems, with their sense of constantly "shifting gears" as the poet makes yet another run at some distant and ever more attenuated target, the following lines from another *eiron*, the so-called monarch of wit, come to mind:

On a huge hill,
Cragged, and steep, Truth stands, and hee that will
Reach her, about must, and about must goe;
And what the hills suddennes resists, winne so . . .

(Donne, "Satyre III," in Poems, 157)

What precisely is Brodsky's relation to the greatest of the English meta-physicals? Can his poetry be called "metaphysical" in any useful or mean-ingful way?[1] Is this poetry a forced and artificial mingling of two bloods, a trained verbal flea whose sole purpose is to "purple the nail" of the impatient reader in an elaborate rhetorical joke? Or can it be called a butterfly, whose unbidden metamorphosis from pedestrian to airy is also a metaphor for poetic speech? These antinomies (flea-butterfly), based on actual conceits taken from each poet's work, could be said to emblema-tize the range of possible reception, from positive to negative, given Donne and Brodsky by their respective cultures. Because Donne was the first English poet to attract Brodsky's attention, and because this pattern of cross-fertilization (Anglo-American/Russian poetic traditions) would prove crucial in Brodsky's later work, it is important that we look care-fully at this instance. Ultimately, the comparison leads to a larger ques-tion—is genuine metaphysical poetry possible within the Russian con-text, and in order to be discovered (as opposed to *rediscovered*) does it need such prior foils as a Milton and such later mediators as Eliot and Grierson?

This, in short, is our topic. In the first part of this chapter we will look briefly at the tradition of Russian meditative or philosophical poetry (*poeziia mysli*), with an eye to how Brodsky both adheres to, and departs from, this tradition. Then we will examine some of the biographical and historico-literary parallels that make Donne and Brodsky, mutatis mu-tandis, kindred spirits. Next we will provide a reading of Brodsky's early masterpiece "The Large Elegy to John Donne," with its striking media-tion by the Russian elegiac tradition. And finally, we will demonstrate how one of Donne's most famous late Renaissance conceits, that of the twin compasses, has been transformed by Brodsky in his own love poetry. As suggested elsewhere in this study, our point is not to identify a case of borrowing or, as Mandelstam urged in his essay on Villon, outright theft, since that much is surely obvious.[2] Rather, it is to find out *why* Brodsky felt compelled to appropriate Donne, how he "russified" him or made him his own, and what exactly this means for his (Brodsky's) ailing and belated tradition. What Helen Gardner has written about Donne's ap-propriation of the great Jewish Platonist Leone Ebreo (the *Dialoghi d'Amore*) as primary source for the "interanimation" of lovers' souls in "The Ecstasy" applies equally forcefully to Brodsky: "One element of

[Donne's] greatness is that certain ideas mattered to him intensely and that he made them wholly his own" ("The Argument," 257).

Russian Poetry of Thought

Russian poetry has a rich philosophic or meditative tradition, but it could hardly be called, at least in the sense in which Samuel Johnson first expressed disapprobation, "metaphysical." To be sure, there was a period in the seventeenth and early eighteenth centuries (that bordered on the one hand by the "Time of Troubles" and on the other by the Petrine reforms) to which scholars have attached the appellation "imported baroque": this was a time of remarkable ferment and even chaos in the arts, one dominated by sermons, school dramas, and, significantly, the so-called *poesis curiosa*—"acrostics, anagrams, carmina figurata, palindromes, paradoxes, paronomasias, 'conceits,' etc." (Titunik, "Baroque," 41). And yet these rhetorical practices, especially the more cerebral and mannered of them,[3] never really "took" as poetic graft onto the bole of the modern lyric tradition. Precisely because they reflected an *imported* intellectual heritage with roots in Polish Jesuit curricula and champions among Ukrainian and Byelorussian clerics at the Kiev Academy, they led only a marginal existence in post-1800 Russian poetry. The works of Simeon of Polotsk, Silvestr Medvedev, Dmitry of Rostov, and Feofan Prokopovich are certainly important as intellectual and cultural history, but they had virtually no impact on the actual verse of Pushkin, Baratynsky, Tyutchev, and Fet, not to speak of their twentieth-century counterparts. And if, for the sake of argument, writers like Simeon (1629–1680) and Feofan (1681–1736) were in some ways Donne's Slavic foils (polyglots, scholars, men of the church, poets, etc.), there was no major modern poet and authority figure such as Eliot to "rediscover" them. Their often labored syntax and syllabic verse forms apparently seemed as unnatural to later generations raised on the elegant iambic tetrameter of Pushkin as the conceits of Donne ("heterogeneous ideas yoked by violence together") must have appeared to English poets trying to peer over the shoulder of Milton—or so went Eliot's logic. In this regard it could be said that the Russian baroque, which does indeed suggest certain parallels with Donne and the English metaphysicals (and hence a provocative "road not taken"), made its way to the wings but not, in the end, to the center stage of modern Russian letters.

Thus abstract thought, when rendered poetically to a Russian audience, has not as a rule had to defend its fortress against the battering ram of genuine medieval scholasticism and strict discursive logic. Various reasons might be advanced to explain this situation. Chief among them would be: the relative absence (or extreme "telescoping") of the legacy of Renaissance humanism in the formation of modern Russian culture, the native tendency to view philosophy not as a secular discipline but as an extension of Orthodox religious thought (at least until the second half of the nineteenth century), and, finally, the fact that John Donne and the tradition he represented were virtually unknown to later Russian writers and cultural figures, who, in any event, were more likely to be acquainted (when they were acquainted at all) with German or French than with English literature. Poets as different in temperament and background as Derzhavin, Zhukovsky, Pushkin, Baratynsky, Venevitinov and the Lovers of Wisdom (*liubomudry*), Tyutchev, and Khodasevich have all written what is usually termed *poetry of thought* (*poeziia mysli*)—a poetry characterized by loftiness of diction, broad speculation on the eternal verities, and, in several cases, firm grounding in German idealistic philosophy, especially Schelling's *Naturphilosophie*. Nevertheless, this poetry, however profound in its own right and crucial for the development of the tradition, is a far cry from the work of Donne, Herbert, or Marvell.

Brodsky himself seems to suggest as much in a radio interview that was taped in 1981 on the occasion of the 350th anniversary of the death of Donne but broadcast only in June 1990 (Brodsky, "S tochki zreniia iazyka," 8 June 1990). About Donne's kindred spirits among the Russians he remarks: "In general, in order to explain to a Russian what John Donne the poet means in stylistic terms I would say he is a combination of Lomonosov, Derzhavin, and, I would add, Gregory Skovoroda—the Skovoroda of the locution 'Don't climb the spheres of Copernicus, / Gaze into the caves of the spirit' (Ne lez' v Kopernikovy sfery, / Vozzri v dukhovnye peshchery) or, even better, 'into the caves of the soul' (dushevnye peshchery)—with the only difference that Donne is a greater poet than all three put together." Brodsky loves the eighteenth century, its sense of a literary language and culture in their roughness and awkward infancy.[4] His verse is full of archaic locutions that could belong to a Derzhavin or a Lomonosov. And Skovoroda's wonderfully picturesque rhyme of new scientific *sfery* with soulful *peshchery* would certainly appeal to Brodsky the paradoxicalist. And yet Brodsky is the first to recognize that, while the potential was there, the "take" did not happen. No John Donne emerged from these precursors, nor indeed apparently could one have.

Let us test out these assumptions on several examples, beginning with Gavrila Derzhavin (1743–1816), one of Brodsky's clearest antecedents among the premoderns. Derzhavin's position on the brink of the modern poetic age, with all that brinkmanship entailed, is inversely symmetrical to Brodsky's position as belated (or possibly postmodern) Acmeist at "the end of a beautiful epoch." The remarkable flux in Derzhavin's language prepared the way for Pushkin just as in Brodsky the superfluity of tone, diction, prosodic structure, intertextual allusion, national history, and personal mythology suggests a poet overladen with tradition and almost deafened by what Mandelstam called the noise of time. Derzhavin's exuberance, the overreaching splendor of his palette, is, so to speak, in anticipation of a poetic Golden Age,[5] while Brodsky's talent is retrospective and ironic, tinctured with the base metals of an Iron (as opposed to Silver or Platinum) Age, and saturated with the spirit of the funeral wreath and the *tombeau*. Having said this, we should not forget that Derzhavin's language, like Brodsky's, can be long-winded, stylistically mixed (e.g., elements of the ode and elegy coexist), and obsessed with the intersection of the carnal and the spiritual, especially death as the moment of the exodus of the spirit from the body. The older poet's flirtation with the baroque, recognized more often in conjunction with his odes, meant that on occasion he also came tantalizingly close to a Russian version of metaphysical verse.

In the poem "In Praise of the Mosquito" (Pokhvala komaru, 1807), he uses the example of an annoying insect to provide a humorous gloss on the rise and fall of the great of the world:

Глас народа мне вещал:
с дуба-де комар упал.
Се по лесу звук раздался,
Холм и дол восколебался,
Океан встал из брегов.
Не на быль ли баснь похожа,
Что упал какой вельможа
Из высоких вниз чинов?
Встав из дрязгу теплым летом,
Под блестящим солнца светом,
Счастья плыл он на крылах.
Комара, мудрец, паденьем
Возгреми нравоученьем:
Суета, скажи, все—ах!

(*Stikh*, 335)

The *vox populi* prophesied to me:
A mosquito allegedly has fallen from an oak.
Behold through the forest a sound rang out,
Hill and dale began to quake,
The ocean rose up from its shores.
Does not this fable resemble the truth
That some grandee has fallen
low from his titled heights?

Having risen from the refuse of a warm summer,
Under the brilliant light of the sun,
He sails on the wings of good fortune.
Look, sage, on the fall of the mosquito
And fulminate with moral teaching:
Proclaim that, ah, everything is vanity!

(my translation)

Here are the elements necessary for the development of an extended conceit (fall of mosquito = demise of grandee), and yet some aspect of the
Donnean formula is still missing. When Donne says—

Oh stay, three lives in one flea spare,
Where wee almost, nay more than maryed are.
This flea is you and I, and this
Our mariage bed, and mariage temple is;
Though parents grudge, and you, w'are met,
And cloysterd in these living walls of jet.

(*Poems*, 40–41)

—he consciously pushes the comparison (flea = amorous union) to the
point of absurdity, to the point where, as Helen Gardner argues, we ad-
mire the "ingenuity" more than the "justness" (*Metaphysical Poets*,
xxvi). "The very ingenuity of [the poem's] argument, ruthlessly cutting
across all facts of the matter by strict deduction of concept from concept,
cries out that the mental mechanism which composed it is easily and readily capable of manipulating mental entities in total separation from the
objects from which they were abstracted" (McCanles, "Paradox in
Donne," 231). In this flea they "more than maryed are" because their
blood is already joined, their marriage bed not an anticipation but a fait
accompli—hence why the scruples over illicit passion? Human beings, if
we allow ourselves to be drawn in by the logic, are no more or no less
than their blood. Donne, like Derzhavin, begins with a version of the
Anacreontic grasshopper, but he goes much farther, leaving behind the
original analogy for the secondary and tertiary issues of the flea's blood,
its body's identification with the marriage chamber and bed (an amazing
metaphor!), its argument for the presence of feeling in the absence of parental authority figures, and so on. Derzhavin's mosquito is charming yet
one-dimensional, and thus could not provide the inspiration (other than
its call to sing the unsingable—"Ia poiu dnes' Komara!" [*Stikh*, 334) for
Brodsky's fly or butterfly.[6]

Evgeny Baratynsky (1800–1844) is one of Brodsky's favorite poets and
one from whom he has presumably learned much. His essential pessimism and doubting cast of mind, flair for what Wallace Stevens might call

the "grand pronunciamento," themes of loss and parting, love of *inso-lubilia*, situation as exile in Finland, interest in philosophy, preference for the elegiac form, a priori conviction that only through rhyme (prosody) can *temps perdu* be redeemed or "restructured,"[7] and tendency to reflect analytically on his own most heartfelt feelings all strike responsive chords in Brodsky. Nevertheless, those poems of Baratynsky to which Brodsky is understandably drawn have something unmistakably "un-Brodskian" about them. Brodsky is not simply a modern Baratynsky; rather, he had to invent a manner which this precursor would have found profoundly alien. In the elegy "Rome" (Rim, 1821) Baratynsky expresses his pessimism about the ephemeral character of the city's glory in a series of questions:

> Ты был ли, гордый Рим, земли самовластитель,
>   Ты был ли, о свободный Рим?
>   К немым развалинам твоим
> Подходит с грустию их чуждый навеститель.
>
> За что утратил ты величье прежних дней?
> За что, державный Рим, тебя забыли боги?
>   Град пышный, где твои чертоги?
> Где сильные твои, о родина мужей?

> *(PSS,* 76)

> Was it you, o proud Rome, who overpowered the earth,
>   Was it you, o free Rome?
>   To your silent ruins
> the alien visitor approaches with sadness.
>
> Why have you lost the greatness of prior days?
> Why, mighty Rome, have the gods forgotten you?
>   Sumptuous city, where are your palaces?
> Where are your powerful ones, o homeland of men?

> (my translation)

Here, too, as in the case of Derzhavin, we find several characteristics that could be seen to relate to Brodsky's personas, including the use of an ancient source to comment allegorically on a modern one, the point of view as being that of someone alien or foreign (*chuzhdyi navestitel'* [alien visitor] and often expressed in the third person, the rhetorical questions that fill the space of the poem but imply no positive answers, and so forth. On the other hand, Baratynsky's syntax (Brodsky's signature) is elegant and simple (N.B. the absence of relative clauses and of enjambement between stanzas)[8] and his word choice uniformly "elevated," both of which mark the poem as distinctly a product of the early nineteenth century.

In "A Halt in the Desert" (Ostanovka v pustyne, 1966), the title poem of Brodsky's second collection, the speaker confronts an analogous situation: a Greek church is being dismantled in his native Leningrad and he is meditating on the significance of the occasion:

Теперь так мало греков в Ленинграде,
что мы сломали Греческую церковь,
дабы построить на свободном месте
концертный зал. В такой архитектуре
есть что-то безнадежное. А впрочем,
концертный зал на тыщу с лишним мест
не так уж безнадежен: это—храм,
и храм искусства. Кто же виноват,
что мастерство вокальное дает
сбор больший, чем знамена веры?
Жаль только, что теперь издалека
мы будем видеть не нормальный купол,
а безобразно плоскую черту.
Но что до безобразия пропорций,
то человек зависит не от них,
а чаще от пропорций безобразья.

(*OVP*, 166)

So few Greeks live in Leningrad today
that we have razed a Greek church, to make space
for a new concert hall, built in today's
grim and unhappy style. And yet a concert hall with more than fifteen hundred seats
is not so grim a thing. And who's to blame
if virtuosity has more appeal
than the worn banners of an ancient faith?
Still, it is sad that from this distance now
we see, not the familiar onion domes,
but a grotesquely flattened silhouette.
Yet men are not so heavily in debt
to the grim ugliness of balanced forms
as to the balanced forms of ugliness.

(*SP*, 131)

George Kline's accurate translation does not, and in fact cannot, give a complete rendering of the stylistic interplay subtly embedded in Brodsky's blank verse. Brodsky, who loves intricate stanzaic patterns and rhyme schemes,[9] has in this instance adopted the blank verse form and a legato syntax (sentences begin and end in mid-line) because presumably he feels that they are most appropriate for the serious, thoughtful, and, as it were, discursive aspect of the situation.[10] Yet he mixes the obsolete or poetically archaic (*daby* [in order to]) with the demonstrably colloquial (*ne tak uzh beznadezhen* [is not so hopeless]) and even substandard (*tyshchu* [normally: *tysiachu*] *s lishnim mest* [a thousand or more seats]). This combination of old and new, poetic and prosaic, would be presumably unthinkable to Baratynsky. For Brodsky, however, it is the only correct response, on the semantic level, to what is being done to his country's cultural and spiritual heritage before his very eyes—that is, the secularization and "Sovietization" not merely of an orphan parish but in a sense of Mandelstam's Christian Hellenicism (cf. "Hagia Sophia"). Brodsky's corrosive irony is of an entirely different order than Baratynsky's pessimism: the older poet would not have placed the wretched Sovietism "concert hall" in juxtaposition with "temple of art," implying that the new church is as devoid of spiritual substance as the old was impregnated with it. But most telling is the philosophical mot contained in the last three lines: man does not depend so much on the "formlessness of proportions" (*bezobrazie proportsii*) as on the "proportions of formlessness" (*proportsii bezobraziia*).[11] What precisely this means (it is formlessness that is in the genitive case and thus "enclosing" proportions?) is perhaps not so important as the need to say it. In any event, this sort of intellectual hairsplitting and arcane syllogizing in poetic form could never have been uttered by Baratynsky, and is one more indication that Brodsky was, even at this relatively early date, in search of entirely different (again, one wants to say "un-Russian") means of expression.

It would take a later poet like Khodasevich, writing in a postrevolutionary ethos that was consciously "living down" the excessive idealism, again largely German, of the Symbolists,[12] to modernize the concept of romantic irony, to mix levels of diction and problematize the rhetorical structure of the lyric. In "The Cork" (Probochka, 1921), Khodasevich's speaker draws parallels between the abstract life of the soul and the domestic existence of the body that might appear farfetched to the traditionalist:

Пробочка над крепким йодом!
Как ты скоро перетлела!
Так вот и душа незримо
Жжет и разъедает тело.

                                                              (*SS*, 87)

Cork on strong iodine!
How soon you have corroded through!
So too does the soul invisibly
burn and eat away the body.

                                                              (my translation)

To compare the body to a moldering cork and the soul, conventionally sacred and pristine, to strong iodine strikes the reader, again, as something eerily close to a modern use of the metaphysical conceit. That this quintessential romantic situation can be located in a medicine chest is a bold gambit on the poet's part and must certainly have raised critical eyebrows at the time. And elsewhere Khodasevich likens the emerging spirit (*dukh*) to a tooth cutting through swollen gums. Be this as it may, the deliberately "witty" use of prosaic imagery (tooth, swollen gums) to present the poet's view of the body-soul debate in its current hypostasis does not of itself constitute a metaphysical poem in the tradition of Donne, Herbert, and their colleagues (see Bethea, *Khodasevich*, 112–13).[13] The intellectual coordinates of Khodasevich's worldview were definitely not "scholastic" in origin, and he would have had little patience with, say, the fine points of the realist-nominalist debate (Ramism) governing Donne's use of paradox or the precise connotations of *ekstasis* (the exodus of the souls of two lovers from their bodies) as they apply to Donne's "The Ecstasy" (McCanles, "Paradox"; Hughes, "Donne's 'Ecstasies'"). Khodasevich did not as a rule erect an elaborate argument, often followed through several stanzas or even an entire poem, on the foundation of a bizarre or ironic analogy (a flea to marriage). His prosaisms, though marshaled to make an abstract or philosophical point, seemed to remain on the level of the phrase or the line. In short, Khodasevich can be considered, in Tynyanov's terminology, an "archaist"— albeit one with clear "modern" tendencies—who continued the nineteenth-century poetry of thought,[14] and not an "innovator" who tried to create a new native tradition ex nihilo or who went outside that tradition altogether.

Joseph Brodsky is, then, as will be argued below, the first and so far the only Russian poet who can be called truly "metaphysical" in the Donnean sense.[15] What this means in context is much more than mere *rediscovery and reinvention*—that is, the oedipal anxiety and Bloomian "belatedness" that trail inevitably in the wake of precursors. Brodsky is, in the first place, a *Russian* whose tradition has no metaphysical roots about which to feel, rightly or wrongly, nostalgic. In this regard, he cannot be compared, at least by simple analogy, to a later English poet, say Eliot, who is trying to heal what he perceives to be *his* tradition's "dissociation of sensibility" by exhuming a prior master putatively capable of "direct sensuous apprehension of thought" and of experiencing ideas "as immediately as the odour of a rose." Brodsky may indeed be nostalgic for prior ages and traditions, but in many instances these are not "his" to begin with (i.e., he need not be concerned with "repeating himself"), and hence the entire vexed issue of poetic genealogy and continuity has to be rethought. This may explain some of the resistance to Brodsky's poetry as excessively cerebral, self-reflexive, overwrought, "un-Russian." These, after all, are the very reasons why Donne himself, under the cloud of Dr. Johnson's stricture, was neglected in his own tradition for centuries until his revival by Grierson and Eliot as a proto-modern. Brodsky has many connections with Donne and his epoch; some of these are consciously cultivated, others are simply "typological," part of larger *Gestalt* patterns that are intriguing and meaningful in their own right. Let us now take a closer look at what these connections entail.

The Donne-Brodsky Dialogue

Brodsky discovered Donne in 1963, the same year in which he first studied the Bible and began to read Dante in Lozinsky's translation.[16] He came upon the poetry of Donne in an anthology of English poetry[17] given him by one of the various Americans who visited Leningrad in those years. In fact, during this period of initial acquaintance, Brodsky, in his own words, "knew extremely little—practically nothing—about Donne . . . some excerpts from the sermons and some verse" (Brodsky, "S tochki zreniia iazyka"). He still had a quite rudimentary command of English, and his method of "translating" Donne was to decode, with the help of a dictionary, the first and last stanzas of a poem and then to reconstruct, through imaginative guesswork, what came in-between.[18] It is fair to assume, therefore, that the young poet, at least at the time he wrote the "Large Elegy," could not have known Donne, or Donne's English, very well. What formally attracted Brodsky to Donne were the "sweep and radius" of the metaphysical poet's vision and his rich stanzaic patterns, which he "wanted to beat" (interview with author, 28–29 March 1991, South Hadley, Mass.). The point here is that Brodsky immediately recognized in Donne a voice that, in the Russian context, was new and arresting, and one that opened up alternative avenues of expression. Not perhaps fortuitously, the same could largely be said for Brodsky's early and abiding interest in the Polish "metaphysicals" Zbigniew Herbert and Milosz.[19] The fact that at roughly the same time Brodsky began reading the Bible (the chief early fruit of which was the long poem "Isaac and Abraham"), Kierkegaard (through the prism of the Russian philosopher Lev Shestov), and Dante indicates that his reading was more or less of a piece—the operative categories being "philosophical" or "speculatively religious," and "non-Soviet."

Brodsky was trying to recapture or, in the case of Donne, take for the first time that intellectual ground which had been effectively lost to the intelligentsia reading public as a result of the policies of Stalinism, especially the literary method known as socialist realism. This ground included in its rich topsoil the entire biblical tradition, with its issues of divine judgment and theodicy, the economy of salvation, the meaning and shape of history, death and resurrection, the relation of soul to body—indeed, an entire religious and philosophical lexicon that had to be exhumed and experimented with *as if for the first time*. We recall that for Brodsky and his Leningrad colleagues[20] the chief living expression of this lost language was the aging Anna Akhmatova, the last great representative of a bygone epoch, the so-called Silver Age of prerevolutionary culture, that still inherited this Judaeo-Christian culture as its rightful patrimony.[21] Brodsky first met Akhmatova in 1961[22] and visited her often before his trial and exile in 1964.[23] By the time of her death in 1966, Akhmatova was considered by many to be the greatest Russian *Christian* poet of the century. She was, in other words, the very embodiment of that historical continuity (*preemstvennost'*) that Brodsky and his orphaned "generation of 1956" so lacked. That Akhmatova served as a godmother figure to these young poets (most of whom were Jews) and that she joined Nadezhda Mandelstam in singling out Brodsky as the most gifted[24] could only be seen as "prefigured" to the author of "Large Elegy." Akhmatova exclaimed upon hearing Brodsky recite the Donne poem that "I fear, Joseph, that you do not understand what you have written" (cited in Polukhina, *Brodsky*, 9).[25]

It is into this vast semantic field and veritable lost Atlantis, which might be termed alternatively *biblical* or *philosophical* (but not yet *metaphysical*), that the Donne discovery falls. Here, for example, is how Brodsky describes his original study of the Bible in a recent interview: "I read the Bible for the first time when I was twenty-three. It leaves me somewhat shepherdless, you see. I wouldn't really know *what to return to*. I don't have any notion of paradise. . . . I went through the severe antireligious schooling in Russia which doesn't leave any kind of notion about afterlife" (Birkerts, "The Art of Poetry," 111; my emphasis). But in fact Brodsky *was* returning—if not personally, then collectively, "mythopoetically"—to a tradition and thematics (otherworldliness) deemed "out of bounds" to his generation, and this realization was (and is) enormously significant for the question of his place in contemporary Russian letters. In effect, Brodsky was "leap-frogging" back over an intermediate generation, the poets of socialist realism/official atheism, to an earlier one (Pasternak, Tsvetaeva, Mandelstam, Akhmatova) that came by this tradition naturally, as part of its cultural baggage.[26] And in the process he was, in his own words, achieving what no one else of his generation had been able to do: the reintroduction of the word *soul* (*dusha*) into Russian poetry as a serious, rather than mock, element of discourse (see Ann Lauterbach, "Genius in Exile," 343).

The semantics of the soul/psyche, often with classical or "muse"-ical linkages, has a well-worn path in Russian verse: precursors with whom Brodsky may have been familiar by 1963 include Baratynsky, Mandelstam, and Khodasevich. The importance of the Donne connection emerges when we place the body/soul dialectic within a specifically Christian scholastic framework. And here there can be no question that Brodsky had fixed on something wholly other to add to what, thematically, was already, according to socialist realist canons, illicit. First, on a purely biographical plane, both poets were in literal and figurative senses *exiles* in their respective cultures. Donne was born a Catholic who from childhood witnessed at close quarters the political dangers (including exile, imprisonment, and death) of living in a Protestant land; as his biographer comments, "he sympathized deeply with their [English Catholics'] dilemma, for it had been his own" (Bald, *A Life*, 66).[27] His thorough study of Church tradition was an attempt to come to terms independently with what each side believed and to ascertain where truth, if it existed at all, lay. To cite Bald, Donne

> had to come to terms both with the world in which he lived and with the conflict of religious faiths into which, by virtue of his family inheritance, he was inevitably plunged. As a Catholic the gates to preferment and success were barred to him; as he knew only too well, his religion offered him nothing in this world but exile or the patient endurance of persecution. Active participation in the life of his age could be purchased at the cost of disloyalty to all that he had been taught to revere. Besides, his restless intellectual curiosity refused to allow him to accept any creed unquestioned [cf. Brodsky's much-discussed "skepticism"], and it eventually drove him to systematic examination of the issues at stake between the conflicting faiths.[28] (*A Life*, 63)

And later on, when he eloped with Ann More against the wishes of her father and thereby lost (again!) all chance of making a career and gaining preferment, Donne was forced into something like "internal exile" at Pyrford,[29] in the home of his friend Sir Francis Wooley. It might even be argued, although for our purposes the trail is perhaps clearer in Brodsky's case, that the young Donne was possessed of a cast of mind inherently *self-estranging*, setting itself against anything corporate or collective that threatened to engulf it in another's embrace, be it church, society, or family. His counsel to a friend—be "thine owne home, and in thy selfe dwell"—has the ring of personal conviction. Indeed, Donne's breaking of the social code (marrying in secret a girl of wealthy family who was still a minor) was no less shocking or, considering the circumstances, ruinous than Brodsky's so-called criminal activity as "parasite."

Like Mandelstam and Pasternak before him, Brodsky was born a Jew into a majority Russian culture that was "Christian" in heritage (with its secular variants).[30] His first recollection of lying, that is, of socially estranging himself, is associated with his Jewishness and with being forced by an officious librarian to fabricate a story in order to avoid ascribing the word *evrei* (Jew), which sounded ugly and foreign, to himself (*Less*, 7–8; see chapter 1). On the other hand, Brodsky appears remarkably uninterested in ethnicity as such, since he has no desire to "belong" to any group that would somehow define or place strictures on his own identity. He is, in short, quite willing to suffer the slings and arrows of ostracism but not use that ostracism as a bond for further "election."[31] Moreover, as we know, Brodsky has experienced firsthand the condition of exile both in the Soviet Union and abroad.[32] In fact, according to earliest records as well as his own statements in essays and interviews Brodsky has always been a loner, has as it were more than met his marginal status halfway.[33] To quote a rather un-Donnean poem written two years before "Large Elegy":

Как хорошо, что некого винить,
как хорошо, что ты никем не связан,
как хорошо, что до смерти любить
тебя никто на свете не обязан.[34]

(*OVP*, 27)

How pleasant that there is no one to blame,
how pleasant that you are tied to no one,
how pleasant that to the grave
no one in this world is obliged to love you.

(my translation)

Russians have a special word, *izgoi*, to describe the socially "odd man out," and Brodsky's sarcasm (e.g., the anaphoric "how pleasant") suggests an almost Dostoevskian embracing of his own pain and torment. Yet the immaturity of this poem and the feelings expressed in it should not blind us to the fact that, even here, Brodsky, like Donne, understands implicitly the bloody rules of martyrdom. Donne could write about pseudo-martyrs because he knew presumably, in his context, how a true martyr should act and how, doctrinally, a subject can be loyal to his king, his church, and his God.[35] In a country where poets are routinely made into martyrs and where sacred values are invested in poetry rather than in officially sanctioned atheism, Brodsky can also write his version of the *via dolorosa*,[36] with its exacting loyalty to a higher intelligence that promises no rewards in this world. Thus, while in regard to the biographical nexus there can be, as far as we know, little possibility of a conscious inheritance or modeling, the sense remains that both poets saw themselves as outsiders and in the fullness of time transposed that perception to the world of their poetry and to the theme of *psychic exile*.[37]

Second, both Donne and Brodsky are voracious cultural consumers who from an early age read widely (Donne more systematically, Brodsky less so) in an attempt to absorb and make their own the chief monuments of Western civilization. Yet this learning, never static or decorative, is made to enter into noisy dialogue with prior traditions. It is inconceivable to imagine a mature work by Donne or Brodsky resulting in unconscious imitation or "monologic" stylization. When Thomas Carew wrote in his famous elegy (1633) to Donne that—

> The Muses garden with Pedantique weedes
> O'rspred, was purged by thee; The lazie seeds
> Of servile imitation throwne away;
> And fresh invention planted, Thou didst pay
> The debts of our penurious bankrupt age.
>
> (Gardner, *Metaphysical Poets*, 116)

—he was in a way forestalling Eliot and laying the groundwork for subsequent reappraisal of Donne as proto-modern. Donne, with all the cultural coding that went with being an Inns-of-Court man, was seemingly incapable of reproducing the mellifluous, highly conventionalized Petrarchan manner of the Spenserian sonnet/love lyric without a sobering or drolly ironic admixture of crude Ovidian amatory realism—an admixture that, as one scholar has argued, was implicated in the amateur poet's questionable social status and vulnerability before those with access to the court (Marotti, *Coterie Poet*, 44–66). Similarly, Brodsky's love poems, some of the most distinctive in Russian verse of this century, are demonstrably "antilyrical" in their diction, self-deflating in their use of rhetorical strategies, and quite often heavily freighted in alternative traditions and intertexts, one of the most salient being that of Donne himself. Hence, even amid moments of "plainspeaking" and intentional coarseness, there is a "scholarly" or academic quality to each poet's verse that sets it apart from that of his immediate contemporaries.[38] Donne's metaphysical speculations were cut straight out of the fabric of learned debates at the time—the common fund of Plato, Aristotle, Proclus, Plotinus, Averroes, St. Thomas Aquinas, Agricola, Ramus, Ockham, Leone Ebreo, and others. But precisely because Brodsky had to reweave this fabric, or something akin to it, from the threads of alien traditions, his major work is a kind of speculation about that which has been conspicuously left *unsaid*, *forgotten*, or worse, simply *unknown* by decades of Soviet rule. Donne was no less alien, and presumably more so, to the young Leningrad cultural community of the fifties and sixties than, say, Ramus or Ockham were to the university-educated population of Donne's London. Of course, it goes without saying that the cultural heritage was more intact in Donne's time (though already showing cracks in its foundation) than in Brodsky's. To put it most broadly, Donne was trying to reconcile the late medieval church tradition with the discoveries rapidly accruing to the new science; Brodsky, living in a no less tumultuous epoch,[39] was likewise trying to wrest a free and genuine speculative inquiry from the grasp of "scientific Marxism" (or secular dogma). Of the paradigmatic affinities between Donne's time and his, Brodsky was, to judge by his own subsequent account, aware.[40]

Third, both Donne and Brodsky initially made their reputations as poets among coteries and small groups of cognoscenti.[41] Their work was rarely published—Donne's because he wanted to cultivate the role of amateur, Brodsky's because his verse was "out of tune" with official literary policy—and circulated from hand to hand in manuscript or "samizdat" form.[42] In a sense their ideal readers were members of their own coteries, ones privy to the "inside" information necessary to decode the elaborate arguments, dense rhetorical structures, and oblique allusions to realia crowding their poems.[43] Here Marotti's characterization of Donne's verse applies, with few reservations, to Brodsky's: "[Donne's] creation of a sense of familiarity and intimacy, his fondness for dialectic, intellectual complexity, paradox and irony, the appeals to shared attitudes and group interests (if not to private knowledge),[44] the explicit gestures of biographical self-referentiality, the styles he adopted or invented all relate to the coterie circumstances of his verse" (Marotti, *Coterie Poet*, 19). This insider ambience partially explains the "hermetic" quality, the *difficilia quae pulchra*, of each poet's verse. It also means that much of their work is unabashedly *occasional*, tethered to a specific time, place, relationship, or event that needs to be contextualized before it can be meaningful. Lady Bedford, Donne's patroness, and "MB," the "dark woman of [Brodsky's] sonnets,"[45] fulfill equivalent roles as the concrete point of departure for metaphysical flights. Both Donne and Brodsky, mutatis mutandis, could take some pride in their amateur or unofficial status because the "professional"[46] in their respective cultures was often compromised, socially or ethically tainted. In this regard it is revealing that Brodsky became a major literary figure in the Soviet Union without publishing a substantial amount (in fact, very little) of his own original verse.[47] His nearly legendary status,[48] augmented by the aureole of martyrdom,[49] is largely a product of that unofficial literary subculture that, with its implicit rules and codes, finds an analogue in the conventions of the Inns-of-Court, where the potential difference between "Jack Donne" and "D. Donne" was understood long before ordination at St. Paul's.

Fourth, Donne and Brodsky are famous travelers; indeed, in Brodsky's case, no Russian poet has traveled more, and lived to tell about it, than he. The occasional character of much of their work is associated with actual journeys from home. Donne and Brodsky are master exegetes of the process of leave-taking (in Russian *rasstavanie, razluka*), with all that implies, including the ultimate separation/border-crossing of death.[50]

Their journeys tend to involve profound musings not only on movement in space but *in time*. The road or path, as well as its shape, topography, and salient landmarks, are physical and metaphysical, literal and figurative. For example, Donne pays the ultimate compliment to his friend Sir Henry Goodyer when he claims in a verse epistle that "Riding I had you, though you still staid there [i.e., at home], / And in these thoughts, although you never stirre, / You came with mee to Micham [i.e., Donne's home], and are here" (*Poems*, 184). And when he travels westward on Good Friday he contemplates what that "natural" movement means both macrocosmically and microcosmically, for the heavenly spheres above and the soul of man below ("let man's soul be a sphere"), since each turns to follow God, the primum mobile (Chambers, "Goodfriday").

Brodsky, too, is constantly involved in the poetic telescoping of physical and metaphysical. He enters into the spirit of a place, whether that place be New York, Venice, Istanbul, Vilnius, Berlin, Yalta, San Francisco, or Kellomäki. Oftentimes he carries on a friendly causerie with an epigraphic native son, say, the Auden of "York" or the Tomas Venclova of "Lithuanian Divertissement." In a visit to Cape Cod, he facetiously describes a fish that rises to a standing position and disappears, amphibianlike,[51] into the bushes on the shore ("Lullaby of Cape Cod"). Not only is his lullaby a birthday gift on the occasion of the country's bicentennial, it is an intricate homage to Robert Lowell (see Montenegro, "An Interview," 533 and chapter 2). Through this seriocomic metaphor of the peripatetic cod Brodsky is telling us how the gift of speech (English) has given him legs and caused him to experience the boundary where land and ocean meet as a temporal *limen*, a cradle (*kolybel'*), since he, like the fish, will eventually pass out of his native element (Russia, Russian language, "Russianness") to move erect into the broad continent of American letters. The poet's tourist trip suddenly explodes into multiple and as it were self-generating (like the primal life in the water) insights about historical necessity and existential freedom, the vastness of empire and the small miracle of poetic speech.[52]

Fifth, regardless of alleged biographical or Gestalt/typological affinities between a seventeenth-century English poet and a twentieth-century Russian one,[53] it is the evidence of Donne's and Brodsky's individual poetic manners that demonstrates most compellingly their kinship. In fact, while Brodsky has in his more than thirty years as a poet "domesticated" many Western sources, including a number of English-language authors (Auden above all), the lessons he learned from Donne were, we can now say, crucial for his subsequent development.[54] All the salient qualities of metaphysical verse distilled by Helen Gardner apply to the kind of poems Brodsky wrote after his initial discovery of Donne: "strong-lined," close-packed, concise or "epigrammatic" (cf. a mutual interest in Martial),[55] elliptical (as category of syntax), deliberately "rough" (as category of versification), curiously wrought, gravitating toward lines of varying length "into which sense [is] packed" and stanzas that are "created for a particular poem" (Gardner, *Metaphysical Poets*, xix–xxxiv). Likewise, Marotti's description of the sparks (the original root of *concetto*) that fly from Donne's studied frustration of logic through logic is instructive to any reader of Brodsky: "Donne used many means to produce such creative discordance in his works, including the deliberate clashing of vehicle and tenor, the noncongruence of statement and tone, the witty misalliance of dramatic situation and actual speech performance, the opposition of rhetorical manner and stylistic decorum" (*Coterie Poet*, 22–23). Brodsky builds entire poems on the basis of such "creative discordance": in "Plato Elaborated" (Razvivaia Platona), for example, each succeeding utterance, undercut by corrosive irony, is meant to be inverted or read "inside out" because what is being described is not an ideal republic but its photographic negative, whose purest form in this world is the very Leningrad that persecuted and spurned the poet (*U*, 8–10).

The heart of the Donne-Brodsky kinship lies at the "macro" level of artistic conception, with how they *prefigure* the material given them by their respective historical moments. Each poet expands, distorts, and refashions the formal expectations of his medium in an attempt to produce "modern versions of classical genres" (Marotti, *Coterie Poet*, 44). In his longer poems especially Brodsky seems to have created a unique (for the Russian context) contemporary hybrid of the Horatian ode, with its philosophic orientation, on the one hand, and the Pindaric ode, usually motivated by a specific occasion, on the other. The elaborate strophic structures and ingenious rhyme schemes in these works suggest additional ties to Pindaric form, which Brodsky could have absorbed either on his own or through the mediation of one of his favorite poets—Mandelstam.[56] Similar arguments could be made about Donne's "conscious attempt to take the [elegiac] form out of its academic humanist setting and put it into his contemporary social world" (Marotti, *Coterie Poet*, 45) and Brodsky's curiously self-regarding elision of the categories of "exile" and "elegy" in his poems on the deaths of others, including Donne and Eliot (see chapter 4). And with their powerful wit and scepticism it is not surprising that Donne and Brodsky, when confronted by the protocol and demands of society and its institutions (whether of the "court" or the "empire"), are capable of inspired satire: witness, for example, the third and fourth satires of Donne or "Anno Domini" of Brodsky.

But perhaps most of all what has made Donne such a rich mine of possibility for Brodsky are three qualities that are distinctive precisely because they appear so intrinsically *un-Russian*: (1) the presence of an essentially *dramatic* (as opposed to lyric) imagination in poetic form,[57] (2) a passion for *paradox* in its most extended and "scholastic" variants (the traditional *insolubilia* of medieval logic), and (3) a tendency to deploy the *metaphysical conceit*—that "hammering out" or "difficult joining" whereby an often bizarre analogy is made the axis of an extended poetic argument or even an entire poem (see Gardner, *Metaphysical Poets*, xxiv). These qualities are manifestly interconnected, and we will have more to comment about them in the final two sections of this chapter. But for now suffice it to say that thanks to the first, Brodsky's work possesses remarkable rhetorical complexity and dialogic interplay; thanks to the second, his exuberant, often "self-canceling" word- and rootplay (paronomasia) and his syntax, some of the most daunting in all Russian verse, carry the reader[58] through Escherlike thickets of illusory attribution in order to advance arguments that, in the end, may appear to common sense or habitual cognition counterintuitive; and thanks to the third, Brodsky has succeeded in finding not only occasional leitmotifs but extended metaphors or visual clusters (fly, butterfly, fish, etc.) on which to base the abstract metaphysics of his major works and books.[59] Like Donne, and presumably through Donne, Brodsky has shown a predilection for expressing the large and the abstract (beauty, mortality) through the small (butterfly). In his "Six Years Later" (Sem' let spustia),[60] as in "The Good-Morrow," love "makes one little room, an every where." Finally and most important, Brodsky's marked use of geometric figures (the triangle) to make the point *visually* of his tragic separation and permanent state of exile, a practice unprecedented in the modern Russian poetic tradition, harks back to the line, circle, and spiral of Donne's twin compasses, with their message of Christian unity and promise of happy endings (see the last section of this chapter ["Brodsky's Use of the Metaphysical Conceit"]).[61] Not perhaps for nothing was the young Brodsky often playfully chided by his Leningrad circle for "overconceptualizing," for making "comparison[s]," as Gardner says of Donne's "conceited" verse, "whose ingenuity [is] more striking than [their] justness" (Gardner, *Metaphysical Poets*, xxiii). Here, however, the profound *differences* between Donne and Brodsky, to be discussed at greater length below, are what are really significant.

"Large Elegy to John Donne"

By now it should be apparent that Joseph Brodsky possesses a pure speculative mind rare in Russian poetry. Like Sir Thomas Browne, the medical doctor-cum-mystic whose work is everywhere marked by oxymoron, paradox, and "double vision," Brodsky might remark that "I love to lose my selfe in a mystery to pursue my reason to an *Oh Altitudo*" (Browne, *Religio Medici*, 334, 338). In this same *Religio Medici*, written in 1634–35 just a few years after Donne's death, Browne goes on in a discursive and, one wants to say, typically "Brodskian" vein:

> 'Tis my solitary recreation to pose my apprehension with those involved aenigma's and riddles of the Trinity, with Incarnation and Resurrection. I can answer all the objections of Satan, and my rebellious reason, with that odde resolution I learned of *Tertullian, Certum est quia impossibile est*. I desire to exercise my faith in the difficultest point, for to credit ordinary and visible objects is not faith, but perswasion . . . where I cannot satisfy my reason, I love to humour my fancy. (*Religio Medici*, 339)

Brodsky, too, loves to pose involved enigmas and riddles to his "apprehension," to exercise his faith in the "difficultest" point, to find out what it means that *Certum est quia impossibile est*.

This, however, is true a fortiori when the subject is the death of a Christian sceptic and fellow poet, for here the body-soul debate emerges in its most dramatic terms. Donne, we recall, who had "contemplated death for many years" (Bald, *A Life*, 528), spent his final days with a drawing of his own enshrouded body, head turned eastward toward Him "Cujus nomen est Oriens." In the seventeenth century it was not uncustomary for a man to pose for his own funeral portrait, to compose his own epitaph, in short, to make a fitting end. It was not the intention, as Bald tells us, "to turn away [one's] face from the facts of death" or "to remove from everyday life all constant reminders of its omnipresence" (Bald, *A Life*, 527). To those who witnessed Donne's final appearance in the pulpit at Whitehall (25 February 1631), it was as though he "had preach't his own Funeral Sermon" (cited in Bald, *A Life*, 526). And here Donne's concern to embrace his own mortality is deeply shared by Brodsky, who is more obsessed with death, his as well as others', than perhaps any other Russian poet with the possible exception of Innokenty Annensky.[62] It should follow, therefore, that the elegy is that form which by definition unleashes in Brodsky the broadest and most "paradoxical" speculation.[63] It is, in his hands, a kind of Jewish prayer for the dead, which, as chance would have it, Donne himself once witnessed, probably in a synagogue in Holland with the Drurys in 1612. Brodsky becomes, as it were, the modern "sonne or some other neere in blood or alliance, [who] comes to the Altar, and there saith and doth some thing in the behalfe of his dead father, or grandfather respectively" (Donne, *Sermons*, 2:169). The absolute nature of death, its total silence and liminal status, makes it an ideal occasion for the presence of poetic speech. For Brodsky, the elegiac genre is a gesture of sublime ventriloquy, since the poet, projecting his words onto the one *who cannot answer back*, must constantly *raise his voice* (if not emotionally, then speculatively) in order to be heard in the deafening quiet.

"Large Elegy" is the second poem in *A Halt in the Desert*. It follows "Christmas Romance" (Rozhdestvenskii romans, 1962), which serves as frontispiece to the collection and underscores, not without irony, the theme of new beginnings.[64] Thus, "Large Elegy" is featured prominently in the first book of verse Brodsky himself had a hand in composing and is, in effect, an announcement of a new voice.[65] To put it simply, Brodsky's emergence as a major poet, his *birth* as it were into the Russian tradition, is directly related to his writing of a poem that celebrates the *death*, or ending, of a great foreign precursor. The poetic *tombeau*, as Lawrence Lipking argues, is both a homage (at times polemical) to literary parents, or perhaps in this instance granduncles, and a declaration of how the speaker intends to carry on in a manner sufficiently distinct from the revered object of the funeral oration (*The Life*, viii–xiii, 138–79). Brodsky's elegy is large, therefore, not only in its thematic scope and compass, which were utterly amazing for 1963, but also in its radical reposing of the issue of what constitutes "greatness" for Russian poetry in the second half of the twentieth century. It is, one could say, seen from the vantage of the Soviet reader of the time, both a major work on a foreign poet and a "foreign" (because unprecedented) work on a major poet. Here, in short, are all the elements—formal, biographical, and historico-literary—for a new legend-in-the-making.

The "Large Elegy" opens with a remarkable verbal rendering of the state of somnolence:

Джон Донн уснул, уснуло все вокруг.
Уснули стены, пол, постель, картины,
уснули стол, ковры, засовы, крюк,
весь гардероб, буфет, свеча, гардины.
Уснуло все. Бутыль, стакан, тазы,
хлеб, хлебный нож, фарфор, хрусталь, посуда,
ночник, белье, шкафы, стекло, часы,
ступеньки лестниц, двери. Ночь повсюду.
Повсюду ночь: в углах, в глазах, в белье,
среди бумаг, в столе, в готовой речи,
в ее словах, в дровах, в щипцах, в угле
остывшего камина, в каждой вещи.

(OVP, 21)

John Donne has sunk in sleep . . . All things beside
are sleeping too; walls, bed, and floor—all sleep.
The table, pictures, carpets, hooks and bolts,
clothes-closet, cupboards, candles, curtains—all

now sleep: the washbowl, bottle, tumbler, bread,
breadknife and china, crystal, pots and pans,
bed-sheets and nightlamp, chest of drawers, a clock,
a mirror, stairway, doors. Night everywhere,
night in all things: in corners, in men's eyes,
in bed-sheets, in the papers on a desk,
in the worm-eaten words of sterile speech,
in logs and fire-tongs, in the blackened coals
of a dead fireplace—in each thing.

(SP, 39)

Death, or in this instance sleep, its simulacrum, requires a special type of controlled overstatement: intellectual, as opposed to lyrical, hyperbole. This is a kind of riddle: how would we imagine a world from which the soul of a great poet has departed? One of Brodsky's favorite techniques, especially with regard to elegy, is to begin a poem on an extraordinarily high note, and then, from, as it were, that end of the tonal scale, to attempt to do the aurally impossible (Certum est quia impossibile est!)—to take the note still higher.

Brodsky seems to have learned this device from, among others, Tsvetaeva:

"Novogodnee" [New Year's Greeting: Tsvetaeva's poem on the death of Rilke] begins in typical Tsvetaeva fashion, at the far right—i.e., highest—end of the octave, on high C . . . with an exclamation directed upward, outward. Throughout the entire poem this tonality, just like the very tenor of this speech, is unvarying: the only possible modification is not a lowering of the register (even in parentheses) but a raising of it. ("Footnote to a Poem," Less, 205)

Like Tsvetaeva, Brodsky possesses the unique ability to direct an idea (death as sleep) "upward" and "outward" in seemingly endless permutations and embellishments. Here, however, the emotion is not maximally high-pitched, but low-pitched (a kind of poetic organ bass), as though the poet were beginning from the other end of the octave. We have gravitated as far as possible away from pure "feeling" in the direction of pure "mind." All bel canto quality—that "lyricism" that modulates its song as it regards itself—is drained out of this opening as the reader is bombarded by the sheer ontological "thingness" of the world.

Of the seventy-one words in these first twelve lines, an incredible forty-two are common nouns (the only proper name being the first two words—"John Donne"). The extended list of things that have, like the great poet, fallen asleep may be Donnean in origin (cf. his Satires). The only verb, other than the implied verb to be, is usnut' (to fall asleep), which, because it is in the perfective aspect, suggests that the result of this activity, the sleep itself, reigns supreme and dominates the present. The verb *to be*—"Night is everywhere. / Everywhere is night"—merely describes the state which has been produced by *usnut'*. The total absence of any other verbs means that there is and can for the moment be no other activity. The world of sleep/death is then a profoundly *nominal* world.[66] The soul, the motive force that provides the verbal adhesive, the logos, to join the things in meaningful human activity, has been effectively removed from this scene. Moreover, there are, in all, only five adjectives or possessive pronouns; each reinforces the "still life" quality of the picture: "all" (*ves'*) the wardrobe (i.e., no part of it is awake), the "bread" (*khlebnyi*) knife (which gives the instrument a "Flemish" quality to go along with the "china, crystal, and dishes"), the "prepared" or "ready-made" (*gotovaia*) speech with "its" (*ee*) words (i.e., the one and the other are already fixed and not free to change in the present), and the "now cool" (*ostyvshii*) hearth (a participle formed from the perfective verb suggesting that the loss of heat is complete). In sum, Brodsky begins his tour de force by showing how, grammatically and syntactically, sleep might be thematized.

But this of course is only the beginning of the poet's conception of Donne's death. Donne is the poet *non plus ultra* of the domestic and the homely. Especially in the aftermath of his disastrous elopement, he loved to set microcosm off against macrocosm, to compare his "little roome" of marital love to an "every where" of other, more practical activities. Hence these details have another function—they are, as Brodsky sees them, the things that comprised the poet's universe. Do these lists, we might ask, add up to anything, or are they simply a random inventory with no higher plot or structure? Does Brodsky use them somehow to "read" Donne? First of all, they all belong *indoors*: we are beginning with the private surroundings that the poet saw and experienced as *his* every day of his life. They are simple and concrete, and yet "generic": that is, none of the domestic objects (bed table, curtains, rugs, clock, etc.) betrays a specifically seventeenth-century English origin. Where these items are used for something, it is for eating (bread, bread knife, dishes), sleeping (bed), keeping warm (hearth, firewood), or self-protection (bolts). In other words, the activities Brodsky ascribes to his hero, at least to judge by these first details, is decidedly quotidian—"prosaic" rather than "poetic." If we were to reconstruct the man from these items, he might be a shopkeeper or a simple parson, not a distinguished church dignitary who, had he survived, would almost certainly have been in line for a bishopric and at the time of his death left a not inconsequential estate valued at between three thousand and four thousand pounds.

And yet, formally, this is still poetry. If we are beginning at one end of the tonal scale, it is still, as Akhmatova immediately recognized, a poetic scale. We know this for several reasons. First, because of the meter: the traditional iambic pentameter, with alternating masculine and feminine rhyme, gives the lines a solemnity and grandeur that accord implicitly with their elegiac message. Moreover, the presence of verse paragraphs, rather than an elaborate stanzaic structure,[67] suggests that Brodsky intends this poem to develop narratively (it is telling the *story* of Donne's death), through dense contiguous images and slow, incremental shifts in voice and perception. Second, and somewhat paradoxically, the descriptive quality of the opening does not imply that there is no word-play, no *poetic* function that can be identified as distinct from the meter and rhyme. The only trope that Brodsky does resort to here, and one that is therefore all the more conspicuous, is a modern version of what a rhetorician like Quintilian might call *chiasmus* or *inversio*: the repeated transposition of phrasal word order for effect. When the speaker says—"Dzhon Donn usnul, usnulo vse vokrug" (lit., John Donne has fallen asleep, asleep has fallen everything around); or "Noch' povsiudu. Povsiudu noch'" (lit., Night is everywhere. Everywhere is night); or "Vse usnulo. Usnulo vse" (lit., Everything has fallen asleep. Asleep has fallen everything)[68]—he is attempting to express poetically that ground swell of centrifugal force that begins with the eternal sleep of the subject.[69] Each transposition closes one circle of description and opens, wavelike, onto another, broader than the first.[70] In this way we pass from the interior to the house itself, to the neighborhood, to the city of London, to the natural world beyond the city, to the larger isle of England, to the upper and lower realms of heaven and hell, and finally to God himself. These syntactic inversions are themselves miniature steps on a ladder and Brodsky's ingenious way of presenting the vertical cosmology inherent in the late Renaissance worldview.[71]

While Brodsky's poem is rich with allusions to Donne texts, it is perhaps the *Devotions upon Emergent Occasions* (1624) that provides the most illuminating gloss on the later work.[72] We can assume that Brodsky was familiar with these exercises on the churchman's expected death and funeral—Donne fell seriously ill in 1623 and was "daily remembered of [his] burial in the funerals of others" (*Devotions*, 102)—because he makes clear reference to the famous island and to the tolling church bells in his Russian elegy.[73] The extended metaphor on which the sixteenth, seventeenth, and eighteenth meditations is based is that of death as a leave-taking from the house of life.[74] Donne's text bears quoting at length:

Here the bells can scarce solemnize the funeral of any person, but that I knew him, or knew that he was my neighbour: we dwelt in houses near to one another before, but now he is gone into that house, into which I must follow him. . . . His soul is gone out . . . he now is entered into the possession of his better estate. His soul is gone, whither? Who saw it come in, or who saw it go

out? Nobody; yet everybody is sure he had one, and hath none. . . . It is the
going out, more than the coming in, that concerns us. This soul, this Bell tells
me, is gone out, whither? . . . That body, which scarce three minutes since was
such a house, as that that soul, which made one step from thence to heaven,
was scarce thoroughly content to leave that for heaven; that body hath lost the
name of a dwelling-house, because none dwells in it, and is making haste to lose
the name of a body, and dissolve to putrefaction. (*Devotions*, 102, 114–16)[75]

Language for the author of these lines is a sharp instrument, both self-
revealing and self-concealing, much like the pocketknife, which was invented during Donne's lifetime. Each *sententia* folds, as it were, into the
handle of the preceding one, yet what is carved on the page is an intricate,
continuously evolving rhetorical design. What has happened to a neighbor could just as soon happen to me (a variation on "love thy neighbor as
thyself"); where is our real estate?—to use a play on words that Nabokov, in this century, would dwell on; a house without an occupant is as
a body without a soul; it is the leave-taking rather than the house-warming that rightly dominates our attention in this life; nobody can witness
this "going out" because no body is a soul, and so forth—these are the
building blocks of Donne's conceit, and his wit shows through even in his
most solemn and inward moments. Unquestionably, such formulations
would have appealed to the young Brodsky because: (1) their subject is
the soul's exodus or exile, (2) their treatment is personal and domestic
(rather than public or community-oriented), and (3) their exposition is a
kind of scholastic riddle or argument (where has the soul gone?), drawn
out through internal punning (no body = nobody, etc.) and verbal maneu-
vering to rather extravagant lengths. Brodsky's elegy is, among other
things, a modern Russian attempt to answer Donne's riddle.

Before proceeding on, however, we need to retrace our steps for a moment. In 1962, perhaps just months before composing "Large Elegy,"[76]
Brodsky wrote a short lyric that resonates intriguingly with this theme of
death as domestic leave-taking. In fact, considering the affinities between
the two poems, one is tempted to see "The tenant finds his new house"
(Vse chuzhdo v dome) as a kind of sketch or rehearsal for the larger piece:

Все чуждо в доме новому жильцу.
Поспешный взгляд скользит по всем предметам,
чьи тени так пришельцу не к лицу,
что сами слишком мучаются этим.
Но дом не хочет больше пустовать.
И, как бы за нехваткой той отваги,
замок, не в состояньи узнавать,
один сопротивляется во мраке.
Да, сходства нет меж нынешним и тем,

кто внес сюда шкафы и стол и думал,
что больше не покинет этих стен,
но должен был уйти; ушел и умер.
Ничем уж их нельзя соединить:
чертой лица, характером, надломом.
Но между ними существует нить,
обычно именуемая домом.

(OVP, 36)

The tenant finds his new house wholly strange.
His quick glance trips on unfamiliar objects
whose shadows fit him so imperfectly
that they themselves are quite distressed about it.
But this house cannot stand its emptiness.
The lock alone—it seems somehow ungallant—
is slow to recognize the tenant's touch
and offers brief resistance in the darkness.
This present tenant is not like the old—
who moved a chest of drawers in, and a table,
thinking that he would never have to leave;
and yet he did: his dose of life proved fatal.
There's nothing, it would seem, that makes them one:
appearance, character, or psychic trauma.
And yet what's usually called "a home"
is the one thing that these two have in common.

(SP, 35)

If Brodsky had never created the magnificent Donne poem, these simple, lapidary verses might have been taken as some early, neo-Acmeist tutelage in the empty houses of Akhmatova. Yet more is going on here than meets the purely Russian eye. Brodsky is already feeling his way toward a pregnant, metaphysical concept of emptiness—that which was once full of life is no more, and what replaces it is qualitatively different than any pristine or virgin emptiness. More abstractly, the tradition Brodsky inherits here in the early sixties is *the emptiness that was once full*: Mandelstam is dead, Akhmatova is in her final years, Petropolis has become Necropolis—has descended to the underworld.[77] The "domestic" (Soviet) can reacquire its authenticity only by inviting in another, "foreign" tenant (John Donne). So the homely images that Brodsky uses to capture this emptiness—the chest, table, and especially lock and thread—will be redeployed in the Donne poem, only with a different semantic orientation: there the departed tenant will be the soul itself. The prosaic imagery becomes "metaphysical" when one lodger becomes the body and the other the soul.[78]

The first ninety-two lines of Brodsky's poem are concerned with how, in words, to describe the sepulchral quiet, from low to high, near to far, small to great, created by the eternal sleep of John Donne. Every living and nonliving thing takes up a frozen pose on a rung of this great cosmological ladder. The vision is almost medieval, quasi-scholastic in its seeming precision, "Dantesque." So far there is no first- or second-person viewpoint in the narration, everything rising in a relentless arc through all the earthly and celestial offices (angels, cherubim, archangels, God Himself) to the very source of poetic language:

> Джон Донн уснул. Уснули, спят стихи.
> Все образы, все рифмы. Сильных, слабых
> найти нельзя. Порок, тоска, грехи,
> равно тихи, лежат в своих силлабах.
> И каждый стих с другим, как близкий брат,
> хоть шепчет другу друг: чуть-чуть подвинься.
> Но каждый так далек от райских врат,
> так беден, густ, так чист, что в них—единство.
> Все строки спят. Спит ямбов строгий свод.
> Хореи спят, как стражи, слева, справа.
>
> (*OVP*, 22–23)

> John Donne has sunk in sleep. His verses sleep.
> His images, his rhymes, and his strong lines
> fade out of view. Anxiety and sin,
> alike grown slack, sleep in his syllables.
> And each verse whispers to its next of kin,
> "Move on a bit." But each stands so remote
> from Heaven's Gates, so poor, so pure and dense,
> that all seems one. All are asleep. The vault
> austere of iambs soars in sleep. Like guards,
> the trochees stand and nod to left and right.
>
> (*SP*, 41)

This is one of Brodsky's earliest and most daring statements about the a priori value of poetic speech, a value that, the poet believes, transcends great men, empires, history itself.[79] Language can go no farther than thoughts of its own empyrean provenance, bumping its head, so to speak, against the sides of its metapoetic cradle/coffin. It determines consciousness, which in turn determines being. Thus "vice, anguish, and sin" (porok, toska, grekhi), all names for human history, lie quietly now within the encompassing frame of their "syllables" (v svoikh sillabakh).[80] On this occasion iambs and trochees "sleep," too, for they are as real as people, perhaps more so. It is difficult to imagine another Russian poet making such a statement in 1963. Only after he has reached this ultimate pitch (there is nothing more to be said about silence) does Brodsky proceed to the second part of his elegy, a dialogue between John Donne's body and soul.

In this section (ll. 93–124), we mount another ladder. Now for the first time direct speech, and therefore other viewpoints, are introduced. Brodsky has cleared the stage for this dialogue, but his almost baroque sense of drama and retardation will not allow his reader/listener to solve the riddle of the soul's departure quickly:

Но, чу! Ты слышишь—там в холодной тьме,
там кто-то плачет, кто-то шепчет в страхе.
Там кто-то предоставлен всей зиме.
И плачет он. Там кто-то есть во мраке.
Так тонок голос. Тонок, впрямь игла.
А нити нет . . .

(OVP, 23)

But hark! Do you not hear in the chill night
a sound of sobbing, whisperings of fear?
There someone stands, disclosed to winter's blast,
and weeps. There someone stands in the dense gloom.
His voice is thin. His voice is needle-thin,
yet without thread . . .

(SP, 41–42)

The vagueness of the potential interlocutor (the repeated "tam" and "kto-to") may owe something to another of Brodsky's early heroes, Dostoevsky, the master of dialogue and suspense. We are drawn further into the mystery precisely because the source of sound is left, for now, unnamed. Yet the image of a voice as a needle in search of thread keeps even this poignant turning point within the semantic field (quotidian, domestic) of the poem's opening.[81] Soon the ladder stretches upward in a series of questions, each directly quoted, each addressed to a representative of the heavenly host. An angel, the cherubim, St. Paul, the Lord, and Gabriel all are asked if it is not one of them who is sobbing in the darkness.[82] The question, for example, posed to God is playfully ironic and therefore all the more striking in the context of Russian religious or philosophical poetry:

«Не ты ль, Господь? Пусть мысль моя дика,
но слишком уж высокий голос плачет.»

(OVP, 24)

"Is it not thou, Lord? No, my thoughts run wild.
And yet how lofty [also 'high-pitched'] is the voice that weeps."

(SP, 42)

Who, finally, is asking these questions, since the quotation marks separate these thoughts from those otherwise attributed to the omniscient narrator?

The answer follows in the next section (ll. 135–90), an extended monologue delivered by the soul of John Donne to his body.[83]

«Нет, это я, твоя душа, Джон Донн.[84]
Здесь я одна скорблю в небесной выси
о том, что создала своим трудом
тяжелые, как цепи, чувства, мысли.

(OVP, 24)

"No, it is I, your soul, John Donne, who speaks.
I grieve alone upon the heights of Heaven,
because my labors did bring forth to life
feelings and thoughts as heavy as stark chains.

(SP, 42–43)

What a stunning gambit for a twenty-three-year-old poet trying to eke out an existence on the margins of Soviet society! Brodsky stakes his reputation and new voice on the imagined words of a soul as it looks down on the world from which it is soon to be exiled. Here, well before the facts of public persecution and physical banishment have become acknowledged topoi of his *vita*, Brodsky has found the theme, through Donne, that will make his mature poetry so distinctive in its native context—that of *psychic* exile. Rather than celebrate its return to God the soul mourns its banishment from the poet's body. The "heavy" thoughts, the mental contortions of the metaphysical poet, did not prevent remarkable flights of fancy during life—

Ты с этим грузом мог вершить полет
среди страстей, среди грехов, и выше.
Ты птицей был и видел свой народ
повсюду, весь, взлетал над скатом крыши.
Ты видел все моря, весь дальний край.
И Ад ты зрел—в себе, а после—в яви.
Ты видел также явно светлый Рай,
в печальнейшей—из всех страстей—оправе.
Ты видел жизнь, она как остров твой.
И с Океаном этим ты встречался:
со всех сторон лишь тьма, лишь тьма и вой.
Ты Бога облетел и вспять помчался.

(OVP, 24)

Bearing this burden, you could yet fly up
past those dark sins and passions, mounting higher.

You were a bird, your people did you see
in every place, as you did soar above
their sloping roofs. And you did glimpse the seas,
and distant lands, and Hell—first in your dreams,
then waking. You did see a jewelled Heaven
set in the wretched frame of men's low lusts.
And you saw Life: your Island was its twin.
And you did face the ocean at its shores.
The howling dark stood close at every hand.
And you did soar past God, and then drop back.

                                                  (*SP*, 43)

—but now, in death, they cannot accompany the soul on its solitary journey. Clearly, what John Donne, with the inspiration of his soul, was able to accomplish is what Brodsky and his generation cannot have: travel on the wings of Renaissance thought. God and Hell and Heaven—all capitalized in defiance of Soviet orthographic practice—were real to Donne. Dispossessed of this heritage, all the *homo sovieticus* can manage is to look on enviously at the forbidden fruit and try to imagine it.

The difference between Donne and Brodsky, a difference that one suspects Brodsky may not have been entirely aware of in 1963, lies in their respective treatments of the soul at the moment of *expiration*. On the day after he preached his final sermon Donne said to a friend: "I am to be judged by a merciful God, *who is not willing to see what I have done amiss*. And, though of my self I have nothing to present to him but sins and misery; yet, I know he looks not upon me now as I am of my self, but as I am in my Saviour, and hath given me even at this present time some testimonies by his Holy Spirit, that I am of the number of his Elect: *I am therefore full of unexpressible joy, and shall dye in peace*" (cited in Bald, *A Life*, 527). In Renaissance cosmology, the soul at the moment of death left the body (*efflatus*) in order to make its way back to the heavenly *spiritus*, anticipating microcosmically the higher movement of the planets or "wandering stars" (*vaga sidera*). "The exile of the soul from its body was thought to last precisely as long as the exile of the planet from its home" (Freccero, "Donne's 'Valediction: Forbidding Mourning,'" 287). From high to low, all rotating bodies and circular/spiral orbits were synchronized, and all "obliquely ran" toward a homecoming (*domicilia*) that was triumphant—"full of unexpressible joy." Even in Donne's secular verse, written at a time of life when he was unsure of his membership in the elect and was only too willing to display his scepticism, the emphasis, as in "A Valediction: Forbidding Mourning," was often on reconciliation, on leave-taking followed by homecoming. In "The Extasie" the lovers' out-of-body experience (*ekstasis*) mixes their two souls, and "makes both one, each this and that." One can argue, given the dramatic situation in the poem and that Donne, "Jack" the rake or "D. Donne" the believer, the critic produces as the mind behind the speaker, that the Platonism of "The Extasie" is either sincere or cynically manipulative (the goal is carnal seduction not spiritual union) or, as Helen Gardner has demonstrated in her fine treatment of the Leone Ebreo subtext (*Dialoghi d'Amore*), something else altogether ("The Argument"). The larger issue, which by now does not seem open to dispute, is that the ecstatic joining of souls is, in seventeenth-century alchemical terms, immutable and "unalloyed," "the union of perfect with perfect"; and yet, to complete the circle of love, this perfection must return to the world of decay, the lovers' bodies, and alloy itself with the lesser, in order that that, too, can be purged and redeemed (Gardner, "The Argument," 253–55). Carnal kisses could then, if properly sanctified, become small versions of cosmic ones, the mingling of two souls (one's inspiration = another's expiration) in this world adumbrating our eventual reuniting in the breath of God.

But Brodsky's emphasis, as befits one of his time and place, is exclusively on the pain of parting, on exile rather than on reunion. His work has no cosmic or microcosmic circles, instead only images of tragic separation, whose geometric form is the triangle (see final section of this chapter). Although Brodsky's poem raises the metaphysics of Donne (the *efflatus* of soul from body), the actual terms of his argument, their combinatory possibilities, are apparently his own, or at least do not owe their derivation to medieval scholasticism. The closest we come to seeing precisely how Brodsky envisions this moment of going-out is in his 1981 essay on Tsvetaeva ("Footnote to a Poem"), which is itself an extended monologue on how her perception of the departure of Rilke's soul from his body is presented in her great long poem *New Year's Greeting* (Novogodnee, 1926).[85] Tsvetaeva's work possesses many qualities that, if read through the prism of the essay, could be seen to apply to "Large Elegy": as a poem on the death of a foreign author, *New Year's Greeting* implies a "further estrangement" than an elegy written strictly within the native tradition; it is a classic *tombeau*, that is, both a tribute to the deceased and a self-searching, "confessional" appropriation of him; the poet's powerful inner ties to German language and culture are implicated, in absentia, in her choice of Russian as medium (yet another "estrangement"); a great poet's death is more than anything a "drama of language as such" and Rilke, in his present out-of-body state, is the "supreme listener"; there is an "absolute quality" to the speaker's monologue, which, as poetic diction, is seen to carry *farther* even than Rilke's soul ("any thought of someone else's soul, as distinct from the soul itself, is *less burdened* than that soul by its deeds"[86]), not after all a Renaissance Christian concept; the soul, as perceived poetically, is not so much concerned with divine reunion and resolution as with eternal wandering and exile (cf.

again the distinction with Donne: "The poetic idea of eternal life on the whole gravitates more toward a cosmogony than toward theology, and what is often put forward as a measure of the soul is not the degree of its perfection essential for achieving likeness and merger with the Creator but rather the physical [and metaphysical] duration and distance of its wanderings in time"); the voice of the poet striving upward is not simply analogous but equivalent,[87] in its "unlimited hierarchism," to the "striving . . . of the soul toward its source," and is "more like a bird than an angel" (cf. "You were a bird, your people did you see / in every place, as you did soar above / their sloping roofs"); and so on (*Less*, 195–267). For Tsvetaeva, as for Brodsky, meters are "animate," like "sacred vessels"; they are, as it were, the rungs of the ladder that the soul of the poet uses to climb out of his existential self. Other stylistic signatures, such as dashes, parentheses, enjambement, and the "infinite subordinate clause," all characteristic of both poets, are ways of leaping ahead and "accelerating" the soul's flight. Chunks of space and time are seen to collapse into missing, because unuttered, chains of associative verbal logic. Birds and Dantesque stars appear prominently in the Tsvetaeva essay and the "Large Elegy" because they provide the aerie, the ulterior vantage and outer radius, from which the soul can look back at the world *without* rejoining God.

In sum, Brodsky's "Large Elegy," like Tsvetaeva's *New Year's Greeting*, is a modern version of *ekstasis*, but not the *ekstasis* of John Donne. Despite the out-of-body experience, the attempt to expire into the air notes that will reach the silent interlocutor and translate into renewed inspiration (the cosmic circle), the poems are actually closer to an ultimate *askesis*, a self-mortification and self-estrangement that can be carried no further. Tsvetaeva's words, the embodiment of her soul, watch Rilke's soul as it turns in outer space to look back at the world it has left. Brodsky's words do something similar in his elegy. In neither case, however, can it be said that the one soul, that of the living poet, *becomes* the soul of the other, the source and focus of the tribute. The souls are "joined," and here is where Brodsky's flair for paradoxical speculation indeed reaches new metaphysical heights, in their state of permanent *exsilium*—what might be called an *ekstasis* of separation. The place where Donne's soul speaks from is not one of the terraces of Dante's Purgatory, with their stairways leading back to earthly paradise and from there to heaven, but a *neiasnyi krai* (murky realm), with no path in sight: "Nu, vot ia plachu, plachu, net puti" (But here I stand and weep. The road is gone) (*OVP*, 25; *SP*, 44). Thus, when Tsvetaeva finally pronounces the name of her god—"*Rainer umer*" (Rainer has died)—she is uttering a kind of mantra of banishment, since Rilke's full name has four *r*'s and the repetition of endings (unrelated grammatically) is an acoustic reminder (a kind of slamming of heaven's gates) of the *rai* (paradise) from which the poet is excluded by her friend's death (see *Less*, 245). What Tsvetaeva says in a letter to Pasternak about the still living Rilke applies a fortiori to the dead Rilke and to this, her last, epistolary gesture to him: "Yes, yes, despite the ardor of letters, the impeccable ear, and the purity of attunement—he doesn't need me, nor does he need you. He is beyond friends" (cited in *Less*, 248). Likewise, Brodsky's intoning of his poet's name—"*Dzhon Donn usnul, usnulo* vse vokrug," which sounds completely foreign in Russian—is not only as low-pitched as Tsvetaeva's is high-pitched but is the verbal equivalent of the famous bells tolling another's death. From Donne's "no man is an island" Brodsky has written a work in which "every man is an island."

The "destructive rationalism" that Brodsky ascribes to Tsvetaeva and that he sees, with characteristic contrariness, as expanding the Russian poetic tradition precisely *by falling outside it* (*Less*, 263–64) is, therefore, his own. But his poem does not end with the end of the soul's monologue. Something happens in the latter part of that monologue that carries over by its own inertia into the finale:

> Ну, вот я плачу, плачу, нет пути.
> Вернуться суждено мне в эти камни.
> Нельзя придти туда мне во плоти.
> Лишь мертвой суждено взлететь туда мне.
> Да, да, одной. Забыв тебя, мой свет,
> в сырой земле, забыв навек, на муку
> бесплодного желанья плыть вослед,
> чтоб сшить своею плотью, сшить разлуку.
> Но, чу, пока я плачем твой ночлег
> смущаю здесь,—летит во тьму, не тает,
> разлуку нашу здесь сшивая, снег,
> и взад-вперед игла, игла летает.
> Не я рыдаю—плачешь ты, Джон Донн.
> Лежишь один, и спит в шкафах посуда,
> покуда снег летит на спящий дом,
> покуда снег летит во тьму оттуда.

> (*OVP*, 25)

> But here I stand and weep. The road is gone.
> I am condemned to live among these stones.
> I cannot fly up in my body's flesh;
> such flight at best will come to me through death
> in the wet earth, when I've forgotten you,
> my world, forgotten you once and for all.

I'll follow, in the torment of desire,
to stitch this parting up with my own flesh.
But listen! While with weeping I disturb
your rest, the busy snow whirls through the dark,
not melting, as it stitches up this hurt—
its needles flying back and forth, back, forth!
It is not I who sob. It's you, John Donne:
you lie alone. Your pans in cupboards sleep,
while snow builds drifts upon your sleeping house—
while snow sifts down to earth from highest Heaven.

(*SP*, 44)

This is one of the most moving laments in all Russian poetry. Body and soul are forever parted, and Brodsky has had to place this Ur-situation on English soil to remind his Russian audience of what it, through historical blindness, can no longer see. And yet this apotheosis of loneliness turns itself, imperceptibly, inside out with the lovely metaphor (the conceit?) of the snow as needle and thread, perhaps the single most important leitmotif in the poem. Brodsky returns to his inventory of homely domestic items to make his ultimate comment about how heaven and earth, God's body and soul, are stitched together, however ephemerally, by the falling needles of snow.[88] Since we can never know our subject, even if he is as important to us as Donne is to Brodsky, all we have in place of psychic *ekstasis* are the images of verbal seams, the words themselves that form on the page, like snowflake-needles, "flying back and forth, back, forth!" It is fitting that Brodsky may have inherited the sewing conceit from the closest thing to a metaphysical in the Russian tradition, Khodasevich, who in one of the later poems ("Without Words" [Bez slov, 1918]) of his first major collection (*Way of Grain*) compared his life to a series of stitches woven along the light fabric of existence by the hand of God. In the end, significantly, the speaker of Khodasevich's poem turns the fabric over to see how the stitchwork on one side—the pattern of life—and the stitchwork on the other—the pattern of death—are interwoven (see Bethea, *Khodasevich*, 157).

In any event, Brodsky's poem ends not with the cavernous tolling of third-person bells and not with the direct speech of departing souls but with a chastened speaker, the voice of the poet himself, whose belated entry into the discourse signals a shift from monologue to dialogue. The contemplation of Donne's death has given rise to this speaker, who announces his arrival graphically (new verse paragraph). Up to this point, we recall, the narrative was sustained first through an omniscient camera eye and then through the soliloquy of Donne's soul. Now Brodsky's speaker asks his first question, "For though our life may be a thing to share, / who is there in this world to share our death?" (*SP*, 45) (Ved' esli mozhno s kem-to zhizn' delit', / to kto zhe s nami nashu smert' razdelit? [*OVP*, 26]), and, poignantly, he addresses his hero for the only time in the poem: "Sleep, John Donne, sleep. Sleep soundly, do not fret / your soul" (*SP*, 45) (Spi, spi, Dzhon Donn. Usni, sebia ne much' [*OVP*, 26]).[89] One would like to think that this is the moment in the poem, the formal occasion, when the consciousness of the English tradition enters into the consciousness of the Russian tradition, when the one, so to speak, awakes to the sound of the other's steady breathing. Brodsky, in a manner that will become characteristic of his "poetics of subtraction" (vychitanie), has not included one detail about Russia or himself in this elegy. Elsewhere he expresses only scorn at those poets who use the death of another for "self-aggrandizement" and "self-portraiture." Be this as it may, it would not be an overstatement to say that the plight of Russian poetry is implicated powerfully in the conclusion:

> Дыра в сей ткани. Всяк, кто хочет, рвет.
> Со всех концов. Уйдет. Вернется снова.
> Еще рывок! И только небосвод
> во мраке иногда берет иглу портного.
> Спи, спи, Джон Донн. Усни, себя не мучь.
> Кафтан дыряв, дыряв. Висит уныло.
> Того гляди и выглянет из туч
> Звезда, что столько лет твой мир хранила.
>
> (*OVP*, 26)

> Man's garment gapes with holes. It can be torn,
> by him who will, at this edge or at that.
> It falls to shreds and is made whole again.
> Once more it's rent. And only the far sky,
> in darkness, brings the healing needle home.
> Sleep, John Donne, sleep. Sleep soundly, do not fret
> your soul. As for your coat, it's torn; all limp
> it hangs. But see, there from the clouds will shine
> that Star which made your world endure till now.
>
> (*SP*, 45)

Life is full of holes, the chief one being death. And the poet, to paraphrase Mandelstam, is interested in what is in the middle of the bagel rather than in its doughy circumference. He is an Akaky Akakievich who by existential definition has his overcoat plucked from him by an arbitrary world order. Whether he be, like Yeats, one who sees more enterprise in walking naked than in embroidering his lyric coat with tired mythologies, or, again like Mandelstam, a defiant contemporary of the Moscow Garment

Trust whose coat bunches awkwardly on him, his only revenge, and haunting return (Akaky Akakievich), is through words. The threads of existence can never hold, but the threads of (poetic) language can. The silent Donne does answer back, otherwise the present poem could not have been written. Thus, when Brodsky says to his subject "Sleep, sleep, John Donne," he is speaking to him as one disembodied linguistic soul to another. This is the only "community" worth having in the first place and restoring in the second. The "destructive rationalism" of Brodsky's voice softens to a kind of lullaby. "You may sleep, John Donne, because I, another lonely soul, have heard you," he seems to say; "I am that needle and thread stitching new meaning out of primordial nothingness." Little wonder that the final image, though distant, is one of protection and guidance—the same guardian star that the poet, now reawakened as *Russian metaphysical*, sees as well.

Brodsky's Use of the Metaphysical Conceit

The lessons that Brodsky learned from Donne did not go idle. In this final section of the chapter we will follow the history of one specific conceit, that of the famous twin compasses in "A Valediction: Forbidding Mourning," as it was adapted by Brodsky in a number of poems he wrote in the wake of the "Large Elegy." Not only did Brodsky know the Donne poem well but he translated it into Russian and therefore wrestled intimately with its vocabulary and formulations (see *OVP*, 224–25).[90] Those Brodsky poems clearly "infected" by the Donne subtext continue to strike even the well-informed native reader by their intricate abstract reasoning, a reasoning that in all likelihood still appears to this day bizarre or anomalous within the tradition. And yet the reasoning and accompanying geometrical imagery are fully "motivated" if we keep in mind their provenance and the use to which Brodsky has put them. Let us begin by quoting the final stanzas of the Donne poem together with Brodsky's translation of them:

> Our two soules therefore, which are one,
> Though I must goe, endure not yet
> A breach, but an expansion,
> Like gold to ayery thinnesse beate.

> If they be two, they are two so
> As stiffe twin compasses are two,
> Thy soule the fixt foot, makes no show
> To move, but doth, if the'other doe.

And though it in the center sit,
Yet when the other far doth rome,
It leanes, and hearkens after it,
And growes erect, as it comes home.

Such wilt thou be to me, who must
Like th'other foot, obliquely runne;
Thy firmnes makes my circle just,
And makes me end, where I begunne.

(Poems, 50–51)

Простимся. Ибо мы—одно.
Двух наших душ не расчленить,
Как слиток драгоценный. Но
Отъезд мой их растянет в нить.

Как циркуля игла, дрожа,
Те будет озирать края,
Не двигаясь твоя душа,
Где движется душа моя.

И будешь ты впиряться в ночь
Там, в центре, начиная вдруг
Крениться, выпрямляться вновь,
Чем больше или меньше круг.

Но если ты всегда тверда
Там, в центре, то должна вернуть
Меня с моих кругов туда,
Откуда я пустился в путь.

(OVP, 225)

Without going into the considerable scholarly industry that has been lavished on the Donne original, certain conceptual dominants can be singled out and recovered straightforwardly, for it was these, we can assume, that initially attracted Brodsky's attention.[91] First, the movement described by the speaker is *both* linear (along radius) *and* circular (along circumference). The poet's beloved (Ann More) remains "fixt" while the poet himself "obliquely runne[s]." Despite the fact that the compass image struck later generations, and in this instance a foreign poet, by its seemingly fantastic ingenuity, Donne had various sources to draw on for it, including Chalcidius' commentary on the *Timaeus* and contemporary *lemmata* (emblem books) (Freccero, "Valediction," 283). Later he returned to this image in one of his sermons: "This life [on earth] is a Circle, made with a Compass, that passes from point to point; That life [in heaven] is a circle stamped with a print, endlesse, and perfect Circle, as soone as it begins" (*Sermons*, 2:200; cited in Freccero, "Valediction," 282). From Donne's seventeenth-century perspective the synchronizing or superimposition of "the linear extension of time and space" and "the circularity of eternity" was not something unique or eccentric but constituted the very "dynamism of humanity" (Freccero, "Valediction," 282). Second, this vortical blending of opposites ("And makes me end, where I begunne") was intended to mirror on earth (i.e., separation of lovers followed by reunion) what one day would happen in heaven (i.e., death as "divorce" of soul from body, followed by resurrection and reunion with God). For Donne, therefore, married love prepares us, through its "gyrations," for immortality: "As farre as man is immortall, he is a married man still, still in possession of a soule, and a body too" (*Sermons*, 7:257; cited in Freccero, "Valediction," 280). Third, it is significant that the perspective in Donne's poem is from *above* (God) *to below* (man); otherwise the motion would not appear circular and the desired effect, reconciliation, would not be achieved. Fourth, love's truth becomes incarnate at its *apex mentis*, the point of articulation where the two legs of the compass meet. In Aristotelian terms (*De Anima*), the fixed left foot (*appetitus*/will) provides the initial thrust while the right foot (*ratio*/reason) steps out, the pushing and pulling motion describing a kind of ball-and-socket joint (*gigglimus*) (*De anima III*, 10:433b, 19ff.; cited in Freccero, "Valediction," 290). At the point where body and soul join, "inter-assured" because their motion reveals a divine intentionality, one finds the *pneuma* or *spiritus* (Freccero, "Valediction," 290–91). And fifth, in medieval Platonism (*Timaeus*), the spiralic movement of the soul in man (microcosm) is seen to recapitulate the planetary movements in the heavens (macrocosm). When the soul has extended as far as it can, in ever widening circles, from the center (i.e., the image of the flatened compass legs), it then proceeds to reverse itself, "growing erect" and "coming home" via narrowing orbits (Freccero, "Valediction," 283).

Before moving to Brodsky's own richly "conceited" verse, a word needs to be said about his translation of the last stanzas of "A Valediction: Forbidding Mourning." As in the Auden-inspired elegy on Eliot, here Brodsky appears loathe to enter into dialogue with the full range of Donne's diction. Perhaps his knowledge of English was still too rudimentary to permit this sort of play. Or perhaps the tradition itself was too new an acquisition, too much an object of reverence, to risk the kind of lexical duel Brodsky would later attempt in his parody of Pushkin in "Twenty Sonnets to Mary Stuart" (Dvadtsat' sonetov k Marii Stiuart). In any event, by retaining Donne's meter and rhyme scheme (iambic tetrameter, *abab*), Brodsky has made Donne's syntax and phrasal counterpoint much simpler than in the original. Indeed, one is tempted to say that he has kept only the skeletal idea of the compasses but in the process has removed the poem's metaphysical guts, its organs and circulatory system. The syntax of Donne's poem is itself rebarbative and compasslike; Brodsky's is, with few exceptions, classically simple and flowing. In the first stanza cited above (the sixth in the original), Donne's thought goes through six delicate modulations: (1) we have two souls, (2) which are as one, (3) and though I must go, (4) they will not endure a breach, (5) but an expansion, (6) like gold which is beaten into airy thinness. Brodsky's thoughts, despite (or actually because of) the full stops, goes through fewer transformations, and those transformations are themselves, in my literal paraphrasing, simpler: (1) we part; (2) for we are one; (3) one cannot pull apart our two souls, (4) as one cannot a precious ingot; (5) but my departure will stretch them into thread/filigree. "To endure not yet a breach but an expansion" is infinitely richer in its expressiveness than the matter-of-fact "one cannot disengage/dismember our two souls," and the "priceless ingot," as inert noun phrase modifying the souls, cannot compare to the marvelous "Like gold to ayery thinnesse beate," with its vivid alchemical connotations. Thus, Brodsky has had to sacrifice much in this transposition. The only two details that could impress the reader of his Russian verse are the same needle and thread image (*nit'*, *igla*), here altered by context, that played such a crucial role in the "Large Elegy," and the poignant invocation of a loved one as fixed center for the poet who is being banished into exile. Ironically, "MB," the dark woman of Brodsky's sonnets, did not remain, à la Ann More, fixed at home as he experienced the outer reaches of empire near the Arctic Circle. Indeed, she became as mutable as her mate. In order to transpose successfully Donne's conceit into his Russian verse, Brodsky would both have to free himself from the enforced sacrifices of working from another language and rethink the geometry of his own painful homecoming.

The first variation on Donne's conceit in Brodsky's verse appears in "For School Age" (Dlia shkol'nogo vozrasta), a poem written in 1964, just a year after the "Large Elegy":

> Ты знаешь, с наступленьем темноты
> пытаюсь я прикидывать на глаз,
> отсчитывая горе от версты,
> пространство, разделяющее нас.
>
> И цифры как-то сходятся в слова,
> откуда приближаются к тебе
> смятенье, исходящее от А,
> надежда, исходящая от Б.
>
> Два путника, зажав по фонарю,[92]
> одновременно движутся во тьме,

разлуку умножая на зарю,
хотя бы и не встретившись в уме.

(OVP, 84)

The setting in of darkness brings, you see,
an effort to divine in the mind's eye,
with misery standing in as point d'appui,
the empty spaces that between us lie.

And numbers coalesce in arch word play,
they form, toward you, their own trajectory—
confusion emanating from point A,
and hope whose derivation is point B.

Two wayfarers, with lamp in hand, in my
pitch darkness move about at the same time,
and by dawn's light this parting multiply,
and can't, if mentally, the other find.

(my translation)

This little poem is found in "Anno Domini," the second section of *A Halt in the Desert*. "Anno Domini," in the year of our Lord, has Akhmatovian resonances (her fifth book of poetry bears this title), and the treatment of love, passion, and betrayal within a largely domestic frame of private memories and fleeting snapshots is also hers. The section is comprised of sixteen poems, one of which is the title poem and all of which, when taken together, trace the trajectory of Brodsky's love affair with "MB," Marina Basmanova, the actual or implied dedicatee. "For School Age" is placed in the first half of "Anno Domini," the sixth of eight poems whose dates of composition range from 1962 to 1965 and whose subject matter is, despite Brodsky's elaborate tropes of indirection, essentially the bright side of the affair. Here we come upon such titles as "A Riddle for an Angel" (Zagadka angelu), "A Slice of Honey-moon" (Lomtik medovogo mesiatsa), "Robin, You'll Flit Off" (Ty vyporkhnesh', malinovka), and "Songs of Happy Winter" (Pesni schastlivoi zimy). The last eight poems in "Anno Domini" are more concerned with the falling trajectory of the affair, sometimes seen through the mediation of a classical or antiquarian subtext (e.g., "To Lycomedes on Scyros" and "Aeneas and Dido"), and with the triangle that has intruded on the earlier scenes of domestic tranquility. These poems bear later dates of composition, from 1967 to 1969.

"For School Age" gets its title from the instructional imprint placed in textbooks for Soviet schoolchildren. Brodsky means to suggest one of those proverbial school-age math problems along the lines of "If Ivan sets off from point A at such-and-such a speed and Katya sets off from point

B at such-and-such a speed, when and where will they meet?" By this time (the previous poem is dated 17 May 1964) the poet has begun his northern exile. He is attempting, as it were, to "vector in" on his beloved's whereabouts, and the lines emerge as an ingenious riddle à la the metaphysical school. The numbers of the elementary math problem become the words of a lyric poem, and from feelings, such as "confusion" and "hope," once associated with specific times and places in their love affair, the speaker extends lines of thought whose hoped-for intersection will produce the living image of her who is absent. As points on a verbal compass, these instances of cascading word-play are all the isolated poet, adrift on his musings, has to perform his dead reckoning. Especially in the last stanza Brodsky's telescoping wit shows through: the pun on "v ume"[93] ("fancifully," "in the imagination") and *um*nozhaia ("multiplying") suggests that the poet is trying, through mental gymnastics, to superimpose the mathematical terms on the poetic ones. What is relevant for our discussion is that even here, in this early incarnation of the Donnean conceit, the net result is on *razluka*, parting, rather than on reunion. Still, the points of view, the wayfarers with their lanterns, though separated by circumstances, are moving and searching for each other. They are trying to come together, even if their efforts for the nonce are insufficient and the math problem, that is, the speaker's loneliness, remains unsolved.

The situation becomes considerably more complex in "Six Years Later" (Sem' let spustia), the final poem in "Anno Domini." Just as the poet appeared to initiate the relationship with "MB" in the famous "I Embraced These Shoulders" (Ia obnial eti plechi, 1962), the first poem in the "Anno Domini" group, so now does he sum up those feelings within the retrospective frame of "Six Years Later." Brodsky did not affix a date of composition in *A Halt in the Desert*, but the poem was written in early 1969. The original Russian title, literally "Seven Years Hence," was altered when Brodsky realized, possibly at the urging of his translator Richard Wilbur, that the anniversary date of January 2 would fall on Tuesday again (a point mentioned in the poem's opening lines) after six, not seven, years.[94] Sometime during Brodsky's peripeties with the authorities (January 1963–February 1964) the shadow of a Girardian rival/mediator imposed itself on the unobstructed "linearity" of the poet's desire. The rival was the Leningrad poet and friend Dmitry Bobyshev, and his affair with "MB," who bore Brodsky his only son after his release from exile in November 1965, seems to have come to a head at that time. To calculate by the dating of poems, this cruel "anno Domini" lasted longer than a calendar year (Brodsky, in retrospect, has postulated that indeed it lasted from 1962 to 1972, his final decade in the Soviet Union[95]) but may have been concentrated in 1966 and, perhaps, in 1967. As Brodsky told one interviewer, "At that time [i.e., the period of his persecution and exile] I had on my hands the first and last major triangle in my life. A *ménage à trois*—the usual thing, two men and a woman—and therefore my mind was occupied mostly by that" (Benedict, "Flight from Predictability," 14). This, at any rate, is how Brodsky looks back at the episode in the final two stanzas of "Six Years Later":

Так долго вместе прожили без книг,
без мебели, без утвари, на старом
диванчике, что—прежде, чем возник—
был треугольник перпендикуляром,
    восставленным знакомыми стойма
    над слившимися точками двумя.

Так долго вместе прожили мы с ней,
что сделали из собственных теней
    мы дверь себе—работаешь ли, спишь ли,
но створки не распахивались врозь,
и мы прошли их, видимо, насквозь
    и черным ходом в будущее вышли.

("Семь лет спустя," OVP, 100)

So long had life together been without
books, chairs, utensils—only that ancient bed—
that the triangle, before it came about,
had been a perpendicular, the head
of some acquaintance hovering above
two points which had been coalesced by love.

So long had life together been that she
and I, with our joint shadows, had composed
a double door, a door which, even if we
were lost in work or sleep, was always closed:
somehow, its halves were split and we went right
through them into the future, into night.

(Part, 3–4; trans. Richard Wilbur)

One might hazard the view that this is perhaps the most cerebral, mathematically formulated, and intellectually teasing description of love's demise in all modern Russian poetry, and in that sense it bears the indelible imprint of the metaphysical verse, and specifically the conceit of the twin compasses, of John Donne. The first four stanzas of "Six Years Later" (not cited here) retell the history of the lovers, how they had grown to nearly preternatural closeness, how each, in a Donnean sense, had moved and responded in utter harmony with the other ("Our two soules therefore, which are one"). The images, such as shielding her eyes from snow-

flakes so that her lashes, cupped in love, flutter like butterflies, are beautiful and touching. To cite the Donne of "The Good-Morrow" and "The
Sunne Rising," the two lovers had made their bed a center and their
apartment walls a sphere, in short, had made their little room an everywhere. But in the first stanza quoted above (actual stanza V) the speaker
recounts, with consummate indirection and paradoxical reasoning worthy of the English master, how the lovers, coalesced into one dot, and the
outside acquaintance, a second dot, had originally formed a perpendicular. That is to say, the shadow of a third "hovered" above them but could
not yet break into their world. The "linearity" of desire, whether of the
rival for the love object or of the speaker for her, did not "triangulate."
When the dots which are one separate, however, a triangle is formed.

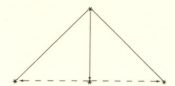

The reader should recall that what for Donne is an image of vortical reconciliation when seen *from above* (God looking down benignly from his
apex mentis on the compass legs) is for Brodsky, with his human perspective, an image of horizontal pain and isolation. Something hovering
above and out of his control (it could be an arbitrary God in another
context) has shattered the harmony and forced him to try to understand
it. By the last stanza the twin compass legs of "A Valediction" have become the two halves of a double door, a door that could not be opened
separately (that is, one *stvorka*, or half, at a time) and that therefore was
a symbol of the seeming inviolable privacy of their little world. Yet even
this is somehow breached, for the lovers are more souls or "shadows"
than bodies, and as a result they find their way into a future of tragic
separation as the fixed points of an eternal isosceles triangle. In the Russian original, they pass all the way through their special double door
(implying they have exited completely their realm of shared experience)
and enter into the future by means of a "backdoor" (lit., "black/dark
way"), which one may take to mean the back-alley deception of an affair
with a rival.

    This adaptation of Euclidean geometry as the basis of an elaborate con-
ceit is not an isolated instance in Brodsky. He will return to precisely the
same terminology—"triangle," "perpendicular," "standing," "to erect/
be erected," "two points/dots"—in the long poem "A Song to No Music"
(Pen'e bez muzyki, 1970) in *The End of a Beautiful Epoch* (1977), his
next collection (*KPE*, 75–82). There the emotional coordinates of his re-

lationship with another woman (Faith Wigzell),[96] all concealed under the mien of a wistful math professor, are given perhaps their most extended and difficult treatment. The first full sentence of the poem stretches out over five stanzas and twenty lines. Between the first line, when it is imagined how she will recall him "in an alien realm," and the twentieth line, when the claim is made that she presides over the "crowd of ciphers" (tolpa nulei) constituting the empty vistas of their separation (in 1970 Brodsky still lived in Leningrad, while Faith Wigzell lived in England), the thoughts of the speaker undergo a remarkable string of mutations, each helped along by Tsvetaevan enjambements, dashes and parentheses, and the ubiquitous trap doors of dependent clauses. It is difficult to "follow" Brodsky along these mountain paths and that is how he, by now a confirmed paradoxicalist, wants it. The seat of the "metaphysical" quality in his poetry has become increasingly lodged in his syntax, something probably suggested to him by both Donne and Tsvetaeva but that he is taking to new heights. Correspondingly, the triangle has become a metaphor for actual, physical separation (not the "future" but the "present"). Whereas in Donne the beloved remains in one place while the poet travels first away, then back to her, now both lovers are *fixed as separate dots*. Parting (*razluka*) is imagined as a straight line (*priamaia*) that rises up the perpendicular between them. The only thing that moves are *their gazes* as they look up from different—again *horizontal*—vantages to the top of the perpendicular: this *zaoblachnyi grot* (grotto beyond the clouds) or *besedka v tuchakh* (summerhouse in the clouds) is their only possible place of meeting, but it too is not of this world.

Hence the given in life ("vot to, chto nam s toboi *DANO*") are these three angles whose joining, paradoxically, is the guarantee of earthly torment and dislocation ("Razluka / est' summa nashikh trekh uglov, / a vyzvannaia eiu muka / est' forma tiagoten'ia ikh / drug k drugu"). The obstacle to desire is not a specific rival but something larger, perhaps the world order itself. And elsewhere in the poem Brodsky calls this triangle, again invoking Euclid and perhaps parodying Donne's Platonism (e.g., the perfection of the circle), nothing less than the "form of [their] marriage" (*forma braka*).[97] Indeed, so much is he aware of the origins of his mental construct and his convoluted tamperings with it that, poking wry fun at himself, he is willing to concede its outrageously precious, almost medieval flavor: "Scholasticism, you'll say. Yes" (Skholastika, ty skazhezh'. Da) (*KPE*, 81). In the end, the truth of Brodsky's modern "scholasticism" is that the apex of the triangle does not integrate the lovers' movements but fixes them on opposite sides of a perpendicular plane (cf. the double door of the earlier poem and the soon-to-appear wall of actual banishment/exile); the *spiritus* emanating from Donne's God, on the other hand, situated at the elevated axis of love, "inter-assures" its subjects that desire will push and pull in an ideal tension of "circular" and "linear" (i.e., *circumference* + *radius*) until that homecoming when the lines again form a single dot.

Brodsky's efforts as metaphysician and poetic Euclid were certainly not over, but he had, virtually singlehandedly, altered the trajectory of contemporary Russian poetry and had, in the process, introduced the educated reading public to a kind of verse it would not soon forget. Let us conclude this chapter with a final example. It is, in my judgment, one of Brodsky's greatest acrobatic feats in the Donnean/Euclidean mode, yet, perhaps not fortuitously, it is also one of his most moving and heartfelt. He is saying goodbye to another woman of initials, "TB" (Tatyana Borovkova), a friend who has died in a recent boating accident in the Finnish Gulf. He asks her, now a heaven-dweller, whether it is even worth the effort to try to convey the storm of feelings that her death has unleashed. The last two stanzas (Brodsky, in general, is one of the most powerful finishers in Russian poetry) are a Roman candle of accelerated emotional modulation, intense metaphysical speculation, and amazingly inventive rhyme (worthy of the best of Mayakovsky). It is also fitting to conclude with them because they contain the touching "Just sleep" (Spi zhe) of the Donne poem. Who says that word-play cannot be both intensely intellectual and passionately alive? Certainly not the poet, or reader, of "In Memory of T. B." (Pamiati T. B., 1968):

> Стоит ли? Вряд ли. Не стоит строчки.
> Как две прямых расстаются в точке,
> пересекаясь, простимся. Вряд ли
> свидимся вновь, будь то Рай ли, Ад ли.
> Два этих жизни посмертной вида
> лишь продолженье идей Евклида.
>
> Спи же. Ты лучше была, а это
> в случае смерти всегда примета,
> знак невозможности, как при жизни,
> с худшим свиданья. Затем, что вниз не
> спустишься. Впрочем, долой ходули—
> до несвиданья в Раю, в Аду ли.

(КРЕ, 28)

> Worth it? Hardly. Not even a line.
> We, the angles and tangents of life's cosine,
> intersect to depart. Be it heaven or hell
> for our next rendezvous, it's hard to tell.
> Yet from whichever point one bids adieu
> the result's an extension of Euclid's view.

So sleep. You whose nature was nearly divine,
which in death is always some sort of sign,
impossibility's token, life's chance to pretend
at meeting those lesser. You could not descend.
So till that non-meeting on some judgment day
let's dispense with the stilts and just walk away.[98]

(my translation)

4

Exile, Elegy, and "Auden-ticity" in Brodsky's "Verses on the Death of T. S. Eliot"

Whatever view we hold, it must be shown
Why every lover has a wish to make
Some other kind of otherness his own:
Perhaps, in fact, we never are alone.
  (W. H. Auden, "Alone")

"[D]EATH," writes Brodsky in his 1982 essay on Akhmatova, "is a good litmus test for a poet's ethics. The 'in memoriam' genre is frequently used to exercise self-pity or for metaphysical trips that denote the subconscious superiority of survivor over victim, of majority (of the alive) over minority (of the dead). Akhmatova [in her poetic cycle *Requiem*] would have none of that" (*Less*, 50). This statement, as it turns out, is itself a kind of litmus test for the author's own ethics and aesthetics. Versions of it reappear at strategic moments in important essays on Tsvetaeva and Auden (*Less*, 195–96, 361), and its central notion plays a conceptual and configural role in several of Brodsky's finest elegiac efforts. Yet the "in memoriam" genre did not always occupy pride of place in Brodsky's oeuvre. As we saw in the Donne elegy, various elements, some biographical and others typological, had to come together before the notion of Russian metaphysical verse could be born. Only when the boundaries symbolized by a poet's death were elided with the borders of a national poetic tradition, only when the issues of exile, whether physical or psychic, and elegy became extensions of each other, could this happen. A number of early texts foreground this process, beginning with the Donne elegy, but perhaps the most striking was written in January 1965, when the young Brodsky was located in internal exile in the far northern village of Norinskaya (Arkhangel Province).[1] Considering the time and place of composition, "Stikhi na smert' T. S. Eliota" (Verses on the Death of T. S. Eliot) is a crucial text not only in Brodsky's career but in the history of post-Stalinist Russian poetry. In it the poet consciously demonstrates what will become a basic principle of his mature *ars poetica*: he adopts a "mourning tongue" and elegiac form from one Western poet (Auden) in order to speak of the death of another (Eliot) and, in this way, to keep "the death of the poet . . . from his poems."[2] He goes out of his native tradition in order, as it were, to reinvent it.

We recall from the previous chapter that Brodsky began his appropriation of the English poetic tradition with Donne. How and why he was drawn to other anglophone poets, Auden above all, is the subject of the present chapter. But before turning to the issue of poetic borrowing, a word needs to be said about Brodsky's idiosyncratic (and belatedly romantic) view of language and national character. English and Russian, argues Brodsky, have different morphological, semantic, and syntactic forms, and these differences have a direct impact on the sort of poetry that each tradition can create. Each language has a different "personality," and this personality underlies anything that is said through the language. Brodsky, it turns out, gravitated toward English for reasons that were simultaneously ethical and aesthetic. Russian was a "magnificently inflected language capable of expressing the subtlest nuances of the human psyche," but its very subtlety, its tendency toward what the poet, using the English phrase, calls "loose ends," left it open to infinite moral compromise. Instead of becoming "a real vessel of civilization," the country of this language "became a drab hell, with a shabby materialist dogma and pathetic consumerist gropings" (*Less*, 26). (Curiously, many thinkers would contend the opposite: Russia's "maximalism" and inability to find an historical middle ground or a middle class has been its greatest undoing.) English, on the other hand, according to Brodsky, is more "analytical" and less "intuitive."[3] In English it is more difficult to lie or, in general, to be ethically ambiguous. This, for example, is why Brodsky prefers to speak of the death of his parents in English: "I write this [his memoiristic essay "In a Room and a Half"] in English because I want to grant them [his parents] a margin of freedom . . . I want Maria Volpert and Alexander Brodsky to acquire reality under a 'foreign code of conscience,' I want English verbs of motion to describe their movements. This won't resurrect them, but English grammar may at least prove to be a better escape route from the chimneys of the state crematorium than the Russian" (*Less*, 460).

The point, which in any event would be almost impossible to prove, is not to agree or disagree with Brodsky but to note his belief in the apriority of language here as well, in, so to speak, its very *ethical* nature. Brodsky's generalizations are significant because they are as close as the reader can come to an explanation of why English became the necessary antidote to the false letter of Soviet reality:

> [I]t's been my impression that any experience coming from the Russian realm, even when depicted with photographic precision, simply bounces off the English language, leaving no visible imprint on its surface. Of course the memory

of one civilization cannot, perhaps should not, become the memory of another. But when language fails to reproduce the negative realities of another culture, the worst kind of tautologies result.

History, no doubt, is bound to repeat itself. . . . But at least one should have the comfort of being aware of what one is falling a victim to when dealing with the peculiar semantics prevailing in a foreign realm such as Russia. One gets done in by one's own conceptual and analytic habits—e.g., using language to dissect experience, and so robbing one's mind of the benefits of intuition. Because, for all its beauty, a distinct concept always means a shrinkage of meaning, a cutting off of loose ends. While the loose ends are what matters most in the phenomenal world, for they interweave.

These words themselves bear witness that I am far from accusing the English language of insufficiency; nor do I lament the dormant state of its native speakers' psyche. I merely regret the fact that such an advanced notion of Evil as happens to be in the possession of Russians has been denied entry into consciousness on the grounds of having a convoluted syntax. One wonders how many of us can recall a plain-speaking Evil that crosses the threshold, saying: "Hi, I'm Evil. How are you?" (*Less*, 30–31)

This notion of the anglophone world as refuge not only in space but also from the "loose ends" of language itself leads directly to the issue of appropriation, an issue which is, *prima facie*, fraught with all manner of Bloomian overtones. If poetic influence is "a disease of self-consciousness" and if every "strong" poet is "condemned to learn his profoundest yearnings through an awareness of *other selves*" (Bloom, *Anxiety*, 26–29), then Brodsky should, by all rights, be feeling considerably under the weather. No other Russian poet of the post-Stalinist era is a better candidate for the Bloomian flu, with its "history of anxiety and self-serving caricature, of distortion, of perverse, wilful revisionism" (*Anxiety*, 30). In fact, readers have to go back to the 1930s and the high modernism of Mandelstam to find another poet so bent on domesticating the foreign and the "other" in order to create a niche for himself, always of course still on the margins, within the mainstream of Russian-Soviet letters. "The Russian language," remarks Mandelstam in his essay "On the Nature of the Word" (1922), "just like the Russian national spirit is formed through ceaseless hybridization, cross-breeding and foreign-born [chuzherodnykh] influences" (*CPL*, 120; *SS*, 2:245). That Mandelstam was a Jew whose family had come to Russia from Central Europe and whose own generation suffered from what the poet called, in *The Noise of Time* (1925), "congenital tongue-tie" are facts that have not been lost on Brodsky, whose debt to this precursor-as-outsider is, as we have seen, very great indeed (see Knox, "Brodskij's Affinity").

The question of outsider does not stop here, however, and that is precisely the point. If we recall that Auden, Brodsky's source in "Verses on the Death of T. S. Eliot," was himself a kind of outsider who labored under the weight of his debt to Yeats, and that Eliot, his subject, was a man "who lived in a condition of permanent exile . . . as if isolation or aloneness were something he was compelled to choose" (Kermode, *Appetite*, 109), then we begin to sense how potentially complex the issue of "cross-breeding and foreign-born influences" is for this Russian poem and the elegiac tradition it represents.[4] Auden, as we know, excised the sections of "September 1, 1939" that sounded too much like the Yeats of "Easter 1916." In fact, he wrestled with the Yeatsian presence to the point where, in this case at least, *he surrendered*—acknowledging that something inauthentic had permeated to the core of the poem and that it could no longer be included in his collected verse (Callan, *Carnival*, 156). Similar analogies could be drawn between a famous Yeatsian occasional elegy such as "In Memory of Major Robert Gregory" and Auden's "In Memory of W. B. Yeats." By the time Auden emigrated to America on the eve of the Second World War, he so feared and resented this symbolic scion of the "last romantics" ("Coole Park and Ballylee, 1931") and the voice Yeats could ventriloquize from afar, against the will of the younger poet, that it is fair to speak of "a kind of obsession" (Callan, *Carnival*, 144). Later, referring to Day Lewis's debt to Hardy, Auden wrote, "I wish I could say the same about Yeats' influence on me. Alas, I think it was a bad influence, for which, most unjustly, I find it difficult to forgive him" (Handley-Taylor and d'Arch Smith, *C. Day Lewis*, v–vi; cited in Callan, *Carnival*, 144).

How much of this background was Brodsky aware of when he wrote his poem in 1965 and then his prose eulogy of Auden, "To Please a Shadow," in 1983?[5] On the one hand, Brodsky seems to have managed the specter of his belatedness and the oedipal demons of prior traditions with the aplomb of a cultural conquistador. Rarely does he openly polemicize with or parody a predecessor, especially if the genre is elegy.[6] When he borrows the themes, images, and indeed meters, cadences, and stanzaic forms of a dead teacher, say a Lowell ("Elegy: for Robert Lowell") or an Akhmatova ("Nunc Dimittis"), he manages a kind of sublime prestidigitation—his voice grows stronger as the master's voice is lovingly recalled. One of Brodsky's greatest achievements, presumably in his own mind and certainly to judge by the collective response of the Russian intelligentsia to his poetry, is that he has *opened up* traditions that, due to the suspended animation of Stalinism, were either insufficiently known or prematurely forgotten. He has never, as far as we can tell by his interviews and written statements, seemed overly concerned with the fact that Donne or Auden or Milosz "got there first." Indeed, Brodsky has gone on record—and defiantly so—as denying the kind of anxiety of which Bloom writes (Knox, "Brodskij's Affinity," 383), and his disclaimers have the ring of authenticity about them, although the psychoanalytic critic could argue that any such statements are really "defense mechanisms" and thus proof a fortiori of the presence of anxiety.[7]

Could it be, on the other hand, that these traditions (especially the Anglo-American) *were not his to begin with* and that, in discovering these poets for the Russians, Brodsky is not a latecomer but rather a newcomer? "Strong" poets, once "ephebes" (in Bloomian terminology), always wrestle with precursors, but that struggle is a good deal less polemical when the alien tradition of the father does not make the son belated in his own native tradition. The "misprision" or "swerve" (*clinamen*) from, or the "completion" (*tessera*) of, the original model works in a Bloomian universe where the later poet, say Auden, feels the full weight— in his own language and native tradition—of the precursor's, say Yeats's, word. But what becomes of that weight and the vexed issue of poetic priority when the model itself is experienced as a word that could not be one's own to begin with?

Exile and Elegy

From early on Brodsky gave evidence of the sort of poetic imagination— "nomadic, decentered, contrapuntal"—which Said and others have identified as characteristic of the exile ("Mind of Winter," 55).[8] In January 1965 Brodsky was located in internal exile in the Arkhangelsk Province of Northern Russia; the previous year he had been tried and sentenced on charges of "social parasitism" (*tuneiadstvo*) and had now begun serving his sentence of five years of hard labor (to be subsequently commuted after twenty months). And yet, despite, or perhaps thanks to, Brodsky's nearly total isolation in the North, he was able to advance substantially as a poet.[9] Indeed, although Brodsky himself rejects the notion of biographical turning points (*Less*, 17), it can be argued that it is this experience that was crucial in the formation of the new, more expansive, "odic" voice that emerged from the frozen chrysalis of the North in the mid-sixties. This growth can now be linked, at least in part, to his reading of modern Anglo-American poetry, Auden in particular.[10] Brodsky, as we know, first read English poetry in Russian translation at home in Leningrad, but exile, he reports in "To Please a Shadow," gave him the chance to become more familiar with it:

> [I]t so happened that my next opportunity to pay a closer look at Auden occurred while I was doing my own time in the North, in a small village lost among swamps and forests, near the polar circle. This time the anthology that I had was in English, sent to me by a friend from Moscow. *It had quite a lot of*

Yeats, whom I then found a bit too oratorical and sloppy with meters, and Eliot, who in those days reigned supreme in Eastern Europe. I was intending to read Eliot. (Less, 361; my emphasis)

We will have more to say about the Auden connection, but for now let us note that: (1) Brodsky was in physical exile; (2) at this time he was drawn to reading Eliot above all other English-speaking poets;[11] (3) Eliot's death in January 1965 caused him to write a poem whose model was Auden's "In Memory of W. B. Yeats," a work about the death of another major figure who had died in another January (1939); and (4) all the poets implicated in this specific concatenation of the "in memoriam" genre were in some sense outcasts or *exiles*—Yeats an Irish nationalist writing in English, Eliot an American who had emigrated to England and Anglicanism, Auden an Englishman who had emigrated to America (and its quintessential city New York), and Brodsky a Russian Jew who was in internal exile but was now beginning his poetic emigration to the Anglo-American tradition.[12] All these border crossings were playing at the edges of Brodsky's mind. If they were not yet present explicitly, the poet was, in his choice and treatment of subject, feeling his way toward them.

Characteristically, Brodsky seems to come closest to defining the term *exile* on an occasion when he distances himself from it. Discussing Auden's "September 1, 1939," he refers to the lines "Exiled Thucydides knew / All that a speech can say / About Democracy" and describes the attempts of a modern Thucydides to muffle self-pity:

> "Exiled" [as in "Exiled Thucydides knew / All that a speech can say / About Democracy"—lines from Auden's poem] is a pretty loaded word, isn't it? It's high-pitched not only because of what it describes but in terms of its vowels also. . . . Now, what in your opinion makes our poet think of Thucydides and of what this Thucydides "knew"? Well, my guess is that it has to do with the poet's [i.e., Auden's] own attempts at playing historian for his own Athens [i.e., England prior to the war]; . . . he too is doomed to be ignored. Hence this air of fatigue that pervades the line, and hence this exhaling feeling in "exiled"—which he could apply to his own physical situation as well, but only in a minor key, for this adjective is loaded with a possibility of self-aggrandizement. (Less 327–28)

As we have seen, "exile" is, for Brodsky, ultimately a non-issue, a dead center off which to move rather than a dead end, which permits no further movement. It is so largely because of *its potential for cliché.*[13] No poet in the twentieth century can use the *topos* of his own loneliness and exile status without first disarming the term's "loaded" nature; if the motif is to be deployed at all, it can be so only "in a minor key," which serves to deflect attention away from the speaker. Brodsky returns to these thoughts in his essays on Tsvetaeva and on Auden, the poets who represent to him the purest essence of elegy and on whose behalf he raises his own eulogistic voice a note higher than anywhere else in *Less Than One*. Here it should be remembered that, according to Brodsky, Tsvetaeva and Auden managed multiple acts of self-creation through self-effacement in their famous works on Rilke ("Novogodnee" [New Year's Greeting]) and Yeats ("In Memory of W. B. Yeats"). The danger of "self-aggrandizement" attending any mention of personal exile is transmuted by them into the disinterested contemplation of psychic *exsilium* confronting us all in the passing of a great poet. The "lyrical" element (the personal loss of a loved one) elides with the "metaphysical" element (the theme of death as universal border crossing) to produce the distilled essence of elegy, what Brodsky calls "the most fully developed genre in poetry" (*Less*, 195).

Brodsky is most revealing on the connection between physical estrangement (exile) and poetic estrangement (elegy) in his analysis of Tsvetaeva's speaker in "New Year's Greeting." By forcing herself to look at the world abandoned by Rilke's soul at his death *as if through the eyes of that soul* she develops the capacity to "look at herself from a distance" (*Less*, 216), to deflect her grief by becoming the other. This stratagem, as any reader would readily acknowledge, is also the Brodskian trope par excellence. Tsvetaeva turns the tables of habitual cognition or reader expectation by *making us the exiles*, the ones stranded in the here and now as Rilke's soul wanders in the empyrean beyond. This is a bold gambit on her part, for we are accustomed to mourning the dead by visualizing the loss from our point of view, through our sorrow at another soul banished from this world (i.e., the bel canto, "self-aggrandizing" element Brodsky so fears). Tsvetaeva, who certainly possessed an ego of monstrous proportions, forestalls this possibility by separating her self from the other mourners and repositioning that self as the eye " 'see[ing]' Rilke 'seeing' all of this" (*Less*, 219). Brodsky attaches primary importance to this stance:

> [T]he knack of estranging—from reality, from a text, from the self, from thoughts about the self—*which may be the first prerequisite for creativity* . . . developed in Tsvetaeva's case to the level of instinct. What began as a literary device became the form (nay, norm) of existence. . . . [E]strangement is at the same time both the method and the subject of this poem. (*Less* 219, 21; my emphasis)[14]

Let us now take a closer look at how the notion of exile is reworked in Auden's and Brodsky's elegies. A cursory examination yields the following thematic and compositional similarities: (1) each poem is divided into three complementary parts, with a distinct progression from first to last; (2) each treats the death, in January, of another poet; (3) each uses the properties of rhyme to "domesticate" the sense of loss; (4) each blends elements of the traditional pastoral elegy and love lyric into its descriptions of a modern cityscape; and (5) each self-consciously situates itself against the notions of national poet ("bard") and national elegiac tradition.

Auden begins "the decade's elegy" (Hynes, *The Auden Generation*, 351) with a description not of the dying Yeats but of the world as it might be seen responding to the news of that dying:

He disappeared in the dead of winter:
The brooks were frozen, the airports almost deserted,
And snow disfigured the public statues;
The mercury sank in the mouth of the dying day.
O all the instruments agree
The day of his death was a dark cold day.

(*CP*, 48–49)[15]

The first verb in the poem is a euphemism, what de Man would call a *prosopon*—a "mask" or "face" that talks around the subject but does not name it ("Lyric Voice," *Lyric Poetry*, 57). It is intimately linked to the later exclamation "O all the instruments agree," which resembles the trope of apostrophe and which has ties to an older, more "rhetorical" tradition. In other words, although the poem is ostensibly about Yeats's death, in actuality it is not. To say that the poet has disappeared is to say that he has gone elsewhere, that he has emigrated. The attributes of death fall instead *on this world*, on the frozen brooks, deserted airports, and snow-covered statues. Even Auden's rhetoric, the sudden surfacing of the iambic cadence in "O all the instruments agree," sounds hollow, as though the traditional participation of nature in a poet's death is by this point in literary history too conscious and awkward a convention, little more than an attempt to calibrate on a thermometer our loss.[16] It follows, therefore, that what is defunct in the line "The *d*ay of his *d*eath was a *d*ark cold *d*ay" is not, in spite of the wording, the poet (he has simply "disappeared") but the traditional language of elegy (the "grand" style). That language, Auden seems to say, no longer rings true, the heavy, alliterative thud of its *d*'s" too close to the organ bass of a funeral dirge.

Lest these remarks sound too much like the idle play of the signifier, I quote from Auden himself on the way his work reflected Yeats. In a 1964 letter to Stephen Spender, Auden wrote, "I am incapable of saying a word about W. B. Yeats because, through no fault of his, he has become for me *a symbol of my own devil of authenticity*, of everything which I must try to eliminate from my own poetry, false emotions, inflated rhetoric, empty sonorities" (Osborne, *W. H. Auden*, 280; my emphasis).[17] To insure his own "authenticity," Auden has taken Yeats's voice, which he prizes but from which he also feels the need to distance himself because of its tendency toward "false emotions" and "inflated rhetoric," and surrounds it in his elegy with the slight whiff of parody. Only through parody can the genuine Yeats, the one who has disappeared beyond the threshold of January 1939, be preserved from the dangers of "self-aggrandizement."[18]

One would expect the twenty-four-year-old author of "Verses on the Death of T. S. Eliot" to be free of the anxiety of influence that plagued Auden. Brodsky confirms such suspicions by telling us exactly how he first reacted to the formal features of Auden's poem, which he encountered in an anthology of English poetry sent to him in exile by a Moscow friend:

> By pure chance the book opened to Auden's "In Memory of W. B. Yeats." I was young then and therefore particularly keen on elegies as a genre, having nobody around dying to write one for. . . . I soon realized that even [the poem's] structure was designed to pay tribute to the dead poet, imitating in reverse order the great Irishman's own modes of stylistic development, all the way down to his earliest: the tetrameters of the poem's third—last—part. (*Less*, 361–62)

There is almost no room here for parody, for the complex polemical relationship that Auden actually felt as he tried to do justice to Yeats without losing his own voice. The "I soon realized that even [the poem's] structure was designed to pay tribute to the dead poet" and "the great Irishman's own modes of stylistic development" appear, at first glance, to overlook the vexed nature of that tribute.

It is not suprising, then, that Brodsky's tone carries over into his poem, whose sonority and ponderous beauty, at least at this outset, seem entirely "on the level":

Он умер в январе, в начале года.
Под фонарем стоял мороз у входа.
Не успевала показать природа
ему своих красот кордебалет.
От снега стекла становились уже.
Под фонарем стоял глашатай стужи.
На перекрестках замерзали лужи.
И дверь он запер на цепочку лет.

(*OVP*, 139)

He died at start of year, in January.
His front door flinched in frost by the streetlamp.
There was no time for nature to display
the splendors of her choreography.

Black windowpanes shrank mutely in the snow.
The cold's town-crier stood beneath the light.
At crossings puddles stiffened into ice.
He latched his door on the thin chain of years.

(*SP*, 99)[19]

We are immediately impressed by the simple syntax of the stanza: only one sentence extends beyond the boundary of a line and there is not a single dependent clause. This is a far cry from the remarkably dense, almost Baroque syntax that Brodsky evinced even in his early works. The reason is, presumably, that the Russian stanza follows the sentence structure of the English original, where each line represents its own self-enclosed thought.[20] Brodsky may also be reinforcing the notion of border-crossing (hence exile) in a formal way: just as sentence and line boundaries are coterminous, so, too, is each thought realized through a "threshold" image (the frost at the *entrance*, the ballet on *stage*, the *windows* framed in snow, the *intersections* reflected in puddles, the closing *door*, etc.). All these thresholds, of course, grow out of the irony inherent in the opening line: the end of a life comes at the beginning of a new year, and the difference between the one and the other is a caesura, a pause for breath, an invisible stepping off or over.

Brodsky's rhyme scheme (AAABCCCB) is as formally complex as Auden's is nonexistent. There are, however, no slant or partial rhymes, which often surface in Brodsky's works in moments of existential doubt and irony, and all the rhyme words, with the exception of *uzhe* (narrower, thinner), are nouns—another rarity.[21] Against Auden's *vers libre* Brodsky counterposes an iambic pentameter, a meter that "throughout much of the twentieth century . . . has rivaled the iambic tetrameter" in popularity among Russian poets (Scherr, *Russian Poetry*, 52). The overall effect is one of simplicity and grandeur. Clearly, Brodsky does not yet sense that the prosodic structures of his language, in this elegiac context, are in danger of casting his enterprise into overstatement or "inflated rhetoric." The marked presence of adjoining rhyme, which would almost certainly sound parodic in modern English, only adds to the poem's acoustic splendor (i.e., "sonority" is not perceived as "empty"). The same may be said of alliterative effects: the *kr* in "emu svoikh *kr*asot *kor*de-balet" and particularly the *st* in "O*t* *s*nega *st*ekla *st*anovilis' uzhe" and "Pod fonarem *st*oial gla*sh*atai *st*uzhi," the last two seeming to announce in advance the naming of the poet ("*Tomas Sterns*") in the third part.

Auden's opening stanza has three examples of what might be called figurative language: the pun on "dead of winter," the "disfigurement" by snow of the public statues, and the striking "The mercury sank in the mouth of the dying day," a line Brodsky calls "astonishing" (*Less*, 362). Brodsky's more elaborate figures, in contrast, despite the "coolness" of

the occasion and the tempo, hide a certain exuberance, especially the ballet image and the perfectly epigrammatic "I dver' on zaper na tsepochku
let." Perhaps because Brodsky is writing in Russian about the death of a
foreign poet, there is a sense of fullness, of balance, between the formal
and semantic features, whereas those same features in Auden suggest an
emptying out of tradition. Brodsky, in effect, like the Tsvetaeva of "New
Year's Greeting," can reinvigorate his native elegiac tradition through a
kind of defamiliarization:

> If . . . the subject [of a Russian elegy] was the demise of a preeminent figure
> belonging to another culture (the death of Byron or Goethe, for example), its
> very "foreignness" seemed to give added stimulus to the most general, abstract
> kind of discussion, viz.: of the role of the "bard" in the life of society, of art in
> general, of, as Akhmatova put it, "ages and peoples." (*Less*, 196–97)

If there is a difference so far in the two elegies, it is in the *added stimulus*
inherent in Brodsky's poem.

This reading is borne out and amplified as the two poems unfold.
Auden hews to his tone of studied understatement and irony: life, epitomized by the wild, unmindful wolves and the "peasant river" of stanza II,
runs on even as the great man dies. "By mourning tongues," that is, by the
words of those left behind, "The death of the poet [is] kept from his
poems." No interest is expressed in the state of Yeats's soul or its present
whereabouts (that, for example, would be too "Yeatsian" a gesture); the
speaker's perspective remains relentlessly tethered to the here and now.
The cityscape of stanza I is reassembled in stanza III, only on this occasion
the urban metaphors refer specifically to the poet and to the absence of
what was once a powerful, magnetic personality:

> The provinces of his body revolted,
> The squares of his mind were empty,
> Silence invaded the suburbs,
> The current of his feeling failed: he became his admirers.
>
> (*CP*, 49)

For Auden what is important, therefore, is the threshold at which the
man "becomes his admirers," the poet his poems. And this threshold is
broached only when there is total absence on one side—for example,
empty squares, *silent* suburbs, and *failed* current. The process of emigra-
tion/exile is completed in stanza 4 as the poet "is scattered among a hundred cities" and given over exclusively to the world of "alterity," that
which is no longer his—the "*unfamiliar* affections," the "happiness in
another kind of wood," and the "*foreign* code of conscience." In short,
Auden's elegizing is, at least thus far, anti-Tsvetaevan; we do not see the
poet seeing Yeats's soul seeing us. Instead, Yeats "becomes" his poems (a
notion he himself expressed in his Byzantium pieces) but in the process

that active, difficult, protean self that gave birth to the poems is, in a sense, *exiled from them*, no longer has a say in what its words mean. "The words of a dead man / Are modified in the guts of the living."

Brodsky, like Auden, raises the Horatian theme of poetic, or secular, immortality—that is, of the verbal "monument" that lives on in this world after the poet's death.[22] But, unlike Auden, he is not against mentioning the nonsecular aspect of that immortality. Here one should note that Auden, in 1939, is weary and impatient with the symbolist heritage, with Yeats's numerous "dialogues of self and soul." Brodsky, however, is writing in 1965, in a world starved for the higher values of a now distant Silver Age.[23] Willing to do battle with facile, state-sponsored atheism, he remarks in another context that his reintroduction of the word *dusha* (soul) into the Russian lyrical lexicon, in a serious and "nonpartisan" framework, is perhaps his greatest achievement as a poet (Lauterbach, "Genius in Exile," 434). Thus when Brodsky says, in stanza III—

> Без злых гримас, без помышленья злого,
> из всех щедрот Большого Каталога
> смерть выбирает не красоты слога,
> а неизменно самого певца.

> (*OVP*, 139)

> With neither grimace nor maliciousness
> death chooses from its bulging catalogue
> the poet, not his words, however strong,
> but just—unfailingly—the poet's self.

> (*SP*, 99)

—he is making the same distinction between life and art, the bard (*pevets*)[24] and his "signature" or style (*krasoty sloga*), as Auden.[25] But it is at this point that Brodsky's and Auden's visions of a dying poet part company. In the last two stanzas of part 1 Brodsky produces a masterly scenario of what it would feel, look, and sound like for the soul of a great poet to depart this world. Note that our angle of vision is directed, except for the final line of stanza V, entirely on the receding Eliot, and that we, à la Tsvetaeva's speaker, set out with him on his journey:[26]

> На пустырях уже пылали елки,
> и выметались за порог осколки,
> и водворялись ангелы на полке.
> Католик, он дожил до Рождества.
> Но, словно море в шумный час прилива,
> за волнолом плеснувши, справедливо
> назад вбирает волны—торопливо
> от своего ушел он торжества.

Уже не Бог, а только время, Время
зовет его. И молодое племя
огромных волн его движенья бремя
на самый край цветущей бахромы
легко возносит и, простившись, бьется
о край земли. В избытке сил смеется.
И январем его залив вдается
в ту сушу дней, где остаемся мы.

(OVP, 140)

Used Christmas trees had flared in vacant lots,
and broken baubles had been broomed away.
Winged angels nested warmly on their shelves.
A Catholic, he lived till Christmas Day.
But, as the sea, whose tide has climbed and roared,
slamming the seawall, draws its warring waves
down and away, so he, in haste, withdrew
from his own high and solemn victory.

It was not God, but only time, mere time
that called him. The young tribe of giant waves
will bear the burden of his flight until
it strikes the far edge of its flowering fringe,
to bid a slow farewell, breaking against
the limit of the earth. Exuberant
in strength, it laughs, a January gulf
in that dry land of days where we remain.

(SP, 99–100)

These verses, regardless of the role of the Auden original, are meta-physical poetry of a high order. Stanza IV breaks into two four-line sentences: in the first, we see details of the Christmas season (another threshold [*porog*], this one of course symbolizing the miracle of the divine word become flesh) that Eliot, a believing Anglican, "lived till" ("Katolik, on dozhil do Rozhdestva"); in the second, we see the now dead poet, or presumably his soul, riding the ebbing waves away from his "solemn victory" (*torzhestvo*). Indeed, the entire stanza is itself in the shape of a wave, with its crest in the center, at the break between *do Rozhdestva* and *No*. The last line—"toroplivo / ot svoego ushel on torzhestva"—is Brodsky's moving, "russified" version of Auden's more matter-of-fact "he became his admirers." That Eliot's soul blends with the vital movement of the sea, which "justly" (*spravedlivo*) recalls its waves from the shore, suggests that there is a divine intentionality or essential rightness to this process. Auden's Yeats merges with his admirers and is thereby lost, at least as a responding self; Brodsky's Eliot looks back at his creation as he is borne away on the wave of time.[27]

Part 2 of each poem contains a figurative ("allegorical" in Brodsky's case) statement about the relation of the poet to his country or countries. These statements function as mid- or turning points of their respective elegiac forms; through them our attention pauses momentarily as it shifts from the literal fact of death in part 1 to the triumphant, cathartic cadences of part 3. Significantly, Auden departs from the pure *vers libre* form of his initial stanzas by beginning, almost imperceptibly, to use "Yeatsian" slant rhyme (another ironic filter). Perhaps, he seems to say, the lyrical elements, the *melos*, in the elegiac tradition have to be broken down (through parody) before they can be reassembled. The poet has to be purged from his poems (what happened in part 1) before his poetry, as poetry, can be celebrated. Brodsky's response—a modified version of a Petrarchan sonnet—is, characteristically, more formally complex and in keeping with the possibilities of an inflected language.

Auden calls Yeats "silly like us," presumably because the latter at some level believed in his personal mythology and willfully blurred the boundaries between life and art. This error, in turn, led Yeats—as it did the young Auden, now looking back self-critically at his Marxist phase—to posit a causal relation between poetry and politics.[28] But by 1939, with the world on the verge of another great war, Auden can say in all seriousness that "poetry makes nothing happen," a position that Yeats, with his Irish nationalism (albeit complicated by various contradictory feelings), could apparently not maintain. "Mad Ireland," therefore, may have "hurt [the poet] into poetry," but that poetry did not hurt, or for that matter console, Ireland back. This is the emotional low point in Auden's elegy, his profound existential denial of the symbolist ethos and all it stands for. Yeats's legacy was founded on a lie—the "parish of rich women [e.g., Lady Gregory], physical decay, / Yourself" which conspired in an unconscionable way to identify poetic truths with historical ones. And yet—and here Auden quietly begins to turn back from his despair—Yeats's art was somehow not compromised by the lie on which it was founded: his "gift survived it all." By the end of this brief ten-line part we have managed, perhaps like the Auden of January 1939 writing about England from America, to distance ourselves from history, the world, and the kind of high modernist logic (poets can be prophets) that brings that world to war, and have begun, sotto voce, to speak of survival and grace. Poetry has no raison d'être beyond itself; it is always and only a "way of happening, a mouth"—that is, a disembodied voice—and for this reason "it survives." Auden is at last ready for the rhymed tetrameters of the concluding part.

Brodsky, as already noted, has a less polemical relationship to his subject, T. S. Eliot, in the Russia of 1965 than Auden has to Yeats in 1939.

Auden left England to avoid the kind of inbred traditionalism and nationalist sentiment, the parish of rich women and the physical decay, that he associated with Yeats. The Anglo-Irish political tensions driving much of Yeats's poetry, especially the "terrible beauty" of a work such as "Easter 1916," were precisely the stuff of the poet-prophet's mentality that Auden, now an outsider residing in America, wished to escape. But for Brodsky, Eliot was *equally* foreign whether viewed as an American expatriate or as a British citizen. Only much later, presumably, did Brodsky fully understand the ironic, inversely symmetrical contrast between Eliot, the naturalized British subject, and Auden, the naturalized American citizen. In any event, as we have seen, Brodsky's perspective in his 1965 poem is not the same as that of his 1983 essay on Auden. Hence Brodsky's part 2 contains none of the withering irony and despair of its counterpart. There is nothing, for example, to correspond to the stylistic descent of "silly like us" or the bitter resignation of "poetry makes nothing happen." Instead, Brodsky's sonnet enacts a solemn pantomime or shadow play:[29] in the octet, two unnamed female mourners stand silently beside the poet's grave; in the sestet, the allegory is decoded and their identities divulged—one is England, the other America. Because the two are equally bereft and because Eliot's poetic identity is an indeterminate composite of both, he belongs to neither. Rather, he becomes—like Brodsky himself—a citizen of the republic of letters, with his grave "bordering" not on any single country but on "the world" (*krai zemli*):

Но каждая могила—край земли.

(OVP, 140)

But each grave is the limit of the earth.

(SP, 100)

Each poem concludes with a third part containing an "exegi monumentum" (the Horatian subtext is explicitly alluded to in Brodsky) to its subject.[30] This is also the first instance in which the respective tones of the poems dovetail. The authors have arrived at this moment of catharsis and celebration via different paths: Auden, the troubled insider, has moved for the moment beyond England and her politics, although, ever the skeptic, he cannot ignore what lies behind:

In the nightmare of the dark
All the dogs of Europe bark,
And the living nations wait,
Each sequestered in its hate.

(CP, 51)

Brodsky, the young poet marginalized and exiled in his own country, has cast his admiring glance at Eliot from his not-so-beautiful afar. Both poems express their celebration through identical trochaic tetrameters and rhyme schemes (*aabb*). Both temper the severity of winter cityscapes by introducing pastoral elements. Auden, in fact, returns the meaning of "verse" to its Latin etymology (*versus* = "furrow"):

> With the farming of a verse
> Make a vineyard of the curse

(*CP*, 51)

And Brodsky, playfully circumlocuting the *urozhai* (harvest) of socialist realist fame, informs his poet that he need not fear time's harvest even in its most primordial guise:

> Томас Стернс, не бойся коз!
> Безопасен сенокос.

(*OVP*, 141)

> Thomas Stearns, don't dread the sheep,
> or the reaper's deadly sweep.[31]

(*SP*, 101)

Still, despite the numerous formal similarities and the final notes of triumphant lyricism, a basic difference remains between the two poems. Auden appears, as it were, congenitally unable to make a positive statement about the power of art without first qualifying it with reference to its tragic origins: the poet must pursue his truth "to the bottom of the night" before he can "persuade us to rejoice"; "healing fountain[s]" must spring up "in the deserts of the heart"; and ultimately the "free man" must learn how to celebrate within "the prison of his days." (In this regard Auden, despite his prior intention to distance himself from his subject, comes intriguingly close to the essence of the mature Yeats's tragic vision. Or perhaps this *is* the point after all?[32])

Although Brodsky is certainly one of the most ironic and questioning of modern Russian poets, this spirit of skepticism is absent from the conclusion to his elegy. The poet, like love, must always leave this world—

> Так любовь уходит прочь.
> Навсегда. В чужую ночь.
> Прерывая крик, слова.
> Став незримой, хоть *жива*.

(*OVP*, 141; my emphasis)

> Thus it is that love takes flight.
> Once for all. Into the night.
> Cutting through all words and cries,
> seen no more, and yet *alive*.

(*SP*, 101; my emphasis)

—but that departure is more than a death, with implications for *there* as well as for *here*. Love may not be visible, but it is, wherever it is, alive. Brodsky seems able to affirm, with his final reference to *krai*, what Auden could not: that we call the other world a "kingdom of darkness" only out of envy, because it is closed to us, and that the world, like a lyre (cf. "Shum shagov i liry zvuk / budet pomnit' les vokrug" [Forests here will not forget / voice of lyre and rush of feet]), will continue to reverberate with, and hence to "remember," Eliot's music just as a body feels the touch of a loved one after that loved one has left.

Ты ушел к другим. Но мы
Называем царством тьмы
этот край, который скрыт.
Это ревность так велит!

Будет помнить лес и луг.
Будет помнить все вокруг.
Словно тело—мир не пуст!—
помнит ласку рук и уст.

(*OVP*, 141)

You have gone where others are.
We, in envy of your star,
call that vast and hidden room,
thoughtlessly, 'the realm of gloom'.

Wood and field will not forget.
All that lives will know you yet—
as the body holds in mind
lost caress of lips and arms.

(*SP*, 101–102)

"Auden-ticity"

Brodsky learned a great deal by tracking his elegiac sentiments at the time of Eliot's death through the filter of Auden's poem on Yeats. In concluding, one might say that the lesson consisted of several main points, all converging ultimately on what I have punningly called poetic authenticity—"Auden-*tichnost'*" (in English, "Auden-ticity"). First, the issue of language and its relation to historical time. Brodsky recalls being struck by Auden's lines, from part 3, that "Time . . . [worships] language and forgives / Everyone by whom it lives" as if by the force of revelation:

I remember sitting there in the small wooden shack, peering through the square porthole-size window at the wet, muddy, dirt road with a few stray chickens on

it, half believing what I'd just read, half wondering whether my grasp of English wasn't playing tricks on me. . . . But for once the dictionary didn't over-
rule me. Auden had indeed said that time (not *the* time) worships language, and
the train of thought that statement set in motion in me is still trundling to this
day. For "worship" is an attitude of the lesser toward the greater. If time worships language, it means that language is greater, or older, than time, which is,
in its turn, older and greater than space. That was how I was taught, and I
indeed felt that way. (*Less*, 363)

It is difficult to say whether this notion of language being prior to history
originated with Auden, since Brodsky repeats it often in his essays on
other poets, but he seems to claim as much, and one would like to think
so. In any event, it is the one cardinal, a priori belief that has accompanied
him through all his wanderings in and out of other belief systems, including Christianity.

The second point, which issues directly from the first, has to do with
Auden's attitude toward language and toward the voice that utters that
language.[33] It is an attitude that seems to have crystallized in the intervening years (1965–83) and is much more explicit in Brodsky's essay "To
Please a Shadow" than in "Verses on the Death of T. S. Eliot." Here one
cannot state too strongly that the qualities Brodsky found in Auden left
their indelible signature on his post-1965 persona. For example, the Englishman's most profound truths (e.g., "time worships language") are
delivered in an "offhand, almost chatty" style—"metaphysics disguised
as common sense, common sense disguised as nursery-rhyme couplets";
there is a "touch of irrelevance" to everything he says; he is "a new kind
of metaphysical poet, a man of terrific lyrical gifts, who disguise[s] himself as an observer of public mores"; his "mask" is dictated not by a single
creed but by "his sense of the nature of language"; the drama of his voice
is not personal but "existential"; he is a master of "indirect speech"; his
sensibility is a unique "combination of honesty, clinical detachment, and
controlled lyricism" (*Less*, 364–65, 369). All these qualities could, in one
form or other, be imputed to the speakers of Brodsky's mature works. In
short, Brodsky found in Auden a poet whose "anti-heroic posture" was
"the *idée fixe* of [Brodsky's] generation" (*Less*, 367). That Auden was a
foreigner in whose language and culture the metaphysical tradition in
poetry was born only added to his already mythical status.

Finally, Auden played the role—first unwitting, then witting—of Virgil
in Brodsky's passage into the world of Anglo-American poetry. He, with
his "indirect speech" and "anti-heroic posture," came to represent the
future of a poetic tradition that Brodsky would soon, unbeknownst to
him, inherit. We know this because Brodsky, upon reflection in the 1983
essay, casts Yeats in the role of the past ("too oratorical and sloppy with
meters"), Eliot in the role of the present (he "reigned supreme in Eastern

Europe" in 1965), and Auden in the role of what Brodsky had still to learn:

> I had yet to read my Auden. Still, after "In Memory of W. B. Yeats," I knew that I was facing an author more humble than Yeats or Eliot, with a soul less petulant than either, while, I was afraid, no less tragic. With the benefit of hindsight I may say now that I wasn't altogether wrong. (*Less*, 364)

Add to all this that the aging Auden took the younger poet under his wing immediately after the latter's exile to the West in 1972, looking after his affairs "with the diligence of a good mother hen" (*Less*, 377), and we begin to see what this man symbolized, and symbolizes, to Brodsky. He was nothing less than the sole reason why Brodsky began, in 1977, four years after Auden's death, to write in the English language in the first place ("to find myself in closer proximity to the man whom I consider the greatest mind of the twentieth century" [*Less*, 357]). It was he, not Eliot, as in the poem, who Brodsky truly believes is "our transatlantic Horace" (*Less*, 382).[34] Brodsky's last mental picture of his hero comes from a dinner party at Stephen Spender's shortly before his death. In order to compensate for a chair that is too low, Auden accepts from the mistress of the house two volumes of the *OED* as a makeshift throne. Brodsky claims to be seeing "the only man who [has] the right to use those volumes as his seat" (*Less*, 382).[35] Given the younger poet's defiant "cosmopolitanism" and his biography as unreconstructed *homo duplex*, perhaps in the end it is not so remarkable that Auden, a foreigner, has come to occupy a niche in Brodsky's pantheon as prominent as that of the native Tsvetaeva?

Still, it would be difficult to find a greater tribute than the one Brodsky paid to Auden in a 1987 interview in *Partisan Review*. Here, the Russian exile seems to expose the kinship, and its ultimate significance, as never before. When asked by the interviewer (David Montenegro) to comment on the role Akhmatova and Auden have played in his life, Brodsky responds with words of gratitude and love that make it fatuous—if not indecent—to speak of anxiety of influence and oedipal struggle between poetic fathers and sons. We would be closer to the mark if we spoke of a catharsis or redemption of influence. What better way to end this chapter than with Brodsky's own words about how he has become more fully himself by becoming the other:

> [Auden and Akhmatova] turned out to be people whom I found that I could love. Or, that is, if I have a capacity for loving, those two allowed me to exercise it, presumably to the fullest. To the extent that I think—oddly enough, not so much about Akhmatova but about Auden—sometimes that I am he. . . .
>
> Essentially, what you do love in a poet like Auden is not the verses. Obviously you remember, you memorize, you internalize the verse, but you internalize it and internalize it and internalize it until the point comes when he occupies

in you more of a place than you yourself occupy. Auden, in my mind, in my
heart, occupies far greater room than anything or anybody else on the earth. As
simple as that. Dead or alive or whatever. . . . I simply think about him too
often. In a sense, I can go as far as to say that, if I could supply an index to my
daily mental operation, I think Auden and his lines would pop up more frequently there, would occupy more pages, so to speak, than anything else. . . .

Both of them I think gave me, whatever was given me, almost the cue or the
key for the voice, for the tonality, for the posture towards reality. In a sense, I
think that their poems to a certain extent—some of Akhmatova's and quite a
lot of Auden's—are written by me, or that I'm the owner. . . . I sort of live their
lives. Not that I'm a postscript to either one of them. Both would rebel against
that. But to myself it's more sensible and more pleasant perhaps to think I'm a
postscript to them than that I'm leading my own life. I happen to think of
myself as somebody who loves Auden or loves Akhmatova more than myself.
It's obviously an exaggeration, but it's an exaggeration I feel comfortable with
sometimes. I know quite clearly one thing about both of them: that they were
both better than I in all possible respects. And that's enough. (Montenegro,
"Interview," 538–39)

5

Judaism and Christianity in Mandelstam, Pasternak, and Brodsky: Exile and "Creative Destiny"

Христианское искусство всегда действие, осно-
ванное на великой идее искупления. Это—
бесконечно разнообразное в своих проявлениях
«подражание Христу», вечное возвращение к един-
ственному творческому акту, положившему начало
нашей исторической эре. Христианское искусство
свободно. Это в полном смысле слова «искусство
ради искусства». Никакая необходимость, даже
самая высокая, не омрачает его светлой внутренней
свободы, ибо прообраз его, то чему оно подражает,
есть само искупление мира Христом. Итак, не
жертва, не искупление в искусстве, а свободное и
радостное подражание Христу—вот краеугольный
камень христианской эстетики.

    (Осип Мандельштам, «Пушкин и Скрябин»)

Christian art is always based on the great idea of redemption. It is an "imitation of Christ" infinitely varied in all its
manifestations, an eternal return to the single creative act
that began our historical era. Christian art is free. It is "art
for art's sake" in its fullest meaning. No necessity of any
kind, not even the highest, darkens its bright inner freedom,
for its prototype, that which it imitates, is the very redemption of the world by Christ. Thus, neither sacrifice, nor
redemption in art, but the free and joyous imitation of
Christ is the keystone of Christian aesthetics.

    (Osip Mandelstam, "Pushkin and Scriabin"; translated
    by Jane Gary Harris)

Века и поколения только после Христа вздохнули
свободно. Только после него началась жизнь в
потомстве, и человек умирает не на улице под
забором, а у себя в истории, в разгаре работ,
посвященных преодолению смерти, умирает, сам
посвященный этой теме.

    (Борис Пастернак, «Доктор Живаго»)

It was not until after the coming of Christ that time and man could breathe freely. It was not until after Him that men began to live toward the future. Man does not die in a ditch like a dog—but at home in history, while the work toward the conquest of death is in full swing; he dies sharing in this work.

    (Boris Pasternak, *Doctor Zhivago*; translated by Max Hayward and Manya Harari)

В Рождество все немного волхвы
    (Иосиф Бродский, «24 декабря 1971 года»)

When it's Christmas we're all of us magi.
    (Joseph Brodsky, "December 24, 1971"; translated by Alan Myers with the author)

AT WHAT POINT does a writer of verse become "the Poet," find his "creative path" (tvorcheskii put'), first walk in step with "destiny"? Where and how does an individual come to see that he has a contractual relationship with fate, a relationship implicating his biography and his word not only in a past and present but in a future? The questions are not fatuous ones but go to the heart of such notions, crucial to Russian poetry, as *sud'ba poeta* (fate of the poet). Mandelstam "accepted life as it was," wrote his widow; "I believe this was because he saw right at the beginning that his poetic gift was a matter of predestination" (N. Mandelstam, *Hope Abandoned*, 12).

Perhaps an example from a poet whose life is still unfolding might provide a logical point of departure for the present chapter. When a young man was (re-)arrested in Leningrad on 13 February 1964 and brought to trial five days later (the crime was social "parasitism"), he had already begun to study those poets (Mandelstam, Tsvetaeva, John Donne), writers and philosophers (Dostoevsky, Kierkegaard, Shestov), and cultural monuments (the Bible) that would, from a purely formal point of view, make possible the birth of "Brodsky." Yet that was not enough. Poets, at least Russian poets, do not usually become themselves through study alone; there must also be a certain recognition of one's place in history. In order to assume the title of "Brodsky" and to fulfill the destiny prepared for him by his poetic (largely Judaeo-Christian) culture, he had to become a victim and the state an angry, unforgiving, and capricious God. The man, in other words, according to a logic that was absolute and irreversible, had *to become the poet.* As Brodsky himself explains the motivation behind his arrest in terms that emphasize, doubly, his outcast status: "I just happened to combine the most inviting characteristics in

that I was writing poetry and I was a Jew" (Atlas, "A Poetic Triumph").[1]
And the precise moment when Brodsky became himself was when Judge
Savelyeva began to probe the issue of his identity:

> Судья: А вообще какая ваша специальность?
> Бродский: Поэт. Поэт-переводчик.
> Судья: А кто это признал, что вы поэт? Кто причислил вас к поэ-
>   там?
> Бродский: Никто. (*Без вызова.*) А кто причислил меня к роду че-
>   ловеческому?
> Судья: Вы учились этому?
> Бродский: Чему?
> Судья: Чтобы быть поэтом? Не пытались кончить Вуз, где готовят
>   . . . где учат . . .
> Бродский: Я не думал, что это дается образованием.
> Судья: А чем же?
> Бродский: Я думаю, это . . . (*растерянно*) . . . от Бога . . .
>
> ("Zasedanie suda," 280)

> Judge: But in general what is your specialty?
> Brodsky: I'm a poet, a poet-translator.
> Judge: And who said you were a poet? Who included you among the ranks of
>   the poets?
> Brodsky: No one. (*Without emphasis.*) And who included me among the ranks
>   of the human race?
> Judge: Did you study this?
> Brodsky: What?
> Judge: To be a poet? You did not try to finish university where they prepare
>   . . . where they teach . . .
> Brodsky: I didn't think you could get this from school.
> Judge: How, then?
> Brodsky: I think that it . . . (*confused*) . . . comes from God . . .
>
> ("Trial," 6–7)

It would be wrong to make light of this situation—since it is just this
sort of life-and-death duel that creates a rich and poignant tension between the life of a simple individual, a "civilian" or "lay person" as it
were, and the life of a poet—but one almost feels sorry for the dull and
stupid judge, nominally in charge of this lower court yet seemingly oblivious to the higher law governing the defendant. It was Brodsky, the help-
less victim, who was, so to speak, holding the cards. The deck had already
been shuffled and the hands layed out by the "fates" of Mandelstam,
Akhmatova, Tsvetaeva, and Pasternak. Judge Savelyeva had no idea that
Brodsky had raised the ante and implicated her in a high-stakes game that
went considerably beyond the boundaries of the courtroom with the

phrase "from God." It was here, as it seems in retrospect, that Brodsky indeed became the Isaac of his earlier (1963) poem, as well as the second "Joseph" (the first being Mandelstam) and Akhmatova's adoptive son. It was here that Brodsky's most cherished notion, echoing Mandelstam, passed through the same crucible that had chastened his adoptive parents: "[V]erses . . . survive whether published or not: because of the prosody, because they are charged with time in both senses of the word. They will survive because language is older than state and because prosody always survives history" (*Less*, 52). And it was here, in a tragic fate that allowed him to read self into national tradition, that Brodsky began to live out the words he would eventually ascribe to Tsvetaeva: "Tsvetaeva the poet was identical to Tsvetaeva the person; between word and deed, between art and existence, there was neither a comma nor even a dash: Tsvetaeva used an equals sign" (*Less*, 219–20). What is ironic (Are not such situations always ironic in a profound, cosmic sense?) is that we would not have these words ("Ia dumaiu, eto . . . ot Boga") had not one courageous woman, Frida Vigdorova, furtively, and against the express command of the judge, written them down and circulated them in the clandestine press, just as Mandelstam's legacy and martyrology had earlier depended on the narrative shaping of another devoted woman. Brodsky could not have become "Brodsky" without Donne and Auden, Kierkegaard and Dostoevsky, but "Brodsky" would have remained Brodsky without Judge Savelyeva.

At the moment when a poet assumes his destiny, if he is at all conscious of it, he enters into a reciprocal agreement—a kind of "potlatch"—that obligates as it uplifts (see Freidin, *A Coat*, xi). The future is never simply "open" to this individual who is truly himself only when he embodies, through his work, "the essential thought of his age" (Lipking, *The Life*, 9).[2] We tend, for example, to forget that the Akhmatova of *Requiem* speaks as the Suffering Mother not—or at least not only—for internal literary reasons but because that is the future, after the death of Mandelstam and the imprisonment of her son, bequeathed to her. The Mother *must survive* to see her Son die on the cross—that is the life, the only authentic life, that comes to model Akhmatova's own. Future biographers will no doubt be interested in how such "disciple" figures as Nadezhda Mandelstam and Lydia Chukovskaya strive to preserve and highlight, perhaps not without competition, the mythic contours (martyred Son, long-suffering Mother) of their respective poets' lives.[3]

Of modern poetic traditions, the Russian has been specially blessed (or cursed) with the notion of tragic destiny and awash in what Khodasevich once called the "bloody repast" (krovavaia pishcha) of its many martyrs. Is there something specifically *Russian*, the Western reader might ask, in the fact that Blok, the poet of a dying order obsessed with his own ambivalent christology, expires from psychic "asphyxiation," or

Mayakovsky, the poet of a new order who once described himself as nailed to the printed page, puts a bullet in his brain at Eastertime? The historical reasons for such homologies, intriguing as they are, lie well beyond the scope of the present study. Instead, what I would like to draw the reader's attention to is the possibility for attempting a new kind of poetic biography, one that would take into account that, for the chosen poet, it is not the individual poem that is crucial but rather the charismatic life informing and narrating the Book (see Freidin, *A Coat*, 1–33; "Sidia na saniakh"). Perhaps Nadezhda Mandelstam said it most pointedly:

> [T]he whole value of poetry is in the quality of the poetic thought behind it, in the poet's view of the world, not in the externals of poetic form. The harmony of verse is only, after all, the concentrated essence of the poet's thought, and what is really new in his work is not the serrated arrangement of his lines, the originality of his rhymes, Futurism, or a return to "classicism," but his exploration of life and death, the fusion of his life story with his poetry, the play of the children with their Father, and the endeavor to link the passing moment with the flow of historical time. The poet's work is but the mirror of his personality. Who made the marvellous remark that the creator is always better than his creations? (*Hope Abandoned*, 399)

The outstanding biographical and textual scholarship of recent years, especially that of Christopher Barnes, Lazar Fleishman, Gregory Freidin, and Omry Ronen, has now made it possible to examine more carefully the enabling myths in the "poetic lives" of Pasternak and Mandelstam.[4] As already mentioned in preceding chapters, it is too early for a scholarly biography of Brodsky. Yet it is not premature to claim that some of these same enabling myths are structuring Brodsky's view of himself qua poet as well as his notion of "destiny." Paramount among these myths are those of Judaism and Christianity, especially that of Logos, of the word-become-flesh. The present chapter will focus on how these three very different poets, Mandelstam, Pasternak, and Brodsky, employ these myths in order to define themselves within and against their respective epochs and to create "destinies" that in turn, *mirabile dictu*, create them. The vectors of "biography," "myth," and "history" intersect for these poets in different concepts of destiny, in different ways to their essential poetic selves. For now, suffice it to say that the Mandelstam, Pasternak, and Brodsky we regard as major, even "great," poets simply would not exist without the mythopoeic paradigms—both enabling and disabling, and often in fierce conflict—of Judaism and Christianity. And it is in the tension across these paradigms (or "cross-breeding," in Mandelstam's phrase [*SS*, 2:345), as potentially hobbling for a poet's life as it is inspiring for his art, that we can best see "destiny" do its work.

The burdens of linguistic destiny were especially heavy for Franz Kafka, the quintessential outsider. And as Robert Alter has recently shown, few writers have been more compelling in their ability "to convert the distinctive quandaries of Jewish existence into images of the existential dilemmas of mankind *überhaupt*, 'as such'" than Kafka (*Necessary Angels*, 53). In an oft-cited 1921 letter to Max Brod, Kafka goes to the heart of the Diaspora Jew's conflicted position vis-à-vis the gentile language of his adoptive culture:

> Most young Jews who began to write German wanted to leave Jewishness behind them, and their fathers approved of this, but vaguely (this vagueness was what was so outrageous to them). But with their posterior legs they were still glued to their fathers' Jewishness and with their waving anterior legs they found no new ground. The ensuing despair became their inspiration . . . The product of their despair could not be German literature, though outwardly it seemed so. They existed among three impossibilities, which I just happen to call linguistic impossibilities . . . These are: the impossibility of not writing, the impossibility of writing German, the impossibility of writing differently. One might also add a fourth impossibility, the impossibility of writing. (*Letters to Friends*, 288–89; cited in Alter, *Necessary Angels*, 33)

The passage offers a virtual textbook case of that potential for "Jewish self-hatred" of which Sander Gilman has written: the "outsiders' acceptance of the mirage of themselves generated by their reference group—that group in society which they see as defining them—as a reality" (*Jewish Self-Hatred*, 2). The assimilated Jewish writer is torn between the "liberal promise" that "anyone is welcome to share in the power of the reference group *if* he abides by the rules that define that group" and the "conservative curse" that "the more you are like me, the more I know the true value of my power, which you wish to share, and the more I am aware that you are but a shoddy counterfeit, an outsider" (Gilman, *Jewish Self-Hatred*, 2). The various scriptive challenges or "impossibilities" facing writers such as Kafka, Walter Benjamin, and Gershom Scholem, caught as they were between the tug of the adoptive *Muttersprache* (German) and the tug of the revelatory *Ursprache* (Hebrew), might therefore be seen as typological for Mandelstam, Pasternak, and Brodsky, poets who have become the most eloquent spokesmen in their own tradition for Russian Christian culture.[5] But does Gilman's formula really apply to the latter? What, if any, is the countervailing role of the Hebrew or of the Yiddish *mauscheln* in their cases? Can we say of our poets that what moves them to write is primarily the urge to prove that they can "both speak an acceptable language [i.e., Russian] and speak it better than their non-Jewish contemporaries" (*Jewish Self-Hatred*, 18)? When they use Russian, is it "always with the anxiety that they use language differently

than their reference group, in a way that is understood by it as 'Jewish'"
(*Jewish Self-Hatred*, 19)? Despite the real and abiding presence, for example, of Jewish stereotypes and anti-Semitism in Russian society, is the
picture at all altered when the majority culture is itself conflicted about its
otherness, its marginalization with regard to the metropolitan centers and
civilization of Western Europe (see Dreizin, *The Russian Soul*)? Finally,
which myth is in this instance the more powerful and more formative—
the myth of Jewish origins, with its corollary of linguistic tongue-tie, or
the myth of the poet as *izgoi*, "Yid" (in Tsvetaeva's phrase), or suffering
kenotic Christ? All these questions are relevant to the comparative concerns of this chapter, and I will attempt to address them as we look more
carefully at the individual poets.

In *The Life of the Poet* Lawrence Lipking identifies three turning points at
which a poem enters into dialogue with destiny and, through its own
making, "constitute[s] the experience of a life": (1) the moment of breakthrough or "initiation"; (2) the moment of summing up or "harmonium"
(the term is Wallace Stevens's); and (3) the moment of passage or the
"tombeau," "when the legacy or soul of the poet's work is transmitted to
the next generation" (Lipking, *The Life*, ix). Moreover, it is, according to
Lipking, through the initiatory poem that the poet first "finds himself,"
through the harmonium piece that he gives an "epic" sense of his life and
times, and through the tombeau that he examines, often elegiacally, the
issue of poetic mortality (*The Life*, xi). Lipking's study offers numerous
examples of fine close reading as he passes some of the great figures and
works of the Western poetic tradition (Virgil's *The Aeneid*, Dante's *La
Vita Nuova*, Goethe's *Faust*, Blake's *Marriage of Heaven and Hell*,
Keats's "On First Looking into Chapman's Homer," Yeats's *Per Amica
Silentia Lunae*, Whitman's *Leaves of Grass*, etc.) through the optic of
initiation-harmonium-tombeau. In many ways his basic premise is one
echoed by Boris Tomashevsky almost sixty years ago: "The poet considers as a premise to his creations not his actual curriculum vitae, but his
ideal biographical legend. Therefore, only this biographical legend
should be important to the literary historian in his attempt to reconstruct
the psychological milieu surrounding a literary work" ("Literature and
Biography," 52).[6] What I propose in the following is to try out Lipking's
typology on the "lives" of Mandelstam, Pasternak, and Brodsky, keeping
in mind all the while that each situates himself differently vis-à-vis the
same national tradition and that each stresses a pattern of beginning
("initiation") or ending ("harmonium," "tombeau") for his own reasons.
Certain texts will be used to illustrate the argument, although it is clear
that, without considerable supporting evidence, such isolated parts cannot be allowed to speak for the whole.

Mandelstam

Let us begin with Mandelstam, a poet obsessed with the pattern of initiation.[7] Of those scholars who have examined the "Jewish theme" in Mandelstam, Kiril Taranovsky, Omry Ronen, Gregory Freidin, and Clare Cavanagh have focused discussion on three poems Mandelstam wrote in 1910, as he was beginning his career and passing muster into the Acmeist camp.[8] These poems, "Iz omuta zlogo i viazkogo" (Out of an evil and miry pool), "V ogromnom omute prozrachno i temno" (The enormous pool is limpid and dark), and "Neumolimye slova" (The implacable words), while published separately, were never collected in any of the editions of *Stone* (Kamen') appearing during the poet's lifetime, presumably because the autobiographical material in them was too raw and unchastened by the poetic of the new and authentic "Mandelstam." In all three poems the "evil and miry pool" is associated with the poet's past, with Judaism, with a history and tradition whose awful, reverse flow[9] pulls the Pascalian and Tyutchevian thinking reed (*trostinka*) back into the dark womb of a *khaos iudeiskii* (Judaic chaos) described a decade later in *Shum vremeni* (The Noise of Time; *SS*, 2:55, 65; see Cavanagh, "Mandel'shtam and the Making," 237–41).[10] On the other hand, the *zapretnaia zhizn'* (forbidden life) which the reed, straw (solominka), or lily (liliia) strives toward in heliotropic fashion is the world of Christian grace, redemption, the fresh start and new word longed for by the young poet referred to by Petersburg literati as *Zinaidin zhidenok* (Zinaida [Gippius's] little Yid).[11] The third poem is the most interesting because it actually superimposes the image of a crucified Christ onto that of the sinister pool:

> Неумолимые слова . . .
> Окаменела Иудея,
> И, с каждым мигом тяжелея,
> Его поникла голова.
>
> Стояли воины кругом
> На страже стынущего тела,
> Как венчик, голова висела
> На стебле тонком и чужом.
>
> И царствовал, и никнул он,
> Как лилия в родимый омут,
> И глубина, где стебли тонут
> Торжествовала свой закон.

(SS, 1:138)

The implacable words . . .
Judea became petrified,
And, heavier with every moment,
His head drooped.

Warriors stood guard
Around the cooling body.
His head, like a corolla, hung
On a slender and alien stem.

And He reigned, and He drooped,
Like a lily into its native pool,
And the deep where stems sink
Was celebrating its law.

(translated by Gregory Freidin)

Here, as Freidin correctly points out, the young poet is caught and paralyzed between his "affinities to two contradictory orders, one of origins and the Law (Judaism), the other of the new faith and Grace (Christianity)" (*A Coat*, 52). The reference to Christ does not resolve anything, as it does for Tyutchev: His head rests on an *alien* stem, that is, it does not belong to the speaker, while the depths of the *native* pool celebrate their iron law. Words are *implacable*, not redemptive, because they constantly invoke a past that exerts its hold on the present. Judea is stony, its weight too much for the head on the slender stalk, and so this second Adam, unlike his counterpart in "Notre Dame," written two years later, is unable to create, to raise the rood of time, to be reborn into a new word ("iz tiazhesti nedobroi / I ia kogda-nibud' prekrasnoe sozdam" [and from the unkind heaviness I too will someday create the beautiful]). The frail, drooping *trostinka* of the one poem has not found the massive, burly *dub* (oak) of the other ("S trostinkoi riadom—dub, i vsiudu tsar'—otves" [Alongside the reed [stands] the oak, and everywhere the plummet is tsar]). In a word, the longed-for initiation does not take place; what reigns instead are verbal confusion and conceptual impasse. Mandelstam has not become "Mandelstam."

Initiation implies incorporation of an outsider into the sacred culture of the majority. Assimilation will come, believes the convert, when the "accent" of one's parents, whether literal or figurative, is fully purged and the initiate at last both speaks an "acceptable language" and "speaks it better than [his] non-Jewish contemporaries" (Gilman, *Jewish Self-Hatred*, 18). Through the first half of his career, that is, through the writing of such works as *Stone I* and *Stone II*, *Tristia*, "Pushkin and Scriabin," and *The Noise of Time*, Mandelstam is obsessed with working out the mechanism of one type of initiation: that from Judaism to Christianity.

"Pushkin and Scriabin" and *The Noise of Time* are crucial texts in this initiation process because they provide prosaic glosses on the poems.[12] In the first, for example, we see how Mandelstam, under the influence of Tadeusz Zielinski, V. V. Gippius, and Vyacheslav Ivanov, came to view death, expressed ultimately in Christ's passion, as a creative act and, more problematic, to conflate Rome with Judaism and Hellas with Christianity (see Freidin, *A Coat*, 76).[13] "Rome has surrounded Golgotha with an iron ring. . . . Rome has risen up against Hellas . . . Hellas must be saved from Rome. If Rome triumphs, it is not even [Rome] that triumphs, but Judaism [iudeistvo]—Judaism always stood behind its [Rome's] back and is only awaiting the hour when it will celebrate its awful, unnatural motion: history will turn back the flow of time" (*SS*, 4:100). This value system most likely came to Mandelstam via Zielinski, the immensely influential Polish classicist who taught at St. Petersburg University from 1885 to 1921 and whose *Drevne-grecheskaia religiia* (Ancient Greek Religion, 1918) advanced the notion that it was Judaism, with its exclusive monotheism and emphasis on nonassimilation, and not Rome, that lay behind the downfall of Hellas, with the latter's ecumenical (from the Greek *oikumene*, "world civilization") culture and acceptance of foreign gods (Cavanagh, "Mandel'shtam and the Making," 243–50). In other words, as Mandelstam, the Jew who was trying to find a place for himself in Russia's Christian culture, went about the task of transferring the seat of Christianity from the Rome of *Stone* to the Byzantium of *Tristia*, he was also, in an irony that could not have been lost on him, citing his own people as being too narrow and nationalistic and the Hellenes as being the more genuine "cosmopolitans" (Cavanagh, "Mandel'shtam and the Making," 247).[14]

Furthermore, in *The Noise of Time* we see for the first time exactly how Mandelstam personalized these painful issues.[15] His lack of a coherent and meaningful past (he had, he claimed, a *znak zianiia* [hiatus] "where a family ought to have been"), his exclusive emphasis on what the critic Edward Said has termed the cultural *affiliation* of books over the biological *filiation* of family or race (*The World*, 16–24), and his descriptions of his parents' (particularly his father's) chronic inability to speak *native* Russian all add up to a composite portrait of a "child of the nineties." That is, the hiatus or existential gap that confronts the young Mandelstam is also, in his willfully romantic version, the same one confronting his entire generation of *raznochinets* intellectuals trying to make a new start for their country *ex nihilo* (see Harris, *Mandelstam*, 48–62).[16]

> My desire is to speak not about myself but to track down the age, the noise, and the germination of time. My memory is inimical to all that is personal. . . . [Its] labor is not to reproduce but to distance the past. A *raznochinets* needs no

memory—it is enough for him to tell of the books he has read, and his biography is done. Where for happy generations the epic speaks in hexameters and
chronicles, I have merely the sign of the hiatus, and between me and the age lies
an abyss, a moat filled with clamorous time, the place where a family and
reminiscences of family ought to have been. What was it my family wished to
say? I do not know. It was tongue-tied from birth—but it had, nevertheless,
something it might have said. Over my head and that of many of my contemporaries hangs congenital tongue-tie. We were not taught to speak but to babble—and only by listening to the swelling noise of the age and the bleached
foam on the crest of its wave did we acquire a language. (*Noise*, 109–10; *SS*,
2:99)

To reinvoke Lipking, *The Noise of Time* is the text that permits us to see
most explicitly how Mandelstam, surveying his past, "gathers strength by
embodying the essential thought of his age."[17] However, the gaps of his
Judaic past that the poet tries to fill through his initiation into Christian
culture are not simple instances of absence, as we know from the three
"pool" poems of 1910, but dark vortices with their own primal undertow.

In the period 1915–16, as Mandelstam wrote "Pushkin and Scriabin"
and contemplated the apocalyptic happenings of his age, he also composed two Phaedra poems that, significantly, conclude *Stone II* and begin
Tristia.[18] Freidin demonstrates how in these poems the ever oblique Mandelstam was manipulating the Greek myth about incest (i.e., Phaedra/
Mother Russia, tormentor and victim, conceives a disastrous passion for
her (step)son, Hippolytus/the poet) as a template for the Christian myth
about mystical marriage (the hierogamy joining Lamb and Bride) (*A
Coat*, 94). What makes Freidin's reading compelling is that Mandelstam
chose precisely this moment to revisit, under the guise of another ritual,
the failed initiation of the "pool" poems.[19] It would not be an overstatement to say that the haunting lyric "Eta noch' nepopravima" (This night
cannot be undone) is a turning point in Mandelstam's efforts to remake
his life within the tradition of *imitatio Christi*.

Эта ночь непоправима,
А у вас еще светло.
У ворот Ерусалима
Солнце черное взошло.

Солнце желтое страшнее—
Баю баюшки баю—
В светлом храме иудеи
Хоронили мать мою.

Благодати не имея
И священства лишены,

В светлом храме иудеи
Отпевали прах жены.

И над матерью звенели
Голоса израильтян.
Я проснулся в колыбели,
Черным солнцем осиян.

(SS, 1:163)

This night cannot be undone,
But you still have light.
At Jerusalem's gate,
The black sun has risen.

The yellow sun is more terrifying.
Lulla-lulla-by,
In a light temple, Judeans
Were burying my mother.

Not possessing grace
And deprived of sanctification,
In a light temple, Judeans
Were holding a wake over the remains of a woman.

And over the mother rang
The voices of the Israelites.
—I awoke in my cradle,
Illuminated by the black sun.

(translated by Gregory Freidin)

The night cannot be undone because, first, the poet is faced with the undeniable fact of his mother's death and because, second, he has embarked on a Christian phase which renders powerless the terrible, backward flow of Jewish origins and Old Testament time (the familiar *omut*). In a reversal of the central act of Christianity, *the poet buries his mother*, but does so *in order to be born*. And whereas in the tradition of the *Nunc Dimittis* it is the Christ Child who must be presented by His Mother in the temple before the righteous old man Simeon, representative of the Old Testament, can depart to die (see discussion of Brodsky's "Sreten'e" below), here the speaker appears to be bidding farewell to the body of his mother, with its ties to the "yellow sun" of Judaism, as a necessary prelude to the Christian era. By contrast, the "black sun" that shines over the new being in its cradle is a sign of redemption, grace (blagodat'), and meaningful end; it is clearly a calque for the "creative deaths" of Pushkin and Scriabin and therefore goes unseen by the benighted "Judeans."[20] Note, moreover, that its emphasis is on a *second, apocalyptic* coming rather than a first (e.g., Pasternak's Christmas star—see below). Hence, in order to be born as a new poet, Mandelstam must shift his allegiance from the yellow to the black sun and must in turn embrace his certain martyrdom (*imitatio Christi*). He must cease being the cool, decorous, and perhaps elitist poet of *Stone* and become instead the "suffering bridegroom" who returns, Antaeus-like, to the soil to replenish it with his blood (Freidin, *A Coat*, 94). In sum, the poem is altogether eerie in the way its formal perfection channels and ritualizes the loss of a close relative into poetic gain. Mandelstam is more calm and in control in these verses, more—despite the pain—"initiated," than in the "pool" poems of 1910. The only ripples in the lyric's placid surface are the slightly absurdist lullaby ("Baiu baiushki baiu") that erupts when the speaker "puts to sleep" thoughts of his own biological and racial origins in the corpse being prepared for burial.

Mandelstam was of course never fully initiated, or in any case not for long, into the new world he felt come into being, and that is perhaps our point. It is thanks to that tension, thanks to the fact that wherever, with the help of his mythic codes and multiple identities, he tried to situate himself, it was always sufficiently "beyond the pale" to require a new poetic name. This became especially true in the second half of his career, when the so-called Christian culture on whose behalf he had been ready to sacrifice himself did not seem to need or want him.[21] By the late twenties Mandelstam begins *to reverse* the mythopoeic course of his earlier work, that is, instead of drawing himself out of the chaotic *omut* of his origins in order to remake himself into the poet as Christian martyr, he ferociously defends the *pochetnoe zvanie iudeia* (honorable calling of Jew) ("Fourth Prose," *CPL*, 321; 2:187) in the name of all that is "other" and "unauthorized" (see Cavanagh, "Mandel'štam, Dante").[22] Gradually rejected by the literary establishment during the New Economic Plan and faced with his own writer's block and loss of bearings, Mandelstam actually *needed* (as harsh as this may sound) the Eulenspiegel affair (and then his "two hundred days in the Sabbath Land" of Armenia) in order to reconfirm his position "on the outside."[23] One may even go so far as to say that, given the confrontational, *à rebours* aspect of Mandelstam's personality and poetics, someone like Arkady Gornfeld—a Jew himself and hardly an ideal candidate for establishment status—was almost "fated" to rise up and torment the poet. That is, and again one does not mean by this to make light of Mandelstam's genuine suffering, had the Eulenspiegel affair not happened, it would have to be, by the "Mandelstam" we recognize as a poet, contrived.

Jewishness as "inclusivity," the "tribal" sights, smells, and sounds associated with the boy's grandparents in Riga, is something negative and confining, something that Mandelstam "feared . . . and from which he fled, always fled" (*SS*, 2:55, 67–69); Jewishness as "exclusivity," the crooked name of "Mandelstam street" and the generic outlaw status of "Fourth Prose" (is it autobiography, anecdote, or jeremiad?), is positive and liberating.[24] Even the Christian poet *non plus ultra* starts to look suspiciously outcast and "Jewish" in "Razgovor o Dante" (Conversation about Dante). Likewise, the "free play" of the child with the Father that Mandelstam thought characteristic of Christianity in "Pushkin and Scriabin" becomes inexorably the "bound play" of a rebellious child with an angry Yahweh in the Stalin ode. The *znak ziianiia* (hiatus) that was a sign of insecurity in *The Noise of Time* becomes an order of merit in "Fourth Prose": "With each passing year I become more crafty. It's as if I have been punched full of holes with a conductor's steel punch and stamped with my own name" (*SS*, 2:190; *CPL*, 323–24). And the voice from within the linguistic doughnut's hollow center, the one that rages "for me a doughnut's value resides in the hole" (*SS*, 2:191; *CPL*, 324), becomes more resonant and authentic than that of the authorized doughnut. Indeed, even the "babble" and "tongue-tie" that the poet equated with his Jewish past in *The Noise of Time* take on a positive valence in the thirties—"unauthorized" language, as the source of all genuine poetry, now has the right to be unclear and unstraightforward. Mandelstam the Acmeist experiments with sound play and etymologies like a Futurist; his poems in the "Moscow Notebooks" become contaminated with foreign and substandard speech, nonsense words, and "infantile" phonetics (Cavanagh, "Mandel'štam, Dante," 333–34).[25] In this way, it might be said that Mandelstam continues his obsession with initiation (now of course in reverse), continues to flirt with his martyrdom, continues to insure that destiny is not only a literary trope. The wolf runs not only from, but to, the wolfhound.

Pasternak

The situation represented by the fate of Boris Pasternak is entirely different. As the new biographies by Barnes and Fleishman make abundantly clear, Pasternak's Moscow family, though by no means unmindful of its roots (Sephardic Jews from Odessa), was more at ease in and assimilated to mainstream Russian culture than Mandelstam's. Pasternak would never say, as Mandelstam does in "Fourth Prose," that "my blood [is] burdened with the heritage of sheep breeders, patriarchs and kings" (*SS*, 2:187; *CPL*, 321). In fact, long before his novel, Pasternak expressed a certain impatience with Jews who wore their ethnic roots too close to the surface.[26] And if his father Leonid was, especially after 1910, sympathetic "toward the awakening of national Jewish sentiment" (Fleishman, *Pas-*

ternak, 15), Boris himself seemed willing for the majority of his career to avoid, even perhaps repress, such issues.[27] Be this as it may, the fact of his Jewishness, as well as the dangers of obstreperous ethnicity in a Stalinist culture that came to use *narodnost'* and "Russianness" as bludgeons, were things the poet had eventually, in *Doctor Zhivago*, to deal with. But his method was always indirection, what Fleishman terms a quiet yet stubborn "noncongruence" (*Pasternak*, ix), rather than Mandelstamian confrontation.[28] Recall, for example, Pasternak's reported response to Mandelstam when the latter recited his poem "My zhivem, pod soboiu ne chuia strany" (We live without feeling the country underneath us) to him on the street: "What you have just read to me has no relation to literature, to poetry. It is not a literary fact, but an act of suicide which I do not condone and in which I do not want to take part. You didn't read me anything, I didn't hear anything, and I ask you not to read these verses to anyone else" ("Zametki o peresechenii," 316; cited in Fleishman, *Trid-tsatye gody*, 144–45). Later Pasternak reproved Mandelstam's wife for this lack of circumspection: "He [Pasternak] brought down a torrent of reproaches on me—O. M. was already in Voronezh. Of these I remember one [in particular]: 'How could he write such verses—*after all, he is a Jew*'" (*Vospominaniia*, 1:168–69; my emphasis; cited in Fleishman, *Tridtsatye gody*, 145).[29]

Two facts about Pasternak's family history are perhaps relevant here. First, his descent (via his father) from Don Isaac ben-Yehuda Abravanel, the celebrated fifteenth-century philosopher and political leader, himself said to be descended from the royal house of David, and Don Isaac's son, Yehuda Abravanel, the Renaissance poet who went by the pen name "Leone Ebreo." Second, his baptism into Christianity as an infant by his nanny,[30] now assumed by most scholars to be legendary, a later embel-lishment by a poet who saw his greatest affinity with Christian values. Fleishman has elegantly telescoped these two facts: just as Yehuda, like his father, had been forced into exile in 1492 and in the process had left his infant son behind to be baptized (as recounted in Leone Ebreo's elegy "Lament on the Times"), so, too, had Pasternak père been faced with no other alternative than to abandon his native land in 1921, with the result that the son left behind was baptized, in his (the son's) mind and in his later creative work, if not in fact (Fleishman, *Pasternak*, 17–20). Thus did Pasternak, according to Fleishman, turn biographical myth into reality and the pain of separation into the balm of Christian incorporation.

This much, then, is clear and by now a matter of record: Pasternak, like Mandelstam, was a Russian poet of Jewish origin who came of age in the years preceding the Revolution and who inscribed his own "created life" onto that of the epoch. He may have experienced some unease about his roots, but that fact plays virtually no role in his early work. The next point in our argument is pivotal and suggests perhaps why Mandelstam was first and foremost a poet of repeated (tragic) initiation while Pasternak was a poet of what Lipking calls "harmonium," or epic sensibility. The difference has to do with how each poet viewed the Revolution as a turning point in his own life and in that of his country. The Revolution marked the end of one empire and the beginning of another, and both Mandelstam and Pasternak were present at the birth of the Soviet era as relatively *young men*. In *Okhrannaia gramota* (Safe Conduct), for example, Pasternak remarks pointedly that "Boys who were about my own age had been thirteen in 1905 and were nearly twenty-two before the war. Both their critical ages coincided with the two red dates of their country's history. Their childhood, adolescence and their calling-up at coming of age were immediately fastened to an epoch of transition" (97; *Proza 1915–1958*, 267). However, as we recall from "This night cannot be undone," Mandelstam's feelings in 1916 were heavily colored by the apocalyptic—that is, still largely symbolist—forebodings in the air, including the profundities of V. V. Gippius and Vyacheslav Ivanov. New life was to come through death, the Christian era was to find its cradle at the wake of Judaism. Even the title of Mandelstam's new book, *Tristia*, with its "science of parting" (nauka rastavan'ia), had a tragic, bittersweet quality, and the accent was more on what was passing into the night, the "twilight of freedom" (sumerki svobody), than on the joy of the coming dawn. Blok, the epoch's "tragic tenor," was more the model here than, say, Mayakovsky, who was Pasternak's.

But Pasternak's first major book, *Sestra moia zhizn'* (My sister, life, 1922), is the opposite in every way to the roughly contemporaneous *Tristia*. Now the revolutionary spring and summer of 1917 stand exclusively for newness, awakening love, the proverbial slate washed clean by *zhizn' v razlive* (life overflowing). Pasternak's speaker employs religious terminology—Christmas, millennium, Holy Scripture, hosanna, passion (in multiple senses), Apocalypse—but he does so freely, allusively, without fixed reference to the Bible and with only marginal self-emplotment (*1912–32*, 4, 6, 10, 21, 39). The way Pasternak marshals his "futurist" lessons to give a unique shape and thrust to *My Sister*, thereby almost instantaneously outgrowing all that is crudely avant-gardist and derivative, has been the subject of much scholarship, but oftentimes the larger, and perhaps more interesting point has been obscured. In *My Sister*, Pasternak has all the elements—personal experience, historic turning point, religious symbolism—to construct the sort of elaborately dovetailing myth of self-presentation we observed in the Mandelstam of *Tristia*.[31] Yet he does not. The reason, in my judgment, is that he is not ready for "destiny." That destiny still lies somewhere up ahead, and is intimately linked with the "harmonium" piece we recognize as *Doctor Zhivago*. It implies a concept of futurity that is inimical to the vivid present-ness of *My Sister*, where every lilac branch or raindrop speaks for and through the poet. In other words, "Pasternak," at least the author who came to see himself as having a destiny, wrote his first great collection not for its own sake but in order to embark on a path that would lead to his self and, which is the same thing, to the novel.[32]

In a well-known passage of *Doctor Zhivago* the narrator says of the young Yury of 1911:

> Yura had a good mind and was an excellent writer. Ever since his school days he had dreamed of composing a book about life which would contain, like buried explosives, the most striking things he had seen so far and thought about. But he was too young to write such a book; instead, he wrote poetry. He was like a painter who was always making sketches for a big canvas he had in mind.[33] (Hayward, 58; *DZh*, 65–66)

These thoughts may be dismissed as sheer literary wishful thinking: Pasternak, who is clearly not the same as his character, is using the life and creative development of that character to rewrite his own. On the other hand, and this, one suspects, is the more valid point, Pasternak was "dream[ing] of composing a book about life" if not from the beginning, then for much longer that we generally give him credit for (see Borisov and Pasternak, "Materialy"). *My Sister, Life* is, in this respect, both a *kniga zhizneopisanii* (book of life-descriptions [*DZh*, 65]) in its own right as well as a "sketch" for the great book to come. "I came to understand," recalls the poet in *Safe Conduct*, ". . . that the Bible is not so much a book with a hard and fast text, as *the notebook of humanity* [zapisnaia tetrad' chelovechestva] . . ." (*Safe Conduct*, 91; my emphasis; *Proza 1915–58*, 263). What interests Pasternak, then, is not the individual poem, or even the book of poems, but *the book of life*. As Lipking concludes, "The modern 'epic' is dominated by one story and one story only: the life of the poet" (*The Life*, 70).

Mandelstam's poetics of initiation do not permit the notion of sketches or drafts of an "harmonium" to come; the martyr's time is now—"creative death" either happens or it does not. But Pasternak's *oeuvre* is strewn with shards and traces that echo in advance the novel: the interleaving of prose and poetry sections in the lost fairy story *Tale of the Carp and Napthalain* (Povest' o Karpe i Naftalene), the presence of rivals in the novella *The Apelles Mark* (Apelleseva cherta) and the chapter "Lovelessness" (Bezliub'e), the lyric poet sick with epic intentions (and hence in need of "Doctor Life") in *Sublime Malady* (Vysokaia bolezn'), and the eponymous hero as Christ figure in *Lieutenant Schmidt*. Thus, one may be able to point to the precise provenance of the novel in the actual recorded life of the author, but what truly counts for Pasternak is that the "book of life" has *always* existed in the *camera obscura* of his imagination and that it is his task to gradually develop it and bring it to light. To be sure, *Doctor Zhivago* as novel could not have been written without the knowledge of intervening years, beginning with the many trials (literal and figurative) of Stalinism and continuing through the correlative lessons of fascism and the ensuing Holocaust, the new sense of religious community and *podvizhnichestvo* (heroic conduct) that emerged from the ashes of the Second World War, the philosophy of Christian "personalism" championed by Stefan Schimanski and the young followers of Herbert Read, and, above all, the love affair with Olga Ivinskaya (see Fleishman, *Pasternak*, 211–300). Yet written it was, and Pasternak, as opposed to Mandelstam, needed the patina of a temporal remove in order to turn the lyric diary of *My Sister* into the epic tale of *Zhivago*.

Wallace Stevens once described the poems he was collecting into his first book as "horrid cocoons from which later abortive insects have sprung" (cited in Lipking, *The Life*, 70). The very process of gathering those poems into a book and giving it a name was instructive, however, as were the first two titles lighted on by the poet-entomologist: *The Grand Poem: Preliminary Minutiae* and *Harmonium*. When we compare these titles to the one with which Stevens chose to end his career—*The Whole of Harmonium: Collected Poems of W. S.*—the analogy with Pasternak becomes strikingly clear. To put it simply, the lyrics of *My Sister* are the work of a young "Doctor Life." As many critics have noted, the description of the "morning of the Revolution" in *Zhivago* corresponds neatly with the spirit of the early collection. What is more, an almost identical "narrative" obtains in both books: a love affair with a beautiful woman, responding to seasonal rhythms, is coterminous with "the sea of life, the sea of spontaneity" (Hayward, 124) that surges over everyone between February and October. Indeed, there are certain poems in *My Sister* that anticipate uncannily the *far niente* mood of the lovers (not to speak of actual motifs—e.g., "intoxication") in the Zhivago cycle. Pasternak himself seems to confirm this while reworking a portion of the novel in galley proofs in June and July of 1953: "Such absorption in what I have been doing and in what is happening to me, I have experienced only once before: during the period of *My Sister, Life*. This has been a recurrence of the same creative bliss" (letter of 16 September 1953 to Valentina Zhuravleva, in *Zhuravlev*, 342; cited in Fleishman, *Pasternak*, 258).

More to the point, however, how are the early book and the culminating cycle *different*? First of all, Boris Pasternak's love for Elena Vinograd is—as is his first love of revolution—purely platonic. It is the infatuation of a young man for a "vestal virgin" (vestalka)—or for the notion of "revolution as revelation"; it is all on the surface, in the impressionistic infinitesimals, emotionally "al fresco"; there is no depth to it, no higher perspective, in a word, no genuine or as yet "Christian" suffering. The eroticism, which is here synonymous with remarkable verbal pyrotechnics, is "feigned" on two counts: (1) it has little or no actual basis in reality, and (2) it has no ties to Christ's "passion."[34] Here, for example, the Shakespearean heroines Desdemona and Ophelia go to their deaths in a kind of pantheistic frenzy—

> Дав страсти с плеч отлечь, как рубищу,
> Входили, с сердца замираньем,
> В бассейн вселенной, стан свой любящий
> Обдать и оглушить мирами.
>
> *(1912–1932, 21)*

> Allowing passion to fall from their shoulders like tatters,
> they entered with sinking heart
> the universe's pool to splash and deafen
> their loving figures with worlds.
>
> (my translation)

—while in the Zhivago poems it will be Hamlet, the male character, who repeats the words of Christ in the Garden of Gethsemane. As a Jew speaking for the majority culture at the moment of its awaited rejuvenation, Pasternak was probably sensitive to the tenuousness and ambiguity of his position. Thus, like Mandelstam, he elides the illicit nature of this love (the sibling of the book's title) with the concept of new life, one that would remain with him throughout his career.

By contrast, the love in *Doctor Zhivago* is equally illicit, perhaps more so: the love of a married man for another married woman and, on a higher level, the love of the Son of Man for a simple prostitute:

> На озаренный потолок
> Ложились тени,
> Скрещенья рук, скрещенья ног,
> Судьбы скрещенья.
>
> И падали два башмачка
> Со стуком на пол.
> И воск слезами с ночника
> На платье капал.
>
> И все терялось в снежной мгле
> Седой и белой.
> Свеча горела на столе,
> Свеча горела.
>
> На свечку дуло из угла,
> И жар соблазна

Вздымал, как ангел, два крыла
Крестообразно.

Мело весь месяц в феврале,
И то и дело
Свеча горела на столе,
Свеча горела.

(DZh, 550–551)

Distorted shadows fell
Upon the lighted ceiling:
Shadows of crossed arms, of crossed legs—
Of crossed destiny.

Two tiny shoes fell to the floor
And thudded.
A candle on a nightstand shed wax tears
Upon a dress.

All things vanished within
The snowy murk—white, hoary.
A candle burned on the table;
A candle burned.

A corner draft fluttered the flame
And the white fever of temptation
Upswept its angel wings that cast
A cruciform shadow.

It snowed hard throughout the month
Of February, and almost constantly
A candle burned on the table;
A candle burned.

(Guerney, 445–46)

The cynosure in this love scene has shifted unmistakably—some would say too transparently so—from the breathless celebration of sister life to the solemn reenactment of Christ's passion. Yury's physical lust for Lara—the outline of tangled legs and arms calling up the beast with two backs from *Othello*—is transformed and chastened *through the poetry* into the "cruciform" image of Christ's sacrifice. The ending and beginning known as biological conception (Is this the moment when Yury and Lara conceive their daughter?) becomes a palimpsest revealing the calendar of Holy Week, from the ending of Good Friday (*Strast*naia Piatnitsa) to the beginning of Easter Sunday. And we know all this because of the prose narrative, *the epic framework*, within which the cycle is set and for which it serves as concluding chapter, a kind of revelation or key to *the Book*.

Pasternak, in short, writes himself into a life that, however replete with lapses and false starts, allows this cycle to be its last word—the distilled meaning of destiny, *sud'by skreshcheniia*. The romantic, Mayakovskian "life of the poet," which the youthful Pasternak had discovered to be self-destructive, a kind of fixed mold or "fair copy" no longer susceptible to "revision" (*Safe Conduct*, 116; *Proza 1915–58*, 281), has been re-placed by the life that finds its expression in being "greater than itself."[35] What is fascinating, in the context of Mandelstam's translation of Judaic and Christian codes into the myth of his life, is that Pasternak does some-thing quite analogous, though reversely symmetrical. The "sheepherder and patriarch" of "Fourth Prose" wears the badge of his origins with truculent pride, taking up residence in the crooked byways of "Mandel-stam street." Yury Zhivago, Pasternak's most autobiographical hero, is in name, word and deed the quintessentially *Russian* and *Christian* char-acter, while the source of his inspiration and the object of his outlaw passion is the *foreign-born* Lara Guishar. In effect, the "Pasternak" who speaks through his hero is spared the tug of competing sympathies. He can deflect the issue of Jewishness and destructive nationality onto other characters, especially Gordon; no longer encumbered by a biographical self that can never fully "assimilate," he can make himself over into the native-born Russian.[36] In fact, the pre-Christian Rome that concealed the backward flow of Judaic time in Mandelstam's "Pushkin and Scriabin" appears in curiously similar guise in *Zhivago*: there the author assigns a negative value to any religion that demands monolithic (or monologic) obedience in the name of an abstract throng or *narod* (people), be they Jewish or Soviet, and proposes in place of the ethic of the Roman Coli-seum—in this context the "dead letter" and *carpe diem* philosophy of tsarist Russia as represented by the cynical lawyer Komarovsky—the new era of the free Christian personality as represented by the good doctor (see Bethea, *Shape*, 251–68).

These points are made not to question Pasternak's motives, which Lazar Fleishman has eloquently defended in his most recent book. Nor does one suspect they are particularly relevant to a discussion of the novel proper. They are raised only because they bear on the way the historical author transcribed his life into national epic. No other Russian poet of this century traversed more fully the Virgilian triad of pastoral-georgic-epic, constantly testing himself and his verbal forms (lyric, narrative poem, story, autobiography, novel) in the crucible of his times until at last he came to a work that drew on all his powers (see Lipking, *The Life*, 68–69). There is, finally, something telling in the fact that Mandelstam's and Pasternak's "creative paths" describe a chiasmus, and that Paster-nak's trajectory is from the lodestar of Lermontov to the lodestar of Pushkin, from the exuberance of Futurism to the restraint and *neslykhan-*

naia prostota (unheard-of simplicity)[37] of "Acmeism,"[38] from the youth of *My Sister* to the old age of *Doctor Zhivago*. The "Pasternak" who lived to write the novel was, in the end, governed by the generic expectations of the epos, and in this respect the summing up and resolution, the sublime retrospection, are everything.

Brodsky

In Joseph Brodsky fate has contrived to give us a third piece to the puzzle. Like Mandelstam and Pasternak, he is a Jew writing in the majority culture, and yet that culture can no longer be called "Christian," at least with the same fierce immediacy that it could for the earlier children of symbolism. Everything in Brodsky's case, including the issue of religious faith, is *belated*. As he once confided to an interviewer: "I read the Bible for the first time when I was twenty-three. It leaves me somewhat shepherdless, you see. I wouldn't really know *what to return to*. I don't have any notion of paradise. . . . I went through the severe antireligious schooling in Russia which doesn't leave any kind of notion about afterlife" (Birkerts, "The Art of Poetry," 111; my emphasis). Hence Brodsky has come to the question of Russia's Christian heritage, in every sense, *after the fact*: that heritage had to be acquired through later reading rather than inculcated naturally in youth.[39] What is more, its orphaned status was a metaphor for the Stalinist state at large, where Christianity existed only in its secularized form—"Marxism-Leninism." Brodsky is more aware of his role as autodidact and "posttraditional" outsider than any other poet, perhaps any other writer, of his era. Whereas Mandelstam and Pasternak translated the tensions between Judaism and Christianity into "the essential thought of [their] age" (Lipking, *The Life*, 9) *at the birth* of the Soviet Empire, Brodsky is the poet par excellence *of the death* of that empire and of all that death symbolizes. And for this reason, he is also the master of the *tombeau*, the tomb piece, about which we shall have more to say in a moment.

How does Brodsky's Jewishness enter into the creation of the "poet's life" and poetics? There is, first of all, no mention in his autobiographical writings or interviews of "Judaic chaos," a "Talmudist's syntax" (*Shum vremeni*, SS, 2:67), or of family myths involving august fifteenth-century philosophers descended from the house of David. Instead, the poet reports undramatically: "In 1950, I think, my father was demobilized in accordance with some Politburo ruling that people of Jewish origin should not hold high military rank . . . the fifties were bad years for the Jews" (*Less*, 469).[40] That Brodsky's statement is striking in its flatness is utterly characteristic and shows how unwilling he is, even in this context, to dramatize what was, after all, a banal fact of life. As far as we know, Brodsky is also typical of his generation in that he has never experienced Jewishness as organized religion or even ethnicity; indeed, he rejects outright—not unlike Mandelstam—membership in any group that defines itself by notions of "inclusivity." On the other hand, Brodsky has never denied or repressed the fact of his origins. A close look at the record indicates that an awareness of those origins may have played some role in the evolution of the boy's naturally "self-estranging" consciousness. Here we might recall a previously cited episode (the boy Brodsky lying about the "nationality" blank in his application for membership to the school library) from the memoir "Less Than One":

> I wasn't ashamed of being a Jew, nor was I scared of admitting it. . . . I was ashamed of the word "Jew" itself—in Russian, "*yevrei*"—regardless of its connotations. . . . I remember that I always felt a lot easier with a Russian equivalent of "kike"—"*zhyd*" (pronounced like André Gide): it was clearly offensive and thereby meaningless, not loaded with allusions. . . . All this is not to say that I suffered as a Jew at that tender age; it's simply to say that my first lie had to do with my identity. (*Less*, 7–8)

Note, for example, that the future poet's first conscious contact with anti-Semitism is connected with another kind of membership, this one into the world of books. Note also that, if we are to believe the memoirist, his repugnance is more linguistic (the unseemly sound of the word *evrei*) than personal or psychological. (Actually, it may be hard to accept the fact that this rejection carried *no* pain—"This is not to say that I suffered as a Jew at that tender age"—and that a later, more "stoical" viewpoint is not "touching up" to some extent the picture and thereby privileging, ex post facto, the linguistic reality over the experiential one.) The response to anti-Semitism is to fabricate a lie, a self-conscious estranging of oneself from the norms of society. Thereafter, each time Brodsky mentions the Jewish theme in "Less Than One" it is in the context of *exclusion*: his inability to join the navy because of the "fifth paragraph" (*Less*, 22) or the *arbitrarily cruel punishment* of a Nazi collaborator, a "Gurewicz or Ginzburg," who is denied a last wish ("to take a leak") before execution (*Less*, 19).[41] Such incidents, regardless of the distancing patina, must have had an impact on the boy growing up in Leningrad in the immediate postwar years. They presumably lie at the core of an ambivalence (but *not* necessarily "self-hatred") that rivals Mandelstam's: "Ambivalence, I think, is the chief characteristic of my [Russian] nation" (*Less*, 10). We have only to look here, it seems, for the first signs of Brodsky's perennial exile status, self-imposed and otherwise, his instinctive penchant for "walking out" (*Less*, 13).

And yet it would be a curiously Western, or perhaps even American, distortion to read too much into the links between Brodsky's Jewishness and his métier. As Brodsky recalls, the anti-Semitism he experienced as a child and young adult was ubiquitous and generic: when it occurred, which was often, it was not really aimed at him personally. It was the sort of "background noise" that he and many of his friends recognized but chose not to single out from the surrounding cacophony or acoustic greyness of everyday life in the Soviet Union. Only in a liberal Western democracy, where an individual's rights are protected through elaborate and time-honored legal guarantees, does the distinction between this and other forms of prejudice matter.

I am a Jew one hundred percent—that is my blood. There is no question to me of what I am. But except in the course of my [everyday] life, I thought very little about it, even when I was young. When you are young it is brought to your attention. . . . It was brought to my attention every five minutes, so to speak, in Russia. . . . On the street you experience all forms of anti-Semitism—petty ones. In the street somebody will just sneer at you. I had the misfortune, I still do, of pronouncing *r* and *l* in the slurred [actually, "burred"] manner that betrays a Jew immediately [so-called *kartavost'*].

So it [anti-Semitism] was there. Except I never paid that much attention to it. . . . How should I put it to you? I never was terribly conscious that I was a Jew. Besides, when you grow up in a totally atheistic context, it matters very little to you whether you are a Jew or a Christian. . . . So, in a sense, that helped [one] to be rather oblivious to the, let's say, tradition or history behind [one's] ethnicity. . . .

[Moreover,] as I grew up, I was interested simply in the things that were not immediately, readily available. The Jewish aspect of existence was available and, if I wanted, presumably I could find some ways of illuminating this subject for myself. But it wasn't very interesting because it was available. . . . [But] Christianity, Christian tradition, wasn't available. . . . Not to mention that a far more important thing, that is, Western culture, wasn't available. So, presumably, I concentrated on those things at the expense of my Jewish identity.

But I always believed, and still do, that a man, a human being, should define himself in the first place not in terms of ethnicity, race, religion, philosophical convictions, citizenship, or geographic situation. But first of all one should ask, "Am I a coward?" "Am I a generous man?" "Or am I a liar?" That sort of thing. That is, the information your body does generate to you, to your mind, rather than the external categories that very often simply don't hold. So to me [the fact] of my Jewishness wasn't of very great consequence. In fact, being a Jew became more of a concern, although [still] a small one, when I moved here, where the delineation between Jew and Gentile is put on a very substantial plane of regard.

So the affinity with, if not the ethnos, then at least with its spiritual byproduct, with the Judaic concept of the Supreme Being, makes itself felt in this line of work [i.e., writing poetry] very strongly. I would say that necessarily, by virtue of the métier, one becomes in many ways a Jew, and not only in the sense that you are being ostracized as a consequence. . . . The medium itself brings it home to you. (Interview with author; 28–29 March 1991, South Hadley, Mass.)

This rambling excerpt from a 1991 interview provides fascinating evidence of precisely how belated Brodsky is, and how aware he is of that belatedness. To be sure, he affirms his Jewish heritage, yet simultaneously distances himself from it. Jewishness was "available" to him but Western culture was not, so he gravitated toward the forbidden without a hint of guilt or insecurity. The ethnic-driven anxiety of self-transcendence that inspired Mandelstam and Pasternak to write themselves into a national myth no longer applies, it would seem, to Brodsky. He refuses to be anxious about any categories imposed from outside. Nor is there any suggestion of taboo-breaking or incest. The unease, for example, experienced by Mandelstam at his father's lack of assimilation or the squeamishness shown by Pasternak at his neighbors' too obvious Jewishness is for Brodsky not personalized. Rather, marginalization is a general existential category—the inevitable byproduct of an arbitrary world order.[42] Brodsky appears, therefore, consciously to opt out of the "double bind" of self-hatred analyzed by Gilman. True, he endorses the myth of language and "rel[ies] on [it] for [his] status (and thus [his] power) in society" (Gilman, *Jewish Self-Hatred*, 19). But at no time does he curry favor or seek to ingratiate himself. Why? Because the "belle époque" mythologized by the majority culture is at this late date not worth the price of initiation. "Creative death" is a powerful alternative for a poet, like Mandelstam, writing on the eve of the Revolution. It has no meaning, however, for a poet like Brodsky, except retrospectively, as a way *back into* the culture of Mandelstam and *away from* the culture of the state. Thus, Brodsky can say, appealing to Tsvetaeva, that poets are the "Yids" of society in a way different than his predecessors. Indeed, the poet becomes the last genuine "Yid" in a society that has, ironically, *lost* its Christian roots.

Above all, Brodsky the belated modern seeks reality not so much in people as in books.[43] This is how the outsider forces the majority to remember what it has forgotten:

Somehow, we [Brodsky and his contemporaries] preferred ideas of things to the things themselves. . . . We were avid readers and we fell into a dependence on what we read. Books, perhaps because of their formal element of finality, held us in their absolute power. Dickens was more real than Stalin or Beria. More than anything else, novels would affect our modes of behavior and conversations, and 90 percent of our conversations were about novels. . . . A relationship could have been broken for good over a preference for Hemingway over Faulkner. . . . Nobody knew literature and history better than these people, nobody could write in Russian better than they, nobody despised our times more profoundly. For these characters civilization meant more than daily bread and a nightly hug. This wasn't, as it might seem, another lost generation. This was the only generation of Russians that had found itself, for whom Giotto and Mandelstam were more imperative than their own personal destinies. (*Less*, 27–29)

Books are not a pastime but *life itself*, with models and plots more "true" and more "sacred" than the reality outside. Brodsky raises his eulogistic voice a note higher in these sentences, coming as they do toward the end of "Less Than One," itself a kind of swan song for this generation that experienced the imperative of "Giotto and Mandelstam" more keenly than their own personal destinies and that hid, like monks, in the catacombs of "Hemingway and Faulkner" as the cultural Visigoths carried out their scorched-earth policy on the populace above. In Brodsky we see a reincarnation of the *raznochinets*-intellectual of *The Noise of Time* who must create his own reality through books and who must reinvent a genuine language and tradition to counter the cant of socialist realism.

As suggested earlier, Brodsky is a master of the *tombeau*. No Russian poet of this century has written more elegies, especially to poets who themselves represent a passing of tradition and a marginal status. "Elegies," argues Lipking, "are the heart of literary history, at once a memorial of the past and an attempt to improve upon it or put it to use. . . . Every *tombeau* represents a collaboration between two poets, the dead and the living, and the interests of the two do not necessarily coincide. The dead poet demands tribute, the living must look to his own art" (*The Life*, 138–39). It might even be said that Brodsky *prefers* a dialogue with the dead to a colloquy with the living.[44] He would not subscribe to Lipking's formula that the *tombeau* is an "improvement" on the past; indeed, he would submit the opposite, that his words are effective to the extent that they do not upstage the departed interlocutor and do not draw attention to his, the poet's, present situation. One thinks of the now famous elegies to Donne and Eliot, the lesser known, but equally striking ones to Akhmatova, Auden, and Lowell, as well as a whole series of valedictory pieces to deceased or dying friends, acquaintances, animals, and insects: "Babochka" (The Butterfly), "Mukha" (The Fly), "Na smert' druga" (On the Death of a Friend), "Na smert' Zhukova" (On the Death of Zhukov), "Pamiati Fedi Dobrovol'skogo" (To the Memory of Fedya Dobrovolsky), "Pamiati T. B." (To the Memory of T. B.), "Pamiati Gennadiia Shmakova" (To the Memory of Gennady Shmakov), "Pokhorony Bobo" (Funeral of Bobo). Being a *serdechnik* (one with a heart condition),[45] Brodsky is especially attuned to the rhythmic approach of death, both personally and, as it were, generationally, epochally. Death for him is not an occasional theme but a genuine idée fixe. His books are extended meditations on the nature of life as *metaphysical* border crossing, with all that implies for the spatial and temporal coordinates of his time and people. Writing poetry simply brings this issue of general psychic exile and of the confrontation between words and death into greater focus.

In time Brodsky came to see himself, as had Pushkin and Mandelstam before him, as a modern Ovid banished to a far corner of the empire and, through fate, charged with commenting on the center. The theme of exile is not exclusively, or even primarily, political, however. For example, many of Brodsky's poems about the decline and eclipse of empire— "Ostanovka v pustyne" (A Halt in the Desert), "Pis'ma rimskomu drugu" (Letters to a Roman Friend), "Konets prekrasnoi epokhi" (The End of a Beautiful Epoch), "Post Aetatem Nostram," and so forth—are punctuated by thoughts of an *exsilium* not only on this earth but ultimately from this earth.[46] Furthermore, the very titles of Brodsky's books constantly hint at corners or edges in space (*A Halt in the Desert*), time (*The End of a Beautiful Epoch*), and language (*A Part of Speech*). Brodsky orients himself naturally toward poets of crossroads and of empires stretched to their outer spatial and temporal limits: the West Indian Derek Walcott, the Alexandrian Constantine Cavafy, the Pole (from Wilno) Czeslaw Milosz. As we have seen, he is probably the most traveled Russian poet ever, endlessly searching space for the answers to time and history. Yet unlike Pasternak and Mandelstam, who had to make meaning from a clamorous temporal *transitio* ("old" to "new" Russia), Brodsky has had to incorporate, on a scale unheard of since Nabokov, an actual physical-cum-linguistic *transitio*: from russophone East to anglophone West, from Soviet to American "Empire."[47]

Let us now, in conclusion, make discussion more concrete with reference to one of Brodsky's finest *tombeaus*, "Sreten'e" (Nunc Dimittis). It is, together with "Natiurmort" (Nature morte), his poem about the crucifixion,[48] a fitting late modern companion to the initiation and harmonium pieces, with their Judaeo-Christian dialectic, of Mandelstam and Pasternak:

Когда она в церковь впервые внесла
дитя, находились внутри из числа
людей, находившихся там постоянно,
    Святой Симеон и пророчица Анна.

И старец воспринял младенца из рук
Марии; и три человека вокруг
младенца стояли, как зыбкая рама,
    в то утро, затеряны в сумраке храма.

Тот храм обступал их, как замерший лес.
От взглядов людей и от взоров небес
вершины скрывали, сумев распластаться,
    в то утро Марию, пророчицу, старца.

И только на темя случайным лучом
свет падал младенцу; но он ни о чем
не ведал еще и посапывал сонно,
    покоясь на крепких руках Симеона.

А было поведано старцу сему
о том, что увидит он смертную тьму
не прежде, чем Сына увидит Господня.
    Свершилось. И старец промолвил: "Сегодня,

реченное некогда слово храня,
Ты с миром, Господь, отпускаешь меня,
затем что глаза мои видели это
    дитя: он—твое продолженье и света

источник для идолов чтящих племен,
и слава Израиля в нем."—Симеон
умолкнул. Их всех тишина обступила.
    Лишь эхо тех слов, задевая стропила,

кружилось какое-то время спустя
над их головами, слегка шелестя
под сводами храма, как некая птица,
    что в силах взлететь, но не в силах спуститься.

И странно им было. Была тишина
не менее странной, чем речь. Смущена,
Мария молчала. "Слова-то какие . . ."
    И старец сказал, повернувшись к Марии:

"В лежащем сейчас на раменах твоих
паденье одних, возвышенье других,
предмет пререканий и повод к раздорам.
    И тем же оружьем, Мария, которым

терзаема плоть его будет, твоя
душа будет ранена. Рана сия
даст видеть тебе, что сокрыто глубоко
    в сердцах человеков, как некое око."

Он кончил и двинулся к выходу. Вслед
Мария, сутулясь, и тяжестью лет

согбенная Анна безмолвно глядели.
  Он шел, уменьшаясь в значеньи и в теле

для двух этих женщин под сенью колонн.
Почти подгоняем их взглядами, он
шел молча по этому храму пустому
  к белевшему смутно дверному проему.

И поступь была стариковски тверда.
Лишь голос пророчицы сзади когда
раздался, он шаг придержал свой немного:
  но там не его окликали, а Бога

пророчица славить уже начала.
И дверь приближалась. Одежд и чела
уж ветер коснулся, и в уши упрямо
  врывался шум жизни за стенами храма.

Он шел умирать. И не в уличный гул
он, дверь отворивши руками, шагнул,
но в глухонемые владения смерти.
  Он шел по пространству, лишенному тверди,

он слышал, что время утратило звук.
И образ младенца с сияньем вокруг
пушистого темени смертной тропою
  душа Симеона несла пред собою,

как некий светильник, в ту черную тьму,
в которой дотоле еще никому
дорогу себе озарять не случалось.
  Светильник светил, и тропа расширялась.

                                                                              (*ChR*, 20–22)

When Mary first came to present the Christ Child
to God in His temple, she found—of those few
who fasted and prayed there, departing not from it—
    devout Simeon and the prophetess Anna.

The holy man took the Babe up in his arms.
The three of them, lost in the grayness of dawn,
now stood like a small shifting frame that surrounded
    the Child in the palpable dark of the temple.

The temple enclosed them in forests of stone.
Its lofty vaults stooped as though trying to cloak
the prophetess Anna, and Simeon, and Mary—
    to hide them from men and to hide them from Heaven.

And only a chance ray of light struck the hair
of that sleeping Infant, who stirred but as yet
was conscious of nothing and blew drowsy bubbles;
    old Simeon's arms held him like a stout cradle.

It had been revealed to this upright old man
that he would not die until his eyes had seen
the Son of the Lord. And it thus came to pass. And
    he said: 'Now, o Lord, lettest thou thy poor servant,

according to thy holy word, leave in peace,
for mine eyes have witnessed thine offspring, this Child—
in him thy salvation, which thou hast made ready,
    a light to enlighten the face of all peoples

and carry thy truths to idolatrous tribes;
bring Israel, thy people, its Glory in time.'
Then Simeon paused. A thick silence engulfed them,
    and only his echoing words grazed the rafters,

to spin for a moment, with faint rustling sounds,
high over their heads in the tall temple's vaults,
like some soaring bird that flies constantly upward
    and somehow is caught and cannot return earthward.

A strangeness engulfed them. The silence now seemed
as strange and uncanny as Simeon's speech.
And Mary, confused and bewildered, said nothing—
    so strange had his words been. The holy man, turning

to Mary, continued: 'Behold, in this Child,
now close to thy breast, is concealed the great fall
and rising again of the many in Israel;
    a source of dissension, a sign to be spoken

against. The same weapon which tears at his flesh
shall pierce through thine own soul as well.
Thy wound, Mary, like a new eye, will reveal to
    thy sight what in men's deepest hearts now lies hidden.'

He ended and moved toward the temple's great door.
Old Anna, bent down with the weight of her years,
and Mary, gazed after him, perfect in silence.
    He moved and grew smaller, in size and in meaning,

to these two frail women who stood in the gloom.
As though driven on by the force of their looks,
he strode through the cold empty space of the temple
    and moved toward the whitening blur of the doorway.

The stride of his old legs was audibly firm.
He slowed his step slightly when Anna began
to speak, far behind him. But she was not calling
        to him; she had started to bless God and praise Him.

The door came still closer. The wind stirred his robe
and touched his cool brow, while the roar of the street,
exploding in life by the door of the temple,
        beat stubbornly into old Simeon's hearing.

He went forth to die. It was not the loud din
of streets that he faced when he flung the door wide,
but rather the deaf-and-dumb fields of death's kingdom.
        He strode through a space that was no longer solid.

The roaring of time ebbed away in his ears.
And Simeon's soul held the form of the Child—
its feathery crown now enveloped in glory—
        aloft, like a torch, pressing back the black shadows,

to light up the path that leads into death's realm,
where never before until this present hour
had any man managed to lighten his pathway.
        The old man's torch glowed and the pathway grew wider.

                                        (*Part*, 55–57)

This poem, like the *zybkaia rama* (shifting frame) of historical forces that it describes, seems almost to shimmer and pulsate with its various beginnings and endings. It was written on the eve of Brodsky's exile to the West, a fact underscored both by its dating and by its subsequent placement in *A Part of Speech* immediately before "Odissei Telemaku" (Odysseus to Telemachus), Brodsky's moving farewell to his son Andrei (one recalls the Yehuda Abravanel connection in Pasternak). Brodsky is quite conscious of the structure of his books, of how their "stories" intermesh with the unfolding of the "life of the poet." To cite only the most obvious example, he begins three of his collections, *Ostanovka v pustyne* (A Halt in the Desert, 1970), *Konets prekrasnoi epokhi* (The End of a Beautiful Epoch, 1977), and *Chast' rechi* (A Part of Speech, 1977), with Christmas poems that examine the speaker's attitude toward this venerable *initium a quo*: "Rozhdestvenskii romans" (Christmas Romance), "Vtoroe Rozhdestvo na beregu" (The Second Christmas on the Shore), and "24 dekabria 1971 goda" (24 December 1971).[49] This poem, too, is such a turning point: the presentation of the Christ Child at the temple may be read as the presentation of the poet at the shrine of his Judaeo-Christian ideals before embarking on the new time, and new ordeals, of life "outside" and "beyond."

"The *tombeau*," Lipking tells us, "[characteristically] incorporates many reminiscences of the poet it memorializes—style, verse forms, images, specific lines—and it may even try, eerily, to impersonate his voice" (*The Life*, 140). This is precisely what Brodsky's poem does. Written between January and March 1972, "Nunc Dimittis" was originally dated 16 February 1972, that is, the Feast Day of Saints Simeon and Anna (Steckler, "The Poetic Word," 55): Brodsky clearly wanted to draw attention to this Russian Anna, who, in the verses of Luke (2:36–38), "was of great age . . . [and] did not depart from the temple, worshiping with fasting and prayer night and day." It was Akhmatova's constancy ("nakhodivsh[aia]sia tam *postoianno*"), her desire to remain in Russia (here the temple) at all costs and to be with her people in their hour of need, that the poet chooses to celebrate at the time of his own ordeal.[50] Yet written for the sixth anniversary of Akhmatova's death (5 March 1966), "Nunc Dimittis" is also a tomb piece, and that may be why Brodsky placed a more general "March 1972" in the actual publication of *A Part of Speech* in 1977. Either way, he takes on, in a solemn stylization, the voice of the "prophetess" whom this poem commemorates: the amphibrachic tetrameter is relatively rare for Brodsky and functions to "impersonate" the Akhmatova of such biblical poems as "Rakhil'" (Rachel), "Lotova zhena" (Lot's Wife), "Melkhola" (Michal), and especially the famous concluding poem of *Requiem* "Opiat' pominal'nyi priblizilsia chas" (Again the memorial hour has approached) (Steckler, "The Poetic Word," 57).[51]

Yet "Nunc Dimittis" is by no means a simple *tombeau*, or two-dimensional dialogue between the departed Akhmatova and the departing Brodsky, although that, to be sure, is its primary level of interpretation. Rather, it contains a complex and multilayered "life of the poet" that shows Brodsky aware of "destiny" and, by 1972, the rightful heir to Mandelstam. Akhmatova may be present as the "prophetess Anna"[52] but her more important role, the one confirmed by her later and greatest work, is the Suffering Mother, Mary herself. It is she who joined with Nadezhda Mandelstam in conferring on Brodsky the honorary hypocoristic of "second Osya," thereby reinforcing her function as intermediary, as last link with a glorious Silver Age past, as *the one who survives* until a new martyred son figure can be born. She is Brodsky's beloved poetic parent (recall that he used to visit Akhmatova's grave twice a year, on the anniversary of her death and on her nameday), and he is burying her with the familiar rhythms of these lines just as surely as Mandelstam had buried his own mother in "This night cannot be undone." So "Nunc Dimittis" is most basically a poem about parentage.

In addition, however, and here the dialogue at the tomb bursts into a kind of symposium or round table, Brodsky's interlocutor is Mandelstam, the crucified son who died two years before the younger poet was born. As soon becomes obvious, there is no Joseph, no mortal father, in this picture of the *Nunc Dimittis*. The reasons are several, each fraught with implications for Brodsky's emerging biographical legend. First, it is unseemly to mention, what is more to foreground oneself, in a poem about someone else: as Brodsky once remarked about the Akhmatova of *Requiem*: "[D]eath is a good litmus test for a poet's ethics. The 'in memoriam' genre is frequently used to exercise self-pity or for metaphysical trips that denote the subconscious superiority of survivor over victim, of majority (of the alive) over minority (of the dead). Akhmatova would have none of that" (*Less*, 50). Thus Brodsky has no wish in a poem honoring Akhmatova to stress his unearned "superiority." Second, and no less significant, "Joseph" is not present because his first namesake, Brodsky's *other* parent figure, has already departed and hence cannot be there, and because his second namesake, that is, Brodsky himself, is soon to depart into the metaphorical death of exile. It is quite characteristic of Brodsky that he says all this *without mentioning a name*. His mature poetics, especially after emigration, are relentlessly oriented toward *absence*, toward a reduction of the historical Brodsky to a disembodied speaking voice.[53] In "Nunc Dimittis," we might say, Brodsky is becoming himself, and embracing his destiny, by absenting himself; "he" is the minuend that remains after the subtraction of the last subtrahend—one of those mathematical formulas for the "whittling away" (*vychitanie*) of existence so dear to Brodsky. Hence to the reminiscences from Akhmatova we can add several motifs from Mandelstam: this temple where the Christ Child is being presented recalls the cavernous womb, *forest*like (cf. "zamershii *les*" and "nepostizhimyi *les*") and flexing its architectural muscles (cf. *rasplastat'sia* and "*rasplastyvaia* nervy"), of "Notre Dame" (*Our Mother*!), where the Acmeist first and second Adam was born.[54]

It is a cardinal requirement of the *tombeau* that it open up new possibilities for the succeeding poet just as it sums up past glories for the poet(s) who has departed. To return to the question with which we began this chapter, how does this particular poem show us "Brodsky," the future laureate and principal voice for the Russian poetic tradition in exile? How does the role entered into here guarantee *avant la lettre* the fate of the subsequent books and the "life" they narrate? The answer lies in the poem's perspective; it is here that we must look for the relationship between poetic "voice" (the words themselves) and what Brodsky calls poetic "vector" (the self projecting the words). What is crucial, then, in this verbal picture (the poem almost has an *iconic* quality to it) of crossing—from Old to New Testament, from life at home to life abroad, from a Russian- to English-speaking world, from literary parents to children—is that *Brodsky is nowhere and he is everywhere*. He is of course the Child himself, the new word for which the "prophetess Anna" has so long waited. As he prepares to go into exile, he is supremely aware that his flesh, at least figuratively, "will be tortured" ("terzaema plot' ego budet"). But he is also the *nekaia ptitsa* (a certain bird), the spirit of flight, perhaps the Dove (or the Mandelstamian swallow?), that has lost its ability to descend and that echoes the soaring soul of John Donne and anticipates the attenuated thoughts of the autumn hawk.

Last but not least, however, he is the righteous old man himself, who "should not see death before he had seen the Lord's Christ" (Luke, 2:26) and who personally announces *the old which remains in the new*: "on— tvoe prodolzhen'e i sveta / istochnik dlia idolov chtiashchikh plemen, / *i slava Izrailia v nem*." Simeon passes through the doorway (Brodsky's ubiquitous *limen*) into the "deaf-and-dumb" realm of death (his greatest theme) as a lone voice (his "words" are all the poet wishes to be remembered for), led only by the lamplight of his soul (a Pasternakian motif). Few poets (perhaps only Emily Dickinson?) have had a more fervent desire to equate the myths of their lives with a *vanishing act*, with a diminution "in size and significance" to a point of absolute zero—the perfect pitch of the Christian cenotaph, the *tombeau* without a body. For what is resurrected out of the maw of death is not the poet but the poetic tradition itself. This, and nothing less, is Simeon-Brodsky's life as he "goes on his way to die."

"This Sex Which Is Not One"
versus This Poet Which Is "Less Than One":
Tsvetaeva, Brodsky, and
Exilic Desire

Ах, вы не братья, нет, не братья!
Пришли из тьмы, ушли в туман . . .
Для нас безумные объятия
Еще неведомый дурман.

Пока вы рядом—смех и шутки,
но чуть умолкнули шаги,
Уж ваши речи странно-жутки,
И чует сердце: вы враги.

Oh, you're not brothers, no, not brothers!
You came from darkness, you depart into mist . . .
Wild embraces are for us
Still an unknown spell.

While you're close, we hear laughter and jokes,
But as soon as your footfall dies away,
Your words seem strangely eerie
And the heart senses that you are enemies.
   (Marina Tsvetaeva, "To the Other Camp")

Жить в зпоху свершений, имея возвышенный нрав,
к сожалению, трудно. Красавице платье задрав,
видишь то, что искал, а не новые дивные дивы.

To exist in the Era of Deeds and to stay elevated, alert
ain't so easy, alas. Having raised a long skirt,
you will find not new wonders but what you expected.
   (Joseph Brodsky, "The End of a Beautiful Epoch")

Eros and language mesh at every point. Intercourse and
discourse, copula and copulation, are subclasses of the
dominant fact of communication. They arise from the life-
need of the ego to reach out and comprehend, in the two
vital senses of "understanding" and "containment,"

another human being. Sex is a profoundly semantic act. Like
language, it is subject to the shaping force of social convention, rules of proceeding, and accumulated precedent. To
speak and to make love is to enact a distinctive twofold
universality: both forms of communication are universals of
human physiology as well as of social evolution. It is likely
that human sexuality and speech developed in close-knit
reciprocity. Together they generate the history of self-consciousness, the process, presumably millenary and marked
by innumerable regressions, whereby we have hammered
out the notion of self and otherness. . . . The seminal and the
semantic functions (is there, ultimately, an etymological
link?) determine the genetic and social structure of human
experience. Together they construe the grammar of being.
  (George Steiner, *After Babel*)

To judge by the essays in *Less Than One*, as well as by other statements
in and out of print, no other Russian poet is closer to Joseph Brodsky, to
his self-image as *izgoi* (outcast), and indeed to his entire creative enterprise than Marina Tsvetaeva (1892–1941). The only other writer to occupy an equivalent place in his thinking is not Russian—W. H. Auden.
This is of some importance, particularly when we realize that the remarkable kinship between Tsvetaeva and Brodsky has been little attended to
and that Brodsky himself has played a not insignificant role in the rees-
tablishment of Tsvetaeva's elevated position on the modern Russian Par-
nassus. Tsvetaeva's linguistic maximalism, her fierce independence of
mind and willingness, at all costs, to swim upstream against the powerful
currents of politics and literary convention, and, to rephrase Mayakovsky's most famous line, her tragic ability (need?) to step on the throat of
her life in order to clear the throat of her song all speak powerfully to
Brodsky. Tsvetaeva also happens to be a woman and, not a casual association in this instance, an exile. This difference (gender) within sameness
(exile status) is both the subject of this chapter and yet another useful
means of defining, through contrast and juxtaposition, what Brodsky is
and, no less important, what he is not.
  The reader should be aware that Brodsky himself would probably not
make gender a, or much less *the*, defining characteristic of Tsvetaeva's
genius, a genius that in any event he would relate to her language and its
prosodic resources and inventiveness rather than to an accident of birth.
Brodsky has little patience for psychoanalytic criticism for the same reasons that Nabokov, with characteristic tetchiness, dismissed the intru-

sions of the "Viennese delegation": it (psychoanalysis) is yet another form of discourse, in a world already well represented by totalitarian and "totalizing" speech acts, that wrests control (and responsibility and freedom) from the author. In a contemporary academic setting where we can now contemplate the demise of the "subject," writers such as Nabokov and Brodsky respond with the most compelling evidence to the contrary— imaginative literature that could only have been written by them, by their unique, historically real, and unreplicatable "subjectivities." Still, as recent work has demonstrated, an accident of birth (gender) and a linguistic code (poetry) are not mutually independent, and in fact Tsvetaeva's personal mythology is constantly implicated in the forms and organizing principles of her poetic oeuvre. One of the most vexed and pressing issues of modern thought in general is how, or even whether, a free subject can exist within the layers of deep structure imputed to our unconscious drives and urges.

Brodsky himself has called Tsvetaeva a "Job in skirts," which means that her role as the tradition's righteous patriarch persecuted by an arbitrary God must be immediately qualified in his mind by the "in skirts," by the fact of her gender. "What art and sexuality have in common," writes Brodsky in his essay on Akhmatova ("The Keening Muse"), "is that both are sublimations of one's creative energy, and that denies them hierarchy" (*Less*, 45). Yet to call Tsvetaeva by some other, preferably "matrilineal" biblical name (Rachel? Lilith? Sarah?) simply will not do, for it is precisely Job that she is, but a Job *in skirts*. This confusion lies at the core of Tsvetaeva's poetic power, as well as her real-life tragedy. By understanding Tsvetaeva's emotional "acceleration" (Brodsky's term) we can better understand Brodsky's ratiocinative or metaphysical "acceleration," since both are deeply held aesthetic responses to real-life situations of exile. These poets' maximalisms[1] are, I will argue, alike but different, just as their personal mythologies, their enacted "lives of the poet," are alike but different. Let us begin with an examination of how the categories of exile, gender, and language interact in Tsvetaeva's poetic world, and then, using this as background, proceed to a closer study of Brodsky and his presentation of desire in, and as, exile.

"Poets are Yids," exclaims Tsvetaeva in one of her most famous lines ("Poema kontsa," *SiP*, 4:185). They are battling and embattled, isolating and isolated, *by definition*. If we see them only as victims, which they can be, then we do not see them whole, for they would choose to be "Yids" even if we called them otherwise. Does this mean that they do not experience real pain, that authoritarian institutions and governments do not ostracize, brutalize, and persecute them? No. It simply means that they, à la the Underground Man, refuse to be "decoded." Any master grid can assert that an analogy exists between the "family romance" in early child-hood development and the demons of desire in their art, but it cannot, however subtle, "explain" them. "$2 \times 2 = 5$" counters the Underground Man, in response to the plot that would make sense of his originary urges. The space between what Julia Kristeva terms the *semiotic* and *symbolic* orders cannot be broached except by "transference," by metaphoric lan-guage itself, which is to say that it can be decoded after the fact, but never *encoded* avant la lettre. It is not replicatable. "The work of art," remarks Kristeva in a recent interview, "cuts off natural filiation, it is patricide and matricide, it is superbly solitary" ("Entretien avec Julia Kristeva," *Le Cahiers du Grif*, 32:23). And Brodsky acknowledges something similar but in completely different language, when he states that as an artistic maximalist he "is trying to see how inhuman you can become and still remain a human being" ("The Acceleration of the Poet," 4).

There is no single entry, no grandly carved and cynosural portal, into the Gothic cathedral novel of Marina Tsvetaeva's life and art. Each door (prosody, syntax, strophic design, genre, poetic myth) leads into a cav-ernous nave of spiritual and metaphysical soaring, of sheer drops at stro-boscopic speed and agonizingly ulterior perspectives, unparalleled in Russian poetry. Yet such soaring comes at the existential cost of its oppo-site—the inevitable gravitational pull, the fall and crash, the fact that, in relations with others, Tsvetaeva was a female Quasimodo or, as one might say today, a mad woman in the attic. Over the image of the maiden who would prefer to wield male weapons of war and who has no interest in rocking cradles in *The Magic Lantern* (Volshebnyi fonar', 1912) looms that of the aging mother and outflanked poet who, worn out by battle, falls on her figurative sword in Elabuga. The entire edifice of Tsvetaeva's creative world is built on a foundation of romantic confrontation and transgression,[2] impossibly high standards, nostalgia for the heroism of bygone days, pity for the underdog, and a fervent conviction bordering at times on white-hot passion that relationships between souls and words must settle for nothing less than total, incinerating integration. Tsvetaeva never occupies a middle ground, nor does she allow her interlocutor to. Like Mayakovsky, with whom she shares several traits, Tsvetaeva "need[s] intensity at any cost" (Feiler, *Double Beat*, viii). In her art this intensity eventuated in some of the most piercing, unexpected, and vital poetry ever written, by man *or* woman; in her life it often resulted in behavior that was "monstrous" not only because threatened males said it was so but because it transgressed any acceptable standards of *human* behavior. To transgress in art can be exhilarating and liberating; to trans-gress in life, as Tsvetaeva sometimes did, can be tragic, because both one-self and others can be trampled in the process.[3]

It is intriguing to look for the sources of Tsvetaeva's maximalism in her family history, for the outline of a profoundly confrontational nature can indeed be found there:

> Mother's youth, like her childhood, was lonely, painful, rebellious, deeply introverted. . . . She had a passion for music and enormous talent (never again do I expect to hear anyone play the piano and the guitar as she did), a gift for languages, a brilliant memory, and magnificent written style, wrote poetry in Russian and German, painted. . . . When she was twenty-two Mother married Father, with the express intention of replacing the mother of his orphaned children—Valeria, who was eight, and Andrei, who was one. Father was then forty-four years old. She loved him without reservation, but the first two years of marriage were filled with torment about his continuing love for his [first wife] V. D. Ilovaiskaya. "We were wed at the grave," Mother wrote in her diary. . . . There was much grief. Mother and Father were totally unlike each other. Each had his own heartache. Mother's was music, poetry, yearning; Father's was scholarship. Their lives moved side by side without merging. But they loved each other very much. Mother died [in 1906] at the age of thirty-seven, discontented, unreconciled. . . . Her tormented soul lives on in us [the daughters Marina and Anastasia], but we reveal what she concealed. Her rebellion, her madness, her longing have grown in us to a scream. (Bakhrakh, "Pis'ma Mariny Tsvetaevoi," 329)

Various biographies of the poet support the claim that the child Marina had to contend with the presence of a powerful and high-strung mother who deeply—but never "simply"—loved her children, who sacrificed her own considerable artistic talents on the altar of "family," and who suffered from an arid relationship with her husband ("an alliance of loneliness" [Efron, *Stranitsy*, 17]), himself a distant older man more married to his dreams of opening an art museum suitable for housing Moscow University's collection of ancient sculpture than to his wife or family.

Maria Alexandrovna Mein-Tsvetaeva passed on her values and emotional register to her daughters, including her contempt for philistine self-aggrandizement and her commitment to "Heroica," but along the way her ennui and languid frustration metamorphosed, in the older daughter, into open revolt ("her longing [has] grown in us to a scream"). In addition, she created a perpetual need for parental love and approval in Marina by withdrawing her affections (especially when Marina's own piano playing was felt wanting) and by favoring the younger and more attractive Asya (Tsvetaeva, *Sochineniia*, [1980] 2:496). When Maria Alexandrovna died prematurely, from consumption, coalescing in the children's minds with the heroines of nineteenth-century novels that had been her lifelong companions and exemplars, her "presence" became even more haunting for her daughter. She was, we might say, the morbid "angel in the house" of Victorian mythology, the one Virginia Woolf felt she had to kill in herself before an authentic self could be born (*The Death of the Moth*, 236–38; cited in Gilbert and Gubar, *Madwoman*, 17). She wore "the face of the spiritualized Victorian woman who, having died to her own desires, her own self, her own life, leads a posthumous existence in her own lifetime" (Gilbert and Gubar, *Madwoman* 25). After death her lineaments congealed into a kind of originary myth: Marina would become what Maria Alexandrovna, because of a despotic father, could not. She would have the artistic career that grandfather A. D. Mein forbade his only daughter; she would have the "illicit" romances denied her mother out of propriety and parental control (the one great love of Maria Alexandrovna's life, which the father again placed his ironclad prohibition on, was with a married man); she would, like her Amazonian Tsar-Maiden, live out her mother's bookish dreams "beyond the law" (bezzakonitsei). In answer to a biographical questionnaire distributed to émigré writers in 1926, Tsvetaeva wrote tellingly: "The dominant influence [in my life] is my mother (music, nature, verse, Germany). A passion for heroism. One against all. Heroica" (cited in Shveitser, *Byt*, 18).

One potentially productive means of reading Tsvetaeva, therefore, is to "historicize" this role conflict and to transpose it onto her poetry (to go *from* life *to* work), much the way that Gilbert and Gubar have done in *The Mad Woman in the Attic* (and their later work) and that Antonina Gove has done in her pioneering early article ("The Feminine Stereotype"). Tsvetaeva's famous role reversals, her sympathy for the Amazonian warrior, her predilection for "weak" and tractable men (beginning with her husband Sergey Efron), her simultaneous use and "abuse" of traditional literary sources (folklore, Shakespeare), her urge to speak for those heroines silenced or fetishized by the stereotypes of male-dominated ("phallocentric"[4]) discourse (Ophelia, Phaedra, Ariadne), her transgression of societal taboos (homosexuality) all lend themselves to the sort of revisionist reading first advocated by Adrienne Rich in her celebrated 1971 essay "When We Dead Awaken: Writing as Re-Vision" (in *Adrienne Rich's Poetry*, 90–98). Tsvetaeva emerges from such feminist emplotment as a kind of Russian H. D. Her exile is not only from her provincial homeland to a European center but from "patriarchy" to "matriarchy";[5] her *The Tsar-Maiden* (Tsar'-Devitsa) and *The Swain* (Molodets) are poetic (folk-inspired) reinventions of sexual relations, just as H. D.'s *Helen in Egypt* is; her father and brother figures (Blok, Vyacheslav Ivanov, Mandelstam, Pasternak) provide points of departure to be incorporated but also to be overcome, polemicized with, and "rewritten," just as Pound and Williams do for H. D. Although their cultural backgrounds were fundamentally different, both H. D. and Tsvetaeva felt "separated from the separated" in such European enclaves as London, Prague, and Paris (*Paint It To-Day*, 456–57; cited in Stanford Friedman, "Exile," 95).[6]

For the sake of experiment, let us take two "moments," one from Tsvetaeva's poetry and one from her life of the same period, and examine them according to the logic of feminist emplotment.[7] As part of the experiment we will reverse the usual order of critical analysis ("close reading"), that is, we will proceed not from the life to the work but from the work to the life. Not only will this help us to resist the tendency, especially powerful in the Russian context, to mythologize the poet-martyr who has overcome "life," it may clarify the borders, too often crossed unconsciously (the "night raids" of desire), between *Wahrheit* and *Dichtung*. The war between the sexes is, to be sure, a struggle over bodies. Yet perhaps equally it is a struggle for and about metaphors.

First, the text. "On the Red Steed" (Na krasnom kone) was written in January 1921 in Moscow, one of a number of Tsvetaeva's works that uses the New Year, and the potential new life springing therefrom, as implicit point of departure. The poem is a telescopic variation on the quest narrative, with the Rider on the Red Steed posing several "challenges" to the lyrical hero so that she, by overcoming them, can become an authentic self. As Karlinsky states, it "is basically a personal and lyrical work, although, alone among Cvetaeva's lyrical *poemy*, it shows marked features of [Russian] epic poetry and folk tradition" (*Cvetaeva*, 208). In addition, with its emphasis on overcoming the biological imperative of gender and on accepting one's fate as a "strong woman," "On the Red Steed" shares certain thematic links with the nearly contemporaneous *The Tsar-Maiden* (Tsar'-Devitsa, 1920), a poem (*poema-skazka*) based on an actual fairy tale collected by Afanasiev. One ostensible motivation for writing the poem was Tsvetaeva's unrequited infatuation for the poet Evgeny Lann, who had recently (November 1920) arrived in Moscow with greetings from Tsvetaeva's sister Asya. Not uncharacteristically, Tsvetaeva responded to Lann's lack of response by experiencing a "huge creative upsurge" ("Pis'ma k Lannu," 167) that served, in turn, to liberate her from him.[8]

Tsvetaeva opens the poem with a transgressive knight's move, an invocation to a tutelary spirit that is decidedly not the Muse of male poetic tradition. Her remarkable ability to summon a presence by describing its absence, *what it is not*,[9] is a quality that will become, mutatis mutandis, crucial to Brodsky's poetics:

Не Муза, не Муза
Над бедною люлькой
Мне пела, за ручку водила.
Не Муза холодные руки мне грела,

Горячие веки студила.
Вихор ото лба отводила—не Муза,
В большие поля уводила—не Муза.

Не Муза, не черные косы, не бусы,
Не басни,—всего два крыла светлорусых
—Коротких—над бровью крылатой.
Стан в латах.
Султан.

К устам не клонился,
На сон не крестил.
О сломанной кукле
Со мной не грустил.
Всех птиц моих—на свободу
Пускал—и потом—не жалея шпор,
На красном коне—промеж синих гор
Гремящего ледохода!

(*SiP*, 4:155)

(It was) not the Muse, not the Muse
(who) over the poor cradle
has sung to me, has led me by the hand.
(It was) not the Muse (who) has warmed my cold hands,
cooled my hot eyelids,
Nor (was it) the Muse (who) brushed the forelock from my brow
and led me away into the broad fields.

(It was) neither the Muse, nor black braids, nor beads,
nor fables, (but) only two blond wings—
short ones—above the arched brow.
(It was) a figure in armor.
(It was) a plume.

It did not bend down to my lips,
nor did it not make the sign of the cross at bedtime.
It did not grieve along with me
over my broken doll.
It released all my birds
and then, not sparing the spurs,
(it set off) on a red steed between blue mountains
of thundering ice-floe.

(my translation)

The Muse of course has a long history of inspiring poets, of being the female occasion for male ventriloquists to project onto, or into.[10] Tsvetaeva links this tradition with the "female" attributes of domesticity, the nursery, lullabies and fairy tales, good-night kisses, support and care during times of illness (the feverish eyelids), and decorative attire (braids, beads). In one sense this is a return to and stock-taking of the sheltered self of *The Magic Lantern*. It may also be an allusion to the more "feminine" poetics of Anna Akhmatova, the poem's original dedicatee, who had a reputation for writing about the Muse and who was Tsvetaeva's chief rival and foil in the modern period (Karlinsky, *Cvetaeva*, 210).[11] But the point is that Tsvetaeva mentions these attributes in order to get past them: they do not add up to her "inspiration."

What drives Tsvetaeva to write this poem is the Rider on the Red Steed, the "male" in herself that is not given voice within the confines of feminine stereotypes.[12] His attributes are all demonstrably "masculine": he is a "figure in armor," where *stan* is masculine in gender (*Muza* of course is feminine) and *laty* and *sultan* imply someone or something whose essence is cold, withdrawn, protected, commanding, chivalric, and noble (Tsvetaeva's "Heroica"). This horseman does *not* kiss the speaker at bedtime or ward away the evil one, nor does he concern himself with broken dolls and fading childhoods. Instead he frees the birds of domesticity and then spurs on his steed (male domination "in the saddle") to ever greater heights and wide-open spaces. Tsvetaeva's use of dashes is an important cue for the Rider: they provide the "acceleration," the sense of space and time to be leapt over at a single bound and therefore, as it were, "left out" (grammatical ellipsis). What the Rider does not do is verbalized (he does not make the sign of the cross, etc.), but what he does do on his horse after he applies the spurs the reader must guess—he *gallops* into the mountainside. It could be argued that Tsvetaeva's "compressive" dash, as opposed to Emily Dickinson's, is not intended to shield a "reclusive, emotionally vulnerable personality" through its multivalent implications of "privacy, camouflage and indirection" (Kammer, "The Art of Silence," 156). Rather, its function is precisely the opposite—to expose that vulnerability and to confront it in a merciless, martial duel fraught with a "masculine" language of aggression/transgression.[13]

Which brings us to the issue of poetic form. On the one hand, prosody would seem to be "logocentric" or even "phallogocentric" (Derrida) by definition. That is, the very notion of the interrelation of meter, rhyme, strophic form, and genre imply a rule-centered approach to artistic creation. And, to be sure, the poetics of such literary legislators as Boileau, Trediakovsky, and Lomonosov are, prima facie, prescriptive, rigorously hierarchical, "classical." On the other hand, the transgressing of these rules (without of course completely abandoning them) lies at the very heart of artistic "pleasure," as only Tsvetaeva knew. By the period of *Craft* (Remeslo, wr. 1921–22), one of the great collections in the modern Russian tradition and the last book Tsvetaeva wrote prior to emigration, we find a mature poet willing to experiment with traditional meters, to mix them within individual lines (so-called logaoedic verse) or within sections of poems. "On the Red Steed," for instance, is remarkably rich in its metrical profile, blending choriambic-, iambic-, and amphibrachic-based meters in lines of varying lengths (Karlinsky, *Cvetaeva*, 211). The amphibrachs of the opening strophe, all of which are realized, may suggest the smooth, rocking rhythms of the nursery and *liul'ka* (cradle):

Не Муза, не Муза
Над бедною люлькой
Мне пела, за ручку водила.

But having introduced this regularity, Tsvetaeva quickly intrudes upon it with the same dash that she uses to imply grammatical ellipsis. This visual device, which should not affect the meter of a given line, forces us to read (aloud) that line in a certain way.[14] It is a "spontaneous," "oral" stimulus to the written word. Moreover, the dash's function on the rhythmic level turns out to be parallel to its function on the grammatical level. In the last four lines of the third strophe, it *breaks into* the smooth flow of the amphibrachs, announcing that the Rider is present not only in his "verblessness" but also in his slipping of syllables, his "syncopated rhythm."

Всех птиц моих—на свободу
Пускал—и потом—не жалея шпор,
На красном коне—промеж синих гор
Гремящего ледохода!

Again, the result is not less, but *more* energy.[15]

In the *Psyche* (Psikheia, 1923) edition of the poem the lyrical speaker must overcome three challenges before she can be worthy of her male "genius" (moi genii). (In a reversal of fairy-tale logic, the prize for "success" is not the maiden but, as it were, the mythopoeticizing "swain.") Each of these is a harrowing confrontation with a gender role that ties her to "life" (as opposed to "art"). The first is with the child in her, the second is with the romantic lover in her, and the third is with the mother in her. The dream-episodes are all analogous in that: (1) each creates an elemental crisis situation wherein some fatal choice must be made (a fire raging through the home, a bridge over a river torrent, a whirlwind in a sheer mountain pass); (2) the "objective correlative" for this choice is what the speaker is being asked to *give up* for her art (doll, lover, child); (3) each time the all-powerful Rider "saves" the object of love only to demand—with the words "Liberate Love!" (Osvobodi Liubov'!)—that the speaker *herself* destroy it. For example, in the first episode the speaker's doll is left behind in a blazing, "revolutionary" fire only to be plucked from the flames by the Rider.[16] By following orders and "liberating love" (i.e., smashing the childhood playmate) the speaker is transformed into a "girl without a doll" (Devochka—bez—kukly). Likewise, by killing the lover rescued from the waters she becomes a "maiden without a friend/suitor" (Devushka—bez—druga!). But the third trial is the most chilling, for, by killing the (male!) child delivered from the eagles' talons, she must admit that she is now a "woman without a womb" (Zhenshchina—bez—chreva!).

Как Царь меж облачных зыбей
Стоит, сдвигает бровь.
— Я спас его тебе, — убей!
Освободи Любовь!

Что это вдруг—хрустнуло—нет!—
Это не сушь-древо.
То две руки—конному—вслед:
Женщина—без—чрева!

(*SiP*, 4:370–71)

Like a Tsar among the ripples of clouds
(he) stands, knitting his brows.
"I saved him for you, (now) kill him!
Liberate Love!"

What is this now? Something crunching . . . No!
This is no dry wood.
There are two hands (reaching) after the rider:
A woman without a womb.

(my translation)

This last episode has powerful links with the death, eleven months earlier, of Tsvetaeva's second daughter Irina (see below). The speaker, who has been driving her "firstborn" (pervenets) up into the whirlwind in order to conquer the summit ("Vys' budet nashei"), must now, for the sake of some higher dispensation, become the ultimate monster and, as Lady Macbeth would say, unsex herself. How paradoxical and potentially "inhuman" that Tsvetaeva appears to associate her access to the poetic word exclusively with the Law of the Father and with a pitiless symbolic order that demands that she destroy her own womanhood.[17]

The speaker's duel with the Rider is not yet finished, however. Later on she follows him into what appears to be a "Blokian" blizzard and loses herself in the wild metonymic (almost "cubist") blurring of equestrian figure and snowy countryside. The connection with Alexander Blok may not be fortuitous.[18] In fact, it has been suggested by Tsvetaeva's daughter that the male hero in the poem is none other than Blok himself, who as St. George of the revolution and self-destructive lover of the elemental fury of the Russian winter represents "the purest and most fearless Genius of poetry, the inhabitant of those [poetic] heights that Tsvetaeva felt were for herself unattainable" (Efron, *Stranitsy*, 65). The assertion has more than perfunctory appeal for several reasons, all of which relate to the specific ("inverted") circumstances of the poem. First, as knight errant of Solovyovian "eternal femininity" (*vechnozhenstvennost'*; cf. Goethe's *Das Ewig-Weibliche*), Blok was obsessed by the "woman question." He was, moreover, lead player in one of the most famous love triangles in Russian literary history. He would not (or could not) consummate his marriage to Lyubov Dmitrievna Mendeleeva, who was thought by Blok and Andrei Bely to be the incarnation of Sophia, and yet he willingly sought out the company of St. Petersburg prostitutes, a fact that suggests how thoroughly torn he was by late Victorian standards of male chivalry and "Heroica." Indeed, it may be said that his poetry is, among others things, a battle (*psychomachia*) for his "feminine" nature—will the winner be the "She," the Beautiful Lady and Maiden of the Iridescent Gates (Deva Raduzhnykh Vorot) of his early phase, or will it be the dark, mutable, succuba-like Astarte, the Stranger of his middle phase? Blok, like Tsvetaeva, found the source of his music and his national myth (violated Beautiful Lady = Stranger = revolutionary Russia) in an internal and all-demanding "other," which he hoped would literally transcribe (write from one to the other) his inert and sinful "maleness." Unlike his symbolist alter ego Bely, he was much less interested in Christology than in Sophiology, and in the end could only reach his music through Her and not through Him (see Bethea, "Poetics of Revelation").

Thus, when Tsvetaeva's speaker follows the snowstorm to a church and prepares to give herself to Christ as a means of salvation, her Rider suddenly reappears and, in a turnabout that seems to play on the ending of Blok's *The Twelve* (a distinctly "feminized" Christ leading the rag-tag band of revolutionary "disciples" out of wintry chaos and, presumably, toward a Soviet New Jerusalem), overwhelms her. By substituting the demonic Rider for the Son of God,[19] Tsvetaeva also changes the erotic dynamics of the scene: Blokian "seduction" imperceptibly migrates into what can only be called a kind of alluring ravishment or "rape fantasy":

Ревнивная длан,—твой праздник!
Прими огонь!
Но что—с высоты—за всадник,
И что за конь?

Доспехи на нем—как солнце . . .
—Полет крутой—
И прямо на грудь мне—конской
Встает пятой.

(*SiP*, 4:158)

Jealous palm, (it is) your holiday!
Accept the fire!
But what rider is this from the heights,
and what steed is this?

His armor is like the sun,
(and with) a sharp flight (down),
he stands directly on my breast
with his equine heel.

(my translation)

This is a richly compelling description of Tsvetaeva's relationship to language in, and one could say, *as* the symbolic order. "As in all rape fantasies," writes Toril Moi, "the delight and *jouissance* spring from the fact that *the woman is blameless*: she didn't want it, so cannot be guilty of any illicit desires. . . . [If] a woman is to write, she will feel guilty about her desire to obtain mastery over language unless *she can fantasize away* her own responsibility for such an unspeakable wish" (*Sexual/Textual Politics*, 118; my emphasis).[20] Here then, the speaker, who was ready to choose Christ, as she had been ready to accept doll, lover, and child, is "liberated" because *it is the Rider* who "takes" and "mounts" her. And it is *his* male signifying weapon, his phallic word, that, in the ultimate battle of the poem, penetrates her, the proud Amazonian warrior: "And [so] it enters and enters like a steel lance / Under my left breast—a beam [of light]" [I vkhodit, i vkhodit stal'nym kop'em / Pod levuiu grud'—luch] (*SiP*, 4:159). This is another way of saying that she becomes his ("This is how I desired you" and "[You are] mine and no other's," he exclaims) only when "she" has been murdered. What the Rider impregnates or "pricks" her with is the death of her self.

Now to turn to the question of Tsvetaeva's biography. To claim that Marina Tsvetaeva lived a full (as opposed to long) life is, first and foremost, to court platitude. She had numerous affairs (both with men and with women) and she tested the limits of romantic love, usually in the role of the mother or the child. Even her "platonic" attachments, those carried on at a safe epistolary remove or otherwise conveniently obstructed by reality, had something oddly vampiric or "appropriative"[21] about them. In 1926, when she and Pasternak entered into their famous triangular correspondence with Rilke, it was Tsvetaeva who "monitored" Pasternak's access to the great German (messages went through her in France because Switzerland as yet had no diplomatic links with Russia), and it was Tsvetaeva who "made Rilke the object of an exquisitely fantasied love" (Barnes, *Pasternak*, 1:373). And this despite the fact that the retiring and otherworldly Rilke, by now stricken with leukemia, had made allusions (apparently in vain) to his doomed condition and was, one imagines, horrified by Tsvetaeva's insistence on an actual meeting, where a union of their souls (and perhaps not only their souls!) was to take place.

In every instance that we know of where some romantic other was concerned, Tsvetaeva insisted on being the controlling agent, the one who dictated the pace (mostly intense, if not frenzied) and trajectory of the affair. She could not, literally for the life of her, accept the notion of reciprocity in love (Feiler, *Double Beat*, 62). She was embroiled in triangle after triangle and "specularized" her lovers with a priori romantic codes and formulas worthy of the most insensitive and misogynist male writer.[22] The other simply did not exist as an independent, self-valuing ego. As one biographer notes, "The object of love or dalliance [was] necessary as long as verses [were] being created—he existed for their sake; but as soon as the verses [were] completed, she could—either painfully or easily—part with him" (Shveitser, *Byt*, 262). Another source, the memoirist Vera Zvyagintseva, who met Tsvetaeva in Moscow in the summer of 1919, tells how, for example, the latter began flirting with—inter alia—V. M. Bebutov, a theater director who also happened to be courting Zvyagintseva:

> She [Tsvetaeva] grabbed Bebutov from me immediately, while he was still warm. When, at night [i.e., after a successful party, when the guests were invited to stay over], I went to the dining room for matches (Marina had taught me to smoke, she and hunger), they were already lying "in position." She lay on top of him and was casting her spell with words. She often said that her main passion was to communicate with people, that sexual relationships were necessary because that was the only way to penetrate a person's soul. (cited in Feiler, *Double Beat*, 159)

In other words, not only has Tsvetaeva taken control by assuming the traditionally male position "in the saddle," she has taken the "male" symbolic order by storm as well (note the reference to penetration). Bebutov is only the silent occasion, the passive or "womblike" soul, that Tsvetaeva's massively signifying ego will act on, project upon, "possess," if only in words.

In the fluid sexual culture of revolutionary Moscow, where all were Pompeians sentenced to live at the base of a live volcano, turnabout was certainly fair play. What is more, it is difficult to imagine that a worldly director could be particularly "violated" or "unmanned" by a momentary liaison with a passionate poet who mounts him and psychically penetrates him. However, Tsvetaeva's boundless energy and daring had other, more dire consequences that were closer to home. She was, in Victoria Schweitzer's words, "a bad mother . . . to all three of her children [Ariadna/"Alya," Irina, Georgy/"Mur"]. . . . She ruined her children with a furious, overwhelming love, with the urge to create, even re-create the child in her own way, as in the cases of Alya and Mur, and with indifference, as in the case of Irina" (*Byt*, 245–46). The story of Irina (1917–20) is particularly poignant and horrifying. Because Irina was born into difficult wartime circumstances and because she was, probably congenitally, weak both mentally and physically, Tsvetaeva had almost insurmountable problems caring for her. It has been argued that at least two aspects of Tsvetaeva's character contributed to the flagrant neglect and eventual death of her daughter: (1) Irina, as opposed to Alya, was not precocious, and therefore could not be displayed before admiring acquaintances as an extension/projection of her mother's talent; indeed, other than the fact that the sickly child had a plaintive singing voice, she was not much of a "subject" (in various senses) at all; (2) Tsvetaeva could never be "simply a mother" (Shveitser, *Byt*, 246), that is, she had a nearly pathological loathing for "nurturing" (precisely what Irina needed) and "homemaking," a situation clearly exacerbated by the absence of her husband and by the primitive living conditions in Moscow. "Marina was a poet. Encompassing the entire world, her soul could not encompass every-day life [*byt*] as well: the sweeping of floors, the washing of dishes, ironing. . . . In every-day life Tsvetaeva's capabilities were below those of the most average mother. And Irina, like every sick person, especially a sick child, demanded care, attention, [and] bound [one] to the home" (Shveitser, *Byt*, 246). Nadezhda Mandelstam was shocked to learn that Tsvetaeva would tie Irina to the leg of her bed when she and Alya would go out somewhere; elsewhere it was rumored that the child had been physically abused (beaten) by her older sister. In any event, that Tsvetaeva felt something like indifference, or perhaps worse, toward her second daughter is borne out by most objective biographers and memoirists.

In November 1919, faced with the terrifying prospect of being unable to provide for *either* daughter, Tsvetaeva gave them up to a state-operated orphanage (Kunstevskii detskii dom) outside Moscow, where it was felt they could be adequately fed and sheltered until the situation in the hungry city improved. But this, too, turned into a nightmare when, about a month later, Tsvetaeva visited Kuntsevo and found Alya seriously ill with a life-threatening fever. She immediately took Alya from the orphanage and tended to her as best she could at home in Moscow. Irina seems to have been forgotten in the frantic daily efforts to save Alya. Efron's sisters are purported to have offered to take Irina from the orphanage and look after her—but under the condition that they be allowed to do so *permanently*, itself a damning assessment of the way Tsvetaeva had raised the child thus far. On 2 or 3 February 1920 (the record is unclear), Tsvetaeva ventured out to the League for the Preservation of Children (Liga Spaseniia Detei) and learned unexpectedly that Irina had died at the Kuntsevo orphanage "not from sickness, but from malnutrition [slabost']" (cited in Shveitser, *Byt*, 249). She did not attend her daughter's funeral, presumably because Alya was still running a fever and could not be left unattended. But that she could not face the corpse of this "other" child, so judgmental in its pitiful silence, is also hinted at. Most traces of the tragedy found in extant correspondence (say, that of Efron's sisters and their friends) condemn Tsvetaeva implicitly (that is, they express compassion for the child and indignation at its plight and treatment but without mentioning the mother by name), and she was well aware of this opinion and understandably sensitive to it. However, it is difficult to sympathize—to understand, yes, to sympathize, no—with the way she presents her dilemma to such friends as Zvyagintseva and A. S. Erofeev: "Now I understand much: in all this it is my Adventurism which is at fault, my frivolous relation to hardship, and lastly, my health, my monstrous endurance" (cited in Shveitser, *Byt*, 250). In her two surviving letters to them she begs for pity and help but says virtually nothing about little Irina, about her suffering, about her aborted life. Even here her daughter's terrible death is an occasion for *self-projection*: "And, finally, I have been so abandoned. Everyone has a husband, father, brother, but I had only Alya, who was sick, and I entered totally into her sickness, and now God has punished [me]" (cited in Shveitser, *Byt*, 251).

What about Irina? one wants to ask. Didn't Tsvetaeva "have" her, too? No, apparently she didn't, if by "having" we mean the sort of possession that psychically compensates and ennobles its genetrix. Irina seems to have been an investment that paid no returns (cf. Moi, *Sexual/ Textual Politics*, 110–13). Thereafter, almost nothing in Tsvetaeva's biography suggests that she sought to keep alive the image of Irina. No "memento" of Irina accompanied her into exile. Instead, the child's life and death became massively repressed and, where glimmers of her prior existence involuntarily surfaced, they were conveniently rewritten: for example, subsequently Tsvetaeva blamed Efron's sisters for Irina's demise (thereby settling the score with her prior "tormentors") and, in the only mention in her verse of that terrible winter, the poem "Two hands, lightly lowered" (Dve ruki, legko opushchennye [1920], (she presents the loss of one daughter and the preservation of the other as a kind of romanticized and unavoidable "Sophie's Choice":

Но обеими—зажатыми—
Яростными—как могла!—
Старшую у тьмы выхватывая—
Младшей не уберегла.

(*SiP*, 2:275)

But with both (hands), clenched,
furious—I did what I could!—
I plucked the older one from the murk,
yet didn't manage to save the younger one.

(my translation)

One recalls that Tsvetaeva was fond of giving her children romantic names (Ariadne, [St.] George). But in this instance she was mistaken. "Perdita," the name H. D. gave to her child, following Leontes' and Hermione's abandoned daughter in *The Winter's Tale*, would have been more fitting than the Slavic version of the Greek for "Peace."

In our efforts, then, to emplot Tsvetaeva in the role of victim—and, to repeat, a great deal in her situation was indeed brutal, dehumanizing, and clearly beyond her control—we do not adequately account for the actual tensions and monstrous *choices* confronting her. Kristeva offers an interesting case in point. In her controversial book *Des Chinoises* (1974), she argues: "By establishing itself as the principle of a symbolic, paternal community in the grip of the superego, beyond all ethnic considerations, beliefs or social loyalties, [Judaic and then Christian] monotheism represses, along with paganism, the greater part of agrarian civilizations and their ideologies, women and mothers. . . . It [monotheism] is thus caught in the grip of an abstract symbolic authority which refuses to recognise the growth of the child in the mother's body" (*Kristeva Reader*, 141–42). At this vertiginous level of abstraction and essentialist analogy, the symbolic order, the paternal community, the superego, and monotheism all dovetail in their efforts to repress paganism, agrarian civilizations, women, and mothers. This nameless and faceless "woman" has no "choice" but to be marginalized by her *jouissance or* to repress her nature and thus be incorporated into the symbolic order (the *Virgin* Mary). Ultimately Kristeva urges women to work within the structures of patriarchal repression (here she parts company with Irigaray) in order to subvert them and keep them open (the notion of a "subject-in-process"). Her ideal readers should listen for the echoes "of our *jouissance*, of our mad words, of our pregnancies," for "whatever remains unsatisfied, repressed, new, eccentric, incomprehensible" (*Kristeva Reader*, 156). In effect, Kristeva has created a provocative tapestry of discourses (Freudian-Lacanian, Marxist, etc.) whose aim, within the regnant vocabulary, is formal consistency, not messy and rebarbative verisimilitude, "lifelikeness" (see Bruner, *Actual Minds*, 11–43).

Interestingly enough, when Kristeva finally does turn to some concrete examples, she examines the phenomenon of female suicide among writers, citing the cases of Virginia Woolf, Sylvia Plath, and Tsvetaeva. Her point is that once the structures of the patriarchal/symbolic order (superego) begin to crumble for the woman artist, the latter's word is placed in direct, potentially volatile contact with "the call of the mother"—the semiotic order:

> For a woman, the call of the mother is not only a call from beyond time, or beyond the socio-political battle. With family and history at an impasse, this call troubles the word: it generates hallucinations, voices, 'madness.' After the

superego, the ego founders and sinks. It is a fragile envelope, incapable of stav-
ing off the irruption of this conflict, of this love which had bound the little girl
to her mother, and which then, like black lava, had lain in wait for her all along
the path of her desperate attempts to identify with the symbolic paternal order.
Once the moorings of the word, the ego, the superego, begin to slip, life itself
can't hang on: death quietly moves in. Suicide without a cause, or sacrifice
without fuss for an apparent cause which, in our age, is usually political: a
woman can carry off such things without tragedy, even without drama, without the feeling that she is fleeing a well-fortified front, but rather as though it
were simply a matter of making an inevitable, irresistible and self-evident transition. (*Kristeva Reader*, 156–57)

One wonders what this passage, apparently intended as prolegomenon to
the more specific discussion of female suicide that follows, has to do with
Marina Tsvetaeva. To *which* call of the mother is Kristeva referring? Certainly not that of the troubled Maria Alexandrovna, who, as we have
seen, represented more control and repression than *choric* "irruption"
(except in her music), more *tristesse* than *jouissance*, more superego than
the "black lava" of id. As Feiler notes, "Marina never got over the fact
that her mother had breast-fed Asya while she [Marina] had been given to
a wet-nurse" (*Double Beat*, 21). Indeed, in the morbid fantasy world of
the young Marina, the Devil, with all that he represented (rebellion, passion, the color red, heat), *became her secret father* and overruled the God-
fearing qualities (obedience, prohibition, whiteness, cold) associated with
Maria Alexandrovna (see Tsvetaeva, "Chert," in *Izbrannaia proza*, 2:151–
66; and Feiler, *Double Beat*, 29–32).[23]

Or perhaps Kristeva is speaking not about specific mothers, but about
the "maternal"—a gendered yet generic metaphor for the Lacanian Imaginary? Because Tsvetaeva is "the most rhythmic of Russian poets," she is
assumed to have hanged herself in order "to dissolve being itself, to free
it of the word, of the self, of God" (*Kristeva Reader*, 157–58). But did
Tsvetaeva commit suicide because the word had begun "to slip" its moorings? In fact, as we have seen, did Tsvetaeva not associate her artistic
impulses more with her "monstrous" maleness (the Rider on the Red
Steed) than with her womanhood? Would it not be more correct to say
that Tsvetaeva did not fall victim to the madness and chaos of an unmedi-
ated semiotic order but something like the opposite—she was consumed
by her own "male" narcissism, her uncontrollable urge to "specularize"
the other, her fatal bonding to the Rider at the expense of any other self?
Nor could one call her death, on her return to the Soviet Union, "quiet,"
a "suicide without a cause." How, then, are we to interpret the destruction of her family (i.e., husband executed and older daughter in the
camps), her crushing poverty (i.e., the four hundred rubles she and Mur
had between them at the time of her death would have bought a loaf of

bread and sack of potatoes at the local market [Shveitser, *Byt*, 13]), her lack of creative work (i.e., the only job available in Elabuga was that of scullery maid in the local cafeteria), her total isolation and rejection by the intelligentsia (i.e., all her requests to potential "benefactors" went unanswered)? Again, these are only some of the questions left dangling by the abstract, essentialist treatment of this suicide by Kristeva.

The words of Tsvetaeva's biographer come to mind as a necessary corrective to Kristeva, written as they were in response to the "inhuman" treatment of Irina that the poet was no less willing to apply to her self: "You pity her [Tsvetaeva] incredibly, and you become indignant at her egocentrism, her absorption in herself [sosredotochennost' na sebe] [that is] unnatural in such a situation. And suddenly you catch yourself on a thought: perhaps it is precisely this which seems to us normal people unnatural and abnormal that makes a poet a poet?" (Shveitser, *Byt*, 251) To blame Tsvetaeva's plight on the war-making tendencies of an abstract patriarchy or on the confining structures of the family is to schematize and reduce the genuine existential tragedy of this woman torn between her art and her life. She is a martyr to her art and, like many martyrs, she is also a fanatic. If the family structure in turn-of-the-century Russia had been different, and if the war and revolution had not taken place, then perhaps Tsvetaeva would not have had to make her choices. On the other hand, if these circumstances had not obtained, we certainly would not have had the poetry that is their residue. The only "predicate" Tsvetaeva was willing to attach to the copula of her desire was that of poet. She wanted to be a *poet* more than she wanted, in the end, *to be*. An austere arithmetic, to be sure, but one that, to her credit, she was willing to live out to the last equation with ferocious consistency. "If there is a Judgment Day of the Word, I am innocent" (*Izbrannaia proza*, 1:406).[24]

After Marina Tsvetaeva, no poet in the modern Russian tradition is more "maximalist" than Joseph Brodsky. Yet their maximalisms, though in each case related to their estrangement from life and their status as permanent exiles, are fundamentally different. Tsvetaeva says at the end of one of her affairs (this one with Abram Vishniak in Berlin in 1922): "There has always been something excessive in me for those close to me; for 'some thing' read a 'large half,' a whole self too much; either my living self or the living self of my poetry" (*Le notti fiorentine*, 60). In this regard, to borrow Irigaray's provocative title, Tsvetaeva belongs not only to a sex but to a class of individuals (poets), which is not countable or neatly classifiable—"which is not one." Tsvetaeva, as Brodsky has said on various occasions, defines her poetic self by constantly spilling over the boundaries of logical discourse. Brodsky also understood early on that this particular quality of Tsvetaeva could not be duplicated or learned:

I remember in my twenties when I was writing poems, that is essentially the time when you are going about this business of writing in the "sportsmanlike" manner. That is, you regard it as sport, as competition, and you try to be this and that. At some point, I remember, I thought that I have to write a "Pasternak poem." And I could write a Pasternak poem, and I did, or at least I convinced myself that I had done so, that I could play the game. . . . Then I thought, presumably, about writing a "Mandelstam poem." That is, you don't think that you are trying to write a Mandelstam poem. I never did. But Mandelstam gets immediately into your bloodstream, and you somehow know that you are creating . . . that you are going more or less in the same direction. . . . I remember once . . . I was under the tremendous impression of some of Tsvetaeva's poems. And I began to write a poem which was indeed Tsvetaeva-like. . . . And I understood that I couldn't do it, that I had either to go for a greater emotional sweep (and presumably I didn't have that in me) or for a greater syntactical job, but that was sort of self-defeating. . . . It simply wasn't my thing. And I realized that I can't beat her. And I thought: I'm not going to engage in that. (Interview with author, South Hadley, Mass., 28–29 March 1991)

If Tsvetaeva's "emotional sweep" could not be added to, neither could the paronomastic, syntactic, and prosodic signatures that give that sweep its poetic incarnation. Bumping up against this outer limit, Brodsky had to create his own, which was in many ways its mirror opposite. Instead of emotional sweep, he fills his verse with emotional contraction/subtraction; instead of the dash that stands in for "acceleration" (grammatical ellipsis) he uses the endlessly modulating relative clause that, paradoxically, attenuates and "whittles away" its subject; instead of polymetrism (emphasis on intralinear variety in sound and rhythm) he turns to the strophe as the seat of elaborate (and often *visually* arresting) patterning. Tsvetaeva "left out" in order to intensify a poem's emotional register; Brodsky "inserts" in order to intensify a poem's cerebral or ratiocinative qualities. And understanding that Tsvetaeva's maximalism always made her more than one, Brodsky has decided to go as far as possible in the other direction, to become "less than one."

In short, Brodsky takes the two categories that are uppermost in Tsvetaeva's verse—exile and gender—and transposes them to his own situation. As jilted lover, as banished soul, as artist who must constantly confront his own monstrous "inhumanity," Brodsky resembles nothing so much as a perfect photographic negative of his heroine. And consequently what he says about Tsvetaeva[25] applies a fortiori to himself: "[Tsvetaeva's poems] contain . . . no poetic *a priority*, nothing which hasn't been questioned. Tsvetaeva's verse is dialectical, but it is the dialectics of dialogue: between meaning and meaning, between meaning and sound. It is as though Tsvetaeva were constantly struggling against the *a priori* authority of poetic speech, constantly trying to 'take the buskins off' her verse" (*Less*, 215). Brodsky, too, is constantly "taking the buskins off" his poetic speech, exposing levels of diction, mixing unlikely rhyme partners and rhyme schemes, trying out more daring enjambements. But this lack of poetic "a priority" also has an existential motivation: "[T]he knack of estranging—from reality, from a text, from the self, from thoughts about the self—which may be the first prerequisite for creativity and is peculiar, to a certain degree, to every man of letters, developed in Tsvetaeva's case to level of instinct. What began as a literary device became a form (nay, norm) of existence" (*Less* 219). Brodsky is not being coy here. Language can be exiled from its center as surely as people can be from theirs. To a poet who has internalized that exile to the "level of instinct," however, it is, one may say, "engendered" differently.[26]

Both Tsvetaeva and Brodsky found themselves in physical exile from Russia at approximately the same age: Tsvetaeva was well into her thirtieth year when she emigrated in spring 1922, Brodsky had just turned thirty-two when he arrived in Vienna almost exactly fifty years later, in June 1972. This sense of being physically separated from one's homeland was also accompanied in each case by a sense of premature aging, as if the poet began to experience his/her body as something "alien" at precisely the moment he/she assumed the title of "foreigner" in Western culture. Thus exile from one empire, the primary experience, was seen as a logical template for *exile from this world*, the secondary (but not secondary in importance) experience. What were essentially their "selves" were discovered to be not necessarily coterminous with the physical subject, and in fact the moment of physical exile was also the moment when the physical subject began to come under merciless attack in their work. "I in no way consider the body to be a fully privileged half of a person," wrote the typically hyperbolic Tsvetaeva to one of her younger correspondents during her early émigré years. "In youth—your body is a garment—in old age—a coffin from which you burst out" (Bakhrakh, "Pis'ma Mariny Tsvetaevoi," 310; cited in Weeks, *Marina Cvetaeva*, 46).[27] Since it is this physical subject through which one experiences the immediate pleasure and pain of carnal desire, the deterioration or gradual destruction of that subject brings in its wake, in these two poets, remarkably rich, "compensatory" speculations on the interrelations of love, exile, and the creative act. Tsvetaeva and Brodsky, along with Mayakovsky (in some ways Tsvetaeva's model), are the great poets in the modern Russian tradition of tragic love triangles: they positively *require* the unhappy affair and the presence of a "third" (*triangulated* desire, in Girard's terms) in order to create their love poetry. At some level, probably unconscious, the object of desire is not so important as the desire, rendered in poetic form, itself. Whatever the precise motivation, the displacement of the object of desire, coupled with the aging of a body that up to this point had been a constant

ally in amorous adventures, brings with it more spacious musings on the
issue of psychic exile. Brodsky and Tsvetaeva manage their musings differently, but their points of departure are, mutatis mutandis, roughly
equivalent.

Ever the rebel, Tsvetaeva cannot allow the notion that physical "gray-
ing" (she was possessed of a kind of female "Samson" myth and placed
great value on the power of her "curls") is a necessary prelude to psychic
or spiritual aging. Indeed, in characteristic *à rebours* fashion, she turns
the depredations of the fading flesh on their head, claiming in a poem
written just a few months before emigration: "As a snake gazes on its old
[molted] skin, / I have outgrown my youth" (Kak zmei na staruiu vziraet
kozhu—/ Ia molodost' svoiu pererosla) (4 October 1921; "Khvala Afro-
dite," in *Remeslo*, SiP, 2:133). She selects mythical incarnations, such as
the wasted but immortal Sibyl, which paradoxically underscore her lack
of a body, so that everything material is consumed in the fire of prophecy
and what is left is pure, "disembodied" voice:

Сивилла: вещая! Сивилла: свод!
Так Благовещенье свершилось в тот

Час не стареющий, так в седость трав
Бренная девственность, пещерой став

Дивному голосу . . .
                        —так в звездный вихрь
Сивилла: выбывшая из живых.

                        (5 August 1922; *PR, SiP*, 3:24)

Sibyl the prophetic one! Sibyl the vault!
Thus did the Annunciation take place in that
moment unaging, thus into the grayness of grasses
(was) mortal virginity (turned), having become a cave

to the wondrous voice . . .
                        —thus into an astral whirlwind
(has turned) the Sibyl, departed from the living.

                        (my translation)

The archetypal platonic cave, rather than a symbol of passive representation and Irigarayan "specularizing," becomes a potent, self-impregnating
echo chamber/womb. All that attaches the speaker to "life" has departed,
been banished, from consciousness. Earlier in the same poem, we find
that, through repeated invocation of the prefix *vy-* (motion "out of"/ac-
tivity taken to its irreducible end point) the Sibyl has been burned up/
away (*vy*zhzhena) and drunk up (*vy*pita); the birds of youth have died off
(*vy*merli); the Sibyl's veins have dried up (*vy*sokhli) and she has exited
(*vy*byla, *vy*byvshaia) the living (*PR, SiP*, 3:24).

The seat of the Sibyl's prophecy and the locus of Tsvetaeva's notion of psychic exile is *the word itself*, its incantatory sound patterns,[28] internal rhythms, etymologies, connotations, and associations. Dried out and drained of all fluids,[29] the poet dissolves, mythopoetically, into her essence—a kind of freely suspended voice box. Physical traits (hands, breasts, eyes, mouth) are reduced to synecdochic constellations (the body joining them is not described and has to be posited, as it were, out of thin air); gradually, as the consciousness expands and the body contracts, they are dispersed throughout the universe like so many meteorites. Inasmuch as they are part of the gravitational process of this world, they have nothing to do with the constant upward, centrifugal movement of the soul. Similarly, the signs of age that would humiliate vanity (*tshcheta*) become badges of honor, medals of (pyrrhic) victory, as in the poem "These are the ashes of treasures" (Eto peply sokrovishch), written within days of Tsvetaeva's thirtieth birthday:[30]

Не удушенный в хламе,
Снам и дням господин,
Как отвесное пламя
Дух—из ранних седин!

И не вы меня предали,
Годы, в тыл!
Эта седость—победа
Бессмертных сил.

(27 September 1922; *PR, SiP*, 3:39)

Not smothered in rubbish,
a lord to dreams and to days,
like a vertical flame is
the spirit [grown] prematurely gray!

It is not you, years,
who have betrayed me to the rear!
This grayness is a victory
of immortal powers.

(my translation)

Here, as elsewhere, the grounding of the poet's body, expressed in a negative construction (that which is smothered, "de-spirited" [u*dush*ennyi], in the rubbish of this world is *not* the true self), is contrasted to the soaring, the *vertical* flame, of her consciousness and joined in a startling rhyme pair where the second member is seen to burst out of, and up from, the first (*v khlame* vs. *plamia*). Indeed, so "cosmic," all-embracing, and dematerialized is Tsvetaeva's exilic consciousness that she can claim in "Provoda" (Wires), her cycle of poems dedicated to the beloved, yet necessarily absent Pasternak, that "I am everywhere: / I am dawns and ores, bread and a sigh, / I am and I will be, and I will obtain [or "mine"] / your lips as God will obtain the soul" (Ia vsiudu: / Zori i rudy ia, khleb i vzdokh, / Esm' ia i budu ia, i dobudu / Guby—kak dushu dobudet Bog) (25 March 1923; *PR*, 3:60). Tsvetaeva's, then, is a world of romantic inversion, taken to its outer, interplanetary limit: defeat is victory, loss is gain, life is death and death life, dry is wet, absence is presence, voice is more substantial than reality itself.

Brodsky, as suggested above, begins with nearly the same set of givens: the pain of exile, the fragility of a displaced tradition, the deterioration of the body, loss, absence, existential orphanhood. But his response is so different that, despite the well-deserved caveats about the dangers of a doctrinaire biologism or essentialism, one could believe that we are in the presence of some fundamental truth about how poetic desire is engendered. Is, after all, anatomy in some sense *poetic* destiny, too? How else to explain an opening so like and unlike Tsvetaeva as that of "The Year 1972" (1972 god)?

Птица уже не влетает в форточку.
Девица, как зверь, защищает кофточку.
Подскользнувшись о вишневую косточку,
я не падаю: сила трения
возрастает с паденьем скорости.
Сердце скачет, как белка, в хворосте
ребер. И горло поет о возрасте.
Это—уже старение.

(*ChR*, 24)

A bird no longer flies into the window.
A girl guards her blouse like some beast.
Slipping on a cherry pit,
I no longer fall: the power of friction
waxes with the loss of speed.
The heart jumps like a squirrel in the underbrush
of one's ribs. And the throat sings of age.
This is already [the process of] aging.

(my translation)

Note, to begin with, that Brodsky has organized his thoughts into an elaborate rhyme scheme—*AAABCCCB*. The various lines work in, around, and against themselves to produce a self-reflexive, even "contrived" construct. In addition, the rhyme itself is "preparoxytonic," hence particularly conspicuous and "deep."[31] (Rhyme is by definition contrived, but rhyme schemes that deploy baroque systems of delay and repetition are doubly contrived and therefore potentially doubly ironic in their intent.

We are constantly reminded of a pattern, *visual* as well as acoustic, that is larger than the individual rhyme word and that militates against the "lyrical," the *ta mele* that hears only itself.) Tsvetaeva, as we remarked however, tends to work at the level of the individual word and individual rhyme partner, where sound (Kristeva's semiotic order/id) can often predominate over sense (symbolic order/ego). *Otvesnoe plamia* erupts out of *v khlame*.

But the rhymes of Brodsky's initial tercet—*fortochku/koftochku/kostochku*—are all intentionally prosaic and ironic and diminished (the *ch* suffix); there is, at least so far, no canceling out, no emotional ascent. Tsvetaeva's word- and rootplay (including paronomasia) is generated more out of a desire (atavistic? shamanistic?) to shatter the bonds of logical discourse and tap primal feelings; conversely, Brodsky's puns and epigrams are almost always "intellectual," based on mental agility and riddling distinctions where emotion is concealed rather than exposed: recall, for the sake of illustration, the "form"/"norm" juxtaposition in the prose passage cited above. When Tsvetaeva says "Sivilla: *vy*zhzhena," followed by "Vse ptitsy *vy*merli," and then "Sivilla: *vy*pita" and "Vse zhily *vy*sokhli," she is intensifying, ratcheting up, the sensation of exit, limit and border-crossing, spatial and emotional *excess*. Here Brodsky's bird is something else altogether, a mock Freudian statement, aimed exactly at his real-life self, about the waning of his attractiveness and sexual prowess. (That the bird refuses to fly into the poet's study may also be a reference to an increasingly absent muse.) What this means, therefore, is that, rhetorically speaking, Tsvetaeva's poetic periods are full of romantic expansion or (its opposite) *sarcastic* reduction (irony aimed *at others*); her work contains very little irony per se, at least in the sense of a playful or wry or self-effacing attitude toward one's personas and their voices. Brodsky, by contrast, with the possible exception of Khodasevich, is as completely and mercilessly self-ironizing as any poet in the Russian lyric tradition. From the frightened woman to the slower bodily movements to the irregular heartbeat (Brodsky's future heart problems?), every detail in this first stanza is meant not to elevate but to deflate its speaker. What captivates us, paradoxically, is the *quickness* of the wit, the precision and clarity of the vision, the irreverent irony toward one's own mortality, the sense that Brodsky is not expanding (the Tsvetaevan mode) but, again, *contracting* as a self. If Tsvetaeva often begins a poem on high C, as Brodsky, following Akhmatova, is fond of saying, then he begins somewhere on the opposite end of the tonal scale.

We can push the comparison considerably farther, however, into each poet's view of the war between the sexes. It is here that the startling differences actually undo themselves and commence to reconverge. Brodsky and Tsvetaeva, despite their respective temperatures (cool-hot) and their gender-bound views of the opposite sex (Are there any other?), are in the end more committed to the *podvig* (heroic feat) of artistic creation than to anything else. Their "humanity," their very lives and any opportunities they might have at personal happiness or security, are less important than their work. Looking down on Prague's Jewish Quarter and thinking about the collapse of her current love affair (this one with Konstantin Rodzevich), Tsvetaeva cries out in anguish in *The Poem of the End* (Poema kontsa, 1 February–8 June 1924):

За городом! Понимаешь? За!
Вне! Перешед вал!
Жизнь, это место, где жить нельзя:
Ев-врейский квартал . . .

("Poema kontsa," in SiP, 4:185)

Out of town! Understand? Out!
Outside! Having crossed beyond the rampart!
Life, that's the place where one can't live—
the Jew ish Quarter . . .

(my translation)

As the notions of exile and banishment telescope at dizzying speed (Prague = place of exile, Jewish Quarter = place of exile within Prague, the hill = place of former love from which the speaker must now be banished), Tsvetaeva insists, figuratively, at standing her ground. The withholding "other," the lover who cannot or will not love in return and thus prefers to remain within the pale of normal or licit domestic relations, is the necessary occasion for the poem we are reading.

In this Brodsky and Tsvetaeva are absolutely equal, androgynous brother and sister. When Brodsky continues in the same poem about the year of his exile—

Я был как все. То есть жил похожею
жизнью. С цветами входил в прихожую.
Пил. Валял дурака под кожею.
Брал, что давали. Душа не зарилась
на не свое. Обладал опорою,
строил рычаг. И пространству впору я
звук извлекал, дуя в дудку полую.
Что бы такое сказать под занавес?!

Слушай, дружина, враги и братие!
Все, что творил я, творил не ради я
славы в эпоху кино и радио,
но ради речи родной, словесности.
За каковое раченье-жречество
(сказано ж доктору: сам пусть лечится)

чаши лишившись в пиру Отечества,
нынче стою в незнакомой местности.

(ChR, 26)

I was like all others. That is, I lived a comparable
life. I came to the door with flowers.
I drank. I screwed around.
I took what they put out. My soul didn't hanker after
what was another's. I possessed my own support/fulcrum,
constructed my own lever. And within my space I
extracted sound, blowing into my hollow pipe.
What is there to say as the curtain falls?

Listen, lads, friends and foes!
All that I created I created not for the sake
of fame in an era of cinema and radio,
but for the sake of native speech, literature.
For which solicitous priesthood
(as is said to the doctor: let him heal himself),
deprived of a cup at the feast of the Fatherland,
now do I stand in an unfamiliar place.

(my translation)

—he is making much the same argument against biography, gender roles, and romantic love that Tsvetaeva did in "On the Red Steed." How different the poets' tones and yet how similar their demand at taking up, *no matter what*, a position beyond the pale! Brodsky could never bring himself to say "This grayness is a victory / of immortal powers" for the simple reason that the statement is too unqualified, free of barriers, "de-clawed" of irony,[32] just as Tsvetaeva could never rhyme (whereas Mayakovsky *could*) "ne radi ia" (I . . . not for the sake of) and "i radio" (and radio). Tsvetaeva was not satisfied with the "angel in the house" and sacrificed her to her male genius, the Rider. She was (self-)penetrated by her male muse in a rape fantasy that made attempts at human love seem vapid source material by comparison. And in the Sibyl poems she has dissolved away into a self-engendering womb. So too Brodsky, mixing levels of diction (the lewd, the mock-heroic) and using racy idioms ("I played the fool beneath her skin" = "I got in her pants / fucked her") in a quite un-Tsvetaevan display of *self*-mockery, was seduced by his own muse *from life* (the blouse, flowers, groping overtures) *to art—rodnaia rech'* (native speech) and *slovesnost'* (literature), both feminine. What he has blown through his hollow pipe—as opposed to Tsvetaeva's cave/echo chamber—has produced only one thing of permanent value, and for that he is willing to take his stand in an unknown land.

Thus, to summarize this brief comparative excursus and bridge section, Brodsky views the exile experience as a continuous process of self-reduction (vychitanie), of growing into a lesser state ("less than one"). His body, like Tsvetaeva's, becomes a thing, aging into insentience, but what sustains the poet's consciousness in this loss is not a myth of the romantic subject. Rather it is a hard-won stoicism and an existentialist conviction, perhaps loosely defined as "Christian," that nothing in this world, except art itself, lasts forever. Brodsky closes "The Year 1972" with themes and images that resonate, rather poignantly one suspects, with certain passages in Tsvetaeva:

Вот оно—то, о чем я глаголаю:
о превращении тела в голую
вещь! Ни горе не гляжу, ни долу я,
но в пустоту—чем ее ни высветли.
Это и к лучшему. Чувство ужаса
вещи не свойственно. Так что лужица
подле вещи не обнаружится,
даже если вещица при смерти.

Точно Тезей из пещеры Миноса,
выйдя на воздух и шкуру вынеся,
не горизонт вижу я—знак минуса
к прожитой жизни. Острей, чем меч его,
лезвие это, и им отрезана
лучшая часть. Так вино от трезвого
прочь убирают, и соль—от пресного.
Хочется плакать. Но плакать нечего.

Бей в барабан о своем доверии
к ножницам, в коих судьба материи
скрыта. Только размер потери и
делает смертного равным Богу.
(Это суждение стоит галочки
даже в виду обнаженной парочки.)
Бей в барабан, пока держишь палочки,
с тенью своей маршируя в ногу!

(ChR, 27)

This is what I am talking about:
the transformation of a body into a naked
thing. It's not up that I'm looking, nor down,
but into emptiness—no matter how you illumine it.
And this too is for the better. The sensation of horror
is not characteristic of a thing. Thus a puddle
cannot be found next to a thing,
even when that thing is near death.

Like a Theseus (come) from the cave of Minos,
having emerged into the air and saved his skin,
it is not the horizon I see, but a minus sign
applied to prior life. Sharper than his sword
is this blade, and by it is cut off
one's better part. Thus is wine taken from
someone sober, and salt from the tasteless.
One feels like weeping. But there's no use crying.

Strike the drum (and announce) your trust
of the shears in which the fate of material
is concealed. It is only the degree of loss
which makes a mortal equal to God.
(This is a judgment worth noting
even in view of a naked couple.)
Strike the drum, while you can still hold the sticks,
marching in step with your own shadow.

(my translation)

Brodsky is a modern Theseus who does not, this time at least, mention Ariadne, possibly because it is she who has left him.[33] (Tsvetaeva, of course, would have given us Ariadne's defiant view of *her* abandonment.[34]) Leaving the cave/labyrinth of his past and emerging into the open sky of the West, he sees only a "minus sign," symbol of the shedding of those inner thoughts and feelings (love, homeland, human connectedness, *uiut*/"coziness") that bind a person to a place and a tradition. His images—sword, blade, shears—are those of castration and the gathering threat of impotence, both physical and, no less important, linguistic. The loss of his "better part" can be either a simple, off-color Freudianism or a painful reference to the loss of his loved one ("MB") and his family (son Andrei).[35] It is preferable to be a thing because things have no feelings, are in effect anesthetized, and "this too is for the better." Tsvetaeva, let us recall, is the poet of the *plach*, the lamentation, and in her passionate farewell to her lover in "The Poem of the End," she cannot, even against her will, keep the tears back. Brodsky would like to cry but has not the lachrymal means: even here there is a *vychitanie* of that which is necessary to display the emotion. And so Brodsky marches ahead stoically, holding on as long as time allows to his drumstick/phallic word and keeping step with his own mortality.

In the final section of this chapter I would like to turn to one of Brodsky's little known texts and analyze it carefully within the framework of previous discussion, keeping in mind all the while the notions of exile, desire and sexuality, and national tradition. Our understanding of the Tsvetaeva-Brodsky axis will never be far below the surface.

Время года—зима. На границах спокойствие. Сны
переполнены чем-то замужним, как вязким вареньем,
и глаза праотца наблюдают за дрожью блесны,
торжествующей втуне победу над щучьим веленьем.

Хлопни оземь хвостом, и в морозной декабрьской мгле
ты увидишь, опричь своего неприкрытого срама—
полумесяц плывет в запыленном оконном стекле
над крестами Москвы, как лихая победа Ислама.

Куполов, что голов, да и шпилей—что задранных ног.
Как за смертным порогом, где встречу друг другу назначим,
где от пуза кумирен, градирен, кремлей, синагог,
где и сам ты хорош со своим минаретом стоячим.

Не купись на басах, не сорвись на глухой фистуле.
Коль не подлую власть, то самих мы себя переборем.
Застегни же зубчатую пасть. Ибо если лежать на столе,
то не все ли равно ошибиться крюком или морем.

(1967–70; KPE, 101)

The time of year is winter. The borders are calm. Dreams
are filled with something out of married life, like thick jam,
and the forefather's eyes keep a watch for the twitch of the lure,
which celebrates in vain its victory over the pike's [magical] command.

Bang the ground with your tail[-fin] and in the frozen December murk
you will see—apart from your unconcealed privy parts [or "shame"]—
a crescent moon floating in the dust covered window-pane
above the crosses of Moscow, like Islam's dashing victory.

As many cupolas as heads, and as many spires as cocked legs.
As if beyond death's threshold, where we will make a date, amid
such a throng of heathen temples, saltworks, kremlins, synagogues,
where you too, with your minaret erect, are handsome/good [or "are a sight"].

Don't be cheated by too deep a bass, don't break off on a falsetto.
If not base power, then at least we can overcome ourselves.
Button your fly [lit., "toothed jaws"]. For if one must lie on a table,
isn't it all the same if you miss by the hook or by the sea.

(my translation)

"The time of year is winter" was composed over a three-year period
after the poet's return from internal exile in November 1965 and before
his expulsion from the Soviet Union in June 1972, that is, at a time when
he was increasingly marginalized and dangerously "superfluous" within
his homeland. Moreover, as a pre-emigration lyric that explores the stern
demands of art in an age and place that make personal love and happiness

impossible, the work occupies a position in Brodsky's oeuvre roughly equivalent to that of "On the Red Steed"[36] in Tsvetaeva's. Equally relevant, this period coincides with the gradual breakup of his relationship with "MB" (Marina Basmanova), the woman to whom he had dedicated, and would continue to dedicate, his love poetry, and the mother of his only son Andrei. The poem was eventually included in the collection *The End of a Beautiful Epoch* (Konets prekrasnoi epokhi), which appeared only in 1977 after Brodsky had emigrated. The scene presented in these lines—the poet is alone and looking out on a cityscape at night and contemplating its meaning for him and for humankind in general—will be repeated in countless other locales (Yalta, London, New York, Ann Arbor, Rome, Florence, etc.) at different times of year and under different meteorological conditions, suggesting that existential isolation and inwardness are, for Brodsky, givens.

The poem is written in a perfectly modulated anapestic pentameter with alternating masculine and feminine rhyme and it is organized in four symmetrical stanzas. Why? By now we know that Brodsky uses meter, rhyme, and strophic design as a classical amphora, a graceful repository for his semantic vitriol and his syntactic contortions. They provide the structure, at times the only structure (and hence coherence, even if formal), in a contemporary world that does not answer back. Here we might say that Brodsky's consummate skill in deploying these forms is equal only to the strangeness of the message they bear; they are the boundary, the firm shoreline, from which the poet pushes off into his various realms of exile.[37] Brodsky has tested out all values, including Christian ones, and has come to the following conclusion: "At certain periods of history it is only poetry that is capable of dealing with reality by condensing it into something graspable, something that otherwise couldn't be retained by the mind" (*Less*, 52). Prosody is "simply a repository of time within language"; it is "older than [the] state" and it "always survives history" (*Less*, 52). We are free of course to question what these statements mean and whether they are defensible, but we are not free to question the poet's conviction in their authority, since everything he has written and every act he has performed so far in his life are, to our knowledge, consistent with it.

Formal or prosodic considerations lead inevitably to semantic ones. One might speculate that the tertiary meter, with its more insistent melodics, somehow complements the folk motifs (e.g., the magical pike) or, when read aloud, better suggests the winter setting, with its domestic mood of "sticky jam" and smothering dreams, than, say, the more conversational iamb. Likewise, the alliteration of "*spokoistvie. Sny*," "*perepolneny*," and "*viazkim varen'em*" seems to reinforce acoustically the semantic notion of viscosity. Why does the speaker commence by singling out the season (winter) and the fact, strange to an outsider, that all is quiet on the borders? Because, first, winter is a marked temporal category in Brodsky. The empire in which he lives is experiencing its literal and figurative winter; everywhere the poet looks in *The End of a Beautiful Epoch* he sees stagnation (*kosnost'*, *zastoi*) and the limbo of moral and aesthetic somnolence.[38] And because second, the borders are sufficiently impenetrable and vigilantly guarded that it is futile to attempt a crossing in either direction. The first two sentences, which take place within one line (a relative rarity in the long-winded Brodsky), are armed only with copulatives—that is, they too lack verbal movement. Thus we conclude, *it is winter inside and it is winter outside*. Time and space coordinates, essential to any lyric, are hammered into six words with a deadly calm worthy of an indifferent emperor or his weary subject.

The enjambement leading from line one to line two ("Sny / perepolneny chem-to zamuzhnim . . .") prods the reader/listener into slow mental movement; like the speaker in the situation being described, we are in a kind of preconscious state somewhere at the border between waking and dreaming, so that images come to us as if through a viscous medium (here the "sticky jam"). The passive construction in the second line ("Dreams / are filled . . .") means that, within the temporal and spatial confines just introduced, the speaker is being acted upon, is not a free agent even here in his private life. (To reinvoke the Tsvetaeva connection, she is much more apt to present herself/her speaker as the source of any activity and, correspondingly, to endow her perceptions with *active* constructions, often in the first person.) This is the "separation as desire" (Seidel, *Exile*, x) essential to the exile, whether that individual is in internal bondage looking over a border into freedom or in a foreign place looking back at what has been lost: in either case the border implies prohibition and hence desire. Note that the poet does not, at least yet, describe himself, his origins, private feelings, loved one(s), something that might normally be expected from the "lyric situation." He is not, apparently, a social creature. What is left out of these first two lines is just as telling as what is left in.

The domestic motif, which makes its first appearance in the second line, has sinister overtones. The "something out of married life" (chem-to zamuzhnim) and the thick jam are, despite their warmth, sweetness, and security, obstacles to movement and barriers to freedom. They are to the inside what snow and ice are to the outside. The empire implied in the first line may be a slatternly, smothering consort who keeps her spouse in bed with the blandishments of an officially sanctioned, albeit deadening relationship (cf. Tsvetaeva's scorn for sanctioned love). Yet on a more literal level, the poet is in bed only with himself: the sticky remnants from nonexistent conjugal life may be a euphemism for cruel self-irony—a wet dream. Whatever the precise meaning, this oneiric border condition captures evocatively the inarticulate gropings of desire (the "chem-to" is intentionally vague and indefinite) that coexist amid the flypaper *kosnost'* (stagnation) of Soviet reality (*byt*).

If the first two lines introduce the distaff side of the family (anti-)romance, then the third and fourth lines introduce the male counterpart. These verses are even more recondite, more estranged thematically, than the first two. Why the forefather and the extended fish metaphor? What have these to do with the married life and the jam? Brodsky belongs to the time-honored tradition of Aesopian language and "other-speaking" (*al* + *goria*) in Russian poetry. Nearly everything he says in this poem can mean at least two things at the same time. The forefather, as ultimate authority figure, might be God, the tester of Job,[39] who has placed the poet in this situation, or he might be the Soviet patriarch, say Lenin, Stalin, or Brezhnev. In any event, he is a fisher of souls, whose arbitrary tug of the line can hook any of the unsuspecting creatures navigating below the surface. To understand the image of the fish for Brodsky, we need to go outside the limits of the poem and cite one of his autobiographical essays:

> The wide river lay white and frozen like a continent's tongue lapsed into silence, and the big bridge arched against the dark blue sky like an iron palate. If the little boy [the young Brodsky] had two extra minutes, he would slide down on the ice and take twenty or thirty steps to the middle. All this time he would be thinking about what the fish were doing under such heavy ice. (*Less*, 32)

We also need to know that the phrase "by the pike's command" (po shchuch'emu velen'iu) means something quite specific, referring to a series of fairy tales about the fool Emelya and his encounter with a magical pike that grants him his wish when, instead of taking him home and cooking him, he returns him to the sea (Afanas'ev, *Narodnye russkie skazki*, 1:401–14). (That we have an arbitrary patriarch who is figured through unmistakable "folk" motifs once again recalls Tsvetaeva.) The wondrous words by whose power the poor are made wealthy and the weak tsarlike are, then, a calque for pure desire.

They are also a surrogate for poetry, the one form of human endeavor in Brodsky's (and Tsvetaeva's) mythology that is more ancient than the state and therefore capable of speaking from a vantage outside its political history.[40] Brodsky has used the fish often in his work as a metaphor for Christian grace and sacrifice: the two fish that together with several loaves filled twelve baskets to feed the multitude, Christ as a fisherman whose miracles take place around boats and the water, and so forth. In his early poem "Fish in the Winter" (Ryby zimoi) the poet, not unlike the little boy in the passage above, describes how the stoical fish (presumably like the unsung Soviet citizenry) swim silently, in darkness, their eyes peering futilely into the thick icy membrane above, and he concludes the poem by comparing the movements of these creatures to swerving lines of verse (*SiP*, 25–26). And in his masterpiece *Lullaby of Cape Cod* (Kolybel'naia Treskovogo Mysa, 1975), written in exile, he presents his own migration from the Soviet to the American Empire as that of the cod which, emerging from the primordial waters, crawls onto linguistic all-fours (Brodsky's newly acquired English) and disappears reptilelike into the brush of a new continent (*ChR*, 99–110). Finally, in one of the essays of *Less Than One* he remarks that "in the fourth century the symbol of the Redeemer was not the cross at all; it was the fish, a Greek acrostic for the name of Christ" (*Less*, 398).

Why, then, is the forefather's lure celebrating *in vain* (vtune) its victory over the pike's command? Because the patriarch may catch the physical fish but he cannot contain the magic of its words, which, once uttered, exist independent of the predator and his prey. Immediately before and after his mention of the fish under the ice in "Less Than One" Brodsky alludes to *the Leader*, here of course Stalin: the "army choir singing a hymn to the Leader" over the radio that greeted the boy every morning at breakfast and "a portrait of the Leader on the wall behind the teacher's chair" that greeted him as he sat down in his classroom "to hear drivel" (*Less*, 32–33).[41] The Leader is fishing for the soul of the boy who in the meantime has explored on his own the life of his fellow creatures under the ice. And the boy become man, has through his contrary linguistic weavings and dartings, outmaneuvered the forefather's line and hook: "Once upon a time there was a little boy. He lived in the most unjust country in the world. Which was ruled by creatures who by all human accounts should be considered degenerates. *Which never happened*" (*Less*, 32; my emphasis).[42] That is, Brodsky employs fairy-tale logic—the pike's command—to deny, through language, that the story of his childhood and its explanation from origins ever happened, at least in the manner of a sanctioned biography.[43] He pointedly places this statement ("Once upon a time . . .") at the end of his autobiographical essay, rather than at the beginning, to show the absurdity of historical causality, "dialectical materialism" if you will, and the futility of those who would live by it.

So far so good. This brings us to the second stanza and to a shift of borders as the speaker crosses from a semidreaming to a waking state. The magic pike slaps its tail to the earth and suddenly the poet, rather than getting his wish, is transported to the world of a cold December night. As both Tsvetaeva and Brodsky know only too well, the gift of poetic speech is never happiness; its magic has no strings attached, as in the fairy tale. The window that frames the view of Moscow (recall that

Brodsky is a quintessential *Petersburg* poet) constitutes yet another border and is a familiar metaphor for psychic alienation in other poets of exile, such as Khodasevich and Georgy Ivanov. The dust (*pyl'*) which is the root for *zapylennyi* (covered in dust) is, as Brodsky has said elsewhere, the "flesh of time" and therefore surfaces in contexts where the poet discusses the wages of history. One phrase in this stanza, however, would confuse any nonspecialist reader: Why is Islam apparently victorious over traditionally Christian Moscow with her crosses?

The speaker sees mortification in his own physical being (*sram* can mean both "privy parts" and "shame") and in the fact that this is where his dream has deposited him, in a "second-class power" (vtorosortnaia derzhava) of which he is "one of the deaf, balding, gloomy ambassadors" (odin iz glukhikh, oblysevshikh, ugriumykh poslov), as he says in the closely related poem "The End of a Beautiful Epoch" (*KPE*, 58). However, the full extent of his shame is not yet decodable; all we are empowered to say at this point is that it is naked, "unconcealed," and hence probably has something to do with the vague and fumbling desire of the first stanza. The obsolete preposition *oprich'* both lends an archaic air to the phrase and possibly "politicizes" the poet's illicit urges by punning on the notorious *oprichnina*, Ivan the Terrible's hooded vigilantes, forerunner of the modern KGB, with which Brodsky was well acquainted by this time.

The reference to the crescent moon floating beyond the window like Islam's victory over the crosses of Moscow is, I believe, the pivot of the poem, the suture joining private and public meanings into one, if you will, ideological message. Brodsky may be an intensely private poet, but his privacy certainly has grave implications for the state that must read and listen to his words. Like all major Russian poets, he writes his own fiercely independent version of his nation's history and, no less important, he continues the tradition of inscribing his own life into that history. Throughout *The End of a Beautiful Epoch*, itself a highly ironic title referring to the decline and eventual eclipse of the Soviet empire (Brodsky was clearly prescient on this point), the "Eastern" values lying at the core of Russia's despotic past and present are repeatedly subjected to the sharp blade of the poet's irony. The first stanza of the long poem *Speech about Spilled Milk* (Rech' o prolitom moloke, 1967)[44] begins with an ironic Christmas message—"Ia prishel k Rozhdestvu s pustym karmanom" (I came to Christmas with an empty pocket)—and then proceeds two lines later to explain why the poet is such a failed Magus—"Kalendar' Moskvy zarazhen Koranom" (Moscow's calendar has been infected by the Koran [*KPE*, 6]).

Yet precisely because poetic language is so condensed and telegraphic, this fear and loathing of the East is not glossed, in any easily retrievable way, in Brodsky's poetry of the period of "The time of year is winter." In order to do such archaeological work we need again to consult his later essays, especially the fascinating and haunting "Flight from Byzantium" (1985, *Less*, 393–446).[45] Perhaps significantly, Brodsky places this piece at the end of his book of essays (as a kind of *summa* to his historical musings?), directly before the concluding "In a Room and a Half," the autobiographical companion to "Less Than One." He confesses from the outset that the dispassionate Western reader ("Flight" was originally published in *The New Yorker*) will, in all likelihood, be put off by the writer's closeness to his subject: "Bearing in mind that every observation suffers from the observer's personal traits . . . I suggest that what follows be treated with a due measure of skepticism, if not total disbelief" (*Less*, 393). Brodsky says this because he knows in advance that his remarks about Istanbul, so important in Russia's collective psyche as the second Rome (Constantinople) anticipating the third (Moscow), will have certain racial overtones, all probably offensive.[46] "Flight," without going too deep into its far-flung and problematic particulars, is both an engaging travelogue (Brodsky's first trip to the area) and an extended disquisition on the meaning of this place, as it looks, sounds, and smells to an outsider, for Russian history. And if someone like Edward Said has attempted to demonstrate in *Orientalism* and other works that we in the West have made people into mysterious and inarticulate others only to better subjugate and colonize them, then Brodsky, coming from a heritage that has historically swallowed up the individual within its "community" and *kosnost'*, argues why the Western tradition is so crucial for the survival of Russian culture and of any Russia worth saving.

The only way to do justice to Brodsky's controversial argument is to quote it at some length:

> For all its Greekness, Byzantium belonged to a world with totally different ideas about the value of human existence from those current in the West: in— however pagan it was—Rome. For Byzantium, Persia, for example, was far more real than Hellas. . . . [I]n Isfahan, say, or Baghdad, . . . Socrates would simply have been impaled on the spot, or flayed, and there the matter would have ended. There would have been no Platonic dialogues, no Neoplatonism, nothing: as there wasn't. There would have been only the monologue of the Koran: as there was. (*Less*, 413)

> [B]y the seventh century what had risen over the entire East and started to dominate it was the crescent of Islam. Thereafter, the military encounters between East and West, whatever their outcome, resulted in a gradual but steady erosion of the cross and in a growing relativism of the Byzantine outlook as a consequence of too close and too frequent contact between the two sacred signs. (*Less*, 415)

Constantine did not foresee that the anti-individualism of Islam would find the soil of Byzantium so welcoming that by the ninth century Christianity would be more than ready to flee to the north. . . . Yet the Christianity that was received by Rus from Byzantium in the ninth century already had absolutely nothing in common with Rome. For, on its way to Rus, Christianity dropped behind it not only togas and statues but also Justinian's Civil Code. (*Less*, 416)

[I]f Byzantine soil turned out to be so favorable for Islam it was most likely because of its ethnic texture—a mixture of races and nationalities that had neither local nor, moreover, overall memory of any kind of coherent tradition of individualism. Dreading generalizations, I will add that the East means, first of all, a tradition of obedience, of hierarchy, of profit, of trade, of adaptability: a tradition, that is, drastically alien to the principles of a moral absolute, whose role—I mean the intensity of the sentiment—is fulfilled here by the idea of kinship, of family. I foresee objections, and am even willing to accept them, in whole or in part. But no matter what extreme of idealization of the East we may entertain, we'll never be able to ascribe to it the least semblance of democracy. (*Less*, 417)

The combination of Roman law, reckoned with more seriously in Rome than in Byzantium, and the specific logic of the Roman Church's inner development evolved into an ethico-political system that lies at the heart of the so-called Western conception of the state and the individual being. . . . The drawback of the system that was worked out in Rome—the drawback of Western Christianity—was the unwitting reduction of its notions of evil. . . . By divorcing Byzantium, Western Christianity consigned the East to non-existence, and thus reduced its own notion of human negative potential to a considerable, perhaps even a perilous, degree. (*Less*, 421–22)

In Constantinople . . . there were Christians; the city churches were crowned with the cross. . . . Persistence brought its rewards, and in the fifteenth century the cross surrendered its cupolas to the crescent. (*Less*, 426)

Istanbul's mosques are Islam triumphant. There is no greater contradiction than a triumphant church—or greater tastelessness, either. . . . These enormous toads in frozen stone, squatting on the earth, unable to stir. Only the minarets, resembling more than anything (prophetically, alas) ground-to-air batteries—only they indicate the direction the soul was once about to take. . . . There is, indeed, something menacing about them—eerie, otherworldly, galactic, totally hermetic, shell-like. . . . From the outside, there is no way to tell it [Hagia Sophia] from the mosques, or them from it, for fate has played a cruel (or was it cruel?) joke on the Hagia Sophia. Under Sultan Whatever-His-Redundant-Name-Was, our Hagia Sophia was turned into a mosque. As transformations go, this one didn't require a great deal of effort: all the Muslims had to do was to erect four minarets on each side of the cathedral. Which they did; and it became impossible to tell the Hagia Sophia from a mosque. . . . This transformation reflected something that one may, without giving the matter much thought, take for profound Eastern indifference to problems of a metaphysical nature. (*Less*, 431–32)

The extent to which this series of passages serves to explain the victory of the Islamic crescent over the Christian cross in the poem is sufficiently clear and need not be belabored.[47] Much more fully in the essay than in the lyric, Brodsky is attempting to retrace the path along which he and his country arrived at their present state. Moral positions imply choices and to remain indefinitely "open" and accommodating to others' historical characters, particularly when those characters involve the traducing of the individual, is to be weak and immoral. Brodsky is indeed "cosmopolitan" and, like Mandelstam, a poet of *Western* civilization; those are the values that his experience has taught him to honor. He is the chastened man fleeing from the "obedient" and "despotic" East (here Mid-East) to the "law-abiding" West rather than Said's arrogant Westerner come to colonize the "Orient" with his institutions. Brodsky's fear of the East is not traditionally Russian in the sense that its source is Byzantium/Constantinople/Istanbul rather than the Tartar Yoke. Moreover, his historico-political statements are almost always colored by his aesthetic tastes, as in his negative description of the mosques. Ethics and aesthetics are, as it were, congenitally intertwined. Last, although space does not allow here for more than an aside, these passages, so essential for reconstructing Brodsky's philosophy of history, are richly polemical, not only with the Hellenicism of Mandelstam (cf. his famous "Hagia Sophia") but also with the Byzantinism of Yeats, who clearly (and to Brodsky perilously) romanticized the East in his famous Byzantium poems (see chapter 2).

We can now return to "The time of year is winter" knowing that the crescent and the cross really form a shorthand for Russian history—the hammer (which, as Brodsky comments, is cruciform) and sickle being merely later secular versions of the same essentially religious confrontation (*Less*, 429). The third stanza adds yet another set of frames to the poem, this one relating to the speaker's love life. The line "As if beyond death's threshold, where we will make a date" seems to come from nowhere and is difficult to decipher within the larger public and ideological meanings of the crescent and the cross. Who is the poet's addressee here? Why does their meeting have to await death's threshold? And why are the spires and cupolas, which recall the skyline of Istanbul cited above, suddenly as numerous as people? Why do they crowd around the poet in various suggestive, even indecent ways (the cocked/raised legs)? The answer seems to lie in the last line of the stanza—"where you too, with your minaret erect, are handsome/good" or, if read with an ironic intonation, "where you too, with your minaret erect, are a sight/are no better." Brodsky has taken the phallic architecture from his thoughts of Byzantium and, as it were, *realized the metaphor*. His desire, hinted at over the first two stanzas, becomes as real and specific as it can be, in fact it is hard to think of a more graphic illustration in all Russian poetry, a more ironic and brutally self-deflating "laying bare of the device." The speaker's erection cannot be distinguished from the politico-ideological message, indeed is that message: beyond the grave, where he will be reunited with the loved one whom this "beautiful epoch" has banished from him (presumably the same "MB"), even this flesh-and-blood minaret will not mark him as an outsider. Temples of worship will exist alongside one another. The differences between circumcised Jew and Muslim, between synagogue and minaret, will not be important. Yet such unity and resolution cannot, by definition, happen in this world, whose status quo is permanent pain and exile. As the poet says in *Conversation with a Heaven-Dweller* (Razgovor s nebozhitelem, 1970), another poem in *The End of a Beautiful Epoch*, "Inasmuch as pain is not a violation of the rules: / suffering is / a capability of bodies, / and man is a tester of pain" (Poskol'ku bol'—ne narushen'e pravil: / stradan'e est' / sposobnost' tel, / i chelovek est' ispytatel' boli [*KPE*, 63]). That is why, short of this ultimate threshold, the speaker is left alone with his "shame" and his illicit desire. He cannot have the woman he wants, but her absence is the occasion for this poem.

Are Tsvetaeva and Brodsky saying essentially the same thing when the former mutilates herself into a "woman without a womb" and the latter reduces the impasse of unrequited desire to an obscene and shameful erection? By the time they emigrate, neither of them has a body worth sharing (this is of course *their* view) or that requires its opposite in some capacity other than that of figure of speech. Their linguistic isolation is autogamous. What truth value is there in a statement that argues that these two poets, in denying their human connectedness and embracing their status as tragic exiles, have *become* their tropes—the echo chamber/womb and the configuring signifier/phallus? Probably very little. What can be said without entirely distorting the picture is that Tsvetaeva, in her romantic urge to break down all borders and boundaries, needed a mythical view of Russia that emphasized its total "otherness":

> Russia is only the limit of earthly understanding; beyond the limit of earthly understanding of Russia lies the limitless understanding of the non-earth. "There is such a country [called] God, [and] Russia borders on it," so said Rilke, himself yearning always outside Russia, for Russia, his entire life. And to this day Russia borders on that country called God. . . . Russia has never been

a country on an earthly map. . . . But even Russia is not enough. Every poet is in essence an emigrant, even in Russia. [He is] an emigrant from the Heavenly Kingdom and from the earthly paradise of nature. ("Poet i vremia" [1932], *Izbrannaia proza*, 1:372)

The Russia that Tsvetaeva evokes here and calls elsewhere "an immutability of blood and memory" (*Izbrannaia proza*, 2:305) is as close to being noncontingent (or, if you will, "preoedipal") as any place on earth, and yet even it cannot exist as pure openness but must border on something (the other world, the Heavenly Kingdom).[48] Knowing this, Tsvetaeva retreated, as much as circumstances allowed, into herself, into the echo chamber of her verbal art, and eventually into suicide. But Brodsky insists on his exile status not to erase boundaries or to deny them but to see and feel and reconfigure them more vividly. He requires lines of demarcation as much as his foil requires openness. His Russia does not border on noncontingency but is that very *kosnost'* which his "phallic" and utterly "Western" poetic word would attempt to remap and reborder.

The final stanza is a lovely example of Brodsky's famous stoicism. "Don't be cheated by too deep a bass, don't break off with a falsetto" means something like "find the right middling note, and don't take yourself too seriously, don't strain your voice in either direction." That is, don't show them your pain and, as a much disillusioned member of the generation of 1956, don't fail to maintain your sly, distanced facade. (An utterly un-Tsvetaevan formulation, to say the least.) One cannot hope to overcome temporal power under the present circumstances, but one can control oneself (line 2). The last two lines are again Aesopian, and return us to the fish metaphor with which the poem began. "Close your toothed/ jagged jaws" can mean literally "close your mouth" (as in stop talking, complaining) or, figuratively, "close your fly [of your pants]." Both make sense and, in context, mean approximately the same thing. To the fish placed on the table to be cleaned or to the corpse laid out on the table to be dressed for burial it makes no difference whether one misses "by the hook or by the sea." In both cases the result is inevitably death. In the man's case the pun implies suicide—the hook on which to hang oneself (here Brodsky's knowledge of Tsvetaeva must have been close to the surface) or the sea in which to drown oneself—thoughts apparently much with the poet during this especially trying period of his life. Yet, to repeat, the pike's command has, despite its message, produced a poem of surpassing richness and haunting beauty. Tsvetaeva has not, nor could she be, "duplicated." Rather she has been fully and resonantly "answered."

7

Exile as Pupation: Genre and Bilingualism in the Works of Nabokov and Brodsky

I confess I do not believe in time. I like to fold my magic carpet, after use, in such a way as to superimpose one part of the pattern upon another. Let visitors trip. And the highest enjoyment of timelessness—in a landscape selected at random—is when I stand among rare butterflies and their food plants.

(Nabokov, *Speak, Memory*)

Не ощущая, не
дожив до страха,
ты вьешься легче праха
над клумбой, вне
похожих на тюрьму
с ее удушьем
минувшего с грядущим,
и потому,
когда летишь на луг
желая корму,
приобретает форму
сам воздух вдруг.

Living too brief an hour
for fear or trembling,
you spin, motelike, ascending
above this bed of flowers,
beyond the prison space
where past and future
combine to break, or batter,
our lives, and thus
when your path leads you far
to open meadows,
your pulsing wings bring shadows
and shapes to air.

(Brodsky, "The Butterfly" [Babochka];
translated by George Kline)

In a 1925 story entitled "Christmas" (Rozhdestvo), the young Russian émigré writer V. Sirin presents the feelings of a character who has come to his manor house outside Petersburg to collect the belongings of his son. The boy has just died unexpectedly, and the father, Sleptsov, is wracked by an overwhelming sense of loss and confusion. The character's loneliness and disorientation are compounded by the setting: he wanders about the vacant house and grounds, as recently as the previous summer alive with the movements of the lepidopterist son but now suspended in thoughts of death, as in a daze. Toward the end of the story, however, something extraordinary happens; a cocoon left behind by the son in a biscuit tin bursts open to reveal a great Attacus moth:

> — ... Смерть,—тихо сказал Слепцов, как бы кончая длинное предложение.
>
> Тикали часы. [. . .] Слепцов зажмурился, и на мгновение ему показалось, что до конца понятна, до конца обнажена земная жизнь—горестная до ужаса, унизительно бесцельная, бесплодная, лишенная чудес ...
>
> И в то же мгновение щелкнуло что-то—тонкий звук—как будто лопнула натянутая резина. Слепцов открыл глаза и увидел: в бисквитной коробке торчит прорванный кокон, а по стене, над столом, быстро ползет вверх черное сморщенное существо величиной с мышь. Оно остановилось, вцепившись шестью черными мохнатыми лапками в стену, и стало странно трепетать. Оно вылупилось оттого, что изнемогающий от горя человек перенес жестяную коробку к себе, в теплую комнату, оно вырвалось оттого, что сквозь тугой шелк кокона проникло тепло, оно так долго ожидало этого, так напряженно набиралось сил и вот теперь, вырвавшись, медленно и чудесно росло. Медленно разворачивались смятые лоскутки, бархатные бахромки, крепли, наливаясь воздухом, веерные жилы. Оно стало крылатым незаметно, как незаметно становится прекрасным мужающее лицо. И крылья—еще слабые, еще влажные—все продолжали расти, расправляться, вот развернулись до предела, положенного им Богом,—и на стене уже была—вместо комочка, вместо черной мыши,—громадная ночная бабочка, индийский шелкопряд, что летает, как птица, в сумрак, вокруг фонарей Бомбея.
>
> И тогда простертые крылья, загнутые на концах, темнобархатные, с четырьмя слюдяными оконцами, вздохнули в порыве нежного, восхитительного, почти человеческого счастья. (*Vozvrashchenie Chorba*, 74–75)

". . . death," Sleptsov said softly, as if concluding a long sentence.

The clock ticked. [. . .] Sleptsov pressed his eyes shut, and had a fleeting sensation that earthly life lay before him, totally bared and comprehensible—and ghastly in its sadness, humiliatingly pointless, sterile, devoid of miracles . . .

At that instant there was a sudden snap—a thin sound like that of an over-stretched rubber band breaking. Sleptsov opened his eyes. The cocoon in the biscuit tin had burst at its tip, and a black, wrinkled creature the size of a mouse was crawling up the wall above the table. It stopped, holding on to the surface with six black furry feet, and started palpitating strangely. It had emerged from the chrysalid because a man overcome with grief had transferred a tin box to his warm room, and the warmth had penetrated its taut leaf-and-silk envelope; it had awaited this moment so long, had collected its strength so tensely, and now, having broken out, it was slowly and miraculously expanding. Gradually the wrinkled tissues, the velvety fringes, unfurled; the fan-pleated veins grew firmer as they filled with air. It became a winged thing imperceptibly, as a maturing face imperceptibly becomes beautiful. And its wings—still feeble, still moist—kept growing and unfolding, and now they were developed to the limit set for them by God, and there, on the wall, instead of a little lump of life, instead of a dark mouse, was a great *Attacus* moth like those that fly, birdlike, around lamps in the Indian dusk.

And then those thick black wings, with a glazy eyespot on each and a purplish bloom dusting their hooked foretips, took a full breath under the impulse of tender, ravishing, almost human happiness. (*Details*, 160–61)

In early 1965 Joseph Brodsky was located in internal exile in the far northern village of Norinskaya (Arkhangelsk Province), where he had begun to serve out his sentence for the crime of "social parasitism" (*tuneiadstvo*).[1] Here his daily routine consisted of carting manure, chopping wood, and working the fields with collective farm workers (Polukhina, *Brodsky*, 23). That January 1 he had composed one of his numerous Christmas poems ("1 ianvaria 1965 goda"), and shortly thereafter he wrote a piece ("Vecherom" [In the Evening]) about an evening visit to a hayloft.[2] The description of the scene might strike the reader of Nabokov's "Christmas" as eerily familiar:

Снег сено запорошил
сквозь щели под потолком.
Я сено разворошил
и встретился с мотыльком.
Мотылек, мотылек.
От смерти себя сберег,
забравшись на сеновал.
Выжил, зазимовал.

Выбрался и глядит,
как «летучая мышь» чадит,
как ярко освещена
бревенчатая стена.
Приблизив его к лицу,
я вижу его пыльцу
отчетливей, чем огонь,
чем собственную ладонь.

Среди вечерней мглы
мы тут совсем одни.
И пальцы мои теплы,
как июньские дни.

(OVP, 116)

Snow had sifted through cracks
and soft-powdered the hay.
When I scattered the stalks
I could see a moth stir.
Little moth, little moth!
You staved off your death,
creeping into this loft:
hibernated, survived.

The moth lived to see how
my lantern made smoke trails,
and how brightly lit up
were the planks of the walls.
When I held him up close
I could see his antennas—
more clearly than the flame
or my own two cupped hands.

We are wholly alone
in the evening gloom.
And my fingers are warm
like the lost days of June.

(SP, 85)

Let us not try the patience of our reader: this is not, as far as we know,
a case of "influence," with the younger poet creatively distorting, or
"veering" from, an illustrious precursor (Bloom, *Anxiety of Influence*).
Any points of contiguity here are typological, the stuff of larger Gestalt
patterns, rather than instances of conscious "borrowing." In the winter
of 1965 Brodsky may possibly have known *The Gift* (Dar), where the

butterfly is an important leitmotif; on the other hand, that he had read the rare (for Soviet readers) "Christmas" is unlikely.[3] What is more, he has stated that he and Nabokov are, at bottom, radically *different* authors and that his use of the butterfly and moth in his work is less obsessive, more ad hoc—a kind of topos he wanted to try his hand at but that was not, in essence, integral to his poetics or worldview. Be this as it may, the butterfly appears numerous times in Brodsky's verse and is the focus of at least two of his poems, one of them—"The Butterfly" (Babochka, 1972)—being a clear masterpiece in its genre.[4] It may be fruitful, therefore, here in the last chapter of our study, to compare these two artists— both of whom have been remarkably successful at turning the decrement of exile into the riches of aesthetic and metaphysical speculation— through the magnifying glass of the entomologist. Two distinct artistic personalities, each representing a very different "Russia," have lighted on a single image of metamorphosis to explain their own "pupations" as exiles and their reincarnations in the Anglo-American tradition. Our focus to start with will be the issues of genre (prose versus poetry) and bilingualism.

Few would contest the pairing of Vladimir Nabokov and Joseph Brodsky as utterly unique stylists and demanding (even "fussy") translators, both of themselves and of others.[5] They are, each in his own way, the highest and most dazzling crests of the "first" and "third" waves of Russian émigré literature. To his credit, each has transformed the loss and pain of exile into the miracle of bilingualism and biculturalism.[6] Yet the similarities stop at this rather porous level of abstraction, for these two writers are more powerful and exemplary when seen as irreconcilable antipodes and mirror opposites. They stand for, respectively, the glories of Russian prose and the glories of Russian poetry, not at all the same things within the Russian literary imagination. Historically, one is defiantly and magisterially *pre-Soviet*; the other, with the requisite loathing, self- and otherwise, a genuine *homo sovieticus*.[7] The paradox here, and one we will be investigating in some detail below, is that Nabokov could never be, as Zinaida Gippius first recognized (*Speak, Memory*, 238), a major poet, and this despite the distinctive "poetic" elements in his prose manner. What he lacked, in the first place, was the kind of experience of tradition, including the high modernism of Mandelstam, Tsvetaeva, Pasternak, and Akhmatova, that made the phenomenon of Joseph Brodsky possible. Nabokov's poetic training is at best late Victorian, or in the Russian context, symbolist (Blok, Bely) and slightly postsymbolist (Gumilyov, Khodasevich), at which point it was, linguistically if not temperamentally, arrested.[8] Moreover, there is no evidence that, *rhythmically, prosodically,* that training could have moved farther. It had no basis in the emotional and psychological *raznochinstvo* of Mandelstam or in the remarkable rhythmic syncopation of Pasternak and Tsvetaeva, both of whom were sophisticated musicians. Tsvetaeva's "Heroica," her one-against-all romanticism and disdain for simple family life, were totally alien to the private and domesticated Nabokov (see chapter 6). Equally relevant, Nabokov's poetic apprenticeship had no roots in *Soviet* time, to which Mandelstam, Pasternak, Tsvetaeva, and Akhmatova were all bonded, however painfully and with whatever degree of recalcitrance. In other words, Nabokov's language, his prose language to be sure but his poetic language especially, did not go through the same crucible of experience that formed and fashioned the idiom of Russian high modernism. Brodsky's language, however, is quite inconceivable outside that idiom, being as it is a logical and perhaps ultimate outgrowth from it.

Although Nabokov had sound reasons for the kind of translation he did of Pushkin's *Eugene Onegin*, one suspects that his motives ran deeper than simple "fidelity." And if Edmund Wilson did not know Russian as well as Nabokov did, he did have his point of view, one that was, regardless of the vitriol spilled on both sides, not indefensible. On numerous occasions Nabokov was willing to perform the sort of "total" translation of his and others' poems—that is, he tried as best he could to transpose the ensemble of rhythm, rhyme, and lexicon—that he decried in the foreword to the *Onegin* translation (see, e.g., Grayson, *Nabokov Translated*, 176). Why was this? Simple capriciousness? No, Nabokov was unwilling to transpose perhaps the greatest work of Russian literature into mediocre English verse, which was, with few exceptions, the only verse he was capable of writing. If we look even briefly at the tone of this polemical foreword, something is already given away. For example, Nabokov presents the three possible ways to translate a work of poetry from one language to another:

(1) Paraphrastic: offering a free version of the original, with omissions and additions prompted by the exigencies of form, the conventions attributed to the consumer, and the translator's ignorance. Some paraphrases may possess the charm of stylish diction and idiomatic conciseness, but no scholar should succumb to stylishness and no reader be fooled by it.

(2) Lexical (or constructional): rendering the basic meaning of words (and their order). This a machine can do under the direction of an intelligent bilinguist.

(3) Literal: rendering, as closely as the associative and syntactical capacities of another language allow, the exact contextual meaning of the original. Only this is a true translation. (Pushkin, *EO*, 1:vii–viii [Foreward])

Notice how any wish on the part of an otherwise responsible and talented translator to preserve the "exigencies of form" is dismissed out of hand,

in fact almost truculently. It seems Nabokov would have only scorn for
Novalis's definition of the translator as "the poet of poetry." The mere
thought that anyone would consider the prosodic structure of the work as
worthy of transposition drives him into a smoldering rage. He is liable to
get abusive very quickly—"consumer," "translator's ignorance"—and to
make statements that are seemingly a priori and admit no qualification—
"no scholar should succumb to stylishness and no reader be fooled by it."
If anything must be sacrificed it is what makes Pushkin's masterpiece a
poem and not prose. To try to render the "feel" of Pushkin's Onegin
stanza is essentially blasphemous, a "traducing" of Russia's finest poet,
for that feel exists only in the original. As Nabokov concludes rather
grandly, "Can a rhymed poem like *Eugene Onegin* be truly translated
with the retention of its rhymes? The answer, of course, is no. To reproduce the rhymes and yet translate the entire poem literally is mathematically impossible" (*EO*, 1:ix). Hence the only correct response and only
"true translation" is 3, whose basis is lexical and contextual precision,
something that Nabokov, a wordsmith to his bones, excelled at as almost
no one else in this century.

The problem with Nabokov's position as it is framed in the foreword
and executed in the translation itself is that of equivalences: *what* prosodic structure in rhyme-poor English would do justice to the riches of the
Onegin stanza? And English of what vintage? The English of Pushkin's
time, now thoroughly dated and, if rendered at all, necessarily stylized?
Nabokov is of course correct that an *exact* rendering in English is mathematically impossible. But that does not foreclose discussion, at least not
for that optimal translator who is both a genuine poet *and* bilingual.[9]
Perhaps some equivalent (but not identical) form exists, even today, that
could vouchsafe the anglophone reader/listener the flavor and feel of
Pushkin's magnificent Russian?[10] Nabokov could not admit this possibility, just as he could not admit that, should it exist, he would not be the
verbal Magellan to come upon it. His bilious attack on the Walter Arndt
translation, which shared Bollingen Prize honors with his own massive
project, suggests that he could not understand why others would attempt
to English *all* of Pushkin, and so was driven to outrage by the very
thought.[11] Either translate that part of Pushkin that could be extricated
intact, that is, *the individual words in their contexts*, or nothing. Even
Nabokov's willingness to part with the poetic elements of Pushkin's
text—his rhetorical question "Can a rhymed poem like *Eugene Onegin*
be truly translated with the retention of its rhymes?"—implies a rather
narrow spectrum of prosodic and phonetic interplay (the rhymes themselves). Poetry emerges in this rendering as a linear string of words filled
at the appointed interval with the necessary rhyme partner, or what might

be called, not entirely unfairly, "rhymed narrative." If Pushkin's great poem were simply or exclusively in the rhymes, we would not have, to name just one example, the magical description of the ballerina Istomina in chapter 1 (stanza XX), itself as "balletic" and choreographed a scudding of metrical and physically imaged feet as anything in Russian (or world) poetry.

Simply put, the precise and "painterly"[12] quality of Nabokov's language, including his celebrated *audition colorée*, is a throwback to a prior age, to the patriarchal splendor of Tolstoy or, to a certain extent, Bunin— another poet-prosaist.[13] Nabokov may link this colored hearing to Rimbaud, as he does in *The Gift*, but in fact its emphasis is decidedly on the visual as opposed to the auditory. "For instance," as Fyodor says to his imaginary interlocutor (Koncheev), "the various numerous '*a*'s of the four languages which I speak differ for me in tinge, going from lacquered-black to splintery-gray—like different sorts of wood. I recommend to you my pink flannel '*m*,' " and so on (*Gift*, 86). These are wonderfully precise visual images ("differ for me *in tinge*"), but they have nothing to do, as Nabokov's own efforts in verse do not, with the *sound* of Rimbaud's poetry. The author's themes, including crime, societal taboo, and abnormal psychology, may be to some extent Dostoevskian in origin; his language, on the other hand, serene and Olympian in its lucidity, begins with Tolstoy. And Tolstoy's language is no place to start in order to understand the language of Mandelstam or Tsvetaeva.[14] Nabokov has little feeling, say, for Mandelstamian opacity, for language in its hieratic guise (Christian logos as an act of metaphorical presentation), just as his sense of poetic sound patterns was distinctly old-fashioned and perennially symbolist—alliteration, assonance, onomatopoeia. In his own verse, despite its occasional charm and "neo-Acmeist" specificity of detail, he was at best a "Blokian" and at worst a "Balmontian." He had a "tin ear" not only for music in general, a fact he was willing to acknowledge, but also for the melodic structures of modern poetry, a fact, for whatever reason (insecurity? the shade of Zinaida Gippius?), he was not.

Clearly, the poems in which Nabokov most "becomes" himself are the ones with a narrative story line.[15] In these, including the fine "Slava" (Glory, 1942), "An Evening of Russian Poetry" (1945), and "K Kn. S. M. Kachurinu" (To Prince S. M. Kachurin, 1947), the poet is more adroit and at ease precisely because he has a tale to tell. Let us demonstrate our point with a passage from *Pale Fire*, a "Poem in Four Cantos" that, despite its imaginary author (John Shade) and its stylistic evocations of Pope and Wordsworth, is nonetheless quite representative of Nabokov qua poet:

A thread of subtle pain,
Tugged at by playful death, released again,
But always present, ran through me. One day,
When I'd just turned eleven, as I lay
Prone on the floor and watched a clockwork toy—
A tin wheelbarrow pushed by a tin boy—
Bypass chair legs and stray beneath the bed,
There was a sudden sunburst in my head.

And then black night. That blackness was sublime.
I felt distributed through space and time:
One foot upon a mountaintop, one hand
Under the pebbles of a panting strand,
One ear in Italy, one eye in Spain,
In caves, my blood, and in the stars, my brain,
There were dull throbs in my Triassic; green
Optical spots in Upper Pleistocene,
An icy shiver down my Age of Stone,
And all tomorrows in my funny bone.

                                                              (*Pale Fire*, 26–27)

This is a moment of so-called cosmic synchronization that the poet
John Shade first experiences at age eleven (see Alexandrov, *Nabokov's
Otherworld*, 27–29). It is analogous to many other such moments in Nabokov, beginning with the autobiographical Ganin's "anticipation" of
Mary as he lies in bed examining the wallpaper and recovering from typhus at his parents' summer house in 1915 (*Mary*, 53–57, see also 73–
75).[16] It recalls perhaps most clearly the combination of poetry, toys, illness (here pneumonia), and supercharged consciousness/clairvoyance
("my mind had been dipped and rinsed only recently in a dangerous, su-
pernaturally clean blackness" [*Gift*, 35]) surrounding Fyodor's childhood
memories in *The Gift*. But for all that, including the seeming sfumato overlay and rhapsodic caressing of details, the moment is described linearly,
discursively, as a linked and sequential series. It does not "self-enclose,"
acquiring the metaphoric depth perception and elaborate, unbidden or
"unsponsored" soundplay (as, say, Wallace Stevens's would) of the experience of the lyric poem. It describes the feeling of synchronization, yet
does not, so to speak, *give in to it*. Tsvetaeva, Pasternak, Mandelstam, and
Akhmatova are, above all else, the residues of their own distinct internal
rhythms (their "lyric signatures"), rhythms that control and consume
them, and not vice versa. Shade's epiphanic moment is, then, *a narrative
about getting outside time* with a presentation that is manifestly "dia-
chronic" and "Tolstoyan." Its studied lucidity is prosaic as opposed to
poetic/lyric.[17] No one statement competes logically with what precedes it;

the details (tin wheelbarrow) are designed to give the "poetic crescendo" ("There was a sudden sunburst in my head") a certain authority and anchor in the past. And, to be sure, this narrative strategy works marvelously *in prose* ("poetic prose"), yet it does not seem to work in and as poetry.

To say, for example, "And then black night. That blackness was sublime. / I felt distributed through space and time" is absolutely unthinkable to Mandelstam, even a Mandelstam translated from Russian into English. The statement is too direct, the narrative too shorthand, the word-fit too neat, the rhyming too pedestrian. In effect, Nabokov/Shade has "plugged in" the requisite rhymes but has not created "poetry." The second stanza improves precisely because it suddenly swerves into *self-parody*: the speaker understands, perhaps implicitly, his failure as lyric voice and therefore saves himself by making fun of himself, that is, by undercutting his pretensions at cosmic expansion. The "one foot . . . one hand . . . one ear . . . one eye" is a half-humorous (but also *half-serious*) takeoff on the ecstatic ending of Khodasevich's famous "Ballad" (Ballada), which Nabokov translated (freely!) and knew well. There is great wit and verve in superimposing body parts on ages and regions,[18] yet the tone lapses almost ineluctably into the mock heroic. (Again, did Nabokov/Shade choose Pope or did Pope, as it were, choose Nabokov/Shade?) "*Pant*ing str*a*nd," despite (or because of?) the *a*-based assonance, is clearly funny, as if the phonetic and semantic levels—the very physical "panting" together with the elevated "strand"—jar and jangle in "poetic" (Balmontian!) overkill. Thus the author, who at some level probably did not consider the poem *Pale Fire* to be self-parody, appears to hedge in the last line by resorting to undisguised humor: "And all tomorrows in my funny bone"—not, finally, words one would normally associate with Orphic breakthrough.[19]

Nabokov is one of the great masters of the exilic imagination. Here, for example, a little later in the poem, the death of a fellow émigré is presented:

Nor can one help the exile, the old man
Dying in a motel, with the loud fan
Revolving in the torrid prairie night
And, from the outside, bits of colored light
Reaching his bed like dark hands from the past
Offering gems; and death is coming fast.
He suffocates and conjures in two tongues
The nebulae dilating in his lungs.

(*Pale Fire*, 39)

The scene is too inherently dramatic, too overripe with pathos, suggesting a replay of Podtyagin's heart attack in *Mary*. Brodsky, by contrast, would

not have placed the phrases "the exile" and "the old man" in close proximity. Such juxtaposition invites a sentimental (or even potentially *po-
shlyi* [vulgar]—Nabokov's *bête noire*) reading, a reading Brodsky will
not give voice to within his lyric world. Nor would Brodsky have mentioned conjuring in two tongues without showing, in some quite vivid
and linguistically felt way, what that means in context. Once again, the
poetic Nabokov comes across as too nominal and adjectival, descriptive
rather than presentational.[20] Worst of all, the exquisitely precise and
vivid "The nebulae dilating in his lungs" is upstaged and, as it were, made
vaudevillian by the neatly symmetrical, rather "wooden" adjoining
rhyme phrases: "in two tongues" versus "in his lungs."

But perhaps most intriguing in this regard is Nabokov/Shade's understanding of the larger process of poetic inspiration. As the speaker summarizes:

> Now I shall spy on beauty as none has
> Spied on it yet. Now I shall cry out as
> None has cried out. Now I shall try what none
> Has tried. Now I shall do what none has done.
> And speaking of this wonderful machine:
> I'm puzzled by the difference between
> Two methods of composing: *A*, the kind
> Which goes on solely in the poet's mind,
> A testing of performing words, while he
> Is soaping a third time one leg, and *B*,
> The other kind, much more decorous, when
> He's in his study writing with a pen.
>
> In method *B* the hand supports the thought,
> The abstract battle is concretely fought.
> The pen stops in mid-air, then swoops to bar
> A canceled sunset or restore a star,
> And thus it physically guides the phrase
> Toward faint daylight through the inky maze.
> But method *A* is agony! The brain
> Is soon enclosed in a steel cap of pain.
> A muse in overalls directs the drill
> Which grinds and which no effort of the will
> Can interrupt, while the automaton
> Is taking off what he has just put on
> Or walking briskly to the corner store
> To buy the paper he has read before.

Why is this so? Is it, perhaps, because
In penless work there is no pen-poised pause
And one must use three hands at the same time,
Having to choose the necessary rhyme,
Hold the completed line before one's eyes,
And keep in mind all the preceding tries?
Or is the process deeper with no desk
To prop the false and hoist the poetesque?
For there are those mysterious moments when
Too weary to delete, I drop my pen;
I ambulate—and by some mute command
The right word flutes and perches on my hand.

(Pale Fire, 45–46)

This is truly a remarkable passage, one in which Nabokov qua poet, through his *porte parole*, is presumably speaking "on the level." There exists, he argues, a state of inspiration (method *A*) in which the muse takes over, drills her pain-looking-for-relief (an abscessed tooth in Khodasevich's tropism) into the poet's skull, and renders unnecessary all mediating structures and controlling mechanisms, such as desks and pens. The poet is being acted upon, is the fulcrum rather than the initiator of the movement, much as Yury Zhivago describes the process of composing the poem "Fairy Tale" at Varykino. Perhaps genuine inspiration as a state exists independent of genuine poetry as a product? The poem is composed in the poet's head as he "ambulates" and carries on his "double life." Here, in method *A*, Nabokov/Shade is a kind of Wallace Stevens putting the poem together—or being put together by the poem—as he walks to the Hartford Accident and Insurance Company.

Yet, and this is our main point, the poem that describes the thralldom of method *A* is, in its manner and structure, a distinct product of method *B*. It is overdetermined. The "right word flutes and perches" on the poet's hand, but it is, in the end, no more and no less than a *right word*. Nabokov's notion of rhythmic unit goes no farther than that. There is, in Kristeva's phrase, no "choric" element. Poetry writing is not, or at least not only, a chess problem, a "knight's move" or "castling" maneuvre that slips one piece onto a verbal square just passed over by another.[21] In this respect, Nabokov shares much with Andrei Bely, another brilliant prose writer and failed "Blokian," whose mathematically precise theories and diagrams on meter and rhythm in *Symbolism* much impressed the young Sirin.[22] Experiencing the rush and force of genuine inspiration, Nabokov cannot reproduce that energy from within the poem itself. "In penless work there is no pen-poised pause" is—shed of course of any "archaic" or stylized trace—a line worthy of Poe, Swinburne, or Balmont. Perhaps Nabokov hears it with Russian or French ears, the French, following Baudelaire (a much greater poet), being more partial to Poe than are his late twentieth-century American inheritors? Whatever the case, it is a tribute to Nabokov that he can describe in such detail, and yet so unpoetically, this condition called inspiration.

The very first thing we bump up against when moving from the bilingualism of Nabokov to the bilingualism of Brodsky is the invisible yet very real wall of genre, of "prosaic" versus "poetic" thinking. Nabokov's bilingualism (or trilingualism) was a natural outgrowth of his special upbringing; when, as Elizabeth Klosty Beaujour has recently established, he made his initial forays into English, first translating himself and then going over entirely to composition in his adoptive (actually, chronologically his "first") language, the transition was more wrenching on a *psychological* than on a sheer linguistic level (*Alien Tongues*, 81–117).[23] Scholars of the "cross-over" Nabokov are wont to point out that it is precisely the "bilingual" quality of his English (*tmesis*—something "foreign" inserting itself between elements that are familiar) that makes his prose both strange ("other") and fresh ("original" in context) (see Grayson, *Nabokov Translated*, 216; Beaujour, *Alien Tongues*, 102, 105–106). Nabokov was traducing the *Muttersprache*, or rather, to use a metaphor he would prefer, betraying his lawful wife for an unlawful mistress. And all the while during this first period as an English-language writer, he would arrange "trysts" with his Russian muse and gladly "sleep with her"—that is, write Russian verse "on the sly"—in order to keep the fires burning even as he was carrying out the "drudgery" of composing prose in another language (Beaujour, *Alien Tongues*, 97). Thus, maintaining the fiction of writing Russian verse helped Nabokov over the barrier of leaving "Russia" behind and of taking on a new persona as great *bilingual* prose writer.

Brodsky's trajectory is, as one could expect, entirely different. His identity in Russia and now, in emigration, has always been that of *poet*. His bilingualism, as opposed to Nabokov's, has nothing "natural" or "nurtured" or "old world" about it. It has been earned, syllable by syllable, word by word, over the heads and against the express wishes of the Soviet literary establishment. It was learned, haltingly and through great personal sacrifice, during periods of intense solitude, for example, in his northern exile (Norinskaya), by poring over an anthology of Anglo-American poetry and by trying to parse and piece together sounds and meanings. When Western Slavists first heard the young Leningrad poet cite lines of verse in English, they could barely understand him, so accented and painfully private was his "training."[24] Brodsky's anglophone (and americanophile) leanings have their source and inspiration in Soviet history, a history of distortion and repression. This disenchanted *homo sovieticus* so despised the cant and cliché that had taken root in his native speech that he looked to English and the great modern poets of that tradition as a kind of "truth serum," a way to cleanse, reinvigorate, and discipline his own and his generation's shabby idiom.[25] Nothing about this process came easy to Brodsky, and one doubts whether he himself, his initial impulses honed to diamond-hard conviction by the years of persecution and internal banishment, ever doubted the rightness and efficacy of his "cosmopolitanism." That he loved the language he inherited from Mandelstam and Tsvetaeva cannot be questioned; that he saw that language as embalmed and fixed in the past and not open to the inoculations of other traditions has, however, been questioned, nearly continually, by his linguistic behavior right up to the present. Nabokov had to "trick himself" through one of his elegant fictions into loving two wives; Brodsky has, from the moment he espied his *tvorcheskii put'* (creative path), been a defiant and unreconstructed bigamist.[26] His place in his own history and poetic tradition gave him no other choice.

Brodsky has, after almost twenty years in exile, come to see some essential differences between the anglophone and russophone traditions:

> The English, for example, experience a nostalgia for spontaneity [as opposed to Mandelstam's famous "nostalgia for world culture"], a spontaneity whose place is in the East. They have an attraction toward orientalism, toward things [East] Indian. In general any culture, as a rule, lacks something and is always striving toward something . . .
>
> But if one is to delve into specifics, the English, for example, are exceedingly rational. At least, externally. That is, they often are likely to lose track of nuances, of all those so-called "loose ends." . . . Just suppose that you cut through an apple and remove the skin. Now you know what is inside the apple but by the same token you lose sight of both its bulges, both its cheeks. Russian culture is interested precisely in the apple itself, taking delight in its color, the smoothness of its skin, and so forth. What is inside the apple it often doesn't know. Speaking crudely, these are different ways of relating to the world—rational and synthetic. (Volkova and Volkov, *Iosif Brodskii v N'iu Iorke*, 120)

What is more, as he confides a little later in the same interview, bilingualism has become absolutely necessary to him. Both a curse and a salvation, it places him, the perennial outsider, *between*, but *never fully in*, the two cultures:

> The fact of the matter is that this attachment to two cultures, or to put it more simply, this bilingualism, either you are condemned to it or the opposite, either it is a blessing or it is a punishment, right? This is, if you wish, a totally wonderful situation psychologically. Because you are perched as it were on a mountain

peak and you see both its slopes. I'm not sure if this is correct in my case or not, but my coign of vantage is not a bad one. . . . You see both slopes and that is a completely unique sensation. If a miracle were to happen and I were to return to Russia to live permanently, I would be exceedingly bothered by the inability to use an additional language. (Ibid., 120, 122)

Nabokov *personalizes* his relations with the Russian language (he sleeps with the muse when he creates Russian verse), but the kind of metaphorical leap made by Brodsky here is alien to his lucid, controlled, ever distancing and "enclosing" psyche. Brodsky has grown up and lived in *all* layers of the Russian language, from the most idiomatic and earthy to the most exalted. He understands and admires the genius of writers such as Andrei Platonov and Yuz Aleshkovsky. He has lived among such individuals and heard them use Soviet Russian "from the bottom up." Platonov's brilliant manipulation of bureaucratese or Aleshkovsky's infinitely regressive cursing is *language used against itself*, language that undermines its own ontological reality. When Adorno, for example, suggests it is barbaric to write poetry after Auschwitz (*Prisms*, 34), his message is immediately translatable to Soviet reality. To Brodsky's post-Stalinist, post-1956 generation, the language of Nabokov, and a fortiori the *poetic* language of Nabokov, no longer reflects reality.

Hence Brodsky is able to mythologize his language relations in a broader, national or "geo-spiritual" framework: the anglophone world is "rational," the russophone world is "synthetic." If he does not speak for the *narod* (people, das Volk), a term hopelessly brutalized into the Soviet period, he does speak for a significant portion of the intelligentsia, and therein lies his still sacred contract and charismatic appeal (see Freidin, *A Coat*, 1–33). He can, in a late modern or postmodern replay of the romantic urge, link language to a myth of national self-identity, which amounts to a Prospero-like leap of faith into the "sea of [linguistic] life" that for Nabokov, the natural aristocrat and anglophile virtually from birth, was impossible, or possible *only through Pushkin*, another natural aristocrat. The *raznochinstvo* of the poet, the *zhid* (Yid) in Russian culture, who has nothing behind him but the "noise of time" and who must erect his own Notre Dames from the ruins of former values, is utterly un-Nabokovian. One can, and indeed probably should, argue with Brodsky about such binaries—is American culture so "rational" and is Russian culture so "synthetic"? Does the one really ignore nuance and the other the "big picture"? At the same time, one mounts such arguments at the risk of "bad faith," for Brodsky has *lived* the chaos of Russian life; he has worked in a morgue and drunk with the proletariat. And he has supported himself in the West now for many years, making his way as teacher, intellectual, and man of letters. Of his distinctly literary and cultural patriotism he might say, as the ancient poets did, *Omne solum vati patria est, ille incola mundi* [The poet is at home in any country, he is a citizen of the world]. His binaries, beginning with the linguistic ones, have the ring of authority, of *genuine experience*, about them. Nabokov's bilingualism, with its emphasis on memory and the caressing of the past, is in a way "prelapsarian," its splendid tmesis motivated to help us from falling into Soviet time; Brodsky's bilingualism takes that fall as its point of departure and struggles and grunts to its mountain aerie in order to see the shifting truth-value of "both slopes."

Also utterly un-Nabokovian is Brodsky's notion of translation, a notion that goes to the heart of their differing bilingualisms. When, for example, Brodsky objects to a translation project, he does so on grounds precisely the opposite of Nabokov's. Paul Schmidt's monumental effort to render Khlebnikov in English is flawed, according to Brodsky, because the translator "tailors the material to his own liking, i.e., according to his own notions of what a successful modern poem should be. . . . [H]e reshuffles the lines [e.g., of the poem 'A Zoo'] like a deck of cards, writes in his own lines, skips rhymes as he pleases, alters the meter, 'straightens' complex images, and juggles chronology—in general he behaves like a spoiled child at his aunt's table" ("The Meaning of Meaning," 33). What annoys Brodsky is not that Schmidt has undertaken to find English equivalents for Khlebnikov ("nobody would reproach Schmidt for taking it [the step of translating the maddeningly 'hermetic' Khlebnikov]" ["The Meaning of Meaning," 33]), but that he has not gone far enough. He has "edited" Khlebnikov, without giving his English reader an adequate sense of the Russian's shaggy genius as well as his equally ungainly howlers. Brodsky focuses on *all* the poetic manifold, on the rhymes, meter, imagery, lexicon. He specifically rejects the notion of poetry as "shuffling" lines. And, significantly, he concludes his review by assailing Schmidt's inattentiveness to Khlebnikov's meter (recall, for the sake of comparison, that Nabokov associated the difficulty of translating *Eugene Onegin* primarily with Pushkin's *rhymes*):

> To be fair to the translator, the original itself resists an accurate evaluation. In a sense, the contents of most of Khlebnikov's writing . . . can be ascertained best by a foreigner who has no particular sentiments about Khlebnikov's notion of Russian prosody as juggling the meter, resorting to atrocious compound rhymes, punning, or creating neologisms that work far less often than one wished they did. . . . Predominantly a tetrametric poet, Khlebnikov would have been better served by his translator if Schmidt had stuck to the literal renditions of his poet's lines, no matter the crypt of footnoting that would have been required. That at least would have given his readers an idea of Khlebnikov's verbal intensity and daring, as well as of his verbosities. . . . [T]o employ a reverse figure, this Pound [i.e., Khlebnikov], too, needed an Eliot to edit his cantos. Instead, he ended up with a Schmidt. ("The Meaning of Meaning," 35)

Just like Nabokov, Brodsky can be blunt and sarcastic to the point of cruelty when the issue is the preservation, however proximate, of poetic greatness. On the other hand, despite his lack of sympathy and at some level appreciation of Futurism and the avant-garde, Brodsky even here is much more aware, *as a major practicing poet*, of how a Khlebnikov verse creation is supposed to work from the inside. Although in theory he is unwilling to sacrifice any part of the poem to the process of transposition, one senses that for Brodsky a work's prosodic character is certainly no less important than its individual lexical items. The *contents* of Khlebnikov's writings can be conveyed through literal, Nabokovian translation. (It is difficult to imagine, by the way, Nabokov ever translating Khlebnikov.) If, however, the corpse of the original is to be brought to life in this Frankensteinian experiment, then one will have to know that the poet is essentially tetrametric, that his compound rhymes can be "atrocious," and that his neologisms, while highly inventive, do not always work.

Before turning back to the image of the butterfly in Brodsky and Nabokov, I would like to broach a somewhat thorny, even painful issue—namely, why Nabokov's prose genius *is* translatable and why Brodsky's poetic genius *is not*, or if so, only partially, and what this means for their respective bilingualisms. As we have just discovered, Brodsky is interested in a poet's overall *vector* (his term), that is, in his multidimensional application of myth, prosody, biography, and tradition to create not only a "poetic world" but a kind of totally unique rhythmic signature. He would accede implicitly to George Steiner's formulation that "Any model of communication is at the same time a model of trans-lation, of a vertical or horizontal transfer of significance. . . . Each living person draws, deliberately or in immediate habit, on two sources of linguistic supply: the current vulgate corresponding to his level of literacy, and a private thesaurus" (*After Babel*, 46). By the same token, no educated reader of modern Russian poetry would mistake Brodsky's voice for that of Voznesensky or even Kushner. That voice is his and his alone. When, for example, the speaker says at the beginning of "Pis'ma rimskomu drugu" (Letters to a Roman friend, 1972) that—

> Нынче ветрено и волны с перехлестом.
>   Скоро осень, все изменится в округе.
> Смена красок этих трогательней, Постум,
>   чем наряда перемена у подруги.

>   (*ChR*, 11)

> Now it's windy and the waves are running crisscross.
>   Soon it will be fall, and nature's face will alter.
> Shifts in these bright colors stir me more profoundly,
>   Postumus, than changes in my lady's wardrobe.

>   (*Part*, 52)

—we know these words to be unmistakably Brodskian. How? To begin with, the downbeat of the autumnal setting with its promise of winter and an end to colors and to lovemaking (the *podruga*) coupled with the vague conspiratorial tone addressed to an Horatian friend, who, when translated, evokes "posthumous." This is Brodsky's lyrical milieu, one he is completely "at home" in—the ancient world that is strangely modern. Here he is both playful and serious, making wry jokes about exile, death, and his lady's wardrobe. There is a subtlety of tone in these four lines, a combination of the world-weary, the self-deprecating, and the stoically precise, that could belong only to Brodsky. The initial rhyme-pair of "s perekhlestom" and "Postum," so wonderfully unexpected and, alas, lost in George Kline's translation, is, as the idiomatic Brodsky himself might say, worth the price of admission into the subsequent lines.

Likewise, when Brodsky muses in the opening of his great exile poem "1972 god" (The Year 1972)—

Птица уже не влетает в форточку.
Девица, как зверь, защищает кофточку.
Подскользнувшись о вишневую косточку,
я не падаю: сила трения
возрастает с паденьем скорости.

(*ChR*, 24)

A bird no longer flies into the window.
A girl guards her blouse like some beast.
Slipping on a cherry pit,
I no longer fall: the power of friction
waxes with the loss of speed.

(my translation)

—we are struck not only by the hilariously self-skewering Freudianism of the first line but by the remarkable triple end-rhymes,[27] part of an elaborate stanzaic scheme, that both make fun of themselves (all are emphatically "prosaic") and celebrate their own sound as poetry. "Fortochku/koftochku/kostochku," seemingly anagrammatic negatives of one another, can exist and indeed fuel the best contemporary Russian poetry,[28] whereas in English such adjoining rhymes, all nominal, could presumably exist only in limericks or doggerel. Brodsky, this opening announces, can make verse out of little ventilating windows and cherry pits, just as he can out of his own physical diminution and aging. These lines, in short, are as distinctively "Brodskian" as those that began "Letters to a Roman Friend."

The barrier to Brodsky's total bilingualism comes when he attempts to translate his "rhythmic signature" into English.[29] If we take one of his English-language poems we immediately recognize certain similarities to elements in, for example, "The Year 1972." In 1986 he published in *Partisan Review* the first installment of a long poem ambitiously (and mockingly) entitled *History of the Twentieth Century (A Roadshow)*. The work is designed as a series of verse paragraphs, or coupleted snapshots, of various actors and events as played out on the stage of the twentieth century: people (John Moses Browning, Sir Arthur Conan Doyle, the Wright Brothers, Stalin, etc.) and years come together as a chorus of dancing girls on a burlesque stage of rhyme. This first installment takes us to the year 1914, that is, to the brink of the First World War. Structurally, *History* recalls another of Brodsky's "processional" works—the flawed but still fascinating *Shestvie* (1961). The epigraph, "The Sun's in its orbit, / yet I feel morbid," with its outrageous rhyme, already prepares us for the buffoonery, or "roadshow" character, of the Prologue:

> Ladies and gentlemen and the gay!
> All ye made of sweet human clay!
> Let me tell you: you are okay.
>
> Our show is to start without much delay.
> So let me inform you right away:
> this is not a play but the end of the play
>
> that has been on for some eighty years.
> It received its boos and received its cheers.
> It won't last for long, one fears.
>
> Men and machines lie to rest or rust.
> Nothing arrives as quick as the Past.
> What we'll show you presently is the cast
>
> of characters who have ceased to act.
> Each of these lives has become a fact
> from which you presumably can subtract
>
> but to which you blissfully cannot add.
> The consequences of that could be bad
> for your looks or your blood
>
> For they are the cause, you are the effect.
> Because they lie flat, you are still erect.
> Citizens! Don't neglect
>
> history! History holds the clue
> to your taxes and to your flu,
> to what comes out of the blue.

(*History*, 327–28)

In his Russian verses Brodsky has virtual "perfect pitch" when it comes to walking a high-wire act between high and low, lyric and odic, sublime and scatological. He pulls back his far-reaching metaphysical speculations from the brink of self-pretension through a carefully modulated irony and he raises up the most mundane and deflating statements about his person or surroundings by couching those statements in rapidly telescoping layers of thought and in syntactic "magic boxes." In "Adieu, Mademoiselle Véronique" (Proshchaite, madmuazel' Veronika, 1967), the speaker goes through syntactic contortions and the most attenuated thought process imaginable in order to explain to his addressee how in twenty years he will return for the chair she sat in when she rejected him. Then he says, in typical Brodskian fashion, "You, of course, will pardon me this / buffoonish tone" (Ty, nesomnenno, prostish' mne etot / gaerskii ton) (*OVP*, 171). The ploy works marvelously, precisely because his real pain, deflected onto the chair as the "objective correlative" of that loss (human emotions turn inevitably into things), is masked by the so-called buffoonery. In fact, by concealing the pain it becomes not less but more sharp-edged.

Here, however, it can be argued that that balance, perhaps intrinsic to Brodsky's "layered" Russian, deserts him. In *History of the Twentieth Century* the buffoonery is closer to poetic slapstick and the subtle, sharper edge is much less in evidence. The triple rhymes, the "gay/clay/okay" of the opening tercet, are not specific and prosaic (clichéd, yes, *prosaic*, no) in the way that "fortochku/koftochku/kostochku" are. The English language's lack of inflected endings has made these rhymes predictable, so that "gay" cannot be used in its original meaning (Is this why the poet separates it from "Ladies and gentlemen"?) and "okay" is clownishly self-parodying. One is tempted to think that Brodsky, despite his astonishing prowess as English essayist, hears Russian endings and Russian syntactical units when he pronounces these words. His tone is much more "Mayakovskian" (Mayakovsky being a poet Brodsky shares little with in terms of temperament and aesthetic values), much more swaggering and blunt (cf. "Citizens! Don't neglect . . ."), than anything he would write in Russian. True, this is a far cry from the poet of *Pale Fire*. Brodsky of course knows this is bad poetry, but so bad that he hopes he can make it good. Can bathos, he seems to be saying, turn itself inside out, miraculously become self-aware? Here and there Brodsky-isms, which work with such epigrammatic power in Russian, flash through like fish (one of the poet's favorite images) suddenly breaking to the surface of a brackish pond. The "men and machines lie to rest or rust," for instance, where a permanent ontological state depends on a vowel shift (rest → rust); or the "For they are the cause, you are the effect. / Because they lie flat, you are still erect," where the statement's logical symmetry and the economy of the sexual pun reinforce each other, are vintage Brodsky, but a Brodsky who cannot be properly appreciated because his linguistic roots are in another language. To use the poet's own binaries, he is attempting to see the inside of the apple, something he can do implicitly in Russian, by biting into its outer skin. He does not feel English the way Auden did, however much he has transferred over to the linguistic mores of his adoptive culture. Unfortunately, the Brodsky who can write so movingly about the vagaries of history in "A Halt in the Desert" (Ostanovka v pustyne, 1966) is here reduced to "History holds the clue /to your taxes and to your flu." Likewise, the master of the disappearing subject in "The Autumn Flight of the Hawk" (Osennii krik iastreba, 1975) and what we have been calling elsewhere the "poetics of subtraction" can only muster in this opening a stale "Each of these lives has become a fact / from which you presumably can subtract / but to which you blissfully cannot add." Little wonder that Brodsky did not provide further installments to this chronological roadshow, its potential Mayakovskian/Tsvetaevan verve and sarcasm flattening out in English to a point beyond repair.

I would not want to leave the impression that Brodsky cannot write good, even important or "major status" verse in English. He can, and here he is truly different from Nabokov. The problem seems to be when he writes in a quasi-civic key, something very difficult in the present cultural climate in America, and when he overcompensates for the serious subject matter (history of the twentieth century) by resorting to markedly casual, at times buffoonish puns and turns of phrase. As most language teachers will affirm, the very last level to be mastered by a student of a foreign language prior to total ("native" or "near-native") fluency is that of humor, of the "buffoon" who can also be serious. By contrast, one of Brodsky's most powerful masks, in both Russian and English, is that of elegist. In this guise, which does not depend on the *gaerskii ton* (buffoonish tone) of the "roadshow," his sensibility is more subtle and sure. He is occasionally able to translate his Russian "rhythmic signature" into successful English terms. First, proof by a negative example, the opening stanza of his elegy to Auden:

> The tree is dark, the tree is tall,
> to gaze at it isn't fun.
> Among the fruits of this fall
> your death is the most grievous one.
>
> (Spender, *A Tribute*, 243)

The heartfelt simplicity is undone by the tight rhyme scheme (*abab*)—the poet would have been better served by something "looser" and more forgiving—and the phrase "to gaze at it isn't fun," so demonstrative in its

casualness (again, Brodsky is trying to make casualness *more* painful),
jars hopelessly with the high-sounding "your death is the most grievous
one." The poem was written to commemorate Auden's death in October
1973, that is, just a year and a half after Brodsky's arrival in the West.
Perhaps his English was not yet up to the task (although the startling
combination of "low" and "high" is certainly characteristic of the "Russian" Brodsky)? Subsequently Brodsky came to understand that, however
much he loved and admired Auden, this particular elegy did not do honor
to its subject, and in this sense was probably much worse than writing
nothing at all. As he confided to an interviewer in 1980, "Why did I give
permission for it to be included in the collection [Stephen Spender's edited
volume *W. H. Auden: A Tribute*] . . . and so I've ruined the whole book"
(cited in Polukhina, *Brodsky*, 89).

In 1977, just four years later, Brodsky was to write another elegy to
one of his favorite English-language poets—Robert Lowell.[30] This time,
however, the poem genuinely seems to work, even reaching the level of
Brodsky's great Russian elegy on the death of T. S. Eliot, on which the
Lowell piece may be, at least partially, modeled. Space does not allow us
to quote the poem in full, but perhaps several stanzas will give the reader
a sense of the "elegiac" Brodsky in English. Here is how "Elegy: for
Robert Lowell" opens:

> I
> In the autumnal blue
> of your church-hooded New
> England, the porcupine
> sharpens its golden needles
> against Bostonian bricks
> to a point of needless
> blinding shine.
>
> White foam kneels and breaks
> on the altar. People's
> eyes glitter inside
> the church like pebbles
> splashed by the tide.
>
> What is Salvation, since
> a tear magnifies like glass
> a future perfect tense?
> The choir, time and again,
> sings in the key of the Cross
> of Our Father's gain,
> which is but our loss.

There will be a lot,
a lot of Almighty Lord,
but not so much as a shred
of your flesh. When man dies
the wardrobe gapes instead.
We acquire the idle state
of your jacket and ties.

(*Part*, 135)

There are no lapses in tone, no forced casualness. Indeed, the "There will
be a lot, / a lot of Almighty Lord," with the wry irony of its slightly Jobian
quantification of deity, is a splendid touch. Brodsky evokes Lowell's Boston and New England with remarkable economy and vividness. The
clean, clipped images—the churches as cowls, the golden needles, the
white foam, and the pebbles—succeed precisely because they are not pinioned too tightly by the rhyme scheme and rhythmic structure. Brodsky's
English has become more pliant and yielding through the discovery of
slant rhymes: "needles" and "needless," "bricks" and "breaks," "People's" and "pebbles," and so on. This freedom gives the poet sufficient
maneuverability to refine and hone his images, out of which grow the
motifs and larger existential issues of the poem. Now, for example, we
recognize the Russian Brodsky shining through the English Brodsky: the
death/funeral of a great poet as the splashing of tide ("Verses on the
Death of T. S. Eliot"), the mystery of the crucifixion and of the Father's
"gain" which is our "loss" ("Nature Morte"), and the departure of the
poet's soul that leaves behind the body as a "gaping wardrobe" ("Large
Elegy to John Donne"). These are Brodsky's cherished themes, and
through them he talks with his departed fellow poets as though with
equals before the court of literary history. These lines possess the sort of
concision and tension, the sense that they are saying a great deal with very
few words, that we associate with the best of Brodsky's Russian verse.
And perhaps most poignant and presumably unnoticed by anglophone
readers, Brodsky is fulfilling a role in English that only he, among his
contemporaries, could ever fulfill in Russian: he, himself a major poet
who understands implicitly what failure and pain mean in this world, is
presenting Lowell's case to that higher court. This is *his* duty, to celebrate
the worthy dead in words that do them honor.

Let us now return to "Christmas" as a possible touchstone for the butterfly motif in Nabokov's work. Recall first of all that the butterfly is the
most distinctive and pervasive of Nabokov's many "signatures": it appears prominently in *Mary* (Mashen'ka), *King, Queen, Knave* (Korol',

dama, valet), "The Aurelian" (Pil'gram), *The Defense* (Zashchita Lu-zhina), *Glory* (Podvig), *Laughter in the Dark* (Camera obscura), *Despair* (Otchaianie), *Invitation to a Beheading* (Priglashenie na kazn'), *The Gift* (Dar), *The Real Life of Sebastian Knight*, "A Discovery," *Bend Sinister*, *Lolita, Pnin, Ada, Transparent Things, Look at the Harlequins!*, and others (Karges, *Nabokov's Lepidoptera*). As Brian Boyd, Nabokov's recent biographer, notes, "Perhaps without butterflies Nabokov's life would have meandered in a different direction, or perhaps he would have found another course through the same fertile plain. At any rate the chan-nels along which his mind ran were gouged out more deeply by his love of lepidoptera—and that would help fix the contours of his mature episte-mology, his metaphysics, even his politics" (*Russian Years*, 82). Within this broad context, "Christmas" suggests itself as a useful point of depar-ture because (1) the theme of the butterfly is so dramatically foregrounded in it, and (2) the work occurs early in Nabokov-Sirin's career, when the naive religiosity of the Cambridge years was still relatively close to the surface and had not yet been thoroughly encoded ("protectively colored") in the author's aesthetics and metaphysics. The details of the story's set-ting, including a wooden gallery,[31] its stained-glass windows, and nearby foot bridge, recall descriptions of Vyra, the Nabokov family estate, in *Speak, Memory*, as well as Ganin's youthful haunts in *Mary*. The point, one may say, is not that Sirin—any more than Sleptsov—is somehow using the occasion to retrieve what has been lost through the vagaries of history or biography: by 1925 he was coming to realize that this place (Vyra) and this time (childhood) belonged exclusively to the domain (the "un-real estate") of art (*Speak, Memory*, 40). In this regard, it is intrigu-ing to speculate that the narrative structure of "Christmas" resembles an elegant chiasmus: the father (Sleptsov) who has lost his son and his hope for the future is not unlike the son (Sirin) who had recently lost a father (the statesman V. D. Nabokov, killed by an assassin's bullet in 1922) and his security in the past. Recall, for example, how in *Speak, Memory* the elder Nabokov rushes into young Vladimir's room at Vyra to borrow his net in order to capture a "magnificent female of the Russian Poplar Admi-rable" just a few lines before the son, projecting forward in time, de-scribes the assassination of the father (*Speak, Memory*, 192–93).

Sleptsov stops at the edge of the footbridge and sees in his mind's eye the following:

Он сразу вспомнил, каким был этот мост летом. По слизким доскам, усеянным сережками, проходил его сын, ловким взмахом сачка срывал бабочку, севшую на перила. Вот он увидел отца. Неповто-римым смехом играет лицо под загнутым краем потемневшей от

солнца соломенной шляпы, рука теребит цепочку и кожаный
кошелек на широком поясе, весело расставлены милые, гладкие,
коричневые ноги в коротких саржевых штанах, в промокших сан-
далиях. (*Vozvrashchenie Chorba*, 69)

He vividly recalled how this bridge looked in the summer. There was his son
walking along slippery planks, flecked with aments, and deftly plucking off
with his net a butterfly that had settled on the railing. Now the boy sees the
father. Forever lost laughter plays on his face, under the turned-down brim of
a straw hat burned dark by the sun; his hand toys with the chainlet of the
leather purse attached to his belt, his dear, smooth, sun-tanned legs in their
serge shorts and soaked sandals assume their usual cheerful wide-spread
stance. (*Details*, 155)

This moment of mutual *cognitio*, punctuated by mention of a captured
butterfly, is crucial to an understanding of how aesthetics and metaphysics interact and interpenetrate in Sirin's works. It is shot through with a
lyrical patina and autobiographical poignancy that Sirin, despite his
many cunning disclaimers, was never able to banish completely from his
texts whenever the thematic nexus of father-son-butterfly appeared. *Father sees son and son sees father*. The two are separated not only by a
spatial bridge but by a temporal one as well (the father is *recollecting* the
incident). At the same time, *within the recollection*, they are attached to
each other by the vividness of the moment and the wealth of details that
seem to exist for that moment only. It is as if the details are tiny stitches
in the fabric of existence, and that fabric forms a distinct and unrepeatable pattern. The son moves along (*prokhodil*) the raised and slippery
surface of the bridge as the Attacus moth (*indiiskii shelkopriad*) will move
(*polzet vverkh*) along the wall. The bright joy of the boy's movement and
gestures ("Nepovtorimym smekhom igraet litso . . .") anticipates the
flight of the moth ("kryl'ia . . . vzdokhnuli v poryve . . . pochti cheloveche-
skogo schast'ia"), just as the "wide-spread stance" of his "dear, smooth,
sun-tanned" legs mimics the creature's wings as they keep "growing and
unfolding . . . to the limit set for them by God." The point is not that the
son, in some crude or doctrinaire way, *becomes* (is reincarnated in) the
moth, but that both the joy of the child and the beauty of the insect attest
to the presence of divine intentionality or "mimicry" in all its possible
guises. The eyespots or little windows (*okontsa*) on the moth's wings actually exist in nature (otherwise Nabokov the entomologist would not
have used them), and yet—and this is the point—they also are *lovely metaphors* for the "view from beyond."

This sensation of miraculously "fitting into" time and space ("cosmic
synchronization" [*Speak, Memory*, 218]) will be repeated often in Nabokov's Russian and English novels and nonfictional prose, usually in con-

nection with the themes of romantic love, artistic inspiration, and death. Perhaps the most well-known discussion of Nabokovian mimicry occurs in *The Gift*, when Fyodor's lepidopterist father, soon to disappear and be presumed dead, explains the intricacies of the phenomenon to his son:

Он рассказывал о запахах бабочек—мускусных, ванильных; о голосах бабочек: о пронзительном звуке, издаваемом чудовищной гусеницей малайского сумеречника, усовершенствовавшей мышиный писк нашей адамовой головы; о маленьком звучном тимпане некоторых арктид; о хитрой бабочке в бразильском лесу, подражающей свиресту одной тамошней птички. Он рассказывал о невероятном художественном остроумии мимикрии, которая не объяснима борьбой за жизнь (грубой спешкой чернорабочих сил эволюции), излишне изысканна для обмана случайных врагов, пернатых, чешуйчатых и прочих (мало разборчивых, да и не столь уж до бабочек лакомых), и словно придумана забавником-живописцем как раз ради умных глаз человека (догадка, которая могла бы далеко увести эволюциониста, наблюдавшего питающихся бабочками обезьян). (*Dar*, 125–26)

He told me about the odors of butterflies—musk and vanilla; about the voices of butterflies; about the piercing sound of a Malayan hawkmoth, an improvement on the mouselike squeak of our Death's Head moth; about the small resonant tympanum of certain tiger moths; about the cunning butterfly in the Brazilian forest which imitates the whir of a local bird. He told me about the incredible artistic wit of mimetic disguise, which was not explainable by the struggle for existence (the rough haste of evolution's unskilled forces), was too refined for the mere deceiving of accidental predators, feathered, scaled and otherwise (not very fastidious, but then not too fond of butterflies), and seemed to have been invented by some waggish artist precisely for the intelligent eyes of man (a hypothesis that may lead far an evolutionist who observes apes feeding on butterflies). (*Gift*, 122)

Note that mimicry is "artistic" in its tendency to provide *more* design, *more* intentionality than necessary. For this creative naturalist, existence cannot be explained by any Darwinian "survival of the fittest" or quasi-Marxist "class struggle" (thus the witticism at the expense of the *chernorabochie sily evoliutsii*). Abstract pattern is not imposed on the butterfly's habitat but always grows *out of* the minute and lavishly decorative details of this world. Recently Vladimir Alexandrov has suggested that Nabokov found confirmation of this idea through his study of Petr Uspensky's *A New Model of the Universe: Psychological Method in Its Application to Problems of Science, Religion, and Art* (1931, 1934). Like Nabokov, Uspensky says that "the principle of utilitarianism ha[s] to be abandoned" when explaining the details of mimicry among insects. "The general tendency of Nature," argues Uspensky, "[is] toward decorativeness, 'theatricality,' the tendency to be or to appear different from what she really is at a given time and place" (44; cited in Alexandrov, *Nabokov's Otherworld*, 229). Hence according to Uspensky, and through him Nabokov, the phenomenon of mimicry is "ultimately 'a miracle' that implies a transcendent 'plan, intention and aim' in nature" (45; Alexandrov, *Nabokov's Otherworld*, 229). Nature and art are *not* opposed as chaos and "messiness" are opposed to artifice; instead both participate in the play of the "waggish artist" (zabavnik-zhivopisets). It is a cardinal point in Nabokov's worldview, as Alexandrov has convincingly shown, that ethics, metaphysics, and aesthetics dovetail precisely in this notion of mimicry and in the "protective coloration" of the butterfly. The ethically good man tries to appreciate and preserve this patterning; the metaphysically astute man tries to find it in God's world; and the aesthetically gifted man tries to create it in his own work.

We might say, therefore, that Sleptsov, grieving over his son's death and pondering his own ("It's Christmas tomorrow . . . and I'm going to die" [*Details*, 160]), has entered a state of suspended animation or abulia, what might be termed metaphorically *pupation*. The same can be said of Cincinnatus, the hero of *Invitation to a Beheading*, who is plagued with thoughts of his own impending execution until he sees the large moth (*nochnaia babochka*)[32] brought by his captor (Rodion) escape its fate (breakfast for a spider) and disappear "as if the very air had swallowed it" (eto bylo tak, slovno samyi vozdukh poglotil ee) (*Invitation*, 204; *Priglashenie*, 199).[33] Not only is this creature a harbinger from beyond, it is able to disappear into its surroundings, suggesting it is endowed to an uncanny degree with that very "mimicry" which is Nabokov's metaphor for transcendent logic. Consequently, immediately after this incident Cincinnatus is able, like Sleptsov, to scratch out the word *death* (*Invitation*, 206; see Davydov, *Teksty-Matreški*, 158–60). In a larger sense, before the miraculous appearance of the *nochnye babochki* both characters are "exiled" in this world; they have nothing to live for, just as, prima facie, their impoverished, deracinated, and fatherless creator would appear to have little to live for. And yet, to repeat, both story and novel end on triumphant notes, as though aglow with a light emanating from an entirely different point of view. Death is not an ending but a larval stage to pass through. That is why the image of delicately wrought *translucent* detail (the eye-spotted butterfly wing, the watermark, stained-glass windows, etc.) is so privileged to Nabokov's work—it is inserted by its maker, *membranelike*, between us and the pure consciousness after death in order that "through the glass darkly" hints of a higher order may reach us.[34]

Before looking at Brodsky, let us summarize our findings: (1) the special bond joining father and son is recollected in the context of butterfly
hunting; (2) the aesthetically marked passages (descriptions of son and
moth) derive their force from the dense weave of details and from the
author's remarkable *visual* imagination—that is, these descriptions recapitulate on a metapoetic plane the theme of mimicry in the work itself;[35]
(3) in a cruel mockery of the Christmas season, Sleptsov has nothing to
celebrate until the cocoon left behind by the son "miraculously" bursts
open and produces the great moth; (4) this quintessentially summer creature, described upon its emergence from the tiny sarcophagus as something small and rather repulsive, spreads its beautiful wings in the middle
of winter; (5) a thematic parallel exists between the cocoon, the coffin
of the dead child ("tiazhelyi, slovno vseiu zhizn'iu napolnennyi grob"
["Rozhdestvo," 69]; cf. *Details,* 155), and the present morbid state of
Sleptsov himself (see Davydov, *Teksty-Matreški,* 160); and (6) the ending
bears unmistakable signs of divine intentionality and grace ("kryl'ia . . .
vot razvernulis' do predela, polozhennogo im Bogom").[36]

Brodsky's poem "In the Evening," cited at the outset of this chapter, offers several interesting parallels to "Christmas," parallels that perhaps
deserve mention before we analyze the larger and more ambitious "The
Butterfly." Let us note briefly that (1) the speaker is alone and the setting
is an abandoned building in the winter; (2) Brodsky's moth, like Sirin's,
has managed to preserve itself into this season of death ("ot smerti sebia
sbereg"), but no mention is made of a cocoon, that is, the poet is not
witnessing the creature's birth *out of* a completely different prior state; (3)
we see the moth close up, but it is "generic," simply a *motylek* (moth),
and its details (*pyl'tsa*) are not endowed with the nomenclatural precision
of the entomologist (cf. Sirin's "six black furry feet," "wrinkled tissues,"
"velvety fringes," "fan-pleated veins," "[four] glazy eyespot[s]," etc.); (4)
this poem, together with the preceding Christmas one, suggests a kind of
miracle, so that the images of snow at the outset are gradually metamorphosed into the hands, now "warm like June days," holding the moth.
We will return to these parallels in due course.

"The Butterfly" is arguably one of Brodsky's greatest metaphysical creations. It was begun in 1972, while the poet was still living in Leningrad,
and completed in emigration the following year. Thus it could be sur-
mised that the theme of exile hovers around the edges of this poem just as
it did around "In the Evening." Brodsky has suggested in a private interview that if he had any artists in mind during composition it was Mozart
and Samuel Beckett (especially the latter's "absurdist" streak) rather than
Nabokov.[37] At the time of writing he attended a symphony concert of
Mozart's works with a lady friend, and upon leaving the concert hall the

woman joked with the poet that the composer's special brand of brilliance was not within his (Brodsky's) reach. Brodsky then responded by penning a verbal butterfly capable of competing with the flight of Mozart's musical notes.

I

Сказать, что ты мертва?
Но ты жила лишь сутки.
Как много грусти в шутке
Творца! едва
могу произнести
«жила»—единство даты
рожденья и когда ты
в моей горсти
рассыпалась, меня
смущает вычесть
одно из двух количеств
в пределах дня.

(ChR, 32)

Should I say that you're dead?
You touched so brief a fragment
of time. There's much that's sad in
the joke God played.
I scarcely comprehend
the words "you've lived"; the date of
your birth and when you faded
in my cupped hand
are one, and not two dates.
Thus calculated,
your term is, simply stated,
less than a day.[38]

(Part, 68)

Several aspects of Brodsky's opening stanza immediately strike the reader familar with Nabokov's butterflies. First, the "precision" of Brodsky's description is of a different order than that of Nabokov's. It has to do with inherent *poetic* qualities, with the elaborate stanza form and metrical scheme, themselves as delicate and carefully wrought as the butterfly wing they mimic. If Nabokov derives his aesthetic pleasure from "the tactile delights of precise delineation" (Appel, "An Interview," 33), it is a pleasure primarily "prosaic" (however "poetically" colored) in origin. Brodsky, on the other hand, proceeds from an *aural* rather than visual stimulus; to him it is less important what the butterfly, scientifically, is called, since its presence in this poetic monologue is motivated primarily by its ability to generate paradox (beauty = mortality). Indeed, Brodsky has advanced the provocative theory that Nabokov's obsession with doubles in his works derives from his inability to become a major poet: the doppelgänger is a projection onto the plane of prose of the author's search for a suitable rhyme pair (something he was denied in his attempts to write poetry).[39]

Second, Brodsky's butterfly is *dead*, while Nabokov's are usually alive and in flight or, as in the case of "Christmas," emerging from a cocoon. That is, Brodsky's focus is on the *death of beauty* ("Kak mnogo grusti v shutke Tvortsa!"), while Nabokov's is on *the beauty that overcomes death*. On the larger plane of literary origins and genealogy, Nabokov's point of departure is the symbolist and postsymbolist "otherworldliness" he inherited from Blok, Bely, Gumilyov, and Khodasevich (see Alexandrov, *Nabokov's Otherworld*, 213–27); the butterfly does not die so much as it is reborn into a higher state of consciousness. Death is a necessary episode in God's plot, hence there is no "sadness" in the "Creator's joke." Brodsky's point of departure is precisely the opposite: what is ironic is that something this lovely must die in the first place. In other words, Brodsky's roots, by 1963 largely Christian existentialist (Kierkegaard, Shestov, the "Abraham and Isaac" episode in the Bible), require that he *question* the design that Nabokov, through his marriage of science and art, is able to affirm. And in this respect, as we recall from previous discussion, Brodsky can be called the first and only Russian poet to have mastered the English metaphysical tradition, with its passion for paradox, its "difficult joining" of the conceit, and its predilection for expressing the large and abstract (beauty, mortality) through the small (butterfly).[40]

II
Затем что дни для нас—
ничто. Всего лишь
ничто. Их не приколешь,—
и пищей глаз
не сделаешь: они
на фоне белом,
не обладая телом,
незримы. Дни,
они как ты; верней,
что может весить
уменьшенный раз в десять
один из дней?

(*ChR*, 32)

It's clear that days for us
are nothings, zeros.
They can't be pinned down near us

to feed our eyes.
Whatever days stand stark
against white borders,
since they possess no bodies
they leave no mark.
They are like you. That is,
each butterfly's small plumage
is one day's shrunken image—
a tenth its size.

(*Part*, 68)

Here in stanza II Brodsky begins to give wings to the paradoxical structure of his butterfly. The butterfly is an embodiment of time, or more precisely, of the integers (days) by which we count and delimit time. It weighs so little, like time itself, that it is difficult to grasp its substantiality. One cannot "pin down" (ikh ne prikolesh') days as one can the wings of a butterfly, and one cannot see them because they, like the butterfly that disappears into the protective coloration of its habitat, get lost against a background of white. Brodsky has shifted attention away from the vehicle (butterfly) to the tenor (time, days). Whereas Nabokov never loses sight of the physical aspects of his lepidoptera (esp. wing size, shape, color), and thus his transcendent logic never leaves behind the natural world in which it is embedded, Brodsky is more intent on the *logical paradoxes* generated by bringing tenor and vehicle together in various formulations. Notice, for example, that Nabokov lingers lovingly over the procedures of butterfly collecting (see *Speak, Memory* 119–39) while Brodsky is content to use the image of transfixing and mounting ("Ikh ne prikolesh' ") purely for its metaphorical resonances.

Stanzas III and IV provide a direct and provocative interface with various of Nabokov's texts:

III
Сказать, что вовсе нет
тебя? Но что же
в руке моей так схоже
с тобой? и цвет—
не плод небытия.
По чьей подсказке
и так кладутся краски?
Навряд ли я,
бормочущий комок
слов, чуждых цвету,
вообразить бы эту
палитру смог.

IV
На крылышках твоих
зрачки, ресницы—
красавицы ли, птицы—
обрывки чьих,
скажи мне, это лиц,
портрет летучий?
Каких, скажи, твой случай
частиц, крупиц
являет натюрморт:
вещей, плодов ли?
и даже рыбной ловли
трофей простерт.

(ChR, 33)

Should I say that, somehow,
you lack all being?
What, then, are my hands feeling
that's so like you?
Such colors can't be drawn
from nonexistence.
Tell me, at whose insistence
were yours laid on?
Since I'm a mumbling heap
of words, not pigments,
how could your hues be figments
of my conceit?

There are, on your small wings,
black spots and splashes—
like eyes, birds, girls, eyelashes.
But of what things
are you the airy norm?
What bits of faces,
what broken times and places
shine through your form?
As for your *nature mortes*:
do they show dishes
of fruits and flowers, or fishes
displayed on boards?

(Part, 68–69)

These two stanzas could be read as ironic or inverted commentary on the ending of Nabokov's "Christmas." The speaker asks where the butterfly, or rather the soul that gave it animation, is now, if this beautiful shell has been left behind. It is painful to say that the butterfly no longer *is*, and yet what was is fundamentally different from what is. In "Christmas" what is left behind is the cocoon (the past) and what is promised (meaning comes from the future) is the beautiful moth that has emerged from the chrysalid. The entire structure of Brodsky's verse is based here on *interrogatives*—questions that, even if they are not answered in the negative, undermine the reality of discourse. The poignancy of Nabokov's ending, on the other hand, is based entirely on a declarative structure and on conjunctions that *affirm* the ontological rightness of the pupation and that *animate* its neuter subject: "Ono [sushchestvo] vylupilos' *ottogo*, *chto* iznemogaiushchii ot goria chelovek perenes zhestianuiu korobku k sebe, v tepluiu komnatu, ono vyrvalos' *ottogo*, *chto* skvoz' tugoi shelk kokona proniklo teplo, ono tak dolgo ozhidalo etogo, tak napriazhenno nabiralos' sil i vot teper', vyrvavshis', medlenno i chudesno roslo." The repeated *ottogo*, *chto* (because, on account of) suggests that the cocoon burst open both because it had been taken into a warm room (the scientific explanation) and, equally important, because the man had been "worn out with grief" and his need was being answered; that is, the "iznemogaiushchii ot goria" and the "perenes . . . v tepluiu komnatu" occupy equal and counterbalancing positions in the sentence, so that meaning, grammatical and existential, emerges from "here" and from "there."

Conversely, in Brodsky the focus is relentlessly on the question of what sort of creator could be responsible for such a status quo. Nabokov delights in the design and demonstrates his delight by naming the colors on the butterfly; Brodsky mentions the presence of colors ("Po ch'ei podskazke / i tak kladutsia kraski?") but before naming them inquires after the reason, the *podskazka*, for placing them in this configuration in the first place. And whereas Nabokov is able to make his leap of faith through the science of entomology and through his own mystical belief, Brodsky, who acknowledges that some signature, some order from above, seems to be present in this creature, cannot connect that knowledge to himself, his mortality, and his understanding of time. That is why the eyespots on Brodsky's butterfly *may* be part of a larger portrait (*portret letuchii*) or system of mimicry, but *he* cannot see it, and hence questions its existence. And perhaps most revealing, Brodsky associates his gift of words with *sound* ("ia, / bormochushchii komok / slov"), sound which by definition is alien to color ("slov, chuzhdykh tsvetu") and incapable of conceiving or creating this sort of beauty. We might say, therefore, that at this stage Nabokov's famous *audition colorée* (*Dar*, 85) has vouchsafed him a superiority in his dialogue with mortality (*if* belief in transcendent meaning is superiority), while Brodsky's remarkable ear for rhyme, meter, and poetic form places him at an existential disadvantage before God's palette (*palitra*) and his colorful, though silent, interlocutor.

V

Возможно, ты—пейзаж,
и, взявши лупу,
я обнаружу группу
нимф, пляску, пляж.
Светло ли там, как днем?
иль там уныло,
как ночью? и светило
какое в нем
взошло на небосклон?
чьи в нем фигуры?
Скажи, с какой натуры
был сделан он?

VI

Я думаю, что ты—
и то, и это:
звезды, лица, предмета
в тебе черты.
Кто был тот ювелир,—
что бровь не хмуря,
нанес в миниатюре
на них тот мир,
что сводит нас с ума,
берет нас в клещи,
где ты, как мысль о вещи,
мы—вещь сама?

(ChR, 34)

Perhaps a landscape smokes
among your ashes,
and with thick reading glasses
I'll scan its slopes—
its beaches, dancers, nymphs.
Is it as bright as
the day, or dark as night is?
And could one glimpse—
ascending that sky's screen—
some blazing lantern?
And tell me, please, what pattern
inspired this scene?

It seems to me you are
a protean creature,
whose markings mask a feature

> of face, or stone, or star.
> Who was the jeweler,
> brow uncontracted,
> who from our world extracted
> your miniature—
> a world where madness brings
> us low, and lower,
> where we are things, while you are
> the thought of things?
>
> (*Part*, 69–70)

The rhetorical figure of romantic irony plays a salient role in both Nabokov[41] and Brodsky: as man looks at flora and fauna through a magnifying glass and holds up his prey in tweezers, so does God, a playful but ultimately indifferent author, look down on his creation, including man. Nabokov was famous for the imperious disdain with which he treated his own characters, calling them at one point, punningly, "galley slaves" (*Strong Opinions*, 69). And yet it is equally true that his positive characters, those such as Cincinnatus, Fyodor, and Pnin, are granted a kind of freedom at the end of their servitude: Cincinnatus walks away from his own beheading in the direction "where, to judge by the voices, stood beings akin to him" (*Invitation*, 223); Fyodor is transformed from the "he" to the "I" of the narrative, that is, he becomes the author of the work whose "gift" we have just finished celebrating and whose concluding sonnet form carries us back to the beginning; Pnin ends by driving off the page of his story and out of the clutches of his author (see Davydov, *Teksty-Matreški*). Put simply, Nabokov's deployment of romantic irony is predicated first of all on his version of theodicy—on the notion that God's (or the author's) design does not thwart the freedom and dignity of the truly creative personality but calls it to live up to its gift. Brodsky, on the other hand, being by nature skeptical and pessimistic, embraces the dark side of romantic irony; like Ivan Karamazov (Dostoevsky is one of Brodsky's favorite authors), he does not question God's existence but the logic of His creation. His God, although a marvelous jeweler (another version of the Cartesian clockmaker) and supremely capable of reproducing this elfin diorama in countless permutations, still holds us in his tweezers ("beret nas v kleshchi").[42] We are vulnerable and He, primarily Old Testament (the tormentor of Job and Abraham) rather than New, is indifferent ("brov' ne khmuria") to our fate. And if this is all true, then we, despite our attempts to find a place for our animate natures in the larger picture, are only a "thing" to God ("my—veshch' sama").

Brodsky goes on in the final stanzas of his poem to address many of the same issues raised by Nabokov, but always from his special angle of vision. Here it is worth reiterating that Dr. Johnson defined the metaphysical conceit opprobriously as a kind of intellectually perverse metaphor wherein "heterogeneous ideas [are] yoked by violence together" (Johnson, *Lives of Poets*, 14). The crux of Brodsky's conceit centers on the forcible joining of the silence of the fluttering butterfly (as opposed to others of God's creatures)[43] and the silence of the pen as it crosses the paper to create a poem. It is at this juncture that the metapoetics of Brodsky and Nabokov intersect. The movements of the butterfly in search of food give form to the air . . .

XI
Так делает перо,
скользя по глади
расчерченной тетради,
не зная про
судьбу своей строки,
где мудрость, ересь
смешались, но доверясь
толчкам руки,
в чьих пальцах бьется речь
вполне немая,
не пыль с цветка снимая,
но тяжесть с плеч.

(*ChR*, 37)

So, too, the sliding pen
which inks a surface
has no sense of the purpose
of any line
or that the whole will end
as an amalgam
of heresy and wisdom;
it therefore trusts the hand
whose silent speech incites
fingers to throbbing—
whose spasm reaps no pollen,
but eases hearts.

(*Part*, 71)

Brodsky cannot *see* God's plan when he looks at the colors and patterns in the butterfly's wing, yet he can *feel* something analogous when his own poetic line, not knowing in advance what will come next, responds to the movement of his hand, which in turn pulsates with the unbidden gift of *nemaia rech'*. The poem is his butterfly, his attempt to impress a design on the blank page of reality. That it removes a "weight from his shoulders," that is, makes life bearable, rather than removes pollen from a flower suggests it has its own inscrutable reason for being. Brodsky's position is

finally existentialist and Christian to the extent that he picks up his pen
and makes his poetic flight (and sacrifice, since he, too, is under a death
sentence) in the face of eternal questioning and equally eternal silence.
Both Nabokov and Brodsky, therefore, recognize the butterfly as an
image for art in an exilic world where meaning is never self-evident. For
the former, however, this image is a link in a grandly conceived chain
leading to transcendence; for the latter it is a small revelation, ad hoc and
inseparable from language itself, that has to be made again and again,
with no guarantee of success.

Hence the lesson each writer draws from the life cycle of the butterfly
is different. At the end of his butterfly chapter in *Speak, Memory* Nabokov recalls beginning a day of collecting in July 1910 "on the vast
marshland beyond the Oredezh" and finishing the same hunt amid "Pon-
derosa pines," "above the timber line" of Longs Peak, Colorado, that is,
in America many decades later (*Speak, Memory*, 137–39). How can this
be? The artist-lepidopterist answers with something as close to an article
of faith as can be found in his work:

> I confess I do not believe in time. I like to fold my magic carpet, after use, in
> such a way as to superimpose one part of the pattern upon another. Let visitors
> trip. And the highest enjoyment of timelessness—in a landscape selected at
> random—is when I stand among rare butterflies and their food plants. This is
> ecstasy, and behind the ecstasy there is something else, which is hard to ex-
> plain. It is like a momentary vacuum into which rushes all that I love. A sense
> of oneness with sun and stone. A thrill of gratitude to whom it may concern—
> to the contrapuntal genius of human fate or to tender ghosts humoring a lucky
> mortal. (*Speak, Memory*, 139)

On his magic carpet or on the wings of butterflies, which is the same
thing, Nabokov can experience as one telescoping and glorious instant
outings on two different continents and in two vastly different epochs and
cultures. He sees himself as a character in a supremely artificial but no less
real, divine comedy. Like Cincinnatus, he can at such moments disrobe
from his body, like the moth, disappear "into thin air," and like the hero
of *The Ballad of Longwood Glen*, climb a tree in search of his prey, leave
the three-dimensional world of history, exile, and death behind, and step
off into an ethereal fourth dimension of pure consciousness:

> What tiaras of gardens! What torrents of light!
> How accessible ether! How easy flight!
> His family circled the tree all day.
> Pauline concluded: "Dad climbed away."
>
> *None saw the delirious celestial crowds*
> *Greet the hero from earth in the snow of the clouds.*
>
> (cited in Field, Nabokov: His Life in Art, 101)

Brodsky's conclusion, exactly the opposite, is no less moving, and shows to what extent he belongs to a later epoch, one marked by increasing scepticism about "transcendental signifiers": "v samom dele / mir sozdan byl bez tseli, / a esli s nei, / to tsel'—ne my. / Drug-entomolog, /dlia sveta net igolok / i net dlia t'my" (the world was made to hold / no end or *telos*, / and if—as some would tell us—/ there is a goal, / it's not ourselves. / No butterfly collector / can trap light or detect where / the darkness dwells) (*CR*, 37; *Part*, 72). If Nabokov is a great postsymbolist, then Brodsky is a great postmodernist, the poet who is orphaned and exiled in every conceivable sense, physical and metaphysical. All he has is his language,[44] the words on the printed page, his metaphorical butterfly wing, and this is the one membrane, the one flimsy barrier, separating him from the *Nichto* [No-thing] of nonbeing:

XIV

Ты лучше, чем Ничто.
Верней: ты ближе
и зримее. Внутри же
на все на сто
ты родственна ему.
В твоем полете
оно достигло плоти;
и потому
ты в сутолке дневной
достойна взгляда
как легкая преграда
меж ним и мной.

(*ChR*, 38)

You're better than No-thing.
That is, you're nearer,
more reachable, and clearer.
Yet you're akin
to nothingness—
like it, you're wholly empty.
And if, in your life's venture,
No-thing takes flesh,
that flesh will die.
Yet while you live you offer
a frail and shifting buffer,
dividing it from me.

(*Part*, 72)

Afterword _____

WHAT MIGHT WE SAY in parting about this poet who has always insisted not only on his own sovereign agency but on *creating his own exile*, both linguistic and experiential, even as he has been created by it? And though his life is still unfolding, what does his "vector" yet promise? Why, finally, does Brodsky's instance strike us as poignantly *exemplary*?

Nadezhda Mandelstam once wrote about the role of poetry in Russian culture: "People can be killed for poetry here [in Russia]—a sign of unparalleled respect—because they are still capable of living by it" (*Hope Abandoned*, 11). It is this relationship to the poetic word, among other things, that we are seeing pass before our eyes as the former Soviet Union, in the wake of the August 1991 coup attempt, makes its halting transition to a modern civil society. No one need be killed for his or her poetry, and that is to the good. In fact, Russians are experiencing a relatively free book trade for the first time in memory, and the sight is not, particularly for intelligentsia tastes, inspiring. A secular saint like Mandelstam has suddenly to compete with pornography and detective fiction. The question is, will people still be capable of living by poetry in a post-*glasnost'* era.

Joseph Brodsky, as clear-eyed and unsentimental about the wages of time, death, and history as any modern Russian poet, would certainly not have us pine for the conditions that gave rise to the sacred "potlatch" between poet and audience. He would be the first to tell us that together with Mandelstam's "nostalgia for world culture" went the state's trampling of cultural memory that made such yearning necessary in the first place. Yet the victory for democratic institutions is, one may observe, bittersweet. When Brodsky says of Mandelstam with a eulogistic passion that takes the reader's breath away—

> He was, one is tempted to say, a modern Orpheus: sent to hell, he never returned, while his widow dodged across one-sixth of the earth's surface, clutching the saucepan with his songs rolled up inside, memorizing them by night in the event they were found by Furies with a search warrant. These are our metamorphoses, our myths. (*Less*, 144)

—one wonders how much *he too* needs these myths. Lest we forget, he grew up and came of age in a world where Nadezhda Mandelstam's scale of values still had currency; indeed, he himself was tested in its crucible. And as much as he despises the use of melodrama, especially with respect to himself, he was, in a sense, the last Russian "bard." By this I mean that he was the last writer of verse whose work so attracted the "unparalleled respect" of the state that the latter, though aging and perhaps not so bloodthirsty as the wolfhound of Mandelstamian memory, still felt compelled to place him in a position of mortal peril. And the charismatic contract was fulfilled: he *and* his verse rose, so to speak, to the occasion.

In the mythic time of the Russian family romance, the presence of a punishing father (say, Stalin) and an elaborate set of political and societal taboos made the choice of charismatic rebellion both tragedy-laden and, at the same time, "simple." Between the words and deeds of a Stalin and the words and deeds of a Mandelstam there was little room for ambiguity (or interpretive pluralism), and the tradition itself of poetry as sacred speech, despite the multitudes who were bent or broken to the official ideology, was rarely questioned. The oedipal struggle for ever new poetic versions of the "American dream," where cultural mythology is implicated but where the state and the poet are not necessarily fatally misaligned, is an entirely different matter. Here the tradition itself has little that can be called sacred left of it. Now, many years later, the poet laureate of his adoptive country, Brodsky is faced with a different sort of *podvig* (spiritual feat)—how to get a country like America to recognize and *live for* its poetry. The prospect is daunting, yet the tone of voice, the combination of irony and "vatic" arrogance, is, for all that, the same. Stepson of Akhmatova, heir to Mandelstam and Tsvetaeva, Brodsky has seen the passing of his native culture's heroic age and of his own personal mythology. But even so, in the antiheroic posture (that is still somehow heroic) internalized from his beloved Auden, and in the extravagant claims for American poetry and in the quixotic demands of the American readership, the Russian bard lives on:

> Poetry must be available to the public in far greater volume than it is. It should be as ubiquitous as the nature that surrounds us, and from which poetry derives many of its similes; or as ubiquitous as gas stations, if not as cars themselves. Bookstores should be located not only on campuses or on main drags, but at the assembly plant's gates also. Paperbacks of those we deem classics should be cheap and sold at supermarkets. This is, after all, a country of mass production, and I don't see why what's done for cars can't be done for books of poetry, which take you quite a bit further. . . .

> American poetry is this country's greatest patrimony. It takes a stranger to see some things clearly. This is one of them, and I am that stranger. The quantity of verse that has been penned on these shores in the last century and a half dwarfs the similar enterprise of any literature, and for that matter, both our jazz and our cinema, rightly adored throughout the world. The same goes, I dare say, for its quality, for this is a poetry informed by the spirit of personal responsibility. There is nothing more alien to American poetry than those great continental specialities: the sensibility of the victim with its wildly oscillating, blamethirsty finger; the incoherence of elevation; the Promethean affectations

and special pleading. To be sure, American verse has its vices—too many a parochial visionary, a verbose neurotic. . . .

No other language accumulates so much of this [i.e., verbal "beauty"] as does English. To be born into it or to arrive in it is the best boon that can befall a man. To prevent its keepers from full access to it is an anthropological crime, and that's what the present system of distribution of poetry boils down to. I don't rightly know what's worse, burning books or not reading them. I think, though, that token publishing falls somewhere in between. I am sorry to put this so drastically, but when I think of the great works by the poets of this language bulldozed into neglect on the one hand, and then consider the mind-boggling demographic vista [i.e., the large number of literate readers] on the other, I feel that we are on the verge of a tremendous cultural backslide. . . .

Fifty million copies of an anthology of American poetry for $2 a copy can be sold in a country of 250 million. Perhaps not at once, but gradually, over a decade or so, they will sell. Books find their readers. And if they will not sell, well, let them lie around, absorb dust, rot, and disintegrate. There is always going to be a child who will fish a book out of the garbage heap. I was such a child, for what it's worth. ("An Immodest Proposal")

Notes

Chapter 1
Joseph Brodsky and the Creation of Exile:
A Polemical Introduction

1. "A poet turning to prose . . . is like the shift from gallop to trot, a time-exposure photograph of a monument, or Apollo's one year's service as shepherd for the flocks of King Admetus" (Brodsky, *Modern Russian Poets*, 8–9).

2. From Tsvetaeva's title, "Poet o kritike," with "o kritike" declined in an oblique case, we cannot tell whether she has in mind *kritik* (critic) or *kritika* (criticism).

3. My thanks to Nicole Monnier, a graduate student in Slavic at Princeton University, for a copy of this list.

4. "Yet Brodsky's response [at his trial in 1964 that his calling came "from God"], if repeated on American soil, would sound provocative here, too. In the Soviet Union you are a poet because you have been granted permission to be one by the appropriate authorities. In the United States you are a poet because no authority can prohibit you from being one (more exactly, from enrolling in a course in creative writing, publishing two poems in *Chattanooga Review*, and winning a grant from the National Endowment for the Arts). In either case, God (who in this context is just shorthand for 'poetic calling') seems to have nothing to do with writing poems" (Baranczak, *Breathing*, 203).

5. In this regard, to repeat, Brodsky resists any attempts to write him into a "plot" that does not begin with the primary fact of his poetic language. See below.

6. The paradox here, about which we will have more to say in due course, is that Brodsky understands implicitly the psychic dangers in the "vatic" mode. He constantly downplays the importance of biography in his own work and, following his hero Auden in the latter's "anti-heroic posture" (*Less*, 367), sees a certain falseness in the apocalyptic rhetoric of, say, Yeats. On the other hand, while both Yeats and the later Mandelstam are thematically kindred (Brodsky, "Beyond Consolation," 16), there is not this same rhetorical overreaching in the Russian. Why? One has to assume that in Brodsky's mind it has something to do with Mandelstam's life of sacrifice to poetry and his personal tragedy. As Brodsky says, in utmost seriousness, in his Nobel Lecture, "These shades [Mandelstam, Tsvetaeva, Frost, Akhmatova, Auden] disturb me constantly, they are disturbing me today as well. In any case, they do not spur one to eloquence. In my better moments, I deem myself their sum total, though invariably inferior to any one of them individually. For it is not possible to better them on the page; nor is it possible to better them in actual life" (Loseff and Polukhina, *Brodsky's Poetics*, 1). Reference to "actual life" presumably has more to do with Mandelstam, Tsvetaeva, and Akhmatova than with Auden and Frost. And yet, and here the paradox comes full circle, Brodsky would not trade the inevitable cultural "leveling" that takes place in a free democracy for the sublime "bardic" art produced under tyranny: "The other thing, of course, is the paradox of the Eastern victim's [i.e.

Milan Kundera's] assumption of cultural superiority over the Western villain, which nonetheless doesn't deter him from aspiring to the benefits of the villain's system. . . . To resolve this paradox, one should bear two things in mind: First, that betrayal, erosion, lowering of standards and so forth are the organic features of civilization, that civilization is an organism that excretes, secretes, degenerates, regenerates [cf. the Mandelstam of 'Lamarck'; and that the dying and rotting of its parts is the price this organism pays for evolution. Second, that the purity of the victim is a forced, i.e., artificial purity that we wouldn't trade the smallest of our liberties to have; that our attraction to the victim's cultural standards is of an elegiac nature because they belong to the past of a civilization put, as it were, into the freezer by ideological tyranny. Live fish always smells; frozen fish does so only when it is cooked" ("Why Milan Kundera Is Wrong," 33). We need look no farther than this statement to see how different Brodsky's views are from those of an angry prophet in the wilderness like Alexander Solzhenitsyn.

7. This thrust, as we shall see, comes from Brodsky himself, who declared (*in absentia*) to a gathering of fellow exiles (Vienna, December 1987) the following: "For the truth of the matter is that exile is a metaphysical condition. At least, it has a very strong, very clear metaphysical dimension, and to ignore or to dodge it is to cheat yourself out of the meaning of what has happened to you, and to doom yourself to remaining forever at the receiving end of things, to ossify into an uncomprehending victim" ("The Condition," 16). See the third section of this chapter "Exile."

8. The poet Evgeny Rein, Brodsky's old friend and teacher, has devised the following metaphor to describe his *dlinnoty*: "There is, let's say, a certain machine that produces precisely [chekanit] Brodsky's verses. Imagine that it's a sort of Linotype. When Brodsky is standing right next to it, it produces poetry of the highest quality. But Brodsky quite often goes out to take a smoke; as we know, he likes to smoke a lot. But the machine continues to work: it produces verse of second- and third-class quality. Then Brodsky returns, the smoke break is over, and once again there appears poetry of the highest quality" (Interview with author; 22 August 1989, Moscow).

9. Brodsky's comments on freedom of speech, delivered twenty years ago, bear repeating in the present context: "I do not pretend to objectivity; it strikes me that objectivity is a certain kind of blindness in which background and foreground are totally indistinguishable from each other. In the final analysis I will rely on the good practices of the free press, although freedom of speech, like any freedom bestowed gratuitously, without struggle, has its shadowy sides. For in any second generation, freedom is an inherited rather than personal achievement. Aristocracy—but impoverished aristocracy. It is that freedom of speech which generates inflation of speech" ("Says poet Brodsky," 11).

10. Likewise, the poet laureate's apparently quixotic recommendation to place cheap editions of verse in supermarket check-out lines next to tabloid coverage of "Elvis sightings" has its own quite consistent logic: good poetry need not be, by definition, elitist or rigidly academic ("The People's Poet," 39; see also "An Immodest Proposal").

11. The discomfort, by the way, that many Slavists feel with the application of a basically French (Barthes-inspired) notion of the "pleasure of the text" to, say,

Mandelstam's later verse might be compared to the sort of viewer unease that accompanies "generic" television coverage from the air—for example, crews shooting at a safe distance from their helicopters—of a riot taking place on the streets below. The people become unreal, illusory, their suffering merely a figment of the visual imagination. So, too, when we make Mandelstam's beautiful and haunting words the "free play of the signifier."

12. Brodsky also mentions Auden and Frost in this context, but presumably his emphasis is on the Russian poets.

13. The last three lines, for example, are disappointingly inexact: literally, they read "It's only with grief that I feel solidarity. / But as long as clay has not yet been stuffed into my mouth / Only gratitude will resound from it."

14. In one of his early articles written in the United States, Brodsky mentions that once in the late 1950s he worked in the Far East shooting "crazed wild bears that had gotten used to feeding on the corpses from labor-camp graves and were now dying off because they could not return to normal food" ("Reflections," 66). One is tempted to see a connection between these "wild beasts" and the potential for madness and mayhem in the speaker himself.

15. To be sure, Heaney's "Muse" seems to be more modest and self-contained, hence more "lyrical," than Brodsky's. His poetry has less of the "centrifugal" element, less pure metaphysical speculation, than his Russian colleague's. Likewise, to use Eikhenbaum's categories, Heaney's verse style might be characterized as a combination of "conversational" (*govornoi*) and "melodious" (*napevnyi*), while Brodsky's might be characterized, at least at times, as possessing a definite admixture of the "declamatory/rhetorical" (*deklamativnyi/ritoricheskii*) (*Eikhenbaum, O poezii*, 331).

16. "[Walcott] was surely lucky to be born at this outskirt, at this crossroads of English and the Atlantic where both arrive in waves only to recoil. The same pattern of motion—ashore, and back to the horizon—is sustained in Walcott's lines, thoughts, life" (Brodsky, *Less*, 174).

17. When speaking of Milosz, whom he describes as "one of the greatest poets of our time, perhaps the greatest," Brodsky has mentioned prominently the former's *metaphysical* understanding of language and his *stoicism* (see "Presentation," 364). These are terms that have been frequently applied to Brodsky himself.

18. Again, literally "But as long as clay has not yet been stuffed into my mouth/ Only gratitude will resound from it."

19. The syntax of the final stanza is particularly complex and difficult to render without becoming prolix in English. The literal gist of the final four lines is "Great soul, a transoceanic bow for having found them [words] to you and that mortal part that sleeps in the native earth, which, thanks to you, has acquired the gift of speech in a deaf-and-dumb universe."

20. To date, the best available introductions to Brodsky's life and times are found in Polukhina, *Joseph Brodsky*, 1–101; Kline and Sylvester, "Iosif Aleksandrovich Brodskii"; and Kline, "The 1987 Nobel Prize."

21. Recall the devil Koroviev's droll response to the woman guarding the doorway at Griboedov House (the official club and restaurant of MASSOLIT—i.e., the Writers' Union) in Bulgakov's *Master and Margarita*. When asked to show his card, Koroviev muses, "Well, then, in order to convince yourself that

Dostoevsky is a writer, must you ask to see his identification card? Why, take any five pages from any of his novels and you will see without any cards that you are dealing with a writer. Beside, I imagine he never had any card anyway!" (*Master and Margarita*, 361–62).

22. This notion of *vychitanie* is taken from Mikhail Epstein, a young Moscow critic and "culturologist" who now teaches at Emory University. Epstein coined the term during a faculty seminar on Brodsky at the Middlebury College Russian School in the summer of 1990. I would like to take this opportunity to thank him for this and other insights. A number of critics have commented on Brodsky's urge toward a kind of "existential synecdoche," of reducing the whole of his person or lyrical "I" to a part. See, for example, Polukhina, "Brodsky's Self-Portrait," 126–27. "It is precisely this preference for the part over the whole . . . which brings Brodsky closest to being categorised as an impersonal poet because the lyrical 'I' is almost totally squeezed out of his poetry. The technique of *pars pro toto* as a metonymical means of self-portrayal is cultivated by Brodsky through-out the whole of his work: 38 per cent of all similes which play a part in the delineation of his lyrical subject rest upon a metonymic basis" (127). We will have more to say about this aspect of Brodsky's lyric profile in due course.

23. To be sure, Brodsky's attitude toward life's stormy weather is considerably less romantic and "otherworldly" than that of his postsymbolist forebears (such as Gumilyov and Nabokov), but in the end it is perhaps not fundamentally different.

24. "Childless couples, orphaned children, aborted childbirths, and unregen-erately celibate men and women populate the world of high modernism with remarkable insistence [think of the Russian symbolists and postsymbolists], all of them suggesting the difficulties of filiation. But no less important in my opinion is the second part of the pattern, which is immediately consequent upon the first, the pressure to produce new and different ways of conceiving human relationships. For if biological reproduction is either too difficult or too unpleasant, is there some other way by which men and women can create social bonds between each other that would substitute for those ties that connect members of the same family across generations" (Said, *The World*, 17). For more on this notion of "filiation" versus "affiliation," see Said, *Beginnings*, 81–88, and *The World*, 16–17.

25. See, for example: "A *raznochinets* needs no memory—it is enough for him to tell of the books he has read, and his biography is done" (Mandelstam, *SS*, 2:99).

26. Gordeeva tests her findings on the following prose writers and poets: Valery Popov, Andrei Bitov, Viktor Golyavkin, Lydia Ginzburg, Brodsky, Alex-ander Kushner, Evgeny Rein, Vadim Shefner, and Elena Shvarts. My thanks to Professor Carol Ueland of Drew University for pointing out this article to me.

27. To be sure, Herbert's "metaphysics" are rather simplistic and marginal when compared to those of Milosz and in fact have relatively little significance for his value system and Weltanschauung. Herbert cannot thus be called a "meta-physical" in the same way the label can be applied to Milosz. The source of Her-bert's ethics lies not, as in Milosz, in asking metaphysical questions reaching back to the origin of evil (*unde malum*), but rather in asking moralistic questions reach-ing, in a sense, *forward*, toward situations that life and history may bring about and that will require a clear sense of what is right and wrong. In other words,

Milosz asks mainly why God puts up with evil that exists in the world; Herbert asks mainly how man should deal with evil. The reason for this is that Milosz's philosophy is undetachable from his Catholic theology, while Herbert's is closer to agnosticism than to any specific faith. My thanks to Stanislaw Baranczak of Harvard for his help in formulating these distinctions. Clearly, in this context Brodsky has more to share with Milosz than with Herbert. Other Poles who seem to have appealed to the young Brodsky include Konstanty Ildefons Galczynski and Cyprian Kamil Norwid.

28. On this occasion Slutsky had good reason to feel shame about his behavior. Not only did he vote to expel Pasternak (as did the vast majority of his colleagues), he went further—at the instigation of the authorities he delivered a verbal denouncement of Pasternak at the general meeting.

29. "The damned trait of understanding and thus forgiving everybody, which started while I was in school, fully blossomed in prison" (*Less*, 23).

30. See, for example, the circular structure of "Plokhie vremena tem khoroshi" (Bad times are good in that) in Smith, *Anthology*, 2–5.

31. This sort of metapoetic punning is quite characteristic of Slutsky. Elsewhere, for example, he plays off the difference between *byt* (everyday life) and *bytie* (existence). See "Plokhie vremena tem khoroshi" (Bad times are good in that) in Smith, *Anthology*, 2–5.

32. The volume appeared at Farrar, Straus and Giroux, Brodsky's publishing house.

33. As Dmitry Likhachev writes, "Kushner is an *intelligent* in the highest sense of the word. He is not only a man of the widest knowledge, he is capable of imaginative empathy [sposoben vchuvstvovat'sia], of reimbodiment [perevoploshchenie]; his verse grows not on naked soil but enters with its roots into the culture of the past. Kushner senses his links to his poetic precursors" ("Kratchaishii put'", 9, in Kushner, *Stikhotvoreniia*).

34. Kushner himself is, of course, not unaware of his kinship with Brodsky. He even seems on occasion to welcome the "competition." At least two of his poems, "In a Cafe" (V kafe) and "Folded Wings" (Slozhiv kryl'ia), can be read as elaborate responses to well-known Brodsky poems—"On a Winter Evening in Yalta" (Zimnim vecherom v Ialte) and "The Butterfly" (Babochka).

35. See Kushner, "Neissiakaemyi siuzhet poezii," 183; cited in Ueland, "Echoes," 6–7. *Taurida* refers to Tauric Chersonesus or the Crimea/Black Sea coast; Ovid was exiled to Tomis, in modern Rumania, but the entire area has since become particularly "magnetized" in the minds of such Petersburg poets as Pushkin, Mandelstam, and Brodsky for its mythical blending of Hellenic and Slavic cultures. *Tavricheskii sad* is also the name of a well-known park in St. Petersburg.

36. Solovyov may be a controversial source but note how he compares the two adolescences of Brodsky and Kushner (the former dropped out of school at fifteen, while the latter finished with a gold metal and the "psychology of one who excels" [psikhologiia otlichnika] [86–87]). And according to Solovyov, Kushner's spiritual trials (his role as Salieri to Brodsky's Mozart) began with a private birthday party during which Yevtushenko, Kushner, and Brodsky were asked to read from their latest work (87). Next to Brodsky's poems Kushner's "had no resonance" (ne zvuchali vovse) (85), and even later, after Brodsky was expelled from

the country, Kushner would, again, in Solovyov's perhaps quite enhanced version, look into his artistic mirror and, like the queen in the fairy tale, ask "who is the fairest in the land?" (85).

37. Kushner is, of course, intimately familiar with Mandelstam's biography; he simply chooses to see the man's poetry as *transcending* his personal tragedy. Perhaps his fullest statement to date on Mandelstam is found in "Vypriamitel'nyi vzdokh," a lecture delivered at the Institute of World Literature (IMLI, Moscow) during the Mandelstam festivities of 1988 (24–26 February) and then published in the journal *Neva* (no. 2 [1989]). In his talk Kushner describes Mandelstam's poetry in ecstatic terms, as a "holiday of all the sense organs" (10) and as a source of delight (voskhishchenie) (12) even when its subject is the most piercing human loss. In Brodsky, if it can be put this way, Mandelstam's life is not transcended in the name of his culture. The one feeds and informs the other. Brodsky has deeply *personalized* Mandelstam's biography and example, despite what he might say about the relative unimportance of how poets live.

38. Note also the image of the flute in Mandelstam's late poem "Fleity grecheskoi teta i iota" (The theta and iota of the Greek flute) (*SS*, 1:265–66).

39. On the subject of Brodsky as exile, see, for example, Kline, "Variations" and Polukhina, "The Self."

40. Paul Tabori's definition is probably close to classic: "The dictionaries define exile as forced separation from one's native country, expulsion from home or the state of being expelled, banishment; sometimes voluntary separation from one's native country. The state of banishment can also be one of devastation and alienation. Enforced removal from one's native land, according to an edict or sentence, penal expatriation or banishment, is another version. . . . The etymological and legal definitions of exile represent only one side, however important, of the semantic problem. The historical, psychological, ideological definitions are equally essential" (*Anatomy of Exile*, 23–26).

41. Cf. Irina Odoevtseva's recollection of this sort of projection in her memoirs of her life with the poet Georgy Ivanov: "It seemed that we lived on the threshold of another world, one to which Georgy Ivanov could on occasion crack the door, and that we lived as though on two planes simultaneously—'here and there.' Moreover, 'there' was for him, and sometimes for me, no less real than 'here'" (*Na beregakh Seny*, 448).

42. "To think of exile as beneficial, as a spur to humanism or to creativity, is to belittle its mutilations" (Said, "Mind of Winter," 50).

43. Organized by the Wheatland Foundation, the conference took place in Vienna in December 1987. Brodsky's less than sympathetic response to the plight of the exiled writer was not well received.

44. See Moi, *Kristeva Reader*, 292–300. The essay first appeared in *Tel Quel* in 1977 (no. 74 [Winter 1977], pp. 3–8) as "Un nouveau type d'intellectuel: le dissident."

45. Originally appeared as *Étrangers à nous-mêmes* (Librairie Artheme Fayard, 1989).

46. One recalls Frost's famous mot that poetry is what is lost in translation.

47. Correlatively, it could be argued that from her various transpositions and refashionings—from Bulgarian émigrée to Parisian *echt* intellectual, from bril

liant analyst and taxonomer in the tradition of Freud and Lacan to "subversive" theorist on maternity and the mother's body ("Stabat Mater"), and so forth—Kristeva has replaced one myth of linguistic origins with another.

48. "Recent critical theory has placed undue emphasis on the limitlessness of interpretation. It is argued that, since reading is misreading, no one reading is better than any other, hence all readings, potentially infinite in number, are in the final analysis equally misinterpretations" (*The World*, 39). The reader should note that the complex interaction between text and context, between the way life models literature and literature life, has long been the subject of investigation of Yury Lotman and the so-called Tartu School of Soviet semiotics.

49. In Said's reading, authority comes from the writer's "strategic location" vis-à-vis the material and from the "strategic formation" of power that one text makes with other texts (*Orientalism*, 19–20). The reason why Byron routinely makes the heroines of his Eastern tales silent victims of male action or why Flaubert *speaks for* his Egyptian courtesan Kuchuk Hanem is, according to Said, pervasively political: Orientalism is "a Western style for dominating, restructuring, and having authority over the Orient." Indeed, "because of Orientalism the Orient was not (and is not) a free subject of thought and action" (*Orientalism*, 3). It follows that the texts with which our Western culture has grown up are governed by, in Foucault's terms, totalizing *epistemes* that suppress, demonize, seal off, and variously control the other. And although Said is quick to point out that he does not endorse a rigorous *assujetissement*, the sense, for example, in *The Archaeology of Knowledge*, that a "discourse—impersonal, systematic, highly regulated by enunciative formations—overrides society and governs the production of culture" (*The World*, 186), it is by no means always clear where, in his model, intentionality enters the argument. "Unlike Michel Foucault, to whose work I am greatly indebted, I do believe in the determining imprint of individual writers upon the otherwise anonymous collective body of texts constituting a discursive formation like Orientalism" (*Orientalism*, 23). See also *The World*, 186–88.

50. We recall, for example, that the author of *Orientalism* makes no secret of the "personal dimension" underlying his study: "The life of an Arab Palestinian in the West, particularly in America, is disheartening. There exists here an almost unanimous consensus that politically he does not exist, and when it is allowed that he does, it is either as a nuisance or as an Oriental. The web of racism, cultural stereotypes, political imperialism, dehumanizing ideology holding in the Arab or the Muslim is very strong indeed, and it is this web which every Palestinian has come to feel as his uniquely punishing destiny" (*Orientalism*, 27).

51. "Constantine did not foresee that the anti-individualism of Islam would find the soil of Byzantium so welcoming that by the ninth century Christianity would be more than ready to flee to the north. . . . Yet the Christianity that was received by Rus from Byzantium in the ninth century already had absolutely nothing in common with Rome. For, on its way to Rus, Christianity dropped behind it not only togas and statues but also Justinian's Civil Code" (*Less*, 416).

52. "Russian poets [today] face the same marginalization as do poets in some other cultures; their historic role and killing burden as the conscience of the nation may well be superfluous in a liberated civil society" (Smith, *Anthology*, xxxiii).

Chapter 2
Brodsky's Triangular Vision: Exile as Palimpsest

1. "Pis'ma rimskomu drugu" (*ChR*, 11–14). Other twentieth-century filters might include: the atypical conjunction of lovemaking and death (stanza XVI) and the "Acmeist" nostalgia for physical objects (stanza XVII). What might be interpreted as the poem's anachronistic placement of Pliny the Elder, who died some twenty years before Martial (stanza XVIII), is in fact only that author's *writings*, as George Kline's translation ("a book of Pliny") makes clear (*Part*, 54). My thanks to Professor Yury Shcheglov of the University of Wisconsin-Madison for pointing out these and other details to me. For more on classical motifs in Brodsky, see, for example, Nivat, "The Ironic Journey"; Vail and Genis, "Ot mira—k Rimu"; Verheul, " 'Enei i Didona' Brodskogo"; and Zelinsky, "Dido und Äneas."

2. Several times in the discussion to follow I will be referring to *homo soviet-icus*. Brodsky is clearly not "typical" of the average Soviet citizen. Indeed, his unique ability to carry the torch of culture is what separates him from the vast majority of his contemporaries. My point, however, is that the poet's irony and intentional crudity are meant to show that, despite the overlay of culture amd sophistication, he is not free of the residue of his epoch. He, too, in a sense he would surely acknowledge, is partly "Soviet."

3. With regard to the "classical motifs" found in major works from 1961 to the present, it can be said that from 1961 to 1968 Brodsky's focus was primarily "Greek," from 1968 to 1970 both "Greek" and "Roman," and from 1970 on "Roman." See, for example, in *SiP*, *OVP*, *KPE*, *ChR*, and *U*: "Velikii Gektor" (Great Hector) (1961), "Gladiatory" (Gladiators) (1962), "Orfei i Artemida" (Orpheus and Artemis) (1964), "K Likomedu, na Skiros" (To Lycomedes on Scyros) (1967), "Podsvechnik" (Candlestick) (1968), "Anno Domini" (1968), "Enei i Didona" (Aeneas and Dido) (1969), "Post Aetatem Nostram" (1970), "Odissei Telemaku" (Odysseus to Telemachus) (1972), "Tors" (Torso) (1972), "Pis'ma rimskomu drugu" (Letters to a Roman Friend) (1972), "Rimskie elegii" (Roman Elegies) (1975), "Biust Tiberiia" (The Bust of Tiberius) (1975), *Mramor* (Marbles) (1984). My thanks to Mr. Dan Ungurianu, a graduate student at the University of Wisconsin-Madison, for compiling this information.

4. "Toward the twenties, the Roman themes [in Mandelstam's poetry] gradually overtake the Greek and biblical references, largely because of the poet's growing identification with the archetypal predicament of 'a poet versus an empire' " (*Less*, 128).

5. The image of triangulation as a central metaphor for the experience of exile is also found in Eva Hoffman's *Lost in Translation: A Life in a New Language*, although the connection in this instance is presumably coincidental. My thanks to Professor Stanislaw Baranczak of Harvard for this information. See Baranczak, *Breathing*, 226: " 'Triangulation' is a word that appears with particular frequency on the pages of this book [*Lost in Translation*]. It is meant to signify the way in which the immigrant, caught between two languages and their two built-in philosophies, uses these two given angles to find a distant resultant: his own position

in life and versus life. As Hoffman points out in the concluding paragraphs of her book, what seems to be the immigrant's deprivation may thus be viewed, at the same time, as a spiritually enriching experience." This notion has particular relevance to Brodsky, as will become evident in this and subsequent chapters.

6. Horace is clearly referred to in Brodsky's poem.

7. See "Sokhrani moiu rech'" in *SS*, 1:175–76.

8. I am indebted to Mr. Adam Weiner, a graduate student in Slavic at the University of Wisconsin-Madison, for the following observations about Lowellian subtexts in Brodsky. Brodsky first met Lowell in 1972, the year of his exile from the Soviet Union. Lowell had offered to help Brodsky by reading the latter's poems in English while the author recited them in Russian at the International Festival of Poetry. Additional meetings took place three years later at the Five Colleges in Massachusetts (where Brodsky teaches to this day at Mount Holyoke) and at Lowell's house in Brooklyn. See Polukhina, *Brodsky*, 35. It was in this same year of 1975 that Brodsky wrote *Lullaby of Cape Cod*, a text awash in Lowellian allusions (see below). When Lowell died two years later, Brodsky wrote one of his first English-language elegies, in which he borrowed phrases from the earlier Russian poem and translated them into his adopted language. Thus, it could be said that Brodsky's lullaby about migration into the English language and American empire anticipates and frames—but only to those readers who understand *both* contexts—the English prayer for the dead ("Elegy: For Robert Lowell").

9. For a helpful overview of Eliot's quite specific Dante, see McDougal, "T. S. Eliot's Metaphysical Dante," in *Dante among the Moderns*, 57–81.

10. Cf.: "Destroying myself, contradicting myself, / Like the moth which flies to the midnight flame, / I want to leave our [native] speech / Beyond everything [or: in exchange for everything] for which I am permanently obliged to it" (*SS*, 1:190).

11. The result of a "*local* self-consciousness" and a "*particular* civilization," that is, provincialism.

12. One assumes that Eliot's statements here possess an ironic overlay: Milton, of course, was blind.

13. As Seamus Heaney writes, "[Eliot and Pound] wore his [Dante's] poem like a magic garment to protect themselves from the contagion of parochial English and American culture; and finally they canonized him as the aquiline patron of international modernism" ("Envies and Identifications," 16).

14. "The definitive Dante of the 1929 essay and the definitive Eliot of *Four Quartets* have established a mutually fortifying alliance. The Dante whom Eliot now prefers and expounds walks in the aura of cultural history and representativeness. He is a figure in whom the commentaries on the *Commedia* are implicit; he stands for the thoroughly hierarchical world of scholastic thought, an imagined standard against which the relativity and agnosticism of the present can be judged" (Heaney, "Envies and Identifications," 13–14).

15. The scholarship on the Dante-Mandelstam connection is considerable. See, for example, Glazova, "Mandel'štam and Dante"; and Meilakh and Toporov, "Akhmatova and Dante." Glazova (331, n. 1) gives a synopsis of the prin-

cipal Russian language sources on this question, including works by such leading Mandelstam specialists as Iu. Levin, G. A. Levinton, D. M. Segal, G. Struve, and Kiril Taranovsky. A more recent study is found in Iliushin, "Dante i Petrarka."

16. The Eulenspiegel Affair [1928–29], in which Mandelstam through a bizarre editorial oversight had been accused of plagiarism, and the poet's subsequent trip to the "Sabbath land" of Armenia (1930), had both steeled his resolve to go his own way and renewed his poetic wellspring.

17. See chapter 5. In addition, see Cavanagh, "Osip Mandel'shtam" and "Mandel'shtam, Dante and the 'Honorable Calling of Jew'"; and Freidin, A Coat and "Sidia na saniakh."

18. Or, as Tsvetaeva puts it with her remarkable epigrammatic power in The Poem of the End (Poema kontsa, 1926): "In this most Christian of worlds / Poets are kikes" (V sem khristianneishem iz mirov / Poety—zhidy) (SiP, 2:185).

19. See Heaney ("Envies and Identifications") for an "English-speaking" perspective on the differences between Eliot's Dante and Mandelstam's Dante. (Heaney, of course, is himself an important poet and critic.)

20. Mandelstam did not, of course, see himself in life as a predatory wolf (that role was better suited to members of the establishment), but as the "wolf hound" age bore down on him, this is the position he found himself in.

21. See discussion of modified terza rima in Brodsky's "December in Florence" below.

22. Noted in Freidin, Coat, 238.

23. The reference to Saturn sounds very much like Andrey Bely, with whom Mandelstam spent time during the summer of 1933.

24. It could be argued that Yevgeny Yevtushenko has traveled more than Brodsky, but whether he qualifies as a serious poet is open to question.

25. Here one could say that Eliot's famous passage back to his roots, the crossing from East Coker to the Dry Salvages off the coast of Cape Ann, is mirrored in Brodsky's transatlantic passage from the most "Western" city (Leningrad) of an "Eastern" empire to the East coast cradle of the Western empire in "Lullaby of Cape Cod," the penultimate poem in A Part of Speech and the one immediately preceding "December in Florence." (See earlier discussion of "Lullaby" in this chapter.) It is in this poem, after all, that Brodsky affirms his most basic nature (the adaptive "cosmopolitan") by being reborn into his adoptive language and culture. Eliot, on the other hand, using similar water and shore imagery, exorcises the specter of his "provincial" Puritan past by embracing its moral fervor and high earnestness in the wake of his conversion. Eliot and Brodsky are also alike in one more significant way: both use a combination of foreign and domestic precursors (Dante, Laforgue, and Donne in Eliot's case; Donne, Eliot himself, Auden, Mandelstam, and Tsvetaeva in Brodsky's) in order to overcome a poetic time of troubles (English poetry since Milton, Russian poetry since the death of Stalin). The antidote for a dissociation of sensibility or a socialist realist aesthetic is, in either case, strikingly similar.

26. "Mandelstam," writes Brodsky, "was a Jew who was living in the capital of Imperial Russia, whose dominant religion was Orthodoxy, whose political structure was inherently Byzantine, and whose alphabet had been devised by two Greek monks" (Less, 130).

27. Brodsky has stated in a personal interview (28–29 March 1991, South Hadley, Mass.; with author) that it was Nadezhda Mandelstam who first called him the "second Osya." There may be some confusion, however, since the phrase has also been attributed to Akhmatova. In any event, Mandelstam had been the only Jew among the original Russian Orthodox Acmeists, just as Brodsky, in an irony that could not have been lost on him, got his start as one of the younger "neo-Acmeist" poets, nearly all of them Jewish (E. Rein, V. Uflyand, A. Naiman, and A. Kushner), who surrounded the great Christian poet Akhmatova in her final years.

28. "Can a thing really be the master of a word. The word is Psyche. The living word does not designate an object but freely chooses, as though it were a living space, this or that objective meaning [predmetnaia znachimost'], thingness [ve-shchnost'], dear body. And around this thing the word roams freely, as a soul around a discarded though not forgotten body" (*SS*, 2:226).

29. All these notions converge in "On the Nature of the Word" (O prirode slova, 1922) where Mandelstam attempts the ultimate metaphoric transfer, equating language with the historical imagination and, finally, with history itself: "The life of language in Russian historical reality outweighs all other facts by the fullness of its phenomenal reality [polnotoiu iavlenii], by the fullness of its being, which represents only the unattainable limit for all other phenomena of Russian life. . . . The Russian language is historical by its very nature, inasmuch as in its totality it is an undulating sea of events, the unbroken embodiment and action of an intelligent and breathing flesh. . . . Such a highly organized and organic language is not merely a door to history, but is history itself" (*SS*, 2:246–47).

30. In this respect, Brodsky, following Mandelstam (and indeed much of the modern Russian lyric tradition), would disagree entirely with the solipsistic definition of "style" offered by a critic like Barthes: "Under the name of style a self-sufficient language is evolved which has its roots only in the depths of the author's personal and secret mythology, that subnature of expression where the first coition of words and things takes place. . . . [Style] is the writer's 'thing,' his glory and his prison, it is his solitude. Indifferent to society and transparent to it, a closed personal process, it is in no way the product of a choice or a reflection on Literature" (*Writing Degree Zero*, 10–11). Because of its religious roots, its "moral purity and firmness," Russian poetry can never be a "closed personal process." The poet can be, and usually is in the Russian context, lonely and es-tranged, but his language cannot.

31. The words of this first line are repeated at the beginning of the seventh stanza, but there *par* (steam) is replaced by *pary* (couples), thereby reinforcing the initial paronomasia.

32. Brodsky links the image of the Dantesque beast with the notion of psychic exile in his discussion of Tsvetaeva's *Novogodnee* (New Year's Greeting): "The tragedy of '*Novogodnee*' lies in the separation, in the almost physical rupture of her [Tsvetaeva's] psychological bond with Rilke, and she sets out on this 'jour-ney,' not frightened by a Dantean leopard blocking her path, but by an awareness of abandonment" (*Less*, 204–205). He also uses the *Commedia* as backdrop in his essay on Eugenio Montale, "In the Shadow of Dante" (*Less*, 95–112).

33. Brodsky read the entire *Commedia* in the famous Lozinsky translation in

1962–63, the same years in which he was reading the Bible for the first time as well as the English metaphysicals.

34. "The pilgrim's story leads to the establishment of the author's status as storyteller, so that the story of the *Divine Comedy* is in part the story of how the story came to be written" (Freccero, "The Significance," 265).

35. Brodsky is obsessed with the notion of what the émigré critic Mikhail Epstein calls *vychitanie* (subtraction, reduction) and his poetry is replete with mathematical metaphors, which in many cases point to the diminution or ultimate disappearance of the poet as physical subject. See chapters 1 and 3.

36. In other words, Brodsky's assertion of absence (in this case the absence of his beloved Leningrad) is almost never the assertion of an innocent lack, of something that was never there, but of something that was once full and is now empty. See Kurrik, *Literature and Negation*, 206–207.

37. Brodsky uses the same dehumanizing formula ("a body in a raincoat") to refer to himself in "Lagoon" (Laguna, 1973), his poem about Venice (*ChR*, 42).

38. It is not clear from the dateline ("1976") whether the poem refers to a visit in December 1975 (and then recalled the next year) or December 1976 (and described virtually simultaneously). In any event, Brodsky was close enough to Dante's age (thirty-five) to make the allusion ("at a certain age") significant.

39. And "mothers": for example, Judge Savelyeva, who presided at Brodsky's show trial for social "parasitism" (*tuneiadstvo*) in spring 1964. For a heavily ironic view of Brodsky's hometown, see "Plato Elaborated" (Razvivaia Platona) in *Uraniia* (*U*, 8–10).

40. For the English translation of the poem, Brodsky took the opening two lines of Akhmatova's lyric as epigraph rather than this, the third line, thereby making the Dante connection more explicit.

41. One of the central themes of Mandelstam's (and Akhmatova's) poetry is that of "return" (vozvrashchen'e), to be taken up by Brodsky in the following generation.

42. Birds play a crucial role in the image networks of both Brodsky and Mandelstam, often serving as calques for the soul or psyche. As Nadezhda Mandelstam has explained, this poem is based on an episode from her husband's life: the poet once made a gift of a goldfinch to a neighbor boy who traded in birds (*Kniga tret'ia*, 220).

43. See discussion of two Josephs in connection with the poem "Nunc Dimittis" (Sreten'e) at the conclusion to chapter 5. A third, satanic "Joseph" could be implied here as well: Stalin.

44. When George Kline was translating "December in Florence" (together with the late Maurice English), he was reminded by the author that the statue of Dante in Ravenna is surrounded by cast-iron grillwork whose configuration is strongly reminiscent of a cage. My thanks to Professor Kline for this information.

45. One of the salient semantic fields in Mandelstam's poetry is "sharpness"/ "pointedness."

46. Here Brodsky (stanza III) may also be playing on the "Symbolist" Dante, especially that of Blok, who during his visit to Italy in 1909 was horrified by Florence's corruption and commercialism and wrote several poems sharply castigating this modern whore and "Judas." One line in particular resonates with Brodsky's description of the marketplace: "You [Florence] cannot resurrect your-

self / In the dust of the mercantile crush" (*Stikh*, 403). For more on the Symbolist Dante, see Davidson, *The Poetic Imagination*, 1–99 and Kopper, "Dante in Russian Symbolist Discourse."

47. "'The unwitting pen strays into drawing—while tackling an 'M'—some eyebrows' alludes to the medieval tradition that facial features represent letters in the phrase OMO DEI" (note to "December in Florence," *Part*, 151). Brodsky does not mention here the passage from *Purgatorio*, XXIII:31–33: "Parean l'occhiaie anella sanza gemme: / chi nel viso delli uomini legge 'omo' / ben avria quivi conosciuta l'emme" (The eye-pits were like rings without the gem. He that reads OMO in men's faces might easily have made out the M there) (Dante, *The Divine Comedy*, 297–99). Thanks are due to my colleague Yury Shcheglov of the University of Wisconsin-Madison for allerting me to the precise allusion in *Purgatorio*.

48. Note how Brodsky's final word, a verb (*ubyl* [has left]), recalls Mandelstam's closing in the goldfinch poem (*uletel* [has flown away]).

Chapter 3
The Flea and the Butterfly: John Donne and the Case for Brodsky as Russian Metaphysical

1. George Kline was the first to make this connection: "[Brodsky's] is a private, not a public muse. What is perhaps even worse, in official Soviet eyes, he is a metaphysical poet, in very much the sense in which Donne is a metaphysical poet. His poetry is intensely personal, meditative, religious, existential, 'suffering'" ("Elegy," 344).

2. "Poetic thinking, which is called metaphorical, is in fact synthetic thinking. As such it contains analysis, but cannot be reduced to analysis. Analysis is neither the only nor the final form of cognition. There is also cognition through revelation, and there is cognition through meditation. Moreover, there is cognition through synthesis. In the case of the poet it is through intuitive synthesis, that is, when the poet—according to the poet—steals left and right and does not even experience a sense of guilt as he does so" (Brodsky, *Modern Poets*, 7).

3. Save for their idiosyncratic expression in the spiritual odes of Lomonosov, Derzhavin, and others. See Titunik, "Baroque," 42.

4. One thing that draws Brodsky to Donne, as the poet says in the Pomerantsev interview, is the *sherokhovatost'* (roughness, ruggedness) of the Englishman's verse.

5. "And Derzhavin, descending into the coffin, gave us his blessing," as Pushkin once said in *Eugene Onegin*.

6. Khlebnikov also wrote a charming four-line poem to a fly of which Brodsky, an astute reader of modern poetry, may be aware. For Brodsky's views on Khlebnikov (e.g., "Velimir Khlebnikov's work is a phenomenon of towering incoherence"), see his "The Meaning of Meaning."

7. See Baratynsky's poem "Rhyme" (Rifma, 1840?), in *PSS*, 193–94. His statement that rhyme is like a living branch brought to the poet on his ark by the dove and that it alone with its echoing of divine purpose can reconcile the poet to God's creation sounds very close to Brodsky.

8. To be sure, Baratynsky's syntax becomes relatively more complex in his later works (Kupreianova, "E. A. Baratynskii," 38, in *PSS*) but is still distinctly a

product of the nineteenth century and cannot compare with the highly wrought, even tortured syntactic constructions of the mature Brodsky.

9. One aspect of Donne that was immediately attractive to the young Brodsky was his elaborate strophic designs: "The fact of the matter is that all Russian poetry is mainly strophic and requires extremely simple strophic units—that is, the stanza, the quatrain. At the same time I detected in Donne a much more interesting and exciting structure. He has exceptionally complicated strophic constructions. This was interesting to me and it was this, I believe, that I learned from Donne" (Brodsky, "S tochki zreniia iazyka"). See below.

10. Khodasevich, for example, would do the same thing in his blank verse narratives in *The Way of Grain* (Putem zerna). His "The House" (Dom, 1919–20), for example, clearly resonates with Brodsky's "A Halt in the Desert."

11. *Bezobrazie* literally means "ugliness" but I have translated it here (and elsewhere) as "formlessness" because Brodsky is playing on its central meaning of "that which lacks form or (proper) image." The ironic reference to "proportions" simultaneously implies in this context a lack of proportion, hence formlessness. The differently stressed adjectival variants show the pun more clearly: "bezóbraznyi" (that which lacks form or *obraz*) and "bezobráznyi" (ugly, disgraceful).

12. Here I have in mind the "younger" generation of Russian Symbolists, especially their chief theorist Andrey Bely, rather than the "older" aesthetic ("decadent") wing of symbolism led by Valery Bryusov.

13. Nor need it. Donne was of course the farthest thing from Khodasevich's mind when he wrote such poems. I am simply trying to demonstrate how Brodsky's reliance on the English (as opposed to French or German) tradition is unique.

14. Prince Mirsky in a moment of pique called him "a little Baratynsky from the underground."

15. "While he might be called the T. S. Eliot or perhaps the W. H. Auden of Eastern Europe, Brodsky is also the John Donne Russian poetry never had" (Baranczak, *Breathing*, 211).

16. Brodsky's serious study of Donne, including his translation of several of the latter's poems, took place only in 1964 when Lydia Chukovsky sent him a "Modern Library" edition of Donne for his birthday (May 24). At that time Brodsky had already begun his sentence (five years of hard labor for "parasitism") and was living in exile in the far north (village of Norinskaya, Arkhangelsk Province). See Pomerantsev, "Poverkh bar'erov."

17. Possibly the Untermeyer.

18. Eventually Brodsky would translate four of Donne's poems into Russian: "The Flea," "A Valediction: Forbidding Mourning," "The Storm," and "The Apparition." To judge by his ability to find ingenious equivalences for Donne's language in Russian, Brodsky's knowledge of English was apparently much improved by the time he attempted these translations. The importance of these particular poems for Brodsky's own poetic practice, especially "A Valediction," will be discussed below.

19. The topic of Brodsky's connection with Milosz and Zbigniew Herbert is a rich one and in need of further investigation. Herbert, to be sure, is not a "metaphysical" in the sense that Milosz and Brodsky are. See note 27 to chapter 1. Herbert's return to classical sources (Thucidides, etc.) in a period of national

stagnation, his ironic poetic demeanor, interest in the body-soul contrast (Pan Cogito poems), themes of exile and spiritual inheritance ("the princes of our senses proudly choose exile"), fear of Slavic formlessness, extended poetic meditations on pedestrian objects (both Herbert and Brodsky have poems dedicated to chairs), use of "heaven dwellers" and angels as interlocutors, and so forth, all suggest that this poet, who is once again from an "alien," non-Russian tradition, is a not insignificant intermediary in Brodsky's dialogue with the West. For more on Herbert, see Stanislaw Baranczak's excellent *A Fugitive from Utopia*. Brodsky has said several times that he considers Milosz one of the greatest living poets. See, for example, his "Presentation of Czeslaw Milosz to the Jury": "I have no hesitation whatever in stating that Czeslaw Milosz is one of the greatest poets of our time, perhaps the greatest. . . . His, after all, is a *metaphysical poetry* [my emphasis] which regards the things of this world as manifestation of a certain superior realm, miniaturized or magnified for the sake of our perception."

20. For example, Evgeny Rein and Anatoly Naiman (who subsequently moved to Moscow), Vladimir Uflyand and Alexander Kushner (who remained in Leningrad), and Dmitry Bobyshev and Lev Loseff (who emigrated to the United States).

21. Among the books Akhmatova always kept close at hand in her old age were, significantly, the Bible and Dante (Naiman, *Rasskazy*, 100). The biblical theme of suffering, especially the kind of suffering that Mary experienced at the sight of her crucified son, is given its ultimate treatment in this century in Akhmatova's cycle *Requiem*.

22. Brodsky himself has not been consistent in fixing the date of his first meeting with Akhmatova. Sometimes he has used the year 1961, sometimes 1962. Kline and Sylvester ("Iosif Aleksandrovich Brodskii," 129), for example, cite the year 1960. Evgeny Rein has reported to the Brodsky scholar Valentina Polukhina that he took Brodsky to Akhmatova's and introduced him to her on 7 August 1961. Private correspondence with author (10 March 1992).

23. Akhmatova was so necessary to Brodsky at this stage of his development that he was drawn to rent a house near her in Komarovo in order to be able to visit her twice a day (Thomas, "Interview," 10).

24. There may be some confusion about who first called Brodsky the "second Osya" (the "first Osya" being Osip Mandelstam). Recently, the poet himself has suggested that it was Mandelstam's widow Nadezhda Yakovlevna rather than Akhmatova. (Personal interview with author, 28–29 March 1991, South Hadley, Mass.) The confusion may have arisen from the fact that Akhmatova said several times to her friends that she had read nothing like Brodsky's work since Mandelstam (Polukhina, *Joseph Brodsky*, 8).

25. Brodsky, it is true, has never had much in common with Akhmatova as far as poetic manner is concerned, but he always revered her memory and thought of her as someone crucial to his own moral and artistic coming-of-age. "I like to think—maybe I am deluding myself—but I like to think that in many ways I owe to her my better human qualities; without her they would have taken longer to develop, if ever" (Thomas, "Interview," 9). See Polukhina, *Brodsky*, 8–10. To state the relationship in terms of a well-known analogy, the bent but not broken Akhmatova was to Brodsky and his coevals what Blok, the "tragic tenor" (Akhmatova's words) of his age, was once to Akhmatova and her generation on the eve of the revolution.

26. Brodsky's friend Anatoly Naiman writes, for example: "The beginning of the 1960s was a time of the posthumous fame of Mandelstam." He then goes on to quote an entry from Akhmatova's diary, "And it turned out that these children [Brodsky's generation] had not been sold to the pock-mocked devil as had their fathers. It turned out that it was impossible to sell out in advance three generations. And now the time had come when the children arrived, found the verse of Osip Mandelstam, and said 'This is our poet'" (Naiman, *Rasskazy*, 81).

27. Bald is quite circumstantial on the problems that Donne's family religion posed for him as he tried to make his way in Anglican England. In his youth especially Donne was made to feel aware of "the sense of being apart from others in his family's fidelity to the old religion" (*A Life*, 41). His brother Henry, for example, with whom he had entered Oxford, was arrested in 1593 for his connection with a young Yorkshire priest, and then, after admitting under cross-examination that he, too, had taken vows, was imprisoned, where he died (from the plague) that same year. See *A Life*, 41–42, 59, 63, 66, 116, 202–207.

28. Something very close to these statements, if we transpose the contexts and terms (Catholic/Protestant → Jew/Russian, religion/free speculative inquiry → "scientific Marxism"/free speculative inquiry, etc.), could be made about Brodsky at the time of his initial infatuation with Donne. For the biographical context on Donne I have used primarily two sources: Bald, *A Life*; and Marotti, *Coterie Poet*.

29. In Marotti's phrase, Donne was "living in virtual social exile" (*Coterie Poet*, 155). On the issue of Donne and exile, see Bald, *A Life*, 23, 25, 32, 44–45, and 46.

30. For more on the issue of Brodsky's Jewishness, see the introduction and chapter 5 of this study.

31. Personal interview with author, 28–29 March 1991, South Hadley, Mass.

32. Again, for Brodsky's understanding of "exile" in its various permutations, see the third section ("Exile") of chapter 1.

33. Brodsky is particularly enamoured of Tsvetaeva's famous phrase (from the *Poem of the End*) that "poets are Yids" (poety—zhidy). That is, poets are both excluded and excluding, banished and elected. Any formulation that stresses one feature (say, their status as victim) over the other is, according to Brodsky, insufficient and reductive. Personal interview with author, 28–29 March 1991, South Hadley, Mass.

34. "You'll return to the motherland" (Vorotish'sia na rodinu, 1961).

35. "I have often such a sickely inclination. And, whether it be, because I had my first breeding and conversation with men of a suppressed and afflicted Religion [i.e., Catholicism], accustomed to the despite of death, and hungry of an imagin'd Martyrdome . . . mee thinks I have the keyes of my prison in mine owne hand, and no remedy presents it selfe so soone to my heart, as mine own sword" (preface to *Biathanatos*; cited in Bald, *A Life*, 231). See also Bald, *A Life*, 222–23.

36. See, for example, his "Nature morte" (Natiurmort, 1971), in *KPE*, 108–12. To be sure, Brodsky's attitude toward his own martyrdom is not unambiguous. See the discussion in section 2 ("The Context") of chapter 1.

37. Similar statements, to be sure, could be made about Brodsky's affinity to such poets as Baratynsky, Mandelstam, Tsvetaeva, and Khodasevich.

38. One exception in Brodsky's case being the poetry of Alexander Kushner,

perhaps the most "academic" of contemporary Soviet poets. See Brodsky's introduction to Kushner's *Apollo in the Snow*, ix–xii. Kushner shares numerous traits with Brodsky, including a Leningrad background and a Mandelstamian "nostalgia for world culture" (especially classicism). But precisely because Brodsky's biography has been dominated by the category of exile in its various ontological and aesthetic guises and Kushner's has not ("[Kushner's] life is not rich in spectacular events and doesn't conform to our image of the poetic biography," as Brodsky says, not without a little self-irony), *and* because Kushner's muse is nearly exclusively lyric while Brodsky's is as often odic and epic, the differences between these neo-Acmeists may be more telling than their similarities.

39. His generation, for example, which was born on the eve of the Second World War, experienced as part of their childhood or early maturity: the death of Stalin (1953), the exposure of the "cult of personality," the crushing of the Hungarian Uprising (1956), the rise and fall of Khrushchev, and several cultural "thaws" followed inevitably by hard freezes.

40. "The Renaissance was a time of colossal spiritual disorder of any and every type, political above all. And this was if for no other reason than the Renaissance was a time when dogmatic thought, the ecclesiastical, theological thought that had dominated man's consciousness over the course of a millennium, that is, the dogmatic thought of Christianity, ceased to satisfy man, that is, it became an object of all sorts of investigations and interrogations and questions. This was connected with the flowering of purely secular science, that is, normal science. Donne lived at a time when the heliocentric (solar) system received its citizenship, when the earth ceased to be the center of the universe, and when that center became the sun, a fact that produced an exceedingly large impression on the general public, in the same way that the splitting of the atom did in our time" (Pomerantsev, "Poverkh bar'erov").

41. Donne's Inns-of-Court coterie is treated in depth in Marotti, *Coterie Poet*. Brodsky's "coterie," as suggested earlier, consisted of those young poets and critics who grouped around Akhmatova in Leningrad in the late 1950s and early 1960s (Brodsky, Loseff, Naiman, Kushner, Bobyshev, the slightly older Rein, etc.).

42. In Donne's time the chief means of "public"-ation were the manuscript commonplace book and "published" poetic miscellany. See Marotti, *Coterie Poet*, 4–8.

43. See, for example, Brodsky's allusion to Fedya Dobrovolsky, a friend who perished in a geological expedition, in two early poems (*SiP*, 36–38).

44. In Brodsky if there is anything that could be called a "group," it is usually not more than two—the poet and his interlocutor (often his absent lover). An important early lyric entitled "Christmas Romance" (Rozhdestvenskii romans, 1962) is dedicated to Evgeny Rein, with the assumption that the scenes presented in the poem may have shared meaning for the dedicatee. Occasionally, especially in longer poems on broad themes of empire, "progress," the meaning of history, and so forth, Brodsky invokes a "we" that stands for his generation. See, for example, the ending of the title poem of *Halt in the Desert* (Ostanovka v pustyne, 1966) (*OVP*, 168).

45. This is how Brodsky refers—ironically—to Marina Basmanova, his great love in the Soviet Union and the mother of his only son Andrey. Interview with author, 28–29 March 1991, South Hadley, Mass.

46. For example, Thomas Nashe in Donne's day or a member in good standing of the Writers' Union in Brodsky's. This is not to say that "professional" status means the same thing in each context. If Brodsky could have published his work in the Soviet Union without making concessions to the establishment or betraying his artistic conscience, he presumably would have. Donne, on the other hand, would not. Hence the amateur/professional opposition is not a neat one, nor need it be. The point is that both poets were situated as *outsiders* vis-à-vis their respective establishments (the court, the literary *nomenklatura*) and both earned their reputations through private or underground means of "public"-ation.

47. Between 1961 and 1987 four of Brodsky's poems, including "Verses on the Death of T. S. Eliot," were published in the Soviet journals *Molodoi Leningrad* (Young Leningrad) (1966) and *Den' poezii* (Day of Poetry) (1967). Following his trial and sentencing in 1964 Brodsky's verse (as opposed to his political plight) did, however, begin to attract the attention of Western readers, primarily specialists. As has so often happened in Soviet times, the first (unauthorized) collection of his poems, *Stikhotvoreniia i poemy* (Lyric and Narrative Verse) was published *abroad*, appearing in 1965 in Washington, D.C., while Brodsky was still in exile in Norinskaya.

48. To this day Brodsky is immensely popular among the educated urban youth in the Soviet Union, and some of his verse has been put to music (on the guitar).

49. For example, enforced confinement in a psychiatric hospital, repeated arrests, trial for "parasitism," harsh sentence in the North. See Polukhina, *Joseph Brodsky*, 1–39.

50. Although numerous poets in the Russian tradition have emphasized parting (e.g., Baratynsky, Mandelstam), and numerous others have written journey literature with meta-commentary (e.g., Pushkin, Mandelstam), Brodsky is apparently unique in his capacity to "infold" so many physical and metaphysical crossings simultaneously. If Donne had not already existed as a source, Brodsky, as the saying goes, would have been forced to invent him. See, too, discussion of Dante, Mandelstam, and Brodsky in chapter 5.

51. Compare Sir Thomas Browne, another paradoxicalist in the tradition of Donne, who wrote in *Religio Medici* (1634–35), "we are onely that amphibious piece betweene a corporall and spirituall essence, that middle forme that links those two together, and makes good the method of God and nature, that jumps not from extreames, but unites the incompatible distances by some middle and participating natures . . . thus is man that great and true *Amphibium*, whose nature is disposed to live not onely like other creatures in divers elements, but in divided and distinguished worlds" (346). Again, I am not suggesting an instance of influence (it is highly unlikely that Brodsky had this passage in mind when he wrote his "Lullaby") but rather a typological likeness, a tendency to frame larger concepts in analogous "paradoxical" terms (e.g., man as intermediary being = amphibian).

52. The fish has definite Christian overtones in much of Brodsky's work. See discussion of lyric "The time of year is winter" (Vremia goda—zima) in chapter 6 of this study.

53. To repeat, affinities that Brodsky could have been aware of but in reality may not have been.

54. The "English theme" first came to Brodsky presumably through two channels: (1) the great interest in the Soviet Union at the time in anything to do with America and the forbidden fruit of Anglo-American culture; (2) Akhmatova's longstanding infatuation with such figures as Shakespeare, Byron, Shelley, Keats, Eliot, and Joyce (see Naiman, *Rasskazy*, 106–107).

55. See, for example, Brodsky's "Pis'ma rimskomu drugu" (Letters to a Roman Friend), which are subtitled "from Martial" (iz Martsiala) (*ChR*, 11–14). The subtitle was added by Brodsky's editor (Lev Loseff) for the publication of *Chast' rechi* but was not included in the English translation (*Part*, 52–54). Thus, the fact that Brodsky appears to take liberties with the historical figure of Martial in order to strengthen the parallels between himself and the Roman writer is actually moot.

56. On Brodsky's varied use of strophic structure, see Scherr, "Strofika Brodskogo."

57. Here Brodsky's chief precursors in the modern Russian context are Tsvetaeva and Khodasevich.

58. It is inconceivable that some of Brodsky's poems, like Donne's, could be understood in recitation without first being silently read by the "listener."

59. See, for example, discussion of the comparative role of the butterfly in Brodsky and Nabokov in chapter 7 of the present study.

60. The difference between the translation (six years) and the original (seven years) is explained in the final section of this chapter ("Brodsky's Use of the Metaphysical Conceit").

61. At first glance one might suspect that Brodsky's interest in geometric figures derives from Khlebnikov, the only other major modern to incorporate mathematical metaphors in his work. But Khlebnikov's analogies are usually *algebraic* and have to do with his utopian project for calculating the laws (numerical rather than visual) of history.

62. Both Annensky and Brodsky, significantly, share the fate of the *serdechnik*, in Russian the person with a bad heart.

63. "[E]legy . . . [is] the most fully developed genre in poetry. . . . Every 'on the death of' poem, as a rule, serves not only as a means for an author to express his sentiments occasioned by a loss but also as a pretext for more or less general speculations on the phenomenon of death per se," as Brodsky says in his Tsvetaeva essay ("Footnote to a Poem," *Less*, 195).

64. Brodsky in general is wont to organize his collections around "Christmas" poems—another challenge to a context of state-sponsored atheism. Every year since 1962 (except when his health prevented it), Brodsky has written a Christmas poem.

65. Brodsky's first collection, *Lyric and Narrative Verse* (Stikhotvoreniia i poemy, 1965), was published without his direct participation.

66. It is perhaps pertinent that Brodsky believes English to be an essentially nominal language and therefore a medium almost impervious to the deception and, by analogy, the potential "evil," of empty rhetoric, false attribution, and the infinite "verbal" disguises of prefixation, infixation, suffixation. Personal inter-

view with author, 28–29 March 1991, South Hadley, Mass. In the same interview Brodsky compared Russian to a diabolically complex chess game and English to a tennis match in which "the ball always comes flying back." For more on Brodsky's notions about the different ethical dimensions embedded in the structures of English and Russian, see, for example, *Less*, 30–31, and his interview with the Swedish Slavist Bengt Jangfeldt in *Expressens kultursida* (3 April 1987).

67. As, for example, in the elegy on Eliot ("Verses on the Death of T. S. Eliot"). See chapter 4.

68. I have contorted the English syntax here and elsewhere to give a sense of what Brodsky is doing in Russian.

69. The "centrifugal" movement of the opening and the attempt at a "gradual broadening of perspective" are mentioned directly in the Pomerantsev interview.

70. Brodsky has likened this use of *chiasmus* to the tidal rhythms of waves. Telephone interview with author, 1990 February 14.

71. Brodsky's "geometric" sense of the higher and lower regions of heaven may be indebted to his reading of Dante (the Lozinzky translation), which, as already stated, took place at roughly the same time as his discovery of Donne and the Bible. The use of the Renaissance perspective in the "Large Elegy" is discussed briefly in Shaitanov, "Predislovie," 58–59.

72. Numerous possible Donnean subtexts in Brodsky's poem are mentioned in Kline, "Elegy," 345–47. Among those listed are: Holy Sonnet, VII; "A Valediction: of Weeping"; Holy Sonnet, III; "Lamentations of Jeremy"; *Epithalamion*, X; and "The Progress of the Soul."

73. "No man is an *island*, entire of itself"; "and therefore never send to know for whom the bell tolls; it tolls for thee" (*Devotions*, 108–109). "Ty videl: zhizn', ona kak *ostrov tvoi*" and "Ne slyshen psinyi lai. / I *kolokol'nyi zvon* sovsem ne slyshen" (*OVP*, 24–25) are rendered in Kline's translation as: "And you saw Life: your Island was its twin" and "No din of baying hound / or tolling bell disturbs the silent air" (*SP*, 43). The first line of Donne's that Brodsky ever knew was the famous "for whom the bell tolls" (Pomerantsev, "Poverkh bar'erov").

74. This notion of "house-cooling" (cf. the "now cool" hearth) compares nicely with the ancient Russian tradition of house-warming (*novosel'e*).

75. On the importance of bells to Donne, particularly in connection with the theme of death, see Bald, *A Life*, 10, 261, 453.

76. Since Donne died on 31 March 1631, it is my assumption that Brodsky wrote his poem in commemoration of that death—probably sometime in the early part of 1963. The snow in the poem would indicate a winter or, by Russian standards, early spring setting. See below.

77. None of this is in the poem, however, at least in so many words. It exists only by implication, as part of the heritage of the modern Soviet poet who must occupy the empty house of his ailing lyric tradition.

78. In another early poem, "Exhaustion now" (Teper' vse chashche, 1960), Brodsky brings together the notions of soul, death, bird's flight, and snow—all vital symbols in "Large Elegy." (This work, by the way, sounds, both in terms of cadence and word choice, quite close to several of Khodasevich's "Psyche" poems.) In this regard, one could hypothesize that the two lyrics ("The tenant finds" and "Exhaustion now"), plus Brodsky's reading of Donne and other metaphysicals, prepared the way for the "Large Elegy."

79. But see, too, the kenotic lives of "verbs" in the short poem by the same name ("Glagoly," *SiP*, 72–73) and the discussion of the heroes' names, including their letters and sounds, in *Isaac and Abraham* (Isaak i Avraam [1963], *OVP*, 46–62).

80. Brodsky may be using "v sillabakh" as a pseudo-Anglicism (the etymology is Latin and Greek) in homage to his subject. "V slogakh" would presumably be expected in the Russian context.

81. And closing. See below.

82. Gabriel seems to be placed after the Lord in this series for strategic reasons: his trumpet sounds the end of human history and the moment when the apocalyptic horsemen mount their steeds (ll. 127–30)—not, to say the least, a very Marxist reading.

83. "I understood that a man could hear questions addressed to him in his sleep or in his bedroom at night, but I didn't understand (yet) from whom those questions could come. And suddenly it came to me, and it fit very well into one line of iambic pentameter verse: 'No, it is I, your soul, John Donne'" (Pomerantsev, "Poverkh bar'erov").

84. This was the first line that came to Brodsky as he began to compose the poem. In this sense, it is the nucleus around which the entire work crystallized. My thanks to Professor George Kline of Bryn Mawr College for this insight, which was communicated to him by the poet.

85. This essay also provides a helpful optic for reading Brodsky's other major elegy on a foreign poet, "Verses on the Death of T. S. Eliot." See discussion in chapter 4 of the present study.

86. Compare the lines "I grieve alone upon the heights of Heaven, / because my labors did bring forth to life / feelings and thoughts as heavy as stark chains."

87. Here we find a further appearance of the Acmeist understanding of Christian logos, which came to Brodsky chiefly from Mandelstam. See discussion in chapter 2 above. The poetic word striving upward is not a metaphor for the soul but *is* the soul, the psyche itself.

88. Donne died in the early spring on 31 March 1631, in London. Nowhere, as far as I know, is there reference to a significant snowfall on that date. This may be, again, Brodsky's "Russian" touch.

89. The speaker's words here anticipate Gorchakov's to the dead Gorbunov in Brodsky's long poem about life and death in a *psikhushka* (psychiatric ward/ insane asylum), *Gorbunov and Gorchakov* (Gorbunov i Gorchakov, 1965–68): "Spi, spi, moi drug" (Sleep, sleep, my friend) (*OVP*, 218).

90. Brodsky's growing familiarity with Donne and his tradition is further corroborated by the fact that in 1968 he had a contract from a Soviet publishing house to do a volume (four thousand lines) of the English metaphysical poets. The project, however, was never realized.

91. For my discussion of the scholastic terms embedded in Donne's image of the twin compasses I am heavily indebted to John Freccero's excellent article "Donne's 'Valediction: Forbidding Mourning,'" especially pp. 279–91.

92. Note the similarity of this formulation/conceit ("Dva putnika, zazhav po fonariu") with that found in "A Song to No Music" (Pen'e bez muzyki, 1970), in *KPE*, 79: "Tak dvukh prozhektorov luchi." See below.

93. Apparently a typographical error was made in the first ("Chekhov") edi-

tion of *Ostanovka,* so that the second and fourth lines of the last stanza of the poem ended with identical rhymes—*v ume* (to calculate "in one's head" vs. "fancifully," "in the imagination"). This was changed in the subsequent Ardis reprinting.

94. My thanks to Professor George Kline for clarifying this matter for me. A dating of 1969 for "Six Years Later" is also suggested by the fact that "Aeneas and Dido," the preceding poem in "Anno Domini," was written in the same year.

95. Phone interview with the author, 3 May 1991.

96. "A Song to No Music" was written roughly at the time that Brodsky and Ms. Wigzell were considering marriage. The couple experienced difficulties with living arrangements (and of course visas) because Brodsky still resided in Leningrad and Wigzell was (and is) British. (Presently Ms. Wigzell is Lecturer in the School of Slavonic and East European Studies at the University of London.) The English translation of the poem (*Part,* 26–33) is dedicated to Faith Wigzell.

97. Again, Brodsky and Faith Wigzell had been considering marriage.

98. Brodsky's Russian is here virtually untranslatable, especially if one attempts to retain all aspects of his poetic manifold. My version, though not as literal as one might like under the circumstances, is intended simply to give the English-speaking reader some sense of what, poetically, Brodsky is trying to accomplish.

Chapter 4
Exile, Elegy, and "Auden-ticity"
in Brodsky's "Verses on the Death of T. S. Eliot"

1. Background for this period of Brodsky's life can be found in various sources. See, for example, Blum, "Reporter at Large," 192–217; Naiman, *Rasskazy,* 5–226 passim; and Polukhina, *Joseph Brodsky,* 20–30. The actual court proceedings, preserved through Frida Vigdorova's stenographic notes, are reproduced in "Zasedanie suda," 279–303, and "The Trial of Iosif Brodsky," 6–17.

2. "Verses on the Death of T. S. Eliot" is treated at some length in Polukhina, *Joseph Brodsky,* 81–88; but see also Janecek, "Comments," 150–53, and Kline's notes on the poem in Brodsky, *Selected Poems,* 102. Brodsky briefly mentions what he was trying to achieve in the poem in Brodsky, "The Muse in Exile," 232. He also compares Auden's and Eliot's "flings" with Christianity, favoring the more existential Auden, in Birkerts, "The Art of Poetry," 110–11. The present chapter differs from Polukhina's useful study in several ways, but chiefly by its emphasis on Auden over Eliot as primary formal as well as philosophical source for the poem. Polukhina's attempts to trace Brodsky's use of water imagery (in fact, a pervasive leitmotif in his work) to Eliot's *Four Quartets,* especially "The Dry Salvages," may be, as Brodsky himself has attested, overstated, since he claims not to have possessed such knowledge of Eliot in 1965 (phone interview, 14 February 1990). On the other hand, Brodsky's friend Anatoly Naiman translated part of *The Waste Land,* as well as "Little Gidding" (*Four Quartets*), in 1962, which means that it is unlikely that Brodsky did not know these works at that time (*Rasskazy,* 30–31). (See, in addition, Janecek, "Comments," 152.) Other friends

and acquaintances familiar with Eliot who may have supplied Brodsky with additional information include Andrei Sergeev, Vladimir Muravyov, and Stanislav Krasovitsky. So, by January 1965 *had* Brodsky progressed beyond the selection of Eliot poems in the Gutner anthology (see note 11, below)? It is difficult to determine conclusively, but probably yes.

3. On the influence of English-language sources on Brodsky, see, for example, his interview with the Swedish Slavist Bengt Jangfeldt: "English has certainly influenced my Russian. It's difficult to determine how, but I've noticed, for example, that unwittingly I try to apply to Russian the precise analytical mechanism characteristic of English. I used to write without deliberation; now I ponder every line" (*Expressens kultursida*, 3 April 1987).

4. Brodsky claims that in January 1965 he knew relatively little about the biographies of Eliot and Auden or, more important, about the "outsider"/"insider" issue in those biographies (telephone interview, 14 February 1990). However, that he personifies the responses of England and America to Eliot's death in the poem (part 2) and invokes Horace in part 3 (in his later essay on Auden he will refer to that poet as "our *transatlantic* Horace" [*Less*, 382]) suggests that at some level these categories may have been operating.

5. Another presumably fortuitous (?) convergence among Eliot, Auden, and Brodsky occurs in their respective treatments of Simeon (see Luke 2:22–36), the old man who "should not see death before he had seen the Lord's Christ" and who represents the transition from Old to New Testament thinking, in "A Song for Simeon," "The Meditation of Simeon" (*For the Time Being*), and "Nunc Dimittis" (Sreten'e). See chapter 5.

6. For example, Brodsky playfully teases the Pushkin of "I loved you" (Ia vas liubil, 1829) in "Twenty Sonnets to Mary Queen of Scots" (Dvadtsat' sonetov k Marii Stiuart, 1974), but he does so in order to demonstrate how the lexicon of Pushkin's love lyrics no longer applies without the imposition of a late-twentieth-century ironic filter. In any event, the parodic sonnet has different generic expectations than the elegy. The elegy that pays tribute to a dead friend or colleague militates against this sort of upstaging play, at least from Brodsky's perspective within the Russian poetic tradition. Auden's elegy to Yeats is, within the Anglo-American tradition, more polemical than, say, Brodsky's elegy to Eliot. See below.

7. For example, "The poet . . . steals left and right and does not even experience a sense of guilt as he does so" (Brodsky, "Preface," in Proffer, *Modern Poets*, 7).

8. Works that have been helpful in the present chapter, particularly in its treatment of the relation in Brodsky between the existential category of "exile" and the aesthetic category of "elegy," include Brodsky, "The Condition"; Levin, "Literature and Exile," in *Refractions*, 62–81; Milosz, "Notes on Exile," 281–84; Said, "The Mind," 49–55 and *The World* 1–30; Seidel, *Exile*, 1–16; and Wittlin, "Sorrow," 99–111. See also the issues of *Books Abroad* and *Mosaic* devoted to exile literature in "Works Cited." For more on the issue of Brodsky and exile, see the third section ("Exile") in chapter 1.

9. Compare Stephanie Sandler's illuminating remarks on Pushkin's relations to his readership while located in exile in *Distant Pleasures*, 1–15, and Edward Said's analysis of the benefits of exile, with specific reference to Auerbach's writing of *Mimesis* in Istanbul, in *The World*, 5–9.

10. The equally important connection with John Donne and the English meta-physicals came earlier, in 1963, when Brodsky first began to read English poetry, primarily *in translation*. See chapter 3.

11. Brodsky's friend Mikhail Meilakh gave the poet an anthology of modern English poetry (*Antologiia novoi angliiskoi poezii* [Anthology of New English Poetry], ed. M. Gutner [Leningrad, 1937]) for his birthday in 1963. The anthology contained the following Eliot poems: "The Love Song of J. Alfred Prufrock," "The Hippopotamus," "The Burial of the Dead" (from *The Waste Land*), "The Hollow Men," and one of the *Choruses from "The Rock"* (the "Unemployed"). My thanks to Mr. Meilakh for this information.

12. On the Jewish theme and its relation to Brodsky's exile status, see chapter 5.

13. "For art doesn't imitate life if only for fear of clichés" (*Less*, 41). It is in this issue of poetic cliché more than anywhere else that we can sense Brodsky's "anxiety of influence." He will go to great lengths to avoid saying what has already been said, or at least to say it in a totally new way. See Kreps, *O poezii*, 2–3.

14. As if to raise the ante one last time, Brodsky makes a statement at the end of the essay that borders on self-revelation, with specific application to "Verses on the Death of T. S. Eliot": "It is precisely on account of its destructive rationalism [i.e., Brodsky's favorite mode] that '*Novogodnee*' falls outside Russian poetic tradition, which prefers to resolve problems in a key that while not necessarily positive is at least consoling. . . . It might be more reasonable to say that '*Novogodnee*' does not fall outside Russian poetic tradition *but expands it*" (*Less*, 263, 264; my emphasis).

15. I am using the version of the poem that Brodsky read and responded to in 1965, although several lines were either emended or removed altogether in the final edition of his verse approved by Auden—once again reflective of the poet's increasing "anxiety of influence" in the face of his subject. It is intriguing to note that these lines, including "O all the instruments agree" and the pivotal "time worships language" formulation, were *precisely the ones that originally attracted Brodsky to Auden*. Hence it could be said that Auden's "anti-heroic" posture (Brodsky, *Less*, 367) possessed just enough lyricism to influence the twenty-four-year-old Russian poet but too much to satisfy the author himself, at least the author of the last version. See below.

16. This is presumably why, for example, an older Auden felt compelled to change the line to the more informal "What instruments we have agree." See previous note.

17. Two texts that are important for Auden's understanding of Yeats after January 1939 are "The Public *vs.* the Late Mr. William Butler Yeats" (1939) and *Elegy for Young Lovers* (1961). The former, a prose dialogue between "the Public Prosecutor" and "The Counsel for the Defence" presenting "pro" and "con" cases for Yeats's "greatness," has particular relevance to "In Memory of W. B. Yeats." See the discussion in Callan, *Carnival of Intellect*, 143–62; Hynes, *The Auden Generation*, 349–53; and Lipking, *Life*, 151–60. See also Brodsky's recollection in *Less*, 374: "[Auden:] 'I have known three great poets, each one a prize son of a bitch.' I: 'Who?' He: 'Yeats, Frost, Bert Brecht.'"

18. If, as Lawrence Lipking remarks in his study of the poem, "Yeats enjoys picturing himself dead . . . [and] expects to lose none of his authority in the grave," then it is Auden's role, first and foremost, to "[rob] Yeats of property rights in his own death" (*Life*, 152–54).

19. George L. Kline's relatively faithful translation in Brodsky's *Selected Poems*, 99–102, which will be used in the remainder of this chapter, preserves the original's meter but attempts to reproduce its elegant rhyme scheme only in part 3.

20. The exception being the last two lines of the stanza.

21. To be sure, Brodsky frequently resorts to nominal rhyme. According to Chris Jones, a graduate student in Russian at Keele University (Staffordshire) who has done statistical research on the poet, nouns comprise at least 50 percent of the rhymes in Brodsky's work. Even so, the percentage is much higher in this instance. My thanks to Dr. Valentina Polukhina for this information.

22. Brodsky plays a subtle game of paronomasia with the Horatian subtext ("Exegi monumentum") in his elegy. The combination of e-o-l in "eoliiskaia nimfa" (Aeolian nymph, as in Sappho and the ancient Greek tribe of Aeolians), "Eliot," and "Eol" (Aeolus) are meant presumably to call up Horace's line "Princeps Aeolium carmen ad Italos / Deduxisse modos" (I first communicated Aeolian song to Italian measures). This, for example, is why Brodsky links Aeolus and Horace Flaccus in the third part of the poem: "Budet pomnit' sam Eol. / Budet pomnit' kazhdyi zlak, / kak khotel Goratsii Flak" (Aeolus himself will remember. Every grain will remember, as Horace Flaccus wanted it). I am indebted to my graduate student Adam Weiner of the University of Wisconsin-Madison for this insight.

23. Brodsky is not enamored of the imprecise diction and self-importance of the Symbolists, but he has great respect for the Acmeists (especially Mandelstam and Akhmatova) and Tsvetaeva. Brodsky's thematics, however, owe much to the Symbolists.

24. A word, in all likelihood, Auden would *not* consider using, except in an ironic context.

25. Poetry (*poeziia*), the central noun in stanza 2, and death (*smert'*), the central noun in stanza 3, can be seen here to complement and define each other. Both nouns are feminine, and the use of pronominal substitutes in the second half of each stanza acts to reinforce this notion of complementarity.

26. Cf. the speaker and the point of view in Brodsky's elegy to Donne (1963), as discussed in chapter 3.

27. This opposition between Auden's and Brodsky's elegiac perspective finds its ultimate expression at the end of Brodsky's stanza 5, when the waves carry the poet to the end/edge of the earth (*krai zemli*), break over this threshold, and send him, joyfully, on his way to the great beyond, only to come crashing back as January "into that dry land of days, where we remain."

28. "In the first version of 'In Memory of W. B. Yeats' Auden had written that time would pardon writers like Kipling and Claudel for their right-wing views; the implication was that the left-wing views held by Auden and his audience were consonant with the force of history and would need no forgiveness whatever. Auden soon found this less easy to believe than he did when he wrote it, and was

less willing to encourage such complacency in his readers" (Mendelson, "Auden's Revision," 118). Mendelson (especially 114–19) is excellent on Auden's gradual move away from the tenets of high modernism, including the poetics of Yeats, the latter providing a prime example of how issues of life and art, politics and aesthetics, could be confused and manipulated under the force of rhetoric. See also Callan, *Carnival*, 148–51.

29. The first two lines of Brodsky's sonnet could, presumably, be read as tongue-in-cheek, although their irony, if that indeed is what it is, seems bright and nonthreatening: "Chitaiushchie v litsakh, magi, gde vy? / Siuda! I podderzhite oreol" (*OVP*, 140). I read these lines as serious, however.

30. Here Auden could be recalling Yeats's self-epitaph in "Under Ben Bulben," with the important difference that the younger poet is invoking the healing powers of verse in time of strife while the older poet is, among other things, settling scores and "scorn[ing] the sort [of poet, including presumably Auden] now growing up / All out of shape from toe to top, / Their unremembering hearts and heads / Base-born products of base beds." Auden's parody, in other words, is not meant in this last part to challenge or polemicize but to forgive and reconcile—his (ultimately Christian) way of exorcizing the "anxiety of influence."

31. Kline's translation takes—perhaps of necessity—certain semantic liberties in this instance. The "reaper's deadly sweep" is a free response to Brodsky's original, which reads simply "[The] hay-mowing/hay-reaping [senokos] is not dangerous."

32. See Hynes, *The Auden Generation*, 351–52, for what is "Yeatsian" and "un-Yeatsian" about the last part of Auden's poem. The combination of an unmotivated joy in the face of tragedy recalls Yeats's beggar-fools ("The Three Hermits," "Tom O'Roughley," "Two Songs of a Fool," "Another Song of a Fool," "The Hero, the Girl, and the Fool," "Tom the Lunatic," "Tom at Cruachan," "Old Tom Again," etc.) and, of course, the Chinamen, looking "on all the tragic scene" with their "ancient, glittering, [and] gay" eyes, of "Lapis Lazuli."

33. In this regard one would do well to compare Auden's notions on "writing," "reading," and the poetic craft in the early essays of *The Dyer's Hand* to Brodsky's statements in *Less Than One* and other interviews and articles. Both poets-cum-critics have a good deal in common: the poet must be a philologist; he/she is dependent on the language he/she inherits; "sincerity," in the sense of "honest feelings," is not as important in a work of art as "authenticity"; the poet must master rhymes, meters, and stanza forms; he/she must understand intuitively the difference between poetry and prose; in order to be properly learned and absorbed, verse must be memorized in large quantities, and so forth.

34. Brodsky may be echoing here Auden's line from "The Cave of Making" in *About the House*: "I should like to become, if possible, / a minor Atlantic Goethe." The Horatian temper of much of Auden's later poetry has often been remarked on. See, for example, Wright, *Auden*, 146–48. The important links between Brodsky and Horace have yet to be studied.

35. Brodsky has written two other elegies to Auden, one in English ("Elegy to W. H. Auden," 1974) and one in Russian ("York," 1977). Both show how much his diction has changed, and continues to change, since 1965. See Polukhina, *Joseph Brodsky*, 90–101.

Chapter 5
Judaism and Christianity
in Mandelstam, Pasternak, and Brodsky:
Exile and "Creative Destiny"

1. Compare, mutatis mutandis, Brodsky's comments—in some ways self-revealing—about Mandelstam: "Mandelstam was a Jew who was living in the capital of Imperial Russia, whose dominant religion was Orthodoxy, whose political structure was inherently Byzantine, and whose alphabet had been devised by two Greek monks" (*Less*, 130).

2. See also Lipking, *The Life*, 18: "The poet realizes that his own personal history, reflected in his poems, coincides with the universal spiritual history of mankind."

3. One would also presumably include in such a listing of faithful disciple figures Tsvetaeva's daughter Ariadna Efron, who in her life after the Gulag was dedicated to preserving the myths and martyrology surrounding her mother.

4. See "Works Cited" for full publication information.

5. The three basic options open to Russian-Jewish cultural figures in the first decades of this century (the so-called Silver Age) were: (1) Zionism (its advocates, including Lev Pinsker and Vladimir Yabotinsky, urged that all Jews emigrate to Palestine); (2) assimilation (here the emphasis, typified by the works of Mandelstam and Pasternak, was on transformation to a Russian identity); and (3) synthesis (the unification of the opposing traditions of Judaism and Christianity together with the preservation of a legitimate Jewish mission in the diaspora). The category of "synthesizers" found its leading spokesman in Semyon Dubnow and was represented by a range of scholars, writers, artists and composers, among them Albert (Abram) Harkavy, Lev Shestov, Mark Antokolsky, and Anton Rubenstein. The above conceptual framework comes from Dr. Brian Horowitz of the University of California-Berkeley, who is currently working on a project entitled "Assimilated Jews in the Russian Intellectual Elite, 1890–1920."

6. Yet for our purposes, despite the richness of its initial conception, Lipking's model is not sufficiently "historicized" or grounded in the poets' respective national traditions. That is, its very elegance, its ability to compare and contrast Dante, Blake, and Yeats (Part 1, "Initiation"), means that the specific national character of their "poetic lives" is of necessity sacrificed to the notion of individual biography. What is "Italian," "English," or "Irish" about these lives is perhaps, to Lipking, not so important as the relative isomorphism of their "breakthroughs." In short, although such sentiments take us too far afield, Lipking's work, like Harold Bloom's, bears the unmistakable imprint of its own national tradition (staunch individualism, Emersonian "self-reliance") and could benefit by taking into account the historical poetics of, say, Lydia Ginzburg and Mikhail Gasparov.

7. "Poetry for Mandelstam was a [sacred] vow [obet], and a literary path the realization of that vow in time and space. The temporal axis was composed of a narrative about the life and fate of the self-sacrificing, kenotic poet, and the spatial coordinates outlined through a broadening of the poetry's thematic compass on a world or even cosmic scale" (Freidin, "Sidia na saniakh," 12).

8. As Freidin remarks, "It is curious that, as opposed to his Acmeist confreres who were Orthodox by birth, Mandelstam, the single Jew among the five founders of the school, defined himself precisely as a Christian poet" ("Sidia na saniakh," 14).

9. "Vremia mozhet idti obratno: ves' khod noveishei istorii, kotoraia so strashnoi siloi povernula ot khristianstva k budizmu i teosofii, svidetel'stvuet ob etom [Time can go backward: witness the entire course of recent history that, with a frightening force, has turned away from Christianity toward Buddhism and theosophy]" ("Pushkin i Skriabin," SS, 2:314; CPL, 90).

10. "Ves' stroinyi mirazh Peterburga byl tol'ko son, blistatel'nyi pokrov, nakinutyi nad bezdnoi, a krugom prostiralsia khaos iudeistva, ne rodina, ne dom, ne ochag, a imenno khaos, neznakomyi utrobnyi mir, otkuda ia vyshel, kotorogo ia boialsia, o kotorom smutno dogadyvalsia i bezhal, vsegda bezhal [The entire elegant mirage of Petersburg was only a dream, a brilliant cloak hurled over the abyss, while all around there extended Judaic chaos, not a motherland, not a home, not a hearth, but precisely chaos, an alien *fetal* world, from whence I came, which I feared, about which I guessed only dimly, and which I fled, always fled]" (*Shum vremeni*, SS, 2:55; my emphasis).

11. This is a perfect illustration of the double bind that Gilman refers to in *Jewish Self-Hatred*: Mandelstam is expected to "speak it [i.e., Russian] better than [his] non-Jewish contemporaries" (18), but when he does, he is ridiculed for it.

12. Other Mandelstam texts touching on the Jewish theme include: "Kiev" (1926), "Iakontov" (1926), "Mikoels" (1927), and "Egipetskaia marka" (The Egyptian stamp, 1928).

13. For the links between Gippius's pamphlet *Pushkin i khristianstvo* (Pushkin and Christianity, 1915), Ivanov's talk "Vzgliad Skriabina na iskusstvo" (Scriabin's View of Art, 1915), and Mandelstam's "Pushkin and Scriabin" (1915–16), see Freidin, A Coat, 68–80. On the importance of the thought system of Zielinski for Mandelstam, see Cavanagh, "Mandel'shtam and the Making," 243–84.

14. Or, according to Gilman's harsh formula, Mandelstam was "attempting to ingratiate himself into European society through self-hatred" (*Jewish Self-Hatred*, 19). But Gilman's argument does not take into account how important Western European civilization was to *all* educated Russians, whether of Jewish extraction or not. To leap ahead of ourselves for a moment, it will be precisely this idea of Jewish nationalism and exclusivity that Pasternak will combat in the notorious "anti-Semitic" sections of *Doctor Zhivago*. Moreover, it will be the same Byzantium-Rome dichotomy that Brodsky will confront head-on in "Flight from Byzantium." See below.

15. Mandelstam's ambiguous feelings about his imperfectly assimilated parents have interesting parallels with the cases of Kafka, Benjamin, and Scholem as discussed by Alter in *Necessary Angels*, 29–35. See, for example, the following: "All three of our writers, then, including the Scholem who announced his estrangement from German, maintained a necessary and, one may say, loving relationship with their native language, but it was not untouched by an awareness of contradictions, especially in the case of Kafka and Scholem. These contradictions arise above all from a perception of the sons that their fathers' roots in German culture were shallow, and perhaps too recent to be anything but shallow" (29).

16. As Freidin puts it, "Christian Russians became Jews, and Osip Mandelstam, a Jew among them, assumed the role of a precursor in reverse, one who, instead of announcing the imminent arrival of the Savior, reminded people that he had already arrived, had died on the cross, and had risen" (*A Coat*, 78; see also "Sidia na saniakh," 17).

17. Not perhaps by chance, such similarly "stock-taking" works—also notably in prose—as *Okhrannaia gramota* (Safe Conduct) and *Less Than One* will perform analogous functions in the "created lives" of Pasternak and Brodsky.

18. Phaedra is also, of course, an important myth in the created life of Tsvetaeva, but she, characteristically, sees the conflict from the point of view of the transgressing mother, herself a victim of her passion, rather than from the point of view of Hippolytus the son. See, for example, "Zhaloba" (The Complaint), in *SiP*, 3:54–55. Tsvetaeva, it is worth recalling, was not averse to recruiting Mandelstam in her own incessant myth-making: he plays Dmitry to her Marina (Maryna Mniszek) in her 1916 poem "Dmitrii! Marina! V mire" about the Time of Troubles (*SiP*, 1:213–14) Correspondingly, Mandelstam casts himself as sacrificial Tsarevich (N.B. the present-tense construction of "Tsarevicha vezut" [the Tsarevich is being carried] in *SS*, 1:59) in a poem ("Na rozval'niakh, ulozhennykh solomoi" [On the sledge covered with straw]) inspired by his meeting with Tsvetaeva. See Taranovsky, *Essays*, 115–20.

19. See also the detailed discussion of two other "Jewish" poems, "Sredi sviashchennikov levitom molodym" (A young Levite among the priests, 1917) and "Vernis' v smesitel'noe lono" (Return to the incestuous bosom, 1920), in Cavanagh, "Mandel'shtam and the Making," 250–84. The same poems are also treated briefly in Freidin, *A Coat*, 78–80, 124–26.

20. The sun (setting or rising) and the redemptive grace associated with Christ's (and the Poet's) death formed an abiding image complex for Mandelstam's generation, being linked first and foremost with its most famous representative—Blok. See, for example, Tsvetaeva's "Ty prokhodish' na zapad solntsa" (You progress into the setting sun, 1916), the third poem of her cycle "Stikhi k Bloku" (Verses to Blok), in *SiP*, 1:228–29. This poem, though written five years before Blok's death, already surrounds its subject with the status of sacrificial or "kenotic" victim (she, as opposed to others, will not drive a nail into his hand, etc.).

21. To cite one of Tsvetaeva's most notorious mots: "V sem khristianneishem iz mirov / Poety—zhidy" (In this most Christian of worlds, poets are Yids) (*SiP*, 4:185; cf. N. Mandel'shtam, *Vospominaniia*, 2:302).

22. "I love only you . . . and Jews," Mandelstam remarks to his wife in a letter of 1926 (*CPL*, 506; cited in Cavanagh, "Mandel'štam, Dante," 320).

23. "Self-hating Jews respond either by claiming special abilities in the discourse of the reference group or *by rejecting it completely and creating a new discourse*, uncontaminated, they believe, by their exclusion from it" (Gilman, *Jewish Self-Hatred*, 19).

24. My discussion here of Mandelstam and the "Jewish theme" in the thirties owes much to Clare Cavanagh's fine article "Mandel'štam, Dante, and the 'Honorable Calling of Jew.'"

25. And this, ironically, at a time when Pasternak was casting off his avantgarde manner and growing simpler, more, as it were, "Acmeist."

26. See episode with Frishman-Adelsons and Pasternak's "purely anti-Semitic theme" as discussed in Barnes, *Pasternak*, 313.

27. "Pasternak," concludes Barnes, "always played down the importance of his racial origins" (*Pasternak*, 2).

28. As Nadezhda Mandelstam remarks in the first volume of her memoirs: "In the cases of both Pasternak and M[andelstam]., destiny was hatched from character, like a butterfly from its chrysalis. Both were doomed to be rejected by the literary establishment, but whereas Pasternak, for a time at any rate, sought points of contact with it, M. always shied away" (*Hope Against Hope*, 151).

29. Compare Boris Eikhenbaum's picture of a Mandelstam poetry reading at Nikolai Khardzhiev's in November 1932: "[Mandelstam] is a poet of genius, of valor, a heroic man. A gray-bearded patriarch . . . he recited every poem that he had written (in the past two years) in chronological order! They were such terrifying exorcisms that many people took fright. Even Pasternak was afraid—he lisped: 'I envy your freedom. For me you are a new Khlebnikov. And just as alien to me as he is. I need a non-freedom'" (cited in Freidin, *A Coat*, 7).

30. By comparison, Mandelstam's "conversion" to the Lutheran faith in order to be able to enter the University of St. Petersburg, appears, if not insignificant, then much less freighted in autobiographical myth.

31. "When *My Sister, Life* appeared, and was found to contain expressions not in the least contemporary as regards poetry, which were revealed to me during the summer of the revolution, I became entirely indifferent to the identity of the power which had brought the book into being because *it was immeasurably greater than myself* and than the poetical conceptions surrounding me" (*Safe Conduct*, 117; my emphasis; *Proza 1915–58*, 282).

32. On this issue of the roots of *Doctor Zhivago* in Pasternak's earlier life and works, see Borisov and Pasternak, "Materialy."

33. In an illuminating paper ("Gradus ad Parnassum") delivered at the Pasternak centennial conference in Stanford on 16 October 1990, the émigré scholar Boris Gasparov makes a convincing case for the poet's abiding emphasis on the *process*, rather than the end result, of creation. Gasparov offers evidence from numerous Pasternak texts to advance the argument that it is the repeated break with the past and the (presumably unending) refinement of displaced "drafts" of a "life's work" that interest the poet. See below.

34. This, of course, in no way diminishes the vitality and charm of *My Sister*.

35. The musician Robert Gladstone, who had dinner with Pasternak at his Peredelkino dacha in 1959 in the wake of the Nobel scandal, reports the author of *Doctor Zhivago* as saying, "When I had finished [the novel], I knew I had created something *greater than myself*. . . . I felt I had put my experience *into a larger form*" (my emphasis). (Gladstone's remarks were made during a commemorative panel at the Pasternak centennial conference [Stanford] on 16 October 1990.)

36. I am indebted to my graduate student Eliot Borenstein for this insight, expressed in a seminar paper on *Doctor Zhivago*.

37. "Nel'zia ne vpast' k kontsu, kak v eres', / V neslykhannuiu prostotu" (Toward the end it is impossible not to fall, as [one would] into heresy, into unheard-of simplicity) (*1912–32*, 327).

38. The style of the later Pasternak has, to be sure, no direct links to historical Acmeism.

39. Again, compare Said's distinction between "filiation" and "affiliation" in *The World*, 16–20, and my earlier discussion in the second section ("In Place of Biography") of chapter 1.

40. Compare, for example, this passage to: "There were three of us in that room and a half of ours: my father, my mother, and I. A family, a typical Russian family of the time . . . we should have considered ourselves lucky, especially since we were Jews" (*Less*, 448).

41. Compare "Evreiskoe kladbishche okolo Leningrada" (Jewish cemetery near Leningrad), in *SiP*, 54–55.

42. Here Brodsky's links with Kafka (as discussed earlier), Beckett, and the literature of the absurd are obvious. Brodsky is not interested in Jewishness per se but, to use Alter's formula for Kafka, in "convert[ing] the distinctive quandaries of Jewish existence into images of the existential dilemmas of mankind *überhaupt*, 'as such'" (*Necessary Angels*, 53).

43. See discussion in the second section ("In Place of Biography") of chapter 1.

44. As Brodsky writes in *Less*, 195: "[Elegy] is the most fully developed genre in poetry."

45. Other prominent examples of modern Russian poets with heart problems are Innokenty Annensky, Anna Akhmatova, and, of course, Pasternak.

46. Here, by the way, his muse joins forces with his favorite Tsvetaeva's. See chapter 6.

47. In this one important respect, Brodsky differs somewhat from Mandelstam: while the latter views Byzantium (via "Hellas") as an ideal in *Tristia*, the former derives Russia's notorious *kosnost'* (stagnation, formlessness) and disrespect for the individual from the Islamic (as opposed to Christian) principles of Byzantium (modern-day Istanbul) in "Flight from Byzantium" (*Less*, 393–446) and in several important poems (e.g., "Vremia goda—zima" [The time of year is winter], in *KPE*, 101). Compare, for example, Mandelstam's description of "Hagia Sophia" in his famous poem to Brodsky's description in "Flight from Byzantium" (*Less*, 431–33). For Brodsky, then, the "East" is a terrifying principle, the epitome of a lack of form, so that we might say that in his anti-Byzantium pieces he is polemicizing in part with Mandelstam but especially with the Yeats of "Byzantium" and "Sailing to Byzantium." See chapter 2.

48. "Nature morte" is also situated, significantly, at the end of *Konets prekrasnoi epokhi* (The End of a Beautiful Epoch).

49. Brodsky may have inherited this tendency from Tsvetaeva, who was wont to structure her works around calendar turning points, particularly the New Year. For example, in the verse play *Konets Kazanovy* (Casanova's End), the aging hero (much like Simeon, see below) departs from the Castle of Dux on the last day of 1799 into a snowstorm and, presumably, death. One also recalls in this connection that Pushkin had the habit of writing poems on the anniversary of the opening of the lyceum at Tsarskoe Selo.

50. Tomas Venclova has informed the author that Brodsky presumably did *not* suspect that he was under threat of imminent banishment when he wrote the poem between January and March 1972. According to Venclova's diary, Venclo-

va spoke to Brodsky by telephone from Moscow on May 1, after having heard a rumor on April 29 that the authorities had made their decision. At this point, Brodsky still did not believe the rumor. All this makes the meaning of the poem both more poignant and "prophetic." My thanks to Professor Venclova for this information.

51. On the issue of "impersonation" Brodsky has said the following in connection with his feelings toward Akhmatova and Auden: "In a sense, I think that their poems . . . —some of Akhmatova's and quite a lot of Auden's—are written by me, or that I'm the owner. . . . I sort of live their lives. Not that I'm a postscript to either one of them. Both would rebel against that. But to myself it's more sensible or more pleasant perhaps to think that I'm a postscript to them than that I'm leading my own life" (Montenegro, "Interview," 538).

52. N.B. her potent conception of herself as modern Cassandra.

53. Recall, for example, Mandelstam's "My memory is inimical to all that is personal" and Tsvetaeva's image of the body melting away into pure voice in "Sivilla" (The Sibyl, 1922). See also Mandelstam's "K nemetskoi rechi" (To German Speech, 1932): "Sebia gubia, sebe protivorecha, / Kak mol' letit na ogonek polnochnyi, / Mne khochetsia uiti iz nashei rechi / Za vse, chem ia obiazan ei bessrochno" (Destroying myself, contradicting myself / As the moth flies to the midnight flame, / I feel like leaving our [native] speech / Beyond [or: For] everything with which I am obliged to it without time limit [SS, 1:190]). Curiously, by the 1930s Tsvetaeva also experienced something similar to Mandelstam's desire to escape native speech: she began to translate some of her earlier work into French (e.g., Molodets [The Swain, 1924] into Le Gars) at a time when her lyric output in Russian had fallen off dramatically.

54. Significantly, Brodsky alludes to Notre Dame de Paris in his poem about crucifixion, "Nature morte." Any such reference in the modern Russian tradition invokes automatically the famous Mandelstamian text (and subtext).

Chapter 6
"This Sex Which Is Not One"
versus This Poet Which Is "Less Than One":
Tsvetaeva, Brodsky, and Exilic Desire

1. "Tsvetaeva is a maximalist, and the vector of her emotional movements is known in advance" (Less, 200).

2. On Tsvetaeva's repeated use of what has been termed a poetics of appropriation and transgression, see Makin, Poetics of Appropriation, esp. 1–11.

3. My argument in what follows is essentially that Tsvetaeva's stature as a poet, which is by now indisputable, has become too neatly "engendered." What we are left with increasingly is the rather predictable picture of a proto-feminist freedom fighter, a kind of Russian Hippolyta, which is to say, Tsvetaeva's penchant for mythopoetic masking has become the reality itself. For this Tsvetaeva, the suffix in "poetess" is more relevant than the root form, a marker both of triumphant difference and a source of self-affirming, as well as self-resisting, parody, as Svetlana Boym has suggested in her recent book (Death, 192–240). The Tsvetaeva who participated in Bryusov's "evening of poetesses" in 1920, we are

told, both refuses to be the object of prurient male "speculation" (i.e., the passive Muse), *and* refuses to join forces with a long line of traditional male subjects (the unsuffixed "poet") (Boym, *Death*, 200–19). She keeps the "-ess" but uses it as a kind of female phallus to taunt those, beginning with the grand manipulator Bryusov himself, who would limit her to certain prescribed roles. Likewise, to use a myth-rich metaphor that Kristeva and Cixous have adopted in their treatments of the poet, Tsvetaeva is the mother of a new poetic word, and she died, in a romantic transference from the literal to the literary, in childbirth (see Boym, *Death*, 221).

What needs to be questioned in these narrations of Tsvetaeva's story is the notion that gender alone, or even primarily, including the myth of motherhood, is *the* constitutive element of the poet's special claim on our attention. At the same time, one wishes to restore a bit of choice (choice never being completely free in these matters) to Tsvetaeva's otherwise overdetermined portrait, for herein lies the essence of her tragedy. The question is this: If Tsvetaeva willfully mixed the "genres" of life and art and was courageous enough to pay the consequences, are we, in our turn, doing the poet and the woman justice by subsuming that romantic hybridization uncritically into the largely ahistorical discourse of post-structuralism?

In this respect, Hélène Cixous's long chapter on Tsvetaeva in her recent book is perhaps the most glaring example to date' of what may be termed irresponsible ahistoricism coopted into the service of poststructuralist rhetoric (*Readings*, 110–51). Cixous repeatedly engages in what can only be called a kind of postructural catachresis—demanding more of her language than the context would seem to permit and indulging in a kind of simplistic paradoxicalism where everything becomes its opposite. She writes, for instance, of Akhmatova's and Tsvetaeva's poetic texts that "Theirs are all texts of despair, that is, of hope" (111), with no supporting evidence as to what she actually means. She is also extremely careless with regard to Tsvetaeva's personal history: Tsvetaeva's mother, Maria Alexandrovna Mein-Tsvetaeva, is described as being a Polish woman who happens to speak German (132), when in fact she was the half-Polish daughter of a prosperous Baltic German businessman; Tsvetaeva, who was nothing if not defiantly bisexual, is said to give advice to Natalie Barney, one of the most famous lesbians of her age, from her position as a heterosexual in "Lettre à l'Amazone" (141); and Tsvetaeva's line "Poety—zhidy" (Poets are Yids), which is mistranslated as "All poets are Jews," is mysteriously declared to refer to Mandelstam (116, 132). Even more problematic is how this virtually nonexistent context is then used by Cixous to support larger statements about Tsvetaeva's creative personality, especially what Boym would call the poet's "self-sacrificial maternity" (*Death*, 221)—statements that are, one suspects, either simply not true or irresponsibly inflated (see *Readings*, 127, 129, 143, 146). This tendency to extrapolate from a specific textual instance to a romantic biological essentialism, which is perhaps more marked in Cixous, is also characteristic of Kristeva.

4. "*Phallocentrism* denotes a system that privileges the phallus as the symbol or source of power. The conjuncture of logocentrism and phallocentrism is often called, after Derrida, *phallogocentrism*" (Moi, *Sexual/Textual Politics*, 179, n. 5).

5. In Tsvetaeva not a simple or universally positive notion. See below.

6. In this sense they share the double estrangement of such black writers as Richard Wright and James Baldwin, who, as a result of their race, both were and were not "Americans" when they took up residence in Paris after the Second World War. Here, however, the distinction between "expatriation" and "exile" must be invoked, for what is "self-imposed," no matter how compelling the reason, is never exactly the same as what is *imposed by others*. That H. D. or Wright opted to leave an inhospitable homeland (and literary tradition) would, of necessity, have a different impact on their revisionary projects (especially with regard to the inevitable feelings of guilt experienced toward those "left behind") than, for example, Tsvetaeva's frantic efforts to reunite her family (her husband had been serving in the White Army and could not therefore return to Russia) through the radical "choice" of political exile.

7. To be sure, not all feminist critics speak in the same voice or endorse a single, monolithic emplotment. In what follows I will be relying primarily on the "continental" flank of feminist criticism, that emphasizing *l'Écriture féminine*, with its so-called "writing the body." As opposed to the historicist and more pragmatic (and textually oriented) American School, these continental feminists (Kristeva, Irigaray, Cixous) are often, as previously noted, defiantly ahistorical. They are, moreover, as linguistically, philosophically, and theoretically sophisticated as they are contextually vague; and they are relentlessly psychoanalytic. Their work is a forceful illustration of what cognitive psychologist Jerome Bruner calls the "top down approach" for ordering data into coherent narratives (*Actual Minds*, 10). The "fathers" of their texts, which they repeatedly revise and "overthrow" (but also then incorporate) in a manner that may suggest bad faith to their American colleagues, are Freud, Lacan, and Derrida. That their interest is primarily language and only secondarily (if at all) history is, for our purposes, a not insignificant consideration.

8. " 'On the Red Steed' is written. The last dash has been placed. Should I send it to you [Lann]? What for? The steed exists, so Lann, too, exists—forever—upward! I didn't want to come to you as a beggar—only with poetry. I didn't want to come to you (feminine pride and Tsvetaeva pride—always post factum) as I had been before, yours, while now I am feeling so free. . . . And so, Comrade Lann . . . I stand before you again as on the day you entered my house for the first time . . . : gay, free, happy—myself" ("Pis'ma k Lannu," 180; cited Feiler, *Double Beat*, 177).

9. But see also Karlinsky, *Cvetaeva*, 210: "The [poem's] introduction and epilogue are based on the trope of 'Slavic antithesis,' or comparison by negation, usual in Slavic folk poetry."

10. "She [woman]," writes Irigaray with her typical irony (she is "deadpanning" the "male" point of view), "wills nothing but what he attributes to her. . . . Woman as womb, the unconscious womb of man's language. . . . A body-matter marked by their signifiers, a prop for their soul fantasies. The place where their encoding as speaking subjects is inscribed and where the 'objects' of their desire are projected" (*This Sex*, 94–96).

11. The question of what Gilbert and Gubar call a woman writer's "anxiety of authorship" as opposed to the male writer's "anxiety of influence" (i.e., Bloom's oedipal model where the son must struggle with and "overthrow" the precursor-father) is acutely felt in Tsvetaeva's case and has some fascinating ramifications.

See, for example, Makin, *Poetics of Appropriation*, which is excellent for its lucid discussion of Tsvetaeva's tendency to "transgress" prior texts.

12. "Caught in the specular logic of patriarchy [the discussion is about Irigaray's notion of 'specularization'], woman can choose either to remain silent, producing incomprehensible babble (any utterance that falls outside the logic of the same will by definition be incomprehensible to the male master discourse), or to *enact* the specular representation of herself as a lesser male. The latter option, the woman as mimic, is, according to Irigaray, a form of hysteria. The hysteric *mimes* her own sexuality in a masculine mode, since this is the only way in which she can rescue something of her own desire. The hysteric's dramatization (or *mise en scène*) of herself is thus a result of her exclusion from patriachal discourse" (Moi, *Sexual/Textual Politics*, 135).

13. What is potentially confusing about the case of Tsvetaeva is the *source* of this language. For Tsvetaeva the so-called semiotic order (Kristeva) or deep structure of a poem was born in its beat, in the drumming of her fingers on a hard surface that grew to drown out all else until it was given verbal expression, thereby entering the realm of the "symbolic order." If, however, as Cixous seems to imply, these rhythmic rumblings bring the poet in contact with a primal "Good Mother," a preoedipal "space" where parent and child are one and all differentiation, enumeration, and appropriation (the male libidinal urge for "property") are dissolved in a flood of maternal "milk and honey" (see Moi, *Sexual/Textual Politics*, 113–19), then why is this space described with male metaphors? Either Tsvetaeva's poetry is not *écriture féminine* (a distinct possibility) or the gender oppositions in her metaphors are reversed (what is "male" is really "female"). Clearly, however, given her context (a late Victorian childhood), what Tsvetaeva saw as "forbidden" in life and art was the "male" in herself. See below.

14. Tsvetaeva seems to have been influenced in this practice by Mayakovsky.

15. Thus Tsvetaeva, as opposed to someone like Irigaray, never "pretend[s] to be writing in some pure feminist realm outside patriarchy" (Moi, *Sexual/Textual Politics*, 140). The mere fact that she masters the rules of Russian prosody *in order to break them* suggests that her poetry is part of a prior, largely patriarchal tradition.

16. The urgent scene with the fire, as Karlinsky has noted, has much in common with a similar melodramatic episode in Mayakovsky's *A Cloud in Trousers* (Oblako v shtanakh) (*Cvetaeva*, 210–11).

17. Again, on being caught in the "specular logic" of patriarchy, where the hysteric mimes her own sexuality in the masculine mode, see Irigaray's *Speculum* and note 12 above.

18. The important links between Tsvetaeva and Blok, especially their shared notion of verse (*stikhi*) as *stikhiinost'* (spontaneity), is treated in Ciepiela, "Leading the Revolution." Ciepiela makes the argument that Tsvetaeva's *Krysolov* (Rat-catcher) is an elaborate response to Blok's famous poem of the revolution, *Dvenadtsat'* (The Twelve).

19. Lily Feiler convincingly posits a connection between the Rider and the devil fantasy that Tsvetaeva experienced as a child. See *Double Beat*, 27–31, 176. Ciepiela ("Leading the Revolution," 15–17) suggests also that the demonic Piper/ poet in *Rat-catcher* is an inverted substitute for the Christ at the end of *The Twelve*.

20. Toril Moi's caveat in this context is worth repeating: "Needless to say, this description [the passage just cited] only concerns rape *fantasies* and has nothing whatsoever to do with the reality of rape" (*Sexual/Textual Politics*, 118).

21. Cixous insists that the masculine and feminine libidinal economies are marked, respectively, by the Realm of the *Proper* and the Realm of the *Gift*. Man appropriates in order to preserve the boundaries of self (castration anxiety); woman "depropriate[s] unselfishly, body without end" (Cixous, "Medusa," 259, in Marks and Courtivron, *New French Feminisms*). As Toril Moi sums up the Cixousean position: "Proper—property—appropriate: signalling an emphasis on self-identity, self-aggrandizement and arrogative dominance, these words aptly characterize the logic of the proper according to Cixous. The insistence on the proper, on a proper return, leads to a masculine obsession with classification, systematization and hierarchization. . . . In the Realm of the Proper, the gift is perceived as establishing an inequality—a difference—that is threatening in that it seems to open up an imbalance of *power*. . . . The woman, however, gives without a thought of return. *Generosity* is one of the most positive words in Cixous's vocabulary" (*Sexual/Textual Politics*, 110–13). According to Cixous's model, Tsvetaeva's libidinal economy is much closer to the "masculine" than to the "feminine."

22. " 'Specularization' suggests not only the mirror-image that comes from the visual penetration of the speculum [Irigaray's metaphor] inside the vagina; it also hints at a basic assumption underlying all Western philosophical discourse: the necessity of postulating a subject capable of *reflecting* on its own being. The philosophical meta-discourse is only made possible, Irigaray argues, through a process whereby the speculating subject contemplates himself; the philosopher's *speculations* are fundamentally narcissistic" (Moi, *Sexual/Textual Politics*, 132). It is difficult to imagine a more "narcissistic" poet than Marina Tsvetaeva.

23. "Although the Devil's body [in Tsvetaeva's essay] is *female* [e.g., absence of fur, physique of lioness], he is clearly perceived as a man—a strong, steely, bold man" (Feiler, *Double Beat*, 29). In other words, almost from the beginning Tsvetaeva was deeply ambivalent in her sexual orientation.

24. Perhaps no better words can end this section than Tsvetaeva's own: "I give no one the right to stand in judgment over a poet. Because no one can know. Only poets know but they won't judge. And a priest would release [the poet from judgment]. The only [allowable] judgment over a poet is self-judgment [samo-sud]" (*Izbrannaia proza*, 1:405). Brodsky would agree.

25. It is worth recalling that Tsvetaeva is Brodsky's favorite poet and probably the one he has learned most from.

26. Genuine marginality, if we are going to be honest about it, means that one is writing for an audience that perhaps has not been born, that is not empowered by any extant group, however small and isolated, that is not "worldly" in the sense meant by the critic Edward Said. Is this possible, or is it simply another version, ironic and inverted, of the Nietzschean will to power? Who is Tsvetaeva writing for *in this world* when late in life she translates her own *poema-skazka The Swain* (Molodets), a work already strangely inverted vis-à-vis the original, into French that, if grammatically correct, syntactically resembles Russian? Her voracious poetic appetite having exhausted the semantic, prosodic, and generic resources of her native speech, she moved into a linguistic no-man's land. By the

same token, who is Brodsky writing for when he smuggles into his Russian verse extended scholastic arguments and elaborate English metaphysical conceits that can only be perceived as profoundly alien to the native tradition? What special brand of exile is this? See discussion in the third section ("Exile") of chapter 1.

27. See also Tsvetaeva's statement: "My soul is monstrously jealous: it could never have endured me as a beautiful woman . . . To speak of physical appearance in my case is foolish: it so obviously and so very much is not the issue" (*Pictorial Biography*, 27; cited in Weeks, *Marina Cvetaeva*, 45).

28. Compare the famous "Emche organa i zvonche bubna" (More capacious than the organ and more ringing than the tamborine) (23 December 1924; *PR*, 3:118–19).

29. See also the contemporaneous "Derev'ia" (Trees) cycle in *PR*, *SiP*, 3:29–35.

30. October 9 on the Gregorian calendar.

31. It is noteworthy that Brodsky uses triple and preparoxytonic or paroxytonic rhymes in two poems whose theme is clearly exile: this one ("1972") and "The Fifth Anniversary" (Piataia godovshchina) (*U*, 70–73), written five years later.

32. Nor, to take another example, could Brodsky say, as Tsvetaeva does of herself and her lover in "Poema gory" (Poem of the hill, 1924) that "The gods take vengeance on their likenesses" (Bogi mstiat svoim podobiiam!) (4:165).

33. Compare "K Likomedu, na Skiros" (To Lycomedes on Scyros, 1967), in *OVP*, 92–93.

34. Like Tsvetaeva and Mandelstam, two of his favorite models, Brodsky uses classical mythology to inform his own created life. This is especially true of Tsvetaeva's and Brodsky's poetic depictions of their own children: for example, Tsvetaeva chose the Demeter-Persephone myth (the "Kore") to describe her relations to her daughter Ariadna, while Brodsky saw his separation from his son as a replaying of the Odysseus-Telemachus relationship. See Weeks, "I Named Her," and *ChR*, 23.

35. To be sure, "better part" alludes first of all to Brodsky's own poetry. In the Russian translation of Ovid that Brodsky read, the poet's work is called his *luchshaia chast'* (translation of either *optima pars* or *maxima pars*). Moreover, in the 1970s Brodsky inscribed copies of *Ostanovka v pustyne* (A Halt in the Wilderness) with phrases such as "Iosif Brodskii vam daet svoiu luchshuiu chast'" (Joseph Brodsky gives you his better part). My thanks to Professor George Kline of Bryn Mawr College for this information.

36. Generically, of course, "On the Red Steed" and "The time of year is winter" are totally different. The former is a longer poem with a skeletal story line, the latter a short lyric.

37. To repeat, Brodsky's strophes are some of the most varied and ingenious in the history of Russian poetry (see Scherr, "Strofika Brodskogo"); in one masterpiece entitled "The Butterfly" (Babochka), he creates a stanza that actually sits on the page in a shape imitating its subject. See chapter 7.

38. See, for example, the opening stanzas of "Konets prekrasnoi epokhi" (End of a Beautiful Epoch): "V etikh grustnykh kraiakh vse rasschitano na zimu: sny . . ." and "Etot krai nedvizhim . . ." (*KPE*, 58).

39. Again, always connected with Tsvetaeva in Brodsky's imagination.

40. Brodsky would alter radically the tenor of Jameson's formulation: the horizon of discourse is indeed "untranscendable," but the only discourse granted that honor is *poetic*.

41. It should come as no surprise that Brodsky quit formal schooling at fifteen and thereafter educated himself.

42. The passage goes on: "And there was a city. The most beautiful city on the face of the earth. With an immense gray river that hung over its distant bottom like the immense gray sky over that river. Along that river there stood magnificent palaces with such beautifully elaborated facades that if the little boy was standing on the right bank, the left bank looked like the imprint of a giant mollusk called civilization. *Which ceased to exist*" (*Less*, 32; my emphasis).

43. It could also be argued, as Brodsky's Russian-language version of this essay suggests, that the "which never happened" phrase refers to the fact that the rulers of the USSR were never considered degenerates.

44. Which, by the way, uses a pun from English to comment on the poet's impecunious plight in the Soviet Union.

45. For additional discussion of "Flight from Byzantium," see chapter 2 and Venclova, "A Journey." Brodsky may also be alluding to James Merrill's love poem "Flight from Byzantium."

46. In fact, it would be difficult to imagine two thinkers more different in linguistic approach and worldview than Edward Said and Joseph Brodsky. See discussion in the third section ("Exile") of chapter 1.

47. *Likhaia* (dashing, gallant/evil) as an attributive for *pobeda* (victory) is of course ironic in the poem.

48. Tsvetaeva writes in one of her letters to Pasternak in anticipation of his return to the Soviet Union in March 1923 that "Russia for me is . . . almost the other world. Were you to leave for Guadeloupe, the land of snakes, of convicts, I would not call you back. Russia is a different matter" (*Vestnik*, 128:173; cited in Feiler, 220).

Chapter 7
Exile as Pupation: Genre and Bilingualism in
the Works of Nabokov and Brodsky

1. Brodsky was deported to Norinskaya on 22 March 1964. There he would spend the next eighteenth months (at which point the original sentence was commuted).

2. The poem "Vecherom" follows immediately "1 ianvaria" in *Ostanovka v pustyne* (115–16).

3. Telephone interview, 9 May 1990.

4. The butterfly is also a rather prominent theme in two of Brodsky's chief foils among contemporaries—Alexander Kushner and Bella Akhmadulina. Kushner's poem "Slozhiv kryl'ia" (Folded Wings), in particular, bears comparison with Brodsky's "The Butterfly" in terms of its metapoetic theme and stanzaic structure. See Kushner, *Stikh*, 54–55; and Akhmadulina, *Taina*, 88–89.

5. One interesting parallel between Brodsky and Nabokov noted recently by a scholar is their recourse to English to frame, in autobiographical prose, their experience as Russians. See Diment, "English as Sanctuary."

6. As Elizabeth Klosty Beaujour has persuasively argued, genuine bilingual writers are much more than writers who have mastered more than one language and culture. They are not simply speakers of two (or more) languages who apply "monolingual" mentalities when they are operating in a given linguistic system. "To be true to themselves, . . ." writes Beaujour, "bilingual writers must somehow remain *actively* bilingual" (*Alien Tongues*, 53). By this she means that, in fact, "there is a third language at their command which overarches the others; and the existence of that third language enables them to reconcile the other two" (54). George Steiner describes this third language as an "eclectic cross-weave": "Thus one of the 'languages' inside me, probably the richest, is an eclectic cross-weave whose patterns are unique to myself though the fabric is quite palpably drawn from the public means and rule-governed realities of English, French, German, and Italian" (*After Babel*; cited in Beaujour, 54–55). It is precisely this "eclectic cross-weave" that is so different in Brodsky and Nabokov. See below.

7. Again, to repeat an earlier caveat, this does not mean that Brodsky's culture is in any way typical of that of the majority of his former countrymen, but simply that the Soviet "epoch" has, willy-nilly, left its mark on his consciousness. He is a product of a specific time and place and in that respect only is he a *homo sovieticus*.

8. This is not simply an argument from or about chronology, although Nabokov's coming-of-age as a writer corresponded with the symbolist and postsymbolist years and movements. The point is that Nabokov, even in his best verse, never advanced beyond the status of talented epigone of Blok or Khodasevich or Gumilyov. That his mature verse has little in common with the high modernist spirit of a Mandelstam or Pasternak or Tsvetaeva goes without saying. (This does not mean, by the way, that in Nabokov's verse of the 1930s and after, one does not occasionally hear a "Pasternakian" note or "Pasternakian" tropes. In a poem such as "K Kn. S. M. Kachurinu" [To Prince S. M. Kachurin, 1947] a Pasternakian intonation is particularly noticeable in stanzas 2 and 3 of part 3, beginning with "Voobrazhaiu shchebetan'e . . . " [I imagine a twittering] [*Stikh*, 280]. The point is that Nabokov the poet could not help but internalize some of the mannerisms of modernist verse, although the latter's psychology and values remained profoundly alien to him.) When as late as 1970, in an epigram on Pasternak, he can claim that that poet possesses a "fatal kinship" (rokovoe rodstvo) with the vulgar Benediktov (a comparison that goes back to debates among émigré circles) suggests just how foreign modernist poetics are to him (*Stikh*, 296).

9. That Nabokov was a bilingual author of surpassing genius is not open to question; that he was a genuine poet, to repeat, is. See below.

10. Here one may wish to take issue with D. Barton Johnson, one of Nabokov's more distinguished critics, who agrees with his subject that phonoaesthetic effects endemic to poetic works cannot be systematically transferred from one language to another, this being the principal reason why Nabokov chose his method of "Englishing" *Eugene Onegin*. See Johnson, "Contrastive Phonoaesthetics." I would simply add that Nabokov's reasons may be well argued and consistent but his *motives* may have something to do with his own limited poetic talent. Likewise, I strongly disagree with Beaujour when she writes that "Still, one cannot help believing that Nabokov, had he so decided, might have done the *best possible* poetic translation of *Onegin*" (*Alien Tongues*, 111).

11. "Even worse [than the available metrical translations] are two rhymed versions, which, like grotesque satellites, accompanied the appearance of the first edition of this work; one is Walter Arndt's, . . . a paraphrase, in burlesque English, with preposterous mistranslations, some of which I discuss in *The New York Review of Books*, April 30, 1964; and the other Eugene M. Kayden's product, . . . of which the less said the better" (*EO*, 2:4). Arndt's translation, now in its second (revised) edition, first appeared in 1963, Nabokov's in 1964. How pristine Nabokov's motives were in all this—after all, he had been laboring on his translation of *Eugene Onegin* for many years and had, whether justifiably or not, been partially upstaged by Arndt's "grotesque satellite"—to invoke his own phrase, the less said the better. Brian Boyd, Nabokov's celebrated biographer, goes to considerable pains to demonstrate how Arndt often distorts Pushkin's precise Russian and even adds completely useless filler words (*American Years*, 322–27). And he is right, according to the logic of his subject. Arndt's attempt is flawed precisely in the area of *semantic precision* (Nabokov's greatest concern). But what Nabokov is willing to sacrifice does not, by the same token, bring us any closer to "Pushkin": "Unquestionably, Nabokov's lines are not only unrhymed but often flat and grotesquely awkward, unlike Pushkin's, and it was this that many reviewers found a cruel betrayal of Pushkin and sufficient reason to prefer Arndt's nonsense jingles. . . . [But] Nabokov pays Pushkin the compliment that his exact meaning matters—and how can we take literature seriously if we do not believe this?—and that his music cannot be matched" (*American Years*, 327).

12. "I think I was born a painter—really!" (*Strong Opinions*, 17). Beaujour goes on to link Nabokov's "gift for drawing and painting" with his emphasis on "the image system" and on "holistic right-hemisphere strategies" (*Alien Tongues*, 103).

13. "I think in images," says Nabokov in *Strong Opinions* (14). "I don't believe that people think in any languages. . . . No, I think in images, and now and then a Russian phrase or an English phrase will form with the foam of the brain-wave, but that's about all." Or: "Yes, I write in three languages, but I think in images. The matter of preference does not really arise. Images are mute, yet presently the silent cinema begins to talk and I recognize its language" (Quennell, *A Tribute*, 123; cited in *Alien Tongues*, Beaujour, 103). See Beaujour, *Alien Tongues*, 34–35, 103.

14. Perhaps a small example will suffice for the purposes of illustration. "All happy families are alike" has nothing in common with "Sisters heaviness and tenderness, your signs are identical" (Sestry tiazhest' i nezhnost', odinakovy vashi primety), a line from an early Mandelstam poem. Both statements are built on their own generalizations (happy families versus semantic sisters), yet one is lucidly discursive and the other is murkily metaphorical. Why are heaviness and tenderness sisters? Why are their signs identical? Mandelstam's locution has its own authority, which begins with how it *sounds—tiazhest'* is, acoustically, a "sister" to *nezhnost'*. For more on Nabokov's conservative poetics, see Smith, "Nabokov."

15. In fairness to Nabokov, the "lapidary" and "narrated" quality of much of his verse was motivated by other aspects of his context as well. Vera Nabokov reminds the reader in her preface to her husband's *Stikhi* (Verse) that he insisted

that each of his poem's have a clear "topic and exposition" (*siuzhet i izlozhenie*) as a reaction to the haphazard, seemingly "spontaneous," and ill-formed poetry of the (Russian émigré) "Parisian School."

16. Compare Yury's similarly "inspirational" bout with typhus in *Doctor Zhivago*.

17. I realize that "poetic" and "prosaic" are tendencies, linguistic "vectors" (as Brodsky might say), and not simply defined and delimited absolutes. Poems can contain "prosaic" elements and prose can become, with the help of certain sound tropes, suddenly "poetic." Some distinguished critics, Jonathan Culler for example, have gone to elaborate lengths to claim that a text (perhaps *any* text) becomes poetic by its physical arrangement on a page (that is, what is "poetic" is a visual orientation toward the words and therefore a request to treat these words more seriously or with a greater intensity of effort). See *Structural Poetics*, 163. My response to this is that it cannot be applied, or if so only marginally, to the Russian literary experience. Mandelstam is primarily a poet even when he writes prose, and Nabokov is primarily a prose writer even when he writes poetry. The "vector" remains in force regardless of the "generic" distinction.

18. Compare, for example, the opening section of Auden's "In Memory of W. B. Yeats" (*Collected Poetry*, 48–49).

19. One may even go so far as to claim that the reason Nabokov applauded Khodasevich as "the greatest Russian poet that the twentieth century has yet produced" (*Gift*; Foreword [n.p.]) was because the latter was, in his own way, the most "unlyrical" poet in the modern tradition, and hence one postsymbolist that Nabokov could understand and appreciate.

20. One of the lessons Brodsky claims to have learned from Evgeny Rein is to depend as little as possible on nouns and adjectives for the effects of soundplay, internal rhyme, and end rhyme.

21. "I'm not interested in games as such. Games mean the participation of other persons; I'm interested in the lone performance—chess problems, for example, which I compose in glacial solitude" (*Strong Opinions*, 117). One might argue that Nabokov is, as a lyrical talent, more a Luzhin than a Nabokov. Poems are his verbal chess problems. He is, in his own severe metapoetic terms, a *character*, but not an *author*, of genius.

22. "Nabokov read the treatise [*Symbolism*] entranced. Twenty-five years later he still regarded it as 'probably the greatest work on verse in any language'; forty years later he made it the basis for his comparison of Russian and English prosody in his *Eugene Onegin*" (Boyd, *The Russian Years*, 149). I would suggest that the link between Bely's theories and Nabokov's militantly "unpoetic" *Eugene Onegin* translation is not fortuitous.

23. "I had spoken English with the same ease as Russian, since my earliest infancy. I had already written one English novel in Europe besides translating in the thirties two of my Russian books. Linguistically, though perhaps not emotionally, the transition was endurable" (*Strong Opinions*, 189–90; cited in Beaujour, *Alien Tongues*, 95).

24. "When Brodsky first shouted an English poem by George Herbert into my ear outside a cafe on Gorky Street [in Moscow] 14 years ago [i.e., circa 1966], I thought he was speaking Lithuanian" (Clarence Brown, "The Best Russian Poetry").

25. As George Steiner writes in *After Babel*, "In certain civilizations there come epochs in which syntax stiffens, in which available resources of live perception and restatement wither. Words seem to go dead under the weight of sanctified usage; the frequence and sclerotic force of clichés, of unexamined similes, of worn tropes increases. Instead of acting as a living membrane, grammar and vocabulary become a barrier to new feeling. A civilization is imprisoned in a linguistic contour which no longer matches, or matches only at certain ritual, arbitrary points, the changing landscape of fact" (21).

26. What Beaujour says of genuine bilingual writers applies with particular force to the post-1972 Brodsky: "Both languages and cultures are wholly theirs, but they do not belong wholly to either" (*Alien Tongues*, 55).

27. The preparoxytonic or "deep rhyme" quality of the rhyme words in "The Year 1972" is discussed in chapter 6.

28. There are, for example, currently practicing Russian poets who consider such lines exemplary, even for Brodsky. Michael Kreps, a middle generation émigré poet and Slavist now teaching at Boston College, has told me in a private interview that this poem in particular shows Brodsky at the height of his powers.

29. George Steiner has argued for a more flexible notion of translation in *After Babel* when he writes "inside or between languages, human consciousness equals translation" (47). In other words, Brodsky may be attempting to translate into English qualities (morphological, etc.) that can only exist in Russian. As D. M. Thomas postulates, "One can translate only into one's mother tongue—at least this is true for poetry, because there is something primordial in poetry which cannot be captured in any other way" ([original in French] *Actes*, 162; cited in Beaujour, *Alien Tongues*, 213 n. 44). Leonid Forster has some interesting comments on the respective merits and deficiencies of such bilingual poets as Stefan George, Rilke, and Yvan Goll. Only Goll was completely bilingual, that is, his idiolect or "signature" translated back and forth from French to German, precisely because he "thought in images." The "German" Rilke did not, however, translate into the "French" or, even more, the "Russian" Rilke. See *The Poet's Tongues*, 50–94.

30. For additional discussion of the Lowell connection in Brodsky, see chapter 2.

31. The description of the gallery sounds very close to that of the "pavilion" in *Speak, Memory*, which Nabokov links etymologically to "papilio" (216).

32. Sleptsov's Attacus moth is also described in the Russian as a *nochnaia babochka*.

33. When Nabokov's father was imprisoned briefly in 1908 he wrote via secret message to his wife and asked her to tell their son that "all I see in the prison yard are Brimstones and Cabbage Whites" (*Speak, Memory*, 176).

34. See, for example, the appearance of the Comma butterfly in the context of the "harlequin pattern of colored panes inset in a whitewashed framework" of the veranda in *Speak, Memory*, 106.

35. This is what Nabokov has to say about the attraction lepidoptery holds for him in an interview with Alfred Appel: "My passion for lepidopterological research, in the field, in the laboratory, in the library, is even more pleasurable than the study and practice of literature, which is saying a good deal. Lepidopterists are obscure scientists. . . . The tactile delights of precise delineation, the silent para-

dise of the camera lucida, and the precision of poetry in taxonomic description represent the artistic side of the thrill that accumulation of new knowledge, absolutely useless to the layman, gives its first begetter. Science means to me above all natural science. . . . There is no science without fancy, and no art without facts" (Appel, "An Interview," in Dembo, *Nabokov*, 33).

36. This presence of a divine design "from beyond" is more obvious in the religiously colored poems Sirin-Nabokov wrote in the late teens and early twenties in the Crimea and at Cambridge than in his later Russian fiction, where his "otherworldliness" (*potustoronnost'*) is subtly encoded into his aesthetics. See, for example, "Arkhangely" (Archangels, 1918), "Tainaia vecheria" (The Last Supper, 1918), and "Paskha" (Easter, 1922), in *Stikh*, 14, 16, 66. "Easter" is written specifically on the death of Nabokov's father.

37. Telephone interview, 9 May 1990. Brodsky's relatively cool feelings toward Nabokov may be connected to the fact that apparently the only comment Nabokov ever made about Brodsky was negative. When Carl Proffer sent a poem of Brodsky's to Nabokov in 1969 as a token of the young poet's appreciation (Nabokov had asked Proffer to deliver a pair of jeans to Brodsky in his name), Nabokov responded: "It [the poem] contains many attractive metaphors and eloquent rhymes . . . but is flawed by incorrectly accented words, lack of verbal discipline and an overabundance of words in general. However, esthetic criticism would be unfair in view of the ghastly surroundings and sufferings implied in every line of the poem" (Nabokov, *Selected Letters*, 461).

38. Here and elsewhere the translation of "The Butterfly" is that of George L. Kline, first printed in *The New Yorker* 52 (15 March 1976) and collected in *A Part of Speech*.

39. Telephone interview, 9 May 1990.

40. For more on the connection between Brodsky, Donne, and the English metaphysical tradition, see chapter 3 of the present study. Brodsky's stanzaic pattern, which sits on the page like a butterfly's wing, suggests parallels with the "Easter-wings" of George Herbert. In his grafting of English poetic habits to the Russian lyric tradition Brodsky can only be compared to someone like Jan van der Noot (1539 or 1540–1595?): "Van der Noot successfully transplants the metre and the diction of the Pléiade into Dutch, thereby giving the Low Countries their first considerable body of renaissance poetry in the vernacular"; "Here, in the early days of renaissance and baroque literature in Northern Europe, stands Jan van der Noot, who by his personal achievement and by his inspiring example gave an important stimulus to the development of a more modern poetry in Dutch, English and German. I can think of no poet of his times who exploited as thoroughly and as successfully as he did the possibilities of auto-translation and none who worked with such consistency and virtuosity in two vernaculars at the same time" (Forster, *Poet's Tongue*, 30, 34–35). Like Brodsky, van der Noot spent a large part of his life in exile.

41. Here Nabokov's chief model was presumably Khodasevich. See discussion of "Gorit zvezda, drozhit efir" (A star shines, the air trembles, 1921) in Bethea, *Khodasevich*, 109.

42. As a point of interpretation, the "beret nas v kleshchi" (takes us in pincers) could refer either to God or to the world (tot mir, chto).

43. Brodsky apparently didn't heed the stories of Fyodor's father about the "voices of butterflies" (*Dar*, 125).

44. The one value that has priority in Brodsky's worldview is language itself. In this he is both like and unlike Nabokov, who also places great emphasis on the patterned play of language but not only on that. See, for example, *Less Than One*, 363: "If time worships language [a line from W. H. Auden's poem 'In Memory of W. B. Yeats'], it means that language is greater, or older, than time, which is, in its turn, older and greater than space. That was how I was taught, and I indeed felt that way. So if time—which is synonymous with, nay, even absorbs deity—worships language, where then does language come from? For the gift is always smaller than the giver. And then isn't language a repository of time? And isn't this why time worships it? And isn't a song, or a poem, or indeed a speech itself, with its caesuras, pauses, spondees, and so forth, a game language plays to restructure time?"

Works Cited

Adorno, Theodor. *Prisms*. Translated by Samuel and Shierry Weber. Cambridge, Mass.: MIT Press, 1981. Translation of *Prismen*, 1967.

Afanas'ev, Aleksandr. *Narodnye russkie skazki (v trekh tomakh)*. Vol. 1. Moscow: Gosudarstvennoe izdatel'stvo khudozhestvennoi literatury, 1957.

Akhmadulina, Bella. Interview with Valentina Polukhina. In Lev Loseff and Valentina Polukhina, eds., Brodsky's *Poetics and Aesthetics*, 194–204 (London: Macmillan, 1990).

———. *Taina*. Moscow: Sovetskii pisatel', 1983.

Akhmatova, Anna. *Sochineniia*. Edited by G. P. Struve and B. A. Filipoff. Washington: Inter-language Literary Associates, 1965–83.

Alexandrov, Vladimir E. *Nabokov's Otherworld*. Princeton, N.J.: Princeton University Press, 1991.

Alter, Robert. *Necessary Angels: Tradition and Modernity in Kafka, Benjamin, and Scholem*. Cambridge, Mass.: Harvard University Press, 1991.

———. "The Revolt Against Tradition: Readers, Writer, Critics." *Partisan Review* 43.2 (1991): 282–314.

Alvarez, A. "Plain human speech: East European poetry and radical *chic*." *Times Literary Supplement* (15 May 1992): 6–7.

Appel, Alfred, Jr. "An Interview with Vladimir Nabokov." In L. S. Dembo, ed., *Nabokov: The Man and His Work*, 19–44 (Madison: University of Wisconsin Press, 1967).

Atlas, James. "A Poetic Triumph." *New York Times Magazine* (21 December 1980): 32–34.

Auden, W. H. *The Dyer's Hand and Other Essays*. New York: Random, 1948.

———. *The Collected Poetry of W. H. Auden*. New York: Random House, 1945.

———. *Collected Shorter Poems, 1927–1957*. New York: Vintage Press-Random, 1975.

———. "Letter of Introduction." *C. Day Lewis, the Poet Laureate: A Bibliography*. Compiled by G. Handley-Taylor and Timothy d'Arch Smith. London: St. James, 1968.

Bakhrakh, A. "Pis'ma Mariny Tsvetaevoi." *Mosty* 5 (1960): 299–318.

Bakhtin, Mikhail. "Forms of Time and of the Chronotope in the Novel." *The Dialogic Imagination: Four Essays*. Translated by Caryl Emerson and Michael Holquist. Austin: University of Texas Press, 1981.

Bald, R. C. *John Donne: A Life*. Oxford: Oxford University Press, 1970.

Baranczak, Stanislaw. *Breathing Under Water and Other East European Essays*. Cambridge, Mass.: Harvard University Press, 1990.

———. *A Fugitive from Utopia: The Poetry of Zbigniew Herbert*. Cambridge, Mass.: Harvard University Press, 1987.

Baratynskii, E. A. *Polnoe sobranie stikhotvorenii*. Edited by E. N. Kupreianova. Leningrad: Sovetskii pisatel', 1957.

Barnes, Christopher. *Boris Pasternak: A Literary Biography.* Vol. 1: 1890–1928. Cambridge: Cambridge University Press, 1989.

Barthes, Roland. *Writing Degree Zero.* Translated by Annette Lavers and Colin Smith. New York: Hill and Wang, 1977.

Beaujour, Elizabeth Klosty. *Alien Tongues: Bilingual Russian Writers of the 'First' Emigration.* Ithaca, N.Y.: Cornell University Press, 1989.

Benedict, Helen. "Flight from Predictability: Joseph Brodsky." *The Antioch Review* 43.1 (1985): 9–21.

Bethea, David M. "Blok, Bely, and the Poetics of Revelation." In Robert Hughes and Irina Paperno, eds., *Christianity and Its Role in the Culture of the Eastern Slavs, Modern Times: Ideologies, Institutions, Cultural Life* (Berkeley: University of California Press, forthcoming).

———. "Exile, Elegy, and Auden in Brodsky's 'Verses on the Death of T. S. Eliot.' " *PMLA* 107 (March 1992): 232–45.

———. "Exile as Pupation: The Image of the Butterfly in Nabokov and Brodsky" [Izgnanie kak ukhod v kokon: Obraz babochki u Nabokova i Brodskogo]." *Russkaia literatura* (St. Petersburg), no. 3 (1991): 167–75.

———. "The Exilic Imagination, Russian Style." In Emory Elliot, Ellen Chances, and Robert Maguire, eds., *Culture/Kultura: Soviet-American Dialogues on Literature* (Durham, N.C.: Duke University Press, forthcoming).

———. "Joseph Brodsky as Russian Metaphysical: A Reading of 'Bol'shaia elegiia Dzhonu Donnu.' " *Canadian-American Slavic Studies* 27.1–4 (1993): 69–89.

———. *Khodasevich: His Life and Art.* Princeton, N.J.: Princeton University Press, 1983.

———. "Mandelstam, Pasternak, Brodsky: Judaism and Christianity in the Making of a Modernist Poetics." In Boris Averin and Elizabeth Neatour, eds., *American Scholars on Twentieth Century Russian Literature* (St. Petersburg: Rif, forthcoming).

———. *The Shape of Apocalypse in Modern Russian Fiction.* Princeton, N.J.: Princeton University Press, 1989.

Birkerts, Sven. "The Art of Poetry XXVIII: Joseph Brodsky." *Paris Review* 83 (Spring 1982): 83–126.

Bloom, Harold. *The Anxiety of Influence.* New York: Oxford University Press, 1973.

Blum, Ralph. "A Reporter at Large: Freeze and Thaw: The Artist in Soviet Russia—III." *New Yorker* (11 September 1965): 168–217.

Borisov, V. M. and E. B. Pasternak. "Materialy k tvorcheskoi istorii romana B. Pasternaka 'Doktora Zhivago.' " *Novyi mir* 6 (1988): 205–48.

Boyd, Brian. *Vladimir Nabokov: The Russian Years.* Princeton, N.J.: Princeton University Press, 1990.

———. *Vladimir Nabokov: The American Years.* Princeton, N.J.: Princeton University Press, 1991.

Boym, Svetlana. *Death in Quotation Marks: Cultural Myths of the Modern Poet.* Cambridge, Mass.: Harvard University Press, 1991.

Brodsky, Joseph. "The Acceleration of the Poet." With Peter Forbes. *Poetry Review* 78.1 (1988): 4–5.

———. "Beyond Consolation." *New York Review of Books* (7 February 1974): 13–16.

———. *Chast' rechi. Stikhotvoreniia 1972–1976.* Ann Arbor: Ardis, 1977.

———. "The Condition We Call Exile." *New York Review Of Books* (21 January 1988): 16–19.

———. "Estetiken äetikens moder." Interview with Bengt Jangfeldt. *Expressens kultursida* (3 April 1987).

———. "History of the Twentieth Century: A Roadshow." *Partisan Review* 53 (1986): 327–43.

———. "An Immodest Proposal." *The New Republic* (11 November 1991): 31–36.

———. Interview with Natalia Gorbanevskaia. *Russkaia mysl'* (3 February 1983).

———. "Joseph Brodsky: The People's Poet." See Montgomery, M. R.

———. *Konets prekrasnoi epokhi. Stikhotvoreniia 1964–1971.* Ann Arbor: Ardis, 1977.

———. *Less Than One: Selected Essays.* New York: Farrar, Straus, and Giroux, 1986.

———. "Literature and War—A Symposium. The Soviet Union." *Times Literary Supplement* (17 May 1985): 544.

———. "The Meaning of Meaning." *New Republic* (20 January 1986): 32–35.

———. "The Muse in Exile: Conversations with the Russian Poet, Joseph Brodsky." With Anne-Marie Brumm. *Mosaic* 8 (1974): 229–46.

———. "Nobel Lecture." In Lev Loseff and Valentina Polukhina, eds., *Brodsky's Poetics and Aesthetics*, 1–11 (London: Macmillan, 1990).

———. *Ostanovka v pustyne.* New York: Chekhov, 1970. Reprint. Ann Arbor: Ardis, 1989.

———. *A Part of Speech.* New York: Farrar, Straus, and Giroux, 1980.

———. "Poetry as a Form of Resistance to Reality." Translated and adapted by Alexander Sumerkin and Jamey Gambrell. *PMLA* 107 (March 1992): 220–25. Translation of "Poeziia kak forma soprotivleniia real'nosti," in *Russkaia mysl'* 3829 (25 May 1990).

———. "Presentation of Czeslaw Milosz to the Jury." *World Literature Today* 52.3 (1978): 364.

———. *Primechaniia paporotnika.* Bromma, Sweden: Hylaea, 1990.

———. "Puteshestvie v Stambul." *Kontinent* 46 (1985): 67–111.

———. "Reflections of a spawn of hell." *New York Times Magazine* (4 March 1973): 10, 66–70.

———. "Says poet Brodsky: 'A writer is a lonely traveler and no one is his helper.' " *New York Times Magazine* (1 October 1972): 11, 78–84.

———. *Selected Poems.* Translated by George Kline. New York: Harper, 1973.

———. "Six Years Later." Translated by Richard Wilbur. *New Yorker* (1 January 1979): 30. Included with revisions in *A Part of Speech*.

———. *Stikhotvoreniia i poemy.* Washington: Inter-language Literary Associates, 1965.

———. "S tochki zreniia iazyka: Interv'iu Igoria Pomerantseva s Iosifom Brodskogo v kanun 350-letiia smerti angliiskogo poeta Dzhona Donna." Radio program "Poverkh bar'erov" from the studio "Svoboda" (London) (8 June 1990). (Interview given in 1981.)

Brodsky, Joseph. *To Urania*. New York: Farrar, Straus, and Giroux, 1988.

———. *Uraniia*. Ann Arbor: Ardis, 1987.

———. "Why Milan Kundera Is Wrong about Dostoevsky." *New York Times Book Review* (17 February 1985): 31–34.

———. Personal interview. 28–29 March 1991.

———. Telephone interview. 14 February 1990.

Brown, Clarence. "The Best Russian Poetry Written Today." *New York Times Book Review* (7 September 1980): 11+.

Browne, Sir Thomas. *Religio Medici*. Edited by Jean-Jacques Denomain. Cambridge: Cambridge University Press, 1953.

Bruner, Jerome. *Actual Minds, Possible Words*. Cambridge, Mass.: Harvard University Press, 1986.

Bulgakov, Mikhail. *The Master and Margarita*. Translated by Mirra Ginsburg. New York: Grove, 1967.

Callan, Edward. *Auden: A Carnival of Intellect*. New York: Oxford University Press, 1983.

Carpenter, Humphrey. *W. H. Auden: A Biography*. London: Allen, 1981.

Cavanagh, Clare. "Osip Mandel'shtam and the Modernist Creation of Tradition." Ph.D. dissertation, Harvard University, 1988.

———. "Mandel'shtam, Dante and the 'Honorable Calling of Jew.' " *Slavic and East European Journal* 35.3 (1991): 317–38.

Chambers, A. B. "Goodfriday, 1613. Riding Westward: The Poem and the Tradition." In John R. Roberts, ed., *Essential Articles for the Study of John Donne's Poetry*, 333–48 (Hamden: Archon, 1975). Reprinted from *English Literary History* 28 (1961): 31–53.

Ciepiela, Catherine. "Leading the Revolution: Cvetaeva's 'Krysolov' and Blok's 'Dvenadcat.' " Article ms.

Cixous, Hélène. *La Jeune Née* (en collaboration avec Catherine Clément). Paris: UGE, 1975.

———. "The Laugh of the Medusa." Translation of "Le Rire de la Méduse." In Elaine Marks and Isabelle de Courtivron, eds., *New French Feminisms: An Anthology*, 245–64 (New York: Schocken, 1981).

———. *Readings: The Poetics of Blanchot, Joyce, Kafka, Kleist, Lispector, and Tsvetayeva*. Minneapolis: University of Minnesota Press, 1991.

Cuddihy, John Murray. *The Ordeal of Civility: Freud, Marx, Levi-Strauss, and the Jewish Struggle with Modernity*. New York: Basic Books, 1974.

Dante Alighieri. *The Divine Comedy*. 3 vols. Translated by John D. Sinclair. New York: Oxford University Press, 1961.

Davidson, Pamela. *The Poetic Imagination of Vyacheslav Ivanov: A Russian Symbolist's Perception of Dante*. Cambridge: Cambridge University Press, 1989.

Davydov, Sergei. *"Teksty-Matreški" Vladimira Nabokova*. München: Verlag O. Sagner, 1982.

de Man, Paul. "Lyric Voice in Contemporary Theory: Riffaterre and Jauss." In Chaviva Hošek and Patricia Parker, eds., *Lyric Poetry: Beyond the New Criticism*, 55–72 (Ithaca: Cornell University Press, 1985).

Dembo, L. S., ed. *Nabokov: The Man and His Work*. Madison: University of Wisconsin Press, 1967.

Derzhavin, Gavrila. *Stikhotvoreniia*. Leningrad: Sovetskii pisatel', 1957.

Diment, G. "English as Sanctuary: Nabokov's and Brodsky's Autobiographical Writings." Manuscript.

Donne, John. *Devotions upon Emergent Occasions*. Ann Arbor: University of Michigan Press, 1959.

———. *The Poems of John Donne*. Edited by Herbert J. C. Grierson. 1st ed., 1912. London: Oxford University Press, 1963.

———. *The Sermons of John Donne*. 10 vols. Edited by George R. Potter and Evelyn M. Simpson. Berkeley: University of California Press, 1962.

Dreizin, Felix. *The Russian Soul and the Jew: Essays in Literary Ethnocentrism*. Edited by David Guaspari. Lanham, Md.: University Press of America, 1990.

Efron, Ariadna. *Stranitsy vospominanii*. Paris: Lev, 1979.

Eikhenbaum, Boris. *O poezii*. Leningrad: Sovetskii pisatel', 1969.

Eliot, T. S. *The Complete Poems and Plays (1909–1950)*. New York: Harcourt Brace, Jovanovich, 1971.

———. *Selected Prose*. Edited by Frank Kermode. New York: Farrar, Strauss, and Giroux, 1975.

Emerson, Caryl. *Boris Godunov: Transpositions of a Russian Theme*. Bloomington: Indiana University Press, 1986.

Feiler, Lily. *Marina Tsvetaeva: The Double Beat of Heaven and Hell*. Manuscript.

Field, Andrew. *Nabokov: His Life in Art*. Boston: Little, Brown, 1967.

Fiut, Alexander. *The Eternal Moment: The Poetry of Czeslaw Milosz*. Translated by Theodosia S. Robertson. Berkeley: University of California Press, 1990.

Fleishman, Lazar. *Boris Pasternak: The Poet and His Politics*. Cambridge, Mass.: Harvard University Press, 1990.

———. *Boris Pasternak v tridtsatye gody*. Jerusalem: Magnes/Hebrew University, 1984.

Forster, Leonard. *The Poet's Tongues: Multilingualism in Literature*. London: Cambridge University Press, 1970.

Freccero, John. "Donne's 'Valediction Forbidding Mourning.' " In John R. Roberts, ed., *Essential Articles for the Study of John Donne's Poetry*, 279–304 (Hamden: Archon, 1975). Reprinted from *English Literary History* 30 (1963): 335–76.

———. "The Significance of *Terza Rima*." In Rachel Jacoff, ed., *Dante and the Poetics of Conversion*, 258–71 (Cambridge, Mass.: Harvard University Press, 1986).

Freidin, Gregory. *A Coat of Many Colors: Osip Mandelstam and His Mythologies of Self-Presentation*. Berkeley: University of California Press, 1987.

———. "Sidia na saniakh: Osip Mandel'shtam i kharizmaticheskaia traditsiia russkogo modernizma." Manuscript.

Friedman, Susan Stanford. "Exile in the American Grain: H. D.'s Diaspora." In Mary Lynn Broe and Angela Ingram, eds., *Women's Writing in Exile*, 88–112 (Chapel Hill: University of North Carolina Press, 1989).

Gardner, Helen. "The Argument about 'The Ecstasy.' " In John R. Roberts, ed., *Essential Articles for the Study of John Donne's Poetry*, 239–58 (Hamden: Archon, 1975). Reprinted from Herbert Davis and Helen Gardner, eds., *Eliza-*

bethan and Jacobean Studies presented to F. P. Wilson, 279–306 (Oxford: Clarendon Press, 1959).

Gardner, Helen, ed. *The Metaphysical Poets*. 2d ed. Oxford: Oxford University Press, 1967.

Gasparov, Boris. "Gradus ad Parnassum." Manuscript.

Gilbert, Sandra M. and Susan Gubar. *The Madwoman in the Attic: The Woman Writer and the Nineteenth-Century Literary Imagination*. New Haven: Yale University Press, 1979.

Gilman, Sander L. *Jewish Self-Hatred: Anti-Semitism and the Hidden Language of the Jews*. Baltimore: Johns Hopkins University Press, 1986.

Glazova, Marina. "Mandel'štam and Dante: *The Divine Comedy* in Mandel'-štam's Poetry of the 1930's." *Studies in Soviet Thought* 28 (1984): 281–335.

Gordeeva, Galina. "Svobodnaia taina, ili davai uletim. Kontury 'leningradskoi' literatury: nabliudeniia i dogadki." *Novyi mir* 7 (1990): 230–39.

Gordon, Lyndall. *Eliot's New Life*. Oxford: Oxford University Press, 1988.

Gove, Antonina Filonov. "The Feminine Stereotype and Beyond: Role Conflict and Resolution in the Poetics of Marina Tsvetaeva." *Slavic Review* 36 (1977): 231–55.

Grayson, Jane. *Nabokov Translated: A Comparison of Nabokov's Russian and English Prose*. Oxford: Oxford University Press, 1977.

H. D. [Hilda Doolittle] *Helen in Egypt*. New York: Grove, 1961. New York: New Directions, 1974 (Reprint).

———. *Paint It To-Day*. Edited by Cassandra Laity. New York: New York University Press, 1992.

Harris, Jane Gary. *Osip Mandelstam*. Boston: Twayne, 1988.

Hartman, Geoffrey. *Beyond Formalism: Literary Essays 1958–1970*. New Haven: Yale University Press, 1970.

Harvey, Sir Paul, ed. *The Oxford Companion to Classical Literature*. London: Oxford University Press, 1937.

Heaney, Seamus. "Envies and Identifications: Dante and the Modern Poet." *Irish University Review* 15 (Spring 1985): 5–19.

———. "The Impact of Translation." *Yale Review* 76.1 (1986): 1–14.

Hollander, John, ed. *Modern Poetry: Essays in Criticism*. Oxford: Oxford University Press, 1968.

Hollander, John. *Vision and Resonance: Two Senses of Poetic Form*. 2d ed. New Haven: Yale University Press, 1985.

Hughes, Merrit Y. "Kidnapping Donne." In John R. Roberts, ed., *Essential Articles for the Study of John Donne's Poetry*, 37–57 (Hamden: Archon, 1975). Reprinted from *Essays in Criticism* (2d series) 4 (1934): 61–89.

———. "Some of Donne's 'Ecstasies.' " In John R. Roberts, ed., *Essential Articles for the Study of John Donne's Poetry*, 259–70 (Hamden: Archon, 1975). Reprinted from *PMLA* 75 (1960): 509–18.

Hynes, Samuel. *The Auden Generation: Literature and Politics in England in the 1930s*. Princeton, N.J.: Princeton University Press, 1972.

Iliushin, A. A. "Dante i Petrarka v interpretatsiiakh Mandel'shtama." In S. S. Averintsev, O. G. Lasunskii, et al., *Zhizn' i tvorchestvo O. E. Mandel'shtama: Vospominaniia, materialy k biografii, 'novye stikhi', issledovaniia*, 367–82 (Voronezh: Izdatel'stvo Voronezhskogo universiteta, 1990).

Irigaray, Luce. *This Sex Which Is Not One*. Translated by Catherine Porter, with Carolyn Burke. Ithaca, N.Y.: Cornell University Press, 1985. Translation of *Ce sexe qui n'en pas un* (Paris: Editions de Minuit, 1977).

———. *Speculum of the Other Woman*. Translated by Gillian C. Gill. Ithaca, N.Y.: Cornell University Press, 1985. Translation of *Speculum de l'autre femme* (Paris: Editions de Minuit, 1974).

Janecek, Gerald. "Comments on Brodskij's 'Stixi na smert' T. S. Eliota.' " *Russian Language Journal* 118 (1980): 145–53. Translated in L. V. Loseff, ed., *Poetika Brodskogo: Sbornik statei* (Tenafly: Hermitage, 1986).

Johnson, D. Barton. "Contrastive Phonoaesthetics; or, Why Nabokov Gave Up Translating Poetry as Poetry." In Carl Proffer, ed., *A Book of Things about Vladimir Nabokov*, 28–41 (Ann Arbor: Ardis, 1974).

Johnson, Samuel. *The Lives of the Poets*. Oxford: Oxford University Press, 1933.

Kammer, Jeanne. "The Art of Silence and the Forms of Women's Poetry." In Sandra M. Gilbert and Susan Gubar, eds., *Shakespeare's Sisters: Feminist Essays on Women Poets*, 153–64 (Bloomington, Indiana University Press, 1979).

Karges, Joann. *Nabokov's Lepidoptera: Genres and Genera*. Ann Arbor: Ardis, 1985.

Karlinsky, Simon. *Marina Cvetaeva: Her Life and Art*. Berkeley: University of California Press, 1966.

———. *Marina Tsvetaeva: The Woman, Her World, and Her Poetry*. Cambridge: Cambridge University Press, 1986.

Kermode, Frank. *An Appetite for Poetry*. Cambridge, Mass.: Harvard University Press, 1989.

———. "Dissociation of Sensibility." In John R. Roberts, ed., *Essential Articles for the Study of John Donne's Poetry*, 66–82 (Hamden: Archon, 1975). Reprinted from *Kenyon Review* 19 (1957): 169–94.

———, ed. *Selected Prose*. New York: Farrar, Straus, and Giroux, 1975.

Khodasevich, Vladislav. *Sobranie stikhov*. Edited by N. Berberova. Munich: Izdatel'stvo I. Bashkirtsev, 1961.

———. *Literatunye stat'i i vospominaniia*. New York: Chekhov, 1954.

———. "Pered kontsom." *Vozrozhdenie* (22 August 1936).

Kline, George L. Introduction and translation of Joseph Brodsky, "Elegy for John Donne." *Russian Review* 24 (1965): 341–53. Included with revisions in Joseph Brodsky, *Selected Poems*.

———. "Joseph Brodsky's 'Verses on the Death of T. S. Eliot.' " *Russian Review* 27 (1968): 195–98. Included with revisions in Joseph Brodsky, *Selected Poems*.

———. "The 1987 Nobel Prize in Literature—Joseph Brodsky." *DLB Yearbook 1987*: 3–13.

———. "Variations on the Theme of Exile." In Lev Loseff and Valentina Polukhina, eds., *Brodsky's Poetics and Aesthetics*, 56–88 (London: Macmillan, 1990).

———, and Richard D. Sylvester. "Iosif Aleksandrovich Brodskii." *Modern Encyclopedia of Russian and Soviet Literature* 3 (1979): 129–37.

Knox, Jane E. "Iosif Brodskij's Affinity with Osip Mandel'štam: Cultural Links with the Past." Ph.D. dissertation, University of Texas, 1978.

Kopper, John M. "Dante in Russian Symbolist Discourse." *Slavic Review*, forthcoming.

Kreps, Mikhail. *O poezii Iosifa Brodskogo*. Ann Arbor: Ardis, 1984.

Kristeva, Julia. "About Chinese Women." In Toril Moi, ed., *The Kristeva Reader*, 138–58 (New York: Columbia University Press, 1986). Translation of *Des Chinoises* (Paris: Editions des Femmes, 1974).

———. "A New Type of Intellectual: The Dissident." In Toril Moi, ed., *The Kristeva Reader*, 292–300 (New York: Columbia University Press, 1986). Translation of "Un nouveau type d'intellectuel: le dissident." *Tel Quel* 74 (Winter 1977): 3–8.

———. "Entretien avec Julia Kristeva." Interview with Francoise Collin. *Le Cahiers du GRIF* 32 (1985): 7–23.

———. "Stabat Mater." In Toril Moi, ed., *The Kristeva Reader*, 160–86 (New York: Columbia University Press, 1986).

———. *Strangers to Ourselves*. Translated by Leon S. Roudiez. New York: Columbia University Press, 1991. Translation of *Etrangers à nous-mêmes* (Librarie Artheme Fayard, 1989).

Kurrik, Marie Jaanus. *Literature and Negation*. New York: Columbia University Press, 1979.

Kushner, Alexander. *Apollo in the Snow*. New York: Farrar, Straus, and Giroux, 1991.

Kushner, Aleksandr. "Neissiakaemyi siuzhet poezii." *Voprosy literatury* 7 (1986): 183.

———. *Stikhotvoreniia*. Leningrad: Khudozhestvennaia literatura, 1986.

———. "Vypriamitel'nyi vzdokh." In S. S. Averintsev, O. G. Lasunskii, et al., *Zhizn' i tvorchestvo O. E. Mandel'shtama: Vospominaniia, materialy k biografii, "novye stikhi," kommentarii, issledovaniia*, 5–14 (Voronezh: Izdatel'stvo Voronezhskogo universiteta, 1990).

Lauterbach, Ann. "Genius in Exile." *Vogue* (February 1988): 386+.

Levin, Harry. "Literature and Exile." In Harry Levin, *Refractions: Essays in Comparative Literature*, 62–81 (New York: Oxford University Press, 1966).

Likhachev, Dmitrii. "Kratchaishii put.' " In Aleksandr Kushner, *Stikhotvoreniia*, 3–12 (Leningrad: Khudozhestvennaia literatura, 1986).

Lipking, Lawrence. *The Life of the Poet: Beginning and Ending Poetic Careers*. Chicago: University of Chicago Press, 1981.

The Literature of Exile. Special issue of *Mosaic* 8.3 (1975).

Loseff, Lev and Valentina Polukhina, eds. *Brodsky's Poetics and Aesthetics*. London: Macmillan, 1990.

Makin, Michael. *Marina Tsvetaeva: Poetics of Appropriation*. Oxford: Oxford University Press, forthcoming.

Mandelstam, Nadezhda. *Hope Abandoned*. Translated by Max Hayward. New York: Atheneum, 1974. Translation of *Vtoraia kniga* (Paris: YMCA, 1972).

———. *Hope Against Hope: A Memoir*. Translated by Max Hayward. New York: Atheneum, 1970. Translation of *Vospominaniia* (New York: Chekhov, 1970).

———. *Kniga tret'ia*. Paris: YMCA, 1987.

Mandelstam, Osip. *The Complete Critical Prose and Letters*. Edited by Jane Gary Harris. Translated by Jane Gary Harris and Constance Link. Ann Arbor: Ardis, 1979.

———. *The Prose of Osip Mandelstam: The Noise of Time, Theodosia, The*

Egyptian Stamp. Translated by Clarence Brown. Princeton, N.J.: Princeton University Press, 1965.

———. *Sobranie sochinenii*. 3 vols. Edited by Gleb Struve and Boris Filipoff. Washington: Inter-language Literary Associates, 1964–69. Vol. 4 (supplementary). Paris: YMCA Press, 1981.

———. *Socheneniia*. 2 vols. Moscow: Khudozhestvennaia literatura, 1990.

Marotti, Arthur F. *John Donne, Coterie Poet*. Madison: University of Wisconsin Press, 1986.

McCanles, Michael. "Paradox in Donne." In John R. Roberts, ed., *Essential Articles for the Study of John Donne's Poetry*, 220–35 (Hamden: Archon, 1975). Reprinted from *Studies in the Renaissance* 13 (1966): 266–87.

McDougal, Stuart Y. "T. S. Eliot's Metaphysical Dante." In Stuart Y. McDougal, ed., *Dante among the Moderns*, 57–81 (Chapel Hill: University of North Carolina Press, 1985).

Medvedev, Pavel N. *The Formal Method in Literary Scholarship*. Translated by Albert J. Wehrle. Baltimore: Johns Hopkins University Press, 1978.

Meilakh, M. B. and V. N. Toporov. "Akhmatova i Dante." *International Journal of Slavic Linguistics and Poetics* 15 (1972). 29 75.

Mendelson, Edward. "Auden's Revision of Modernism." In Harold Bloom, ed., *W. H. Auden*, 111–19 (New York: Chelsea, 1986). Originally published as "Preface," in *W. H. Auden, Selected Poems: New Edition* (New York: Vintage-Random, 1979).

Milosz, Czeslaw. *The Captive Mind*. Translated by Jane Zielonko. New York: Vintage, 1981.

———. *Native Realm: A Search for Self-Definition*. Berkeley: University of California Press, 1981.

———. "Notes on Exile." *Books Abroad* 52.2 (Spring 1976): 281–84.

———. *Prywatne obowiązki* [Private Obligations]. Paris: Instytut Literacki, 1972.

———. *The Witness of Poetry*. Cambridge, Mass.: Harvard University Press, 1983.

Moi, Toril, ed. *The Kristeva Reader*. New York: Columbia University Press, 1986.

Moi, Toril. *Sexual/Textual Politics: Feminist Literary Theory*. London and New York: Methuen, 1985.

Montenegro, David. "An Interview with Joseph Brodsky." *Partisan Review* 54.4 (1987): 527–40.

Montgomery, M. R. "Joseph Brodsky: The People's Poet." *The Boston Globe* (2 October 1991): 39, 44.

Morson, Gary Saul and Caryl Emerson. *Mikhail Bakhtin: Creation of a Prosaics*. Stanford: Stanford University Press, 1990.

Nabokov, Vladimir. *Dar*. 1952. Reprint. Ann Arbor: Ardis, 1975.

———. *Details of a Sunset and Other Stories*. New York: McGraw-Hill, 1976.

———. *The Gift: A Novel*. Translated by Michael Scammell. New York: Putnam, 1963.

———. *Invitation to a Beheading*. Translated by Dmitri Nabokov. New York: G. P. Putnam's Sons, 1959.

Nabokov, Vladimir. "An Interview with Vladimir Nabokov." With Alfred Appel, Jr. In L. S. Dembo, ed., *Nabokov: The Man and His Work*, 19–44 (Madison: University of Wisconsin Press, 1967).

———. *Mary*. Translated by Michael Glenny, in collaboration with author. Greenwich: Fawcett, 1970.

———. *Pale Fire: A Novel*. New York: Berkley, 1962.

———. *Priglashenie na kazn'*. 1938. Reprint. Paris: Editions Victor, n.d.

———. *Selected Letters*. Edited by Dmitri Nabokov and Matthew J. Bruccoli. New York: Harcourt, Brace, Jovanovich, 1989.

———. *Speak, Memory: An Autobiography Revisited*. New York: Putnam's Sons, 1966.

———. *Stikhi*. Ann Arbor: Ardis, 1979.

———. *Strong Opinions*. New York: McGraw-Hill, 1973.

———. *Vozvrashchenie Chorba*. Berlin: Slovo, 1930. Reprint. Ann Arbor: Ardis, 1976.

Naiman, Anatolii. *Rasskazy o Anne Akhmatovoi*. Moscow: Khudozhestvennaia literatura, 1989.

Nivat, Georges. "The Ironic Journey into Antiquity." In Lev Loseff and Valentina Polukhina, eds., *Brodsky's Poetics and Aesthetics*, 89–97 (London: Macmillan, 1990).

Odoevtseva, Irina. *Na beregakh Seny*. Paris: La Presse Libre, 1983.

Olesha, Iurii. *Zavist'*. Moskva: Khudozhestvennaia literatura, 1989.

Osborne, Charles. *W. H. Auden: The Life of a Poet*. New York: Harcourt, 1979.

Ouspensky, P. D. *A New Model of the Universe: Principles of the Psychological Method in Its Application to Problems of Science, Religion, and Art*. 2d ed. 1934. Reprint. New York: Knopf, 1943.

Pasternak, Boris. *Doctor Zhivago*. Translated by Max Hayward, Manya Harari, and Bernard Guilbert Guerney. New York: Signet, 1958.

———. *Doktor Zhivago*. Ann Arbor: University of Michigan Press, 1958.

———. *Proza 1915–1958. Povesti, rasskazy, avtobiograficheskie proizvedeniia*. Edited by G. P. Struve and B. A. Filippov. Ann Arbor: University of Michigan Press, 1961.

———. *Safe Conduct: An Autobiography and Other Writings*. New York: New Directions, 1958.

———. *Stikhi i poemy 1912–1932*. Edited by G. P. Struve and B. A. Filippov. Ann Arbor: University of Michigan Press, 1961.

Polukhina, Valentina. "Brodsky's Self-Portrait." In S. Grahem, ed., *Russian Literature since 1917: New Directions*, 122–35 (London: Macmillan, 1992).

———. *Joseph Brodsky: A Poet for Our Time*. Cambridge: Cambridge University Press, 1989.

———. "The Self in Exile." In M. Millington, ed., *Writing in Exile. Renaissance and Modern Studies* series (University of Nottingham) 34 (1991): 9–18.

Proffer, Carl R., ed. *Modern Russian Poets on Poetry*. Ann Arbor: Ardis, 1976.

Pushkin, Aleksandr Sergeevich. *Eugene Onegin: A Novel in Verse*. Translated by Vladimir Nabokov. Revised edition. Princeton, N.J.: Princeton University Press, 1975.

Quennell, Peter, ed. *Vladimir Nabokov, His Life, His Work, His World: A Tribute*. New York: Morrow, 1980.

Rich, Adrienne. "When We Dead Awaken: Writing as Re-Vision." In Barbara Charlesworth Gelpi and Albert Gelpi, eds., *Adrienne Rich's Poetry*, 90–98 (New York: Norton, 1975). The Adrienne Rich article is reprinted from *College English* 34, no. 1 (October 1972): 18–25.

Ronen, Omry. *An Approach to Mandel'štam*. Jerusalem: Magnes/Hebrew University, 1983.

Rooney, William J. " 'The Canonization'—The Language of Paradox Reconsidered." In John R. Roberts, ed., *Essential Articles for the Study of John Donne's Poetry*, 271–78 (Hamden: Archon, 1975). Reprinted from *English Literary History* 23 (1956): 36–47.

Said, Edward W. *Beginnings: Intention and Method*. New York: Basic Books, 1975.

———. "The Mind of Winter: Reflections on Life in Exile." *Harper's* 269, #1612 (September 1984): 49–55.

———. *Orientalism*. New York: Vintage, 1979.

———. *The World, the Text, and the Critic*. Cambridge, Mass.: Harvard University Press, 1983.

Sandler, Stephanie. *Distant Pleasures: Alexander Pushkin and the Writing of Exile*. Stanford: Stanford University Press, 1989.

Scherr, Barry P. *Russian Poetry: Meter, Rhythm, and Rhyme*. Berkeley: University of California Press, 1986.

———. "Strofika Brodskogo." In Lev Loseff, ed., *Poetika Brodskogo*, 97–120 (Tenafly: Hermitage, 1986).

Shaitanov, Igor'. "Predislovie k znakomstvu." *Literaturnoe obozrenie* (August 1988): 55–62.

Seidel, Michael. *Exile and the Narrative Imagination*. New Haven: Yale University Press, 1986.

Shveitser (Schweitzer), Viktoriia. *Byt i bytie Mariny Tsvetaevoi*. Fontenay-aux-Roses, France: Syntaxis, 1988.

Smith, G. S., ed. and trans. *Contemporary Russian Poetry: A Bilingual Anthology*. Bloomington: Indiana University Press, 1993.

Smith, G. S. "Nabokov and Russian Verse Form." *Russian Literature Triquarterly* 24 (1991): 271–305.

Solov'ev, Vladimir. *Roman s epigrafami*. New York: Slovo, 1990.

Spender, Stephen, ed. *W. H. Auden: A Tribute*. London: Weidenfeld and Nicolson, 1975.

Steckler, Irene M. "The Poetic Word and the Sacred Word: Biblical Motifs in the Poetry of Joseph Brodsky." Ph.D. dissertation, Bryn Mawr College, 1982.

Steiner, George. *After Babel*. New York: Oxford University Press, 1975.

———. "Extraterritorial." *Triquarterly* 17 (1970): 119–27.

Stevens, Wallace. *Collected Poems*. New York: Knopf, 1967.

Tabori, Paul. *The Anatomy of Exile: A Semantic and Historical Study*. London: Harrap, 1972.

Taranovsky, Kiril. *Essays on Mandel'štam*. Cambridge, Mass.: Harvard University Press, 1976.

Thomas, D. M. "Interview with Brodsky." *Quarto* 24 (December 1981): 9–11.

Titunik, I. R. "The Russian Baroque." In Victor Terras, ed., *Handbook of Russian Literature*, 40–42 (New Haven: Yale University Press, 1985).

Tomashevsky, Boris. "Literature and Biography." In Ladislav Matejka and Krystyna Pomorska, eds., *Readings in Russian Poetics: Formalist and Structuralist Views*, 47–55 (Cambridge, Mass.: MIT Press, 1971).

"The Trial of Iosif Brodsky" (English language transcript of Brodsky's trial). *New Leader* (31 August 1964): 6–17.

Tsvetaeva, Marina. *Foto-biografiia / A Pictorial Biography*. Edited by Ellendea Proffer. Translated by J. Marin King. Ann Arbor: Ardis, 1980.

———. *Izbrannaia proza v dvukh tomakh: 1917–1937*. Edited by Aleksandr Sumerkin. New York: Russica, 1979.

———. *Neizdannye pis'ma*. Edited by Gleb Struve and Nikita Struve. Paris: YMCA Press, 1972.

———. *Le notti fiorentine*. Translated by Serena Vitale. Milan: Mondadori, 1981.

———. "Pis'mo B. Pasternaku." *Vestnik russkogo khristianskogo dvizheniia* 128:173.

———. "Pis'ma Mariny Tsvetaevoi Evgeniiu Lannu." In V. M. Volosov and I. V. Kudrova, eds., *Marina Cvetaeva: Studien und Materialien. Wiener Slawistischer Almanach* 3 (1981): 161–94.

———. *Sochineniia v dvukh tomakh*. Moskva: Khudozhestvennaia literatura, 1980.

———. *Stikhotvoreniia i poemy v piati tomakh*. New York: Russica, 1980–83.

Ueland, Carol. "Aleksandr Kushner and the Re-emergence of the Leningrad School." *Studies in Comparative Communism* 21 (Autumn/Winter 1988): 369–78.

———. "Echoes of Mandel'štam in the Poetry of Aleksandr Kušner." Article manuscript.

Uspensky, Petr. See Ouspensky, P. D.

Vail, Petr and Aleksandr Genis. "Ot mira—k Rimu." In Lev Loseff, ed., *Poetika Brodskogo*, 198–206 (Tenafly: Hermitage, 1986).

Venclova, Tomas. "A Journey from Petersburg to Istanbul." In Lev Loseff and Valentina Polukhina, eds., *Brodsky's Poetics and Aesthetics*, 135–49 (London: Macmillan, 1990).

Verheul, Kees. " 'Enei i Didona' Iosifa Brodskogo." In Lev Loseff, ed., *Poetika Brodskogo*, 121–31 (Tenafly: Hermitage, 1986).

Volkova, Marianna and Solomon Volkov. *Iosif Brodskii v N'iu-Iorke: fotoportrety i besedy s poetom*. New York: Slovo, 1990.

Weeks, Laura D. " 'I Named Her Ariadna . . .': The Demeter-Persephone Myth in Tsvetaeva's Poems for her Daughter." *Slavic Review* 49 (1990): 568–84.

———. *Marina Cvetaeva: The Search for the Self*. Manuscript.

Wittlin, Joseph. "Sorrow and Grandeur of Exile." *Polish Review* 2.2–3 (Spring–Summer 1957): 99–111.

Woolf, Virginia. *The Death of the Moth and Other Essays*. New York: Harcourt, Brace, Jovanovich, 1942.

Wright, George T. *W. H. Auden*. New York: Twayne, 1969.

"The Writer in Exile." Special section of *Books Abroad* 50, #2 (1976): 271–328.

"Zasedanie suda Dzerzhinskogo raiona goroda Leningrada" (Russian language transcript of Brodsky's trial). *Vozdushnye puti* 4 (1965): 279–303.

Zeeman, Peter. *The Later Poetry of Osip Mandelstam*. Amsterdam: Rodopi, 1988.

Zelinsky, Bobo. "Dido und Äneas bei Anna Achmatova und Iosif Brodskij." In Gerhard Gieseman et al., eds., *Jubiläumsschrift zum 25-jährigen Bestehen des Instituts für Slavistik der Universität Giessen*, 265–78 (New York: Peter Lang, 1987).

Zhuravlev, D. N. *Zhizn', isskustvo, vstrechi*. Moscow: Vserossiiskoe teatral'noe obshchestvo, 1985.

Index